Sursum Corda:
Documents and Readings
on the Traditional Latin Mass

Edited by

David Pietrusza

a createspace book

Sursum Corda:
Documents and Readings on the Traditional Latin Mass

For information email: dap@davidpietrusza.com.

ISBN: 1438256175
EAN-13: 9781438256177

Printed in the United States of America

www.the-latinmass.com
www.createspace.com

10-24-08

Contents

Contents

Introduction

The following collection of readings, while hardly exhaustive on the subject of the Roman Catholic Church's traditional Latin Mass (aka the Tridentine Mass or the extraordinary form of the Latin rite), nonetheless, presents a basic sampling of core documents on a topic vitally important to Catholic worship and, indeed, to the vitality of Holy Mother Church. "For the Church," observed Pius XI in *Officiorum Omnium* in August 1922, "precisely because it embraces all nations and is destined to endure until the end of time . . . of its very nature requires a language which is universal, immutable, and non-vernacular."

And as Paul VI noted in *Sacrificium Laudis in 1966:* "The Latin language is assuredly worthy of being defended with great care instead of being scorned; for the Latin Church it is the most abundant source of Christian civilization and the richest treasury of piety . . . we must not hold in low esteem these traditions of your fathers which were your glory for centuries."

With Pope Benedict XVI's actions to widen the use of this form (painfully circumscribed though never formally banned in the wake of the Second Vatican Council), a collection of this nature becomes more essential than ever to serious Catholics.

The volume at hand begins with key documents from the days of Pope St. Pius V and the Council of Trent outlining the Tridentine Mass itself and the Roman Catholic doctrine of the Eucharist underlying the Mass. Yet, this is not the era from which the traditional Mass dates. Recently, the Vatican has taken to terming the traditional Mass not the Tridentine Mass nor the Mass of Pius V, but rather the "Gregorian Mass," a reference to Pope St. Gregory the Great (590-604) and to its far more substantial antiquity. As Fr. Adrian Fortescue noted at the beginning of the twentieth century: "There is, moreover, a constant tradition that St. Gregory was the last to touch the essential part of the Mass, namely the Canon. Benedict XIV (1740-58) says: "No pope has added or to or changed the Canon since St. Gregory."

The section encompassing the Council of Trent also includes key documents defining Catholic doctrine regarding the Eucharist. To some this may seem a detour. It is not. To not understand the Eucharist (or, at least to understand It as much as the Church teaches us regarding this Mystery of Faith), is to not understand the Holy Sacrifice of the Mass, traditional or otherwise.

Our collection progresses to include essays on the Latin Mass (most particularly on the efficacy of tradition and the Latin language), penned in the late nineteenth and early twentieth centuries, including works by such pre-eminent scholars as John Henry Cardinal Newman (then still an Anglican, but, obviously, a perceptive one), Fr. Adrian Fortescue, and the Rt. Rev. Dom Fernand Cabrol. A later work by Blessed John XXII, *Veterum Sapientia*, promulgated on the very eve of the Second Vatican Council, that "the Church's language must be not only universal but also immutable." An additional work on Latin as a unifying force, authored by Fr. Uwe Michael Lang, brings a contemporary perspective to the topic.

As sacred music comprises such an essential portion of worship, three documents—by St. Pius X, Pius XI, and the Venerable Pius XII—are included on the subject, as is Pius XII's landmark 1947 encyclical on the sacred liturgy, *Mediator Dei*.

It may surprise some to see Pope Paul VI's Constitution on the Sacred Liturgy *Sacrosanctum Concilium*—the Second Vatican Council's pronouncements on the liturgy. But it is necessary to see what Vatican II said ("the use of the Latin language is to be preserved in the Latin rites") and did not say on the subject (as well as its noticeable changes in tone, proportion, and emphasis from what preceded it; as well as its remarkable ambiguities) in order to rightly judge what followed. Another remarkable document from those times is Blessed John XXIII's unequivacle 1962 Apostolic Constitution *Veterum Sapientia: On the Promotion of the Study of Latin.*

We also include documents and essays on issues so very intimately involved in discussions of the Traditional Latin Mass: on Eucharistic fasting from Pius XII; on church architecture from Michael S. Rose; on the issue of orientation during worship by Maurice Hassett from the invaulable *Catholic Encyclopedia* and from Fr. John T. Zuhlsdorf; and on the reception of Holy Communion

Introduction

on the tongue from contemporary Canadian Church scholar, Father Paul McDonald and by His Excellency Athanasius Schneider, Auxiliary Bishop of Karaganda, Kazakhstan.

Addresses by cardinals Joseph Ratzinger (Benedict VXI) and Alfons Strickler analyze developments that followed the Second Vatican Council. Also included is a July 1971 protest of the effective "abolition" of the Latin Mass by fifty prominent English intellectuals—many of whom were non-Catholic. The result was the highly grudging so-called "English" indult of November 1971 (issued by the Congregation for Divine Worship's Archbishop *Annibale Bugnini;* following in 1984 by the nearly-equally reluctant general indult *Quattuor Abhinc Annos*).

We conclude with historic documents issued by Pope John Paul II and Benedict XVI restoring the Traditional Latin Mass to full legality and respect. "Let me say this plainly:" Dario Cardinal Castrillon Hoyos, President of the Pontifical Commission "Ecclesia Dei," told the Latin Mass Society of England and Wales in June 2008, "the Holy Father wants the ancient use of the Mass to become a normal occurrence in the liturgical life of the Church so that all of Christ's faithful—young and old—can become familiar with the older rites and draw from their tangible beauty and transcendence."

A new generation of Catholics is indeed discovering the beauty, reverence, appropriateness, and efficacy of the traditional Mass. That Mass, as the saying goes, is "the Mass the martyrs died for." It is also the Mass the faithful lived for and which gave life to them and to the Church itself. It is, as the English convert Fr. Frederick Faber once so famously noted, 'the most beautiful thing this side of heaven. It came forth out of the grand mind of the Church and lifted us out of earth and out of self, and wrapped us round in a cloud of mystical sweetness and the sublimities of a more than angelic liturgy, and purified us almost without ourselves, and charmed us with celestial charming so that our very senses seemed to find vision, hearing, fragrance, taste and touch more than ear can give."

May this volume humbly guide you in an appreciation of the Traditional Latin Mass's beauties, coherence, logic, aesthetics, and, of course, its multitude of graces. The phrase "Sursum Corda"—found in the Preface of the Canon of the Mass—means

"Lift Up Your Hearts." The response to it being "Habemus ad Dominum"—"We have lifted them up to the Lord." The Traditional Latin Mass has indeed lifted up our hearts and souls for nearly two thousand years.

David Pietrusza
October 2008

The Council of Trent
The canons and decrees of the
sacred and ecumenical Council of Trent

SESSION THE THIRTEENTH

**Being the third under the Sovereign Pontiff, Julius III,
celebrated on the eleventh day of October, 1551.**

DECREE CONCERNING
THE MOST HOLY SACRAMENT OF THE EUCHARIST

The sacred and holy, oecumenical and general Synod of Trent—lawfully assembled in the Holy Ghost, the same Legate, and nuncios of the Apostolic See presiding therein, although the end for which It assembled, not without the special guidance and governance of the Holy Ghost, was, that It might set forth the true and ancient doctrine touching faith and the sacraments, and might apply a remedy to all the heresies, and the other most grievous troubles with which the Church of God is now miserably agitated, and rent into many and various parts; yet, even from the outset, this especially has been the object of Its desires, that It might pluck up by the roots those tares of execrable errors and schisms, with which the enemy hath, in these our calamitous times, oversown the doctrine of the faith, in the use and worship of the sacred and holy Eucharist, which our Saviour, notwithstanding, left in His Church as a symbol of that unity and charity, with which He would fain have all Christians be mentally joined and united together. Wherefore, this sacred and holy Synod delivering here, on this venerable and divine sacrament of the Eucharist, that sound and genuine doctrine, which the Catholic Church—instructed by our Lord Jesus Christ Himself, and by His apostles, and taught by the Holy Ghost, who day by day brings to her mind all truth, has always retained, and will preserve even to the end of the world, forbids all the faithful of Christ, to presume to believe, teach, or preach henceforth concerning the holy Eucharist, otherwise than as is explained and defined in this present decree.

CHAPTER I.
On the real presence of our Lord Jesus Christ
in the most holy sacrament of the Eucharist.

In the first place, the holy Synod teaches, and openly and simply professes, that, in the august sacrament of the holy Eucharist, after the consecration of the bread and wine, our Lord Jesus Christ, true God and man, is truly, really, and substantially contained under the species of those sensible things. For neither are these things mutually repugnant—that our Saviour Himself always sitteth at the right hand of the Father in heaven, according to the natural mode of existing, and that, nevertheless, He be, in many other places, sacramentally present to us in his own substance, by a manner of existing, which, though we can scarcely express it in words, yet can we, by the understanding illuminated by faith, conceive, and we ought most firmly to believe, to be possible unto God: for thus all our forefathers, as many as were in the true Church of Christ, who have treated of this most holy Sacrament, have most openly professed, that our Redeemer instituted this so admirable a sacrament at the last supper, when, after the blessing of the bread and wine, He testified, in express and clear words, that He gave them His own very Body, and His own Blood; words which—recorded by the holy Evangelists, and afterwards repeated by Saint Paul, whereas they carry with them that proper and most manifest meaning in which they were understood by the Fathers—it is indeed a crime the most unworthy that they should be wrested, by certain contentions and wicked men, to fictitious and imaginary tropes, whereby the verity of the Flesh and Blood of Christ is denied, contrary to the universal sense of the Church, which, as the pillar and ground of truth, has detested, as satanical, these inventions devised by impious men; she recognising, with a mind ever grateful and unforgetting, this most excellent benefit of Christ.

CHAPTER II.
On the reason of the Institution of this most holy Sacrament.

Wherefore, our Saviour, when about to depart out of this world to the Father, instituted this Sacrament, in which He poured forth as it were the riches of His divine love towards man, making a remembrance of his wonderful works; and He commanded us, in the participation thereof, to venerate His memory, and to show forth his death until He come to judge the world. And He would also that this sacrament should be received as the spiritual food of souls, whereby may be fed and strengthened those who live with His life who said, He that eateth Me, the same also shall live by Me; and as an antidote, whereby we may be freed from daily faults, and be preserved from mortal sins. He would, furthermore, have it be a pledge of our glory to come, and everlasting happiness, and thus be a symbol of that one body whereof

He is the head, and to which He would fain have us as members be united by the closest bond of faith, hope, and charity, that we might all speak the same things, and there might be no schisms amongst us.

CHAPTER III.
On the excellency of the most holy Eucharist over the rest of the Sacraments.

The most holy Eucharist has indeed this in common with the rest of the sacraments, that it is a symbol of a sacred thing, and is a visible form of an invisible grace; but there is found in the Eucharist this excellent and peculiar thing, that the other sacraments have then first the power of sanctifying when one uses them, whereas in the Eucharist, before being used, there is the Author Himself of sanctity. For the apostles had not as yet received the Eucharist from the hand of the Lord, when nevertheless Himself affirmed with truth that to be His own body which He presented (to them). And this faith has ever been in the Church of God, that, immediately after the consecration, the veritable Body of our Lord, and His veritable Blood, together with His soul and divinity, are under the species of bread and wine; but the Body indeed under the species of bread, and the Blood under the species of wine, by the force of the words; but the Body itself under the species of wine, and the Blood under the species of bread, and the soul under both, by the force of that natural connexion and concomitancy whereby the parts of Christ our Lord, who hath now risen from the dead, to die no more, are united together; and the divinity, furthermore, on account of the admirable hypostatical union thereof with His body and soul. Wherefore it is most true, that as much is contained under either species as under both; for Christ whole and entire is under the species of bread, and under any part whatsoever of that species; likewise the whole (Christ) is under the species of wine, and under the parts thereof.

CHAPTER IV.
On Transubstantiation.

And because that Christ, our Redeemer, declared that which He offered under the species of bread to be truly His own Body, therefore has it ever been a firm belief in the Church of God, and this holy Synod doth now declare it anew, that, by the consecration of the bread and of the wine, a conversion is made of the whole substance of the bread into the substance of the Body of Christ our Lord, and of the whole substance of the wine into the substance of His Blood; which conversion is, by the holy Catholic Church, suitably and properly called Transubstantiation.

CHAPTER V.
On the cult and veneration to be shown to this most holy Sacrament.

Wherefore, there is no room left for doubt, that all the faithful of Christ may, according to the custom ever received in the Catholic Church, render in veneration the worship of latria, which is due to the true God, to this most holy sacrament. For not therefore is it the less to be adored on this account, that it was instituted by Christ, the Lord, in order to be received: for we believe that same God to be present therein, of whom the eternal Father, when introducing Him into the world, says; And let all the angels of God adore Him; whom the Magi falling down, adored; who, in fine, as the Scripture testifies, was adored by the apostles in Galilee.

The holy Synod declares, moreover, that very piously and religiously was this custom introduced into the Church, that this sublime and venerable sacrament be, with special veneration and solemnity, celebrated, every year, on a certain day, and that a festival; and that it be borne reverently and with honour in processions through the streets, and public places. For it is most just that there be certain appointed holy days, whereon all Christians may, with a special and unusual demonstration, testify that their minds are grateful and thankful to their common Lord and Redeemer for so ineffable and truly divine a benefit, whereby the victory and triumph of His death are represented. And so indeed did it behove victorious truth to celebrate a triumph over falsehood and heresy, that thus her adversaries, at the sight of so much splendour, and in the midst of so great joy of the universal Church, may either pine away weakened and broken; or, touched with shame and confounded, at length repent.

CHAPTER VI.
On reserving the Sacrament of the sacred Eucharist, and bearing it to the Sick.

The custom of reserving the holy Eucharist in the sacrarium is so ancient, that even the age of the Council of Nicaea recognised that usage. Moreover, as to carrying the sacred Eucharist itself to the sick, and carefully reserving it for this purpose in churches, besides that it is exceedingly conformable to equity and reason, it is also found enjoined in numerous councils, and is a very ancient observance of the Catholic Church. Wherefore, this holy Synod ordains, that this salutary and necessary custom is to be by all means retained.

CHAPTER VII.
On the preparation to be given that one may worthily receive the sacred Eucharist.

If it is unbeseeming for any one to approach to any of the sacred functions, unless he approach holily; assuredly, the more the holiness and divinity of this heavenly sacrament are understood by a Christian, the more diligently ought he to give heed that he approach not to receive it but with great reverence and holiness, especially as we read in the Apostle those words full of terror; He that eateth and drinketh unworthily, eateth and drinketh judgment to himself. Wherefore, he who would communicate, ought to recall to mind the precept of the Apostle; Let a man prove himself. Now ecclesiastical usage declares that necessary proof to be, that no one, conscious to himself of mortal sin, how contrite soever he may seem to himself, ought to approach to the sacred Eucharist without previous sacramental confession. This the holy Synod hath decreed is to be invariably observed by all Christians, even by those priests on whom it may be incumbent by their office to celebrate, provided the opportunity of a confessor do not fail them; but if, in an urgent necessity, a priest should celebrate without previous confession, let him confess as soon as possible.

CHAPTER VIII.
On the use of this admirable Sacrament.

Now as to the use of this holy sacrament, our Fathers have rightly and wisely distinguished three ways of receiving it. For they have taught that some receive it sacramentally only, to wit sinners: others spiritually only, those to wit who eating in desire that heavenly bread which is set before them, are, by a lively faith which worketh by charity, made sensible of the fruit and usefulness thereof: whereas the third (class) receive it both sacramentally and spiritually, and these are they who so prove and prepare themselves beforehand, as to approach to this divine table clothed with the wedding garment. Now as to the reception of the sacrament, it was always the custom in the Church of God, that laymen should receive the communion from priests; but that priests when celebrating should communicate themselves; which custom, as coming down from an apostolical tradition, ought with justice and reason to be retained. And finally this holy Synod with true fatherly affection admonishes, exhorts, begs, and beseeches, through the bowels of the mercy of our God, that all and each of those who bear the Christian name would now at length agree and be of one mind in this sign of unity, in this bond of charity, in this symbol of concord; and that mindful of the so great majesty, and the so exceeding love of our Lord Jesus Christ, who gave His own beloved soul as the price of our salvation, and gave us His own flesh to eat, they would believe and venerate these sacred mysteries of His Body and Blood with such constancy and firmness of faith, with such devotion of soul, with such piety and worship as to be able frequently to receive that supersubstantial bread, and that it may be to them truly the life of the soul, and the perpetual health of their mind; that being invigorated by the strength thereof, they may, after the journeying of this miserable pilgrimage, be able to arrive at their heavenly country, there to eat, without any veil, that same bread of angels which they now eat under the sacred veils.

But forasmuch as it is not enough to declare the truth, if errors be not laid bare and repudiated, it hath seemed good to the holy Synod to subjoin these canons, that all—the Catholic doctrine being already recognised—may now also understand what are the heresies which they ought to guard against and avoid.

ON THE MOST HOLY SACRAMENT OF THE EUCHARIST

CANON I.—If any one denieth, that, in the sacrament of the most holy Eucharist, are contained truly, really, and substantially, the Body and Blood together with the soul and divinity of our Lord Jesus Christ, and consequently the whole Christ; but saith that He is only therein as in a sign, or in figure, or virtue; let him be anathema.

CANON II.—If any one saith, that, in the sacred and holy sacrament of the Eucharist, the substance of the bread and wine remains conjointly with the Body and Blood of our Lord Jesus Christ, and denieth that wonderful and singular conversion of the whole substance of the bread into the Body, and of the whole substance of the wine into the Blood—the species Only of the bread and wine remaining—which conversion indeed the Catholic Church most aptly calls Transubstantiation; let him be anathema.

CANON III.—If any one denieth, that, in the venerable sacrament of the Eucharist, the whole Christ is contained under each species, and under every part of each species, when separated; let him be anathema.

The Council of Trent:
Decree Concerning the Most Holy Sacrament of The Eucharist

CANON IV.—If any one saith, that, after the consecration is completed, the Body and Blood of our Lord Jesus Christ are not in the admirable sacrament of the Eucharist, but (are there) only during the use, whilst it is being taken, and not either before or after; and that, in the hosts, or consecrated particles, which are reserved or which remain after communion, the true Body of the Lord remaineth not; let him be anathema.

CANON V.—If any one saith, either that the principal fruit of the most holy Eucharist is the remission of sins, or, that other effects do not result therefrom; let him be anathema.

CANON VI.—If any one saith, that, in the holy sacrament of the Eucharist, Christ, the only-begotten Son of God, is not to be adored with the worship, even external of latria; and is, consequently, neither to be venerated with a special festive solemnity, nor to be solemnly borne about in processions, according to the laudable and universal rite and custom of holy church; or, is not to be proposed publicly to the people to be adored, and that the adorers thereof are idolators; let him be anathema.

CANON VII.—If any one saith, that it is not lawful for the sacred Eucharist to be reserved in the sacrarium, but that, immediately after consecration, it must necessarily be distributed amongst those present; or, that it is not lawful that it be carried with honour to the sick; let him be anathema.

CANON VIII.—If any one saith, that Christ, given in the Eucharist, is eaten spiritually only, and not also sacramentally and really; let him be anathema.

CANON IX.—If any one denieth, that all and each of Christ's faithful of both sexes are bound, when they have attained to years of discretion, to communicate every year, at least at Easter, in accordance with the precept of holy Mother Church; let him be anathema.

CANON X.—If any one saith, that it is not lawful for the celebrating priest to communicate himself; let him be anathema.

CANON XI.—If any one saith, that faith alone is a sufficient preparation for receiving the sacrament of the most holy Eucharist; let him be anathema. And for fear lest so great a sacrament may be received unworthily, and so unto death and condemnation, this holy Synod ordains and declares, that sacramental confession, when a confessor may be had, is of necessity to be made beforehand, by those whose conscience is burthened with mortal sin, how contrite even soever they may think themselves. But if any one shall presume to teach, preach, or obstinately to assert, or even in public disputation to defend the contrary, he shall be thereupon excommunicated.

The Council of Trent
*The canons and decrees of the
sacred and ecumenical Council of Trent*

SESSION THE TWENTY-SECOND

Being the sixth under the Sovereign Pontiff, Pius IV,
celebrated on the seventeenth day of September, 1562.

DOCTRINE ON THE SACRIFICE OF THE MASS.

The sacred and holy, ecumenical and general Synod of Trent—
lawfully assembled in the Holy Ghost, the same Legates of the
Apostolic See presiding therein—to the end that the ancient,
complete, and in every part perfect faith and doctrine touching the
great mystery of the Eucharist may be retained in the holy Catholic
Church; and may, all errors and heresies being repelled, be preserved
in its own purity; (the Synod) instructed by the illumination of the
Holy Ghost, teaches, declares; and decrees what follows, to be
preached to the faithful, on the subject of the Eucharist, considered as
being a true and singular sacrifice.

CHAPTER I.
On the institution of the most holy Sacrifice of the Mass.

Forasmuch as, under the former Testament, according to the
testimony of the Apostle Paul, there was no perfection, because of the
weakness of the Levitical priesthood; there was need, God, the Father
of mercies, so ordaining, that another priest should rise, according to
the order of Melchisedech, our Lord Jesus Christ, who might
consummate, and lead to what is perfect, as many as were to be
sanctified. He, therefore, our God and Lord, though He was about to
offer Himself once on the altar of the cross unto God the Father, by
means of his death, there to operate an eternal redemption;
nevertheless, because that His priesthood was not to be extinguished
by His death, in the last supper, on the night in which He was
betrayed—that He might leave, to His own beloved Spouse the
Church, a visible sacrifice, such as the nature of man requires,
whereby that bloody sacrifice, once to be accomplished on the cross,
might be represented, and the memory thereof remain even unto the
end of the world, and its salutary virtue be applied to the remission of

those sins which we daily commit—declaring Himself constituted a priest for ever, according to the order of Melchisedech, He offered up to God the Father His own Body and Blood under the species of bread and wine; and, under the symbols of those same things, He delivered (His own Body and Blood) to be received by His apostles, whom He then constituted priests of the New Testament; and by those words, Do this in commemoration of Me, He commanded them and their successors in the priesthood, to offer (them); even as the Catholic Church has always understood and taught. For, having celebrated the ancient Passover, which the multitude of the children of Israel immolated in memory of their going out of Egypt, He instituted the new Passover, (to wit) Himself to be immolated, under visible signs, by the Church through (the ministry of) priests, in memory of His own passage from this world unto the Father, when by the effusion of His own Blood He redeemed us, and delivered us from the power of darkness, and translated us into His kingdom. And this is indeed that clean oblation, which cannot be defiled by any unworthiness, or malice of those that offer (it); which the Lord foretold by Malachias was to be offered in every place, clean to His name, which was to be great amongst the Gentiles; and which the apostle Paul, writing to the Corinthians, has not obscurely indicated, when he says, that they who are defiled by the participation of the table of devils, cannot be partakers of the table of the Lord; by the table, meaning in both places the altar. This, in fine, is that oblation which was prefigured by various types of sacrifices, during the period of nature, and of the law; in as much as it comprises all the good things signified by those sacrifices, as being the consummation and perfection of them all.

CHAPTER II.
That the Sacrifice of the Mass is propitiatory both for the living and the dead.

And forasmuch as, in this divine sacrifice which is celebrated in the Mass, that same Christ is contained and immolated in an unbloody manner, who once offered Himself in a bloody manner on the altar of the Cross; the holy Synod teaches, that this sacrifice is truly propitiatory and that by means thereof this is effected, that we obtain mercy, and find grace in seasonable aid, if we draw nigh unto God, contrite and penitent, with a sincere heart and upright faith, with fear and reverence. For the Lord, appeased by the oblation thereof, and granting the grace and gift of penitence, forgives even heinous crimes and sins. For the victim is one and the same, the same now offering by the ministry of priests, who then offered Himself on the Cross, the manner alone of offering being different. The fruits indeed of which oblation, of that bloody one to wit, are received most plentifully through this unbloody one; so far is this (latter) from derogating in any way from that (former oblation). Wherefore, not only for the sins, punishments, satisfactions, and other necessities of the faithful who are living, but also for those who are departed in Christ, and who are not as yet fully purified, is it rightly offered, agreeably to a tradition of the apostles.

CHAPTER III.
On Masses in honour of the Saints.

And although the Church has been accustomed at times to celebrate, certain masses in honour and memory of the saints; not therefore, however, doth she teach that sacrifice is offered unto them, but unto God alone, who crowned them; whence neither is the priest wont to say, "I offer sacrifice to thee, Peter, or Paul;" but, giving thanks to God for their victories, he implores their patronage, that they may vouchsafe to intercede for us in heaven, whose memory we celebrate upon earth.

CHAPTER IV
On the Canon of the Mass.

And whereas it beseemeth, that holy things be administered in a holy manner, and of all holy things this sacrifice is the most holy; to the end that it might be worthily and reverently offered and received, the Catholic Church instituted, many years ago, the sacred Canon, so pure from every error, that nothing is contained therein which does not in the highest degree savour of a certain holiness and piety, and raise up unto God the minds of those that offer. For it is composed, out of the very words of the Lord, the traditions of the apostles, and the pious institutions also of holy pontiffs.

CHAPTER V.
On the solemn ceremonies of the Sacrifice of the Mass.

And whereas such is the nature of man, that, without external helps, he cannot easily be raised to the meditation of divine things; therefore has holy Mother Church instituted certain rites, to wit that certain things be pronounced in the mass in a low, and others in a louder, tone. She has likewise employed ceremonies, such as mystic benedictions, lights, incense, vestments, and many other things of this kind, derived from an apostolical discipline and tradition, whereby both the majesty of so great a sacrifice might be recommended, and the minds of the faithful be excited, by those visible signs of religion and piety, to the contemplation of those most sublime things which are hidden in this sacrifice.

CHAPTER VI.
On Mass wherein the priest alone communicates.

The sacred and holy Synod would fain indeed that, at each Mass, the faithful who are present should communicate, not only in spiritual desire, but also by the sacramental participation of the Eucharist, that thereby a more abundant fruit might be derived to them from this most holy sacrifice: but not therefore, if this be not always done, does It condemn, as private and unlawful, but approves of and therefore commends, those Masses in which the priest alone communicates sacramentally; since those Masses also ought to be considered as truly common; partly because the people communicate spiritually thereat; partly also because they are celebrated by a public minister of the Church, not for Himself only, but for all the faithful, who belong to the body of Christ.

CHAPTER VII.
On the water that is to be mixed with the wine to be offered in the chalice.

The holy Synod notices, in the next place, that it has been enjoined by the Church on priests, to mix water with the wine that is to be offered in the chalice; as well because it is believed that Christ the Lord did this, as also because from His side there came out blood and water; the memory of which mystery is renewed by this commixture; and, whereas in the apocalypse of blessed John, the peoples are called waters, the union of that faithful people with Christ their head is hereby represented.

CHAPTER VIII.
On not celebrating the Mass every where in the vulgar tongue; the mysteries of the Mass to be explained to the people.

Although the mass contains great instruction for the faithful people, nevertheless, it has not seemed expedient to the Fathers, that it should be everywhere celebrated in the vulgar tongue. Wherefore, the ancient usage of each church, and the rite approved of by the holy Roman Church, the mother and mistress of all churches, being in each place retained; and, that the sheep of Christ may not suffer hunger, nor the little ones ask for bread, and there be none to break it unto them, the holy Synod charges pastors, and all who have the cure of souls, that they frequently, during the celebration of mass, expound either by themselves, or others, some portion of those things which are read at Mass, and that, amongst the rest, they explain some mystery of this most holy sacrifice, especially on the Lord's days and festivals.

CHAPTER IX.
Preliminary Remark on the following Canons.

And because that many errors are at this time disseminated and many things are taught and maintained by divers persons, in opposition to this ancient faith, which is based on the sacred Gospel, the traditions of the Apostles, and the doctrine of the holy Fathers; the sacred and holy Synod, after many and grave deliberations maturely had touching these matters, has resolved, with the unanimous consent of all the Fathers, to condemn, and to eliminate from holy Church, by means of the canons subjoined, whatsoever is opposed to this most pure faith and sacred doctrine.

ON THE SACRIFICE OF THE MASS.

CANON I.—If any one saith, that in the Mass a true and proper sacrifice is not offered to God; or, that to be offered is nothing else but that Christ is given us to eat; let him be anathema.

CANON II.—If any one saith, that by those words, Do this for the commemoration of Me (*Luke* xxii. 19), Christ did not institute the apostles priests; or, did not ordain that they, and other priests should offer His own Body and Blood; let him be anathema.

CANON III.—If any one saith, that the sacrifice of the Mass is only a sacrifice of praise and of thanksgiving; or, that it is a bare commemoration of the sacrifice consummated on the Cross, but not a propitiatory sacrifice; or, that it profits him only who receives; and that it ought not to be offered for the living and the dead for sins, pains, satisfactions, and other necessities; let him be anathema.

CANON IV.—If any one saith, that, by the sacrifice of the Mass, a blasphemy is cast upon the most holy sacrifice of Christ consummated on the Cross; or, that it is thereby derogated from; let him be anathema.

CANON V.—If any one saith, that it is an imposture to celebrate Masses in honour of the saints, and for obtaining their intercession with God, as the Church intends; let him be anathema.

CANON VI.—If any one saith, that the canon of the Mass contains errors, and is therefore to be abrogated; let him be anathema.

CANON VII.—If any one saith, that the ceremonies, vestments, and outward signs, which the Catholic Church makes use of in the celebration of Masses, are incentives to impiety, rather than offices of piety; let him be anathema.

CANON VIII.—If any one saith, that Masses, wherein the priest alone communicates sacramentally, are unlawful, and are, therefore, to be abrogated; let him be anathema.

CANON IX.—If any one saith, that the rite of the Roman Church, according to which a part of the canon and the words of consecration are pronounced in a low tone, is to be condemned; or, that the Mass ought to be celebrated in the vulgar tongue only; or, that water ought not to be mixed with the wine that is to be offered in the chalice, for that it is contrary to the institution of Christ; let him be anathema.

DECREE CONCERNING THE THINGS TO BE OBSERVED, AND TO BE AVOIDED, IN THE CELEBRATION OF MASS.

What great care is to be taken, that the sacred and holy sacrifice of the Mass be celebrated with all religious service and veneration, each one may easily imagine, who considers, that, in holy writ, he is called accursed, who doth the work of God negligently; and if we must needs confess, that no other work can be performed by the faithful so holy and divine as this tremendous mystery itself, wherein that life-giving victim, by which we were reconciled to the Father, is daily immolated on the altar by priests, it is also sufficiently clear, that all industry and diligence is to be applied to this end, that it be performed with the greatest possible inward cleanness and purity of heart, and outward show of devotion and piety. Whereas, therefore, either through the wickedness of the times, or through the carelessness and Corruption of men, many things seem already to have crept in, which are alien from the dignity of so great a sacrifice; to the end that the honour and cult due thereunto may, for the glory of God and the edification of the faithful people, be restored; the holy Synod decrees, that the ordinary bishops of places shall take diligent care, and be bound to prohibit and abolish all those things which either covetousness, which is a serving of idols, or irreverence, which can hardly be separated from impiety; or superstition, which is a false imitation of true piety, may have introduced. And that many things may be comprised in a few words: first, as relates to covetousness:—

they shall wholly prohibit all manner of conditions and bargains for recompenses, and whatsoever is given for the celebration of new Masses; as also those importunate and illiberal demands, rather than requests, for alms, and other things of the like sort, which are but little removed from a simonical taint, or at all events, from filthy lucre.

In the next place, that irreverence may be avoided, each, in his own diocese, shall forbid that any wandering or unknown priest be allowed to celebrate mass. Furthermore, they shall not allow any one who is publicly and notoriously stained with crime, either to minister at the holy altar, or to assist at the sacred services; nor shall they suffer the holy sacrifice to be celebrated, either by any Seculars or Regulars whatsoever, in private houses; or, at all, out of the church, and those oratories which are dedicated solely to divine worship, and which are to be designated and visited by the said Ordinaries; and not then, unless those who are present shall have first shown, by their decently composed outward appearance, that they are there not in body only, but also in mind and devout affection of heart. They shall also banish from churches all those kinds of music, in which, whether by the organ, or in the singing, there is mixed up any thing lascivious or impure; as also all secular actions; vain and therefore profane conversations, all walking about, noise, and clamour, that so the house of God may be seen to be, and may be called, truly a house of prayer.

Lastly, that no room may be left for superstition; they shall by ordinance, and under given penalties, provide, that priests do not celebrate at other than due hours; nor employ other rites, or other ceremonies and prayers, in the celebration of Masses, besides those which have been approved of by the Church, and have been received by a frequent and praiseworthy usage. They shall wholly banish from the Church the observance of a fixed number of certain Masses and of candles, as being the invention of superstitious worship, rather than of true religion; and they shall instruct the people, what is, and whence especially is derived, the fruit so precious and heavenly of this most holy sacrifice. They shall also admonish their people to repair frequently to their own parish churches, at least on the Lord's days and the greater festivals. All, therefore, that has been briefly enumerated, is in such wise propounded to all Ordinaries of places, as that, by the power given them by this sacred and holy Synod, and even as delegates of the Apostolic See, they may prohibit, ordain, reform, and establish, not only the things aforesaid, but also whatsoever else shall seem to them to have relation hereunto; and may compel the faithful people inviolably to observe them, by ecclesiastical censures and other penalties, which at their pleasure they may appoint; any privileges, exemptions, appeals, and customs whatsoever, to the contrary notwithstanding.

The Catechism of the Council of Trent: The Sacrament of The Eucharist: Importance of Instruction on the Eucharist

Edited Under St. Charles Borromeo
Published by Decree of Pope St. Pius V

As of all the sacred mysteries bequeathed to us by our Lord and Saviour as most infallible instruments of divine grace, there is none comparable to the most holy Sacrament of the Eucharist; so, for no crime is there a heavier punishment to be feared from God than for the unholy or irreligious use by the faithful of that which is full of holiness, or rather which contains the very author and source of holiness. This the Apostle wisely saw, and has openly admonished us of it. For when he had declared the enormity of their guilt who discerned not the Body of the Lord, he immediately subjoined: *Therefore are there many infirm and weak among you, and many sleep.*

In order that the faithful, therefore, aware of the divine honors due to this heavenly Sacrament, may derive therefrom abundant fruit of grace and escape the most just anger of God, pastors should explain with the greatest diligence all those things which may seem calculated more fully to display its majesty.

Institution of the Eucharist

In this matter it will be necessary that pastors, following the example of the Apostle Paul, who professes to have delivered to the Corinthians what he had received from the Lord, first of all explain to the faithful the institution of this Sacrament.

That its institution was as follows, is clearly inferred from the Evangelist. Our Lord, *having loved His own, loved them to the end.* As a divine and admirable pledge of this love, knowing that the hour had now come that He should pass from the world to the Father, that He might not ever at any period be absent from His own, He accomplished with inexplicable wisdom that which surpasses all the order and condition of nature. For having kept the supper of the

Paschal lamb with His disciples, that the figure might yield to the reality, the shadow to the substance, *He took bread, and giving thanks unto God, He blessed, and brake, and gave to the disciples, and said: "Take ye and eat, this is My Body which shall be delivered for you; this do for a commemoration of Me."* In like manner also, He took the chalice after He had supped, saying: *"This chalice is the new testament in My Blood; this do, as often as you shall drink it, in commemoration of Me."*

Meaning of the Word "Eucharist"

Wherefore sacred writers, seeing that it was not at all possible that they should manifest by one term the dignity and excellence of this admirable Sacrament, endeavoured to express it by many words.

For sometimes they call it *Eucharist*, which word we may render either by good grace, or by *thanksgiving*. And rightly, indeed, is it to be called *good grace*, as well because it first signifies eternal life, concerning which it has been written: *The grace of God is eternal life*; and also because it contains Christ the Lord, who is true grace and the fountain of all favours.

No less aptly do we interpret it thanksgiving; inasmuch as when we immolate this purest victim, we give daily unbounded thanks to God for all His kindnesses towards us, and above all for so excellent a gift of His grace, which He grants to us in this Sacrament. This same name, also, is fully in keeping with those things which we read were done by Christ the Lord at the institution of this mystery. For *taking bread He brake it, and gave thanks*. David also, when contemplating the greatness of this mystery, before he pronounced that song: *He hath made a remembrance of his wonderful works, being a merciful and gracious Lord, he hath given food to them that fear him*, thought that he should first make this act of thanksgiving: *His work is praise and magnificence.*

Other Names of This Sacrament

Frequently, also, it is called *Sacrifice*. Concerning this mystery there will be occasion to speak more at length presently.

It is called, moreover, *Communion*, the term being evidently borrowed from that passage of the Apostle where we read: *The chalice of benediction which we bless, is it not the communion of the Blood of Christ? And the bread which we break, is it not the partaking of the Body of the Lord?* For, as Damascene has explained, this Sacrament unites us to Christ, renders us partakers of His flesh and Divinity, reconciles and unites us to one another in the same Christ, and forms us, as it were, into one body.

Whence it came to pass, that it was called also *the Sacrament of peace and love*. We can understand then how unworthy they are of the name of Christian who cherish enmities, and how hatred, dissensions and discord should be entirely put away, as the most destructive bane of the faithful, especially since by the daily Sacrifice of our religion, we profess to preserve nothing with more anxious care, than peace and love.

It is also frequently called the *Viaticum* by sacred writers, both because it is spiritual food by which we are sustained in our pilgrimage through this life, and also because it paves our way to eternal glory and happiness. Wherefore, according to an ancient usage of the Catholic Church, we see that none of the faithful are permitted to die without this Sacrament.

The most ancient Fathers, following the authority of the Apostle, have sometimes also called the Holy Eucharist by the name of *Supper*, because it was instituted by Christ the Lord at the salutary mystery of the Last Supper.

It is not, however, lawful to consecrate or partake of the Eucharist after eating or drinking, because, according to a custom wisely introduced by the Apostles, as ancient writers have recorded, and which has ever been retained and preserved, Communion is received only by persons who are fasting.

The Eucharist Is a Sacrament Properly So Called

The meaning of the name having been explained, it will be necessary to show that this is a true Sacrament, and one of those seven which the holy Church has ever revered and venerated religiously. For when the consecration of the chalice is effected, it is called *a mystery of faith*.

Besides, to omit the almost endless testimonies of sacred writers, who have invariably thought that this was to be numbered among the real Sacraments, the same thing is proved from the very principle and nature of a Sacrament. For there are in it signs that are external and subject to the senses. In the next place it signifies and produces grace. Moreover, neither the Evangelists nor the Apostle leave room for doubt regarding its institution by Christ. Since all these things concur to establish the fact of the Sacrament, there is obviously no need of any other argument.

In What Respect the Eucharist Is a Sacrament

But pastors should carefully observe that in this mystery there are many things to which sacred writers have from time to time attributed the name of Sacrament. For, sometimes, both the consecration and the Communion; nay, frequently also the Body and Blood itself of our Lord, which is contained in the Eucharist, used to be called a Sacrament. Thus, St. Augustine says that this Sacrament consists of two things, the visible species of the elements, and the invisible Flesh and Blood of our Lord Jesus Christ Himself. And it is in the same sense that we say that this Sacrament is to be adored, meaning the Body and Blood of our Lord.

Now it is plain that all these are less properly called Sacraments. The species of bread and wine themselves are truly and strictly designated by this name.

How the Eucharist Differs From All the Other Sacraments

How much this Sacrament differs from all the others is easily inferred. For all the other Sacraments are completed by the use of the material, that is, while they are being administered to some one. Thus, Baptism attains the nature of a Sacrament when the individual is actually being washed in the water. For the perfecting of the Eucharist on the other hand, the consecration of the material itself suffices, since neither (species) ceases to be a Sacrament, though kept in the pyx.

Again in perfecting the other Sacraments there is no change of the matter and element into another nature. The water of Baptism, or the oil of Confirmation, when those Sacraments are being administered, do not lose their former nature of water and oil; but in the Eucharist, that which was bread and wine before consecration, after consecration is truly the substance of the Body and Blood of the Lord.

The Eucharist Is But One Sacrament

But although there are two elements, as bread and wine, of which the entire Sacrament of the Eucharist is constituted, yet guided by the authority of the Church, we confess that this is not many Sacraments, but only one.

Otherwise, there cannot be the exact number of seven Sacraments, as has ever been handed down, and as was decreed by the Councils of Lateran, Florence, and Trent.

Moreover, by virtue of the Sacrament, one mystical body is effected; hence, that the Sacrament itself may correspond to the thing which it effects, it must be one.

It is one not because it is indivisible, but because it signifies a single thing. For as food and drink, which are two different things, are employed only for one purpose, namely, that the vigor of the body may be recruited; so also it was but natural that there should be an analogy to them in the two different species of the Sacrament, which should signify the spiritual food by which souls are supported and refreshed. Wherefore we have been assured by our Lord the Saviour: *My Flesh is meat indeed, and My Blood is drink indeed.*

The Eucharist Signifies Three Things

It must, therefore, be diligently explained what the Sacrament of the Eucharist signifies, that the faithful, beholding the sacred mysteries with their eyes, may also at the same time feed their souls with the contemplation of divine things. Three things, then, are signified by this Sacrament. The first is the Passion of Christ our Lord, a thing past; for He Himself said: *Do this for a commemoration of Me,* and the Apostle says: *As often as you shall eat this bread, and drink the chalice, you shall show the death of the Lord, until He come.*

It is also significant of divine and heavenly grace, which is imparted at the present time by this Sacrament to nurture and preserve the soul. Just as in Baptism we are begotten unto newness of life and by Confirmation are strengthened to resist Satan and openly to profess the name of Christ, so by the Sacrament of the Eucharist are we nurtured and supported.

It is, thirdly, a foreshadowing of future eternal joy and glory, which, according to God's promises, we shall receive in our heavenly country.

These three things, then, which are clearly distinguished by their reference to past, present and future times, are so well represented by the Eucharistic mysteries that the whole Sacrament, though consisting of different species, signifies the three as if it referred to one thing only.

Constituent Parts of the Eucharist

The Matter

It is particularly incumbent on pastors to know the matter of this Sacrament, in order that they themselves may rightly consecrate it, and also that they may be able to instruct the faithful as to its significance, inflaming them with an earnest desire of that which it signifies.

The First Element of The Eucharist Is Bread

The matter of this Sacrament is twofold. The first element is wheaten bread, of which we shall now speak. Of the second we shall treat hereafter. As the Evangelists, Matthew, Mark, and Luke testify, Christ the Lord *took bread* into His hands, *blessed, and brake, saying: This is My Body*; and, according to John, the same Saviour called Himself bread in these words: *I am the living bread, that came down from heaven.*

The Sacramental Bread Must Be Wheaten

There are, however, various sorts of bread, either because they consist of different materials, such as wheat, barley, pulse, and other products of the earth; or because they possess different qualities, some being leavened, others altogether without leaven. It is to be observed that, with regard to the former kinds, the words of the Saviour show that the bread should be wheaten; for, according to common usage, when we simply say *bread*, we are sufficiently understood to mean wheaten bread. This is also declared by a figure in the Old Testament, because the Lord commanded that the loaves of proposition, which signified this Sacrament, should be made of fine flour.

The Sacramental Bread Should Be Unleavened

But as wheaten bread alone is to be considered the proper matter for this Sacrament a doctrine which has been handed down by Apostolic tradition and confirmed by the authority of the Catholic Church so it may be easily inferred from the doings of Christ the Lord that this bread should be unleavened. It was consecrated and instituted by Him on the first day of unleavened bread, on which it was not lawful for the Jews to have anything leavened in their house.

Should the authority of John the Evangelist, who says that all this was done before the feast of the Passover, be objected to, the argument is one of easy solution. For *by the day before the pasch* John understands the same day which the other Evangelists designate as *the first day of unleavened bread.* He wished particularly to mark the natural day, which commences at sunrise; whereas they wanted to point out that our Lord celebrated the Pasch on Thursday evening just when the days of the unleavened bread were beginning. Hence, St. Chrysostom also understands the first day of unleavened bread to be the day on the evening of which unleavened bread was to be eaten.

The peculiar suitableness of the consecration of unleavened bread to express that integrity and purity of mind which the faithful should bring to this Sacrament we learn from these words of the Apostle: *Purge out the old leaven, that you may be a new paste, as you are unleavened. For Christ our Passover is sacrificed. Therefore, let us feast, not with the old leaven, nor with the leaven of malice and wickedness, but with the unleavened bread of sincerity and truth.*

Unleavened Bread Not Essential

This quality of the bread, however, is not to be deemed so essential that, if it be wanting, the Sacrament cannot exist; for both kinds are called by the one name and have the true and proper nature of bread. No one, however, is at liberty on his own private authority, or rather presumption, to transgress the laudable rite of his Church. And such departure is the less warrantable in priests of the Latin Church, expressly obliged as they are by the supreme Pontiffs, to consecrate the sacred mysteries with unleavened bread only.

Quantity of The Bread

With regard to the first matter of this Sacrament, let this exposition suffice. It is, however, to be observed, that the quantity of the matter to be consecrated is not defined, since we cannot define the exact number of those who can or ought to receive the sacred mysteries.

The Second Element of the Eucharist Is Wine

It remains for us to treat of the other matter and element of this Sacrament, which is wine pressed from the fruit of the vine, with which is mingled a little water.

That in the institution of this Sacrament our Lord and Saviour made use of wine has been at all times the doctrine of the Catholic Church, for He Himself said: *I will not drink from henceforth of this fruit of the vine until that day.* On this passage Chrysostom observes: *He says, "Of the fruit of the vine," which certainly produced wine not water*; as if he had it in view, even at so early a period, to uproot the heresy which asserted that in these mysteries water alone is to be used.

Water Should Be Mixed With the Wine

With the wine, however, the Church of God has always mingled water. First, because Christ the Lord did so, as is proved by the authority of Councils and the testimony of St. Cyprian; next, because by this mixture is renewed the recollection of the blood and water that issued from His side. Waters, also, as we read in the Apocalypse, signify the people; and hence, water mixed with the wine signifies the union of the faithful with Christ their Head. This rite, derived as it is from Apostolic tradition, the Catholic Church has always observed.

But although there are reasons so grave for mingling water with the wine that it cannot be omitted without incurring the guilt of mortal sin, yet its omission does not render the Sacrament null.

Again as in the sacred mysteries priests must be mindful to mingle water with wine, so, also, must they take care to mingle it in small quantity, for, in the opinion and judgment of ecclesiastical writers, that water is changed into wine. Hence, these words of Pope Honorius on the subject: *A pernicious abuse has prevailed in your district of using in the sacrifice a greater quantity of water than of wine; whereas, according to the rational practice of the universal Church, the wine should be used in much greater quantity than the water.*

No Other Elements Pertain to This Sacrament

These, then, are the only two elements of this Sacrament; and with reason has it been enacted by many decrees that, although there have been those who were not afraid to do so, it is unlawful to offer anything but bread and wine.

Peculiar Fitness of Bread and Wine

We have now to consider the aptitude of these two symbols of bread and wine to represent those things of which we believe and confess they are the sensible signs.

In the first place, then, they signify to us Christ, as the true life of men; for our Lord Himself says: *My Flesh is meat indeed, and My Blood is drink indeed.* As, then, the body of Christ the Lord furnishes nourishment unto eternal life to those who receive this Sacrament with purity and holiness, rightly is the matter composed chiefly of those elements by which our present life is sustained, in order that the faithful may easily understand that the mind and soul are satiated by the Communion of the precious Body and Blood of Christ.

These very elements serve also somewhat to suggest to men the truth of the Real Presence of the Body and Blood of the Lord in the Sacrament. Observing, as we do, that bread and wine are every day changed by the power of nature into human flesh and blood, we are led the more easily by this analogy to believe that the substance of the bread and wine is changed, by the heavenly benediction, into the real Flesh and real Blood of Christ.

This admirable change of the elements also helps to shadow forth what takes place in the soul. Although no change of the bread and wine appears externally, yet their substance is truly changed into the Flesh and Blood of Christ; so, in like manner, although in us nothing appears changed, yet we are renewed inwardly unto life, when we receive in the Sacrament of the Eucharist the true life.

Moreover, the body of the Church, which is one, consists of many members, and of this union nothing is more strikingly illustrative than the elements of bread and wine; for bread is made from many grains and wine is pressed from many clusters of grapes. Thus, they signify that we, though many, are most closely bound together by the bond of this divine mystery and made, as it were, one body.

Form of the Eucharist

The form to be used in the consecration of the bread is next to be treated of, not, however, in order that the faithful should be taught these mysteries, unless necessity require it; for this knowledge is not needful for those who have not received Holy Orders. The purpose (of this section) is to guard against most shameful mistakes on the part of priests, at the time of the consecration, due to ignorance of the form.

Form to Be Used In the Consecration of The Bread

We are then taught by the holy Evangelists, Matthew, and Luke, and also by the Apostle, that the form consists of these words: This is My Body; for it is written: *Whilst they were at supper, Jesus took bread, and blessed it, and brake, and gave to His disciples, and said: Take and eat, This is My Body.*

This form of consecration having been observed by Christ the Lord has been always used by the Catholic Church. The testimonies of the Fathers, the enumeration of which would be endless, and also the decree of the Council of Florence, which is well known and accessible to all, must here be omitted, especially as the knowledge which they convey may be obtained from these words of the Saviour: *Do this for a commemoration of Me.* For what the Lord enjoined was not only what He had done, but also what He had said; and especially is this true, since the words were uttered not only to signify, but also to accomplish.

That these words constitute the form is easily proved from reason also. The form is that which signifies what is accomplished in this Sacrament; but as the preceding words signify and declare what takes place in the Eucharist, that is, the conversion of the bread into the true body of our Lord, it therefore follows that these very words constitute the form. In this sense may be understood the words of the Evangelist: *He blessed*; for they seem equivalent to this: *Taking bread, he blessed it, saying: "This is My Body."*

Not All the Words Used Are Essential

Although in the Evangelist the words, *Take and eat,* precede the words (*This is My Body*), they evidently express the use only, not the consecration, of the matter. Wherefore, while they are not necessary to the consecration of the Sacrament, they are by all means to be pronounced by the priest, as is also the conjunction for in the consecration of the Body and Blood. But they are not necessary to the validity of the Sacrament, otherwise it would follow that, if this Sacrament were not to be administered to anyone, it should not, or indeed could not, be consecrated; whereas, no one can lawfully doubt that the priest, by pronouncing the words of our Lord according to the institution and practice of the Church, truly consecrates the proper matter of the bread, even though it should afterwards never be administered.

Form to Be Used in the Consecration of the Wine

With regard lo the consecration of the wine, which is the other element of this Sacrament, the priest, for the reason we have already assigned, ought of necessity to be well acquainted with, and well understand its form. We are then firmly to believe that it consists in the following words: *This is the chalice of My Blood, of the new and eternal testament, the mystery of faith, which shall be shed for you and for many, to the remission of sins.* Of these words the greater part are taken from Scripture; but some have been preserved in the Church from Apostolic tradition.

Thus, the words, *this is the chalice*, are found in St. Luke and in the Apostle; but the words that immediately follow, *of My Blood*, or *My Blood of the new testament, which shall be shed for you and for many to the remission of sins*, are found partly in St. Luke and partly in St. Matthew. But the words, *eternal*, and *the mystery of faith*, have been taught us by holy tradition, the interpreter and keeper of Catholic truth.

Concerning this form no one can doubt, if he here also attend to what has been already said about the form used in the consecration of the bread. The form to be used (in the consecration) of this element, evidently consists of those words which signify that the substance of the wine is changed into the Blood of our Lord. Since, therefore, the words already cited clearly declare this, it is plain that no other words constitute the form.

They moreover express certain admirable fruits of the Blood shed in the Passion of our Lord, fruits which pertain in a most special manner to this Sacrament. Of these, one is access to the eternal inheritance, which has come to us by right *of the new and everlasting testament.* Another is access to righteousness by *the mystery of faith*; for God hath set forth Jesus to be *a propitiator through faith in His blood, that he himself may be just, and the justifier of him, who is of the faith of Jesus Christ.* A third effect is *the remission of sins.*

Explanation of the Form Used in the Consecration of the Wine

Since these very words of consecration are replete with mysteries and most appropriately suitable to the subject, they demand a more minute consideration.

The words: *This is the chalice of My Blood*, are to be understood to mean: *This is My Blood, which is contained in this chalice.* The mention of the chalice made at the consecration of the Blood is right and appropriate, inasmuch as the Blood is the drink of the faithful, and this would not be sufficiently signified if it were not contained in some drinking vessel.

Next follow the words: *Of the new testament.* These have been added that we might understand the Blood of Christ the Lord to be given not under a figure, as was done in the Old Law, of which we read in the Epistle to the Hebrews that without blood a testament is not dedicated; but to be given to men in truth and in reality, as becomes the New Testament. Hence, the Apostle says: *Christ therefore is the mediator of the new testament, that by means of His death, they who are called may receive the promise of eternal inheritance.*

The word eternal refers to the eternal inheritance, the right to which we acquire by the death of Christ the Lord, the eternal testator.

The words *mystery of faith*, which are subjoined, do not exclude the reality, but signify that what lies hidden and concealed and far removed from the perception of the eye, is to be believed with firm faith. In this passage, however, these words bear a meaning different from that which they have when applied also to Baptism. Here the mystery of faith consists in seeing by faith the Blood of Christ veiled under the species of wine; but Baptism is justly called by us *the Sacrament of faith*, by the Greeks, *the mystery of faith*, because it embraces the entire profession of the Christian faith.

Another reason why we call the Blood of the Lord *the mystery of faith* is that human reason is particularly beset with difficulty and embarrassment when faith proposes to our belief that Christ the Lord, the true Son of God, at once God and man, suffered death for us, and this death is designated by the Sacrament of His Blood.

Here, therefore, rather than at the consecration of His Body, is appropriately commemorated the Passion of our Lord, by the words, *which shall be shed for the remission of sins.* For the Blood, separately consecrated, serves to place before the eyes of all, in a more forcible manner, the Passion of our Lord, His death, and the nature of His sufferings.

The additional words *for you and for many*, are taken, some from Matthew, some from Luke, but were joined together by the Catholic Church under the guidance of the Spirit of God. They serve to declare the fruit and advantage of His Passion. For if we look to its value, we must confess that the Redeemer shed His Blood for the salvation of all; but if we look to the fruit which mankind have received from it, we shall easily find that it pertains not unto all, but to many of the human race. When therefore (our Lord) said: *For you*, He meant either those who were present, or those chosen from among the Jewish people, such as were, with the exception of Judas, the disciples with whom He was speaking. When He added, *And for many*, He wished to be understood to mean the remainder of the elect from among the Jews or Gentiles.

With reason, therefore, were the words *for all* not used, as in this place the fruits of the Passion are alone spoken of, and to the elect only did His Passion bring the fruit of salvation. And this is the purport of the Apostle when he says: *Christ was offered once to exhaust the sins of many*; and also of the words of our Lord in John: *I pray for them; I pray not for the world, but for them whom Thou hast given Me, because they are Thine.*

Beneath the words of this consecration lie hid many other mysteries, which by frequent meditation and study of sacred things, pastors will find it easy, with the divine assistance, to discover for themselves.

Three Mysteries of the Eucharist

We must now return to an explanation of those truths concerning the Eucharist about which the faithful are on no account to be left in ignorance. Pastors, aware of the warning of the Apostle that those who discern not the Body of the Lord are guilty of a most grave crime, should first of all impress on the minds of the faithful the necessity of detaching, as much as possible, their mind and understanding from the dominion of the senses; for if they believe that this Sacrament contains only what the senses disclose, they will of necessity fall into enormous impiety. Consulting the sight, the touch, the smell, the taste and finding nothing but the appearances of bread and wine, they will naturally judge that this Sacrament contains nothing more than bread and wine. Their minds, therefore, are as much as possible to be withdrawn from subjection to the senses and excited to the contemplation of the stupendous might and power of God.

The Catholic Church firmly believes and professes that in this Sacrament the words of consecration accomplish three wondrous and admirable effects.

The first is that the true body of Christ the Lord, the same that was born of the Virgin, and is now seated at the right hand of the Father in heaven, is contained in this Sacrament.

The second, however repugnant it may appear to the senses, is that none of the substance of the elements remains in the Sacrament.

The third, which may be deduced from the two preceding, although the words of consecration themselves clearly express it, is that the accidents which present themselves to the eyes or other senses exist in a wonderful and ineffable manner without a subject. All the accidents of bread and wine we can see, but they inhere in no substance, and exist independently of any; for the substance of the bread and wine is so changed into the Body and Blood of our Lord that they altogether cease to be the substance of bread and wine.

The Mystery of the Real Presence

To begin with the first (of these mysteries), pastors should give their best attention to show how clear and explicit are the words of our Saviour which establish the Real Presence of His Body in this Sacrament.

Proof from Scripture

When our Lord says: *This is My Body, this is My Blood*, no person of sound mind can mistake His meaning, particularly since there is reference to Christ's human nature, the reality of which the Catholic faith permits no one to doubt. The admirable words of St. Hilary, a man not less eminent for piety than learning, are apt here: *When our Lord Himself declares, as our faith teaches us, that His Flesh is food indeed, what room can remain for doubt concerning the real presence of His Body and Blood?*

Pastors should also adduce another passage from which it can be clearly seen that the true Body and Blood of our Lord are contained in the Eucharist. The Apostle, after having recorded the consecration of bread and wine by our Lord, and also the administration of Communion to the Apostles, adds: *But let a man prove himself, and so eat of that bread and drink of the chalice; for he that eateth and drinketh unworthily, eateth and drinketh judgment to himself, not discerning the Body of the Lord*. If, as heretics continually repeat, the Sacrament presents nothing to our veneration but a memorial and sign of the Passion of Christ, why was there need to exhort the faithful, in language so energetic, to prove themselves? By the terrible word *judgment*, the Apostle shows how enormous is the guilt of those who receive unworthily and do not distinguish from common food the Body of the Lord concealed in the Eucharist. In the same Epistle St.

Paul had already developed this doctrine more fully, when he said: *The chalice of benediction which we bless, is it not the communion of the Blood of Christ?* and the bread which we break, is it not the participation of the Body of the Lord? Now these words signify the real substance of the Body and Blood of Christ the Lord.

Proof from the Teaching of the Church

These passages of Scripture are therefore to be expounded by pastors; and they should especially teach that there is nothing doubtful or uncertain about them. All the more certain are they since the infallible teaching of God's Church has interpreted them, as may be ascertained in a twofold manner.

Testimony of the Fathers

The first is by consulting the Fathers who flourished in the early ages of the Church and in each succeeding century, who are the most unexceptionable witnesses of her doctrine. All of these teach in the clearest terms and with the most entire unanimity the truth of this dogma. To adduce the individual testimony of each Father would prove an endless task. It is enough, therefore, that we cite, or rather point out a few, whose testimony will afford an easy criterion by which to judge of the rest.

Let St. Ambrose first declare his faith. In his book *On Those Who are Initiated into the Mysteries* he says that the true Body of Christ is received in this Sacrament, just as the true Body of Christ was derived from the Virgin, and that this truth is to be believed with the firm certainty of faith. In another place he teaches that before consecration there is only bread, but after consecration there is the Flesh of Christ.

St. Chrysostom, another witness of equal authority and gravity, professes and proclaims this mysterious truth in many passages, but particularly in his sixtieth homily, *On Those Who Receive the Sacred Mysteries Unworthily*; and also in his forty-fourth and forty-fifth homilies on St. John. *Let us*, he says, *obey, not contradict God, although what He says may seem contrary to our reason and our sight. His words cannot deceive, our senses are easily deceived.*

With this doctrine fully agrees the uniform teaching of St. Augustine, that most zealous defender of Catholic faith, particularly when in his explanation of the thirty-third Psalm he says: *To carry himself in his own hands is impossible to man, and peculiar to Christ alone; He was*

carried in His own hands when, giving His Body to be eaten, He said,
This is My Body.

To pass by Justin and Irenaeus, St. Cyril, in his fourth book on St. John, declares in such express terms that the true Body of our Lord is contained in this Sacrament, that no sophistry, no captious interpretations can obscure His meaning.

Should pastors wish for additional testimonies of the Fathers, they will find it easy to add St. Denis, St. Hilary, St. Jerome, St. Damascene, and a host of others, whose weighty teaching on this most important subject has been collected by the labor and industry of learned and pious men.

Teaching of the Councils

Another means of ascertaining the belief of the holy Church on matters of faith is the condemnation of the contrary doctrine and opinion. It is manifest that belief in the Real Presence of the Body of Christ in the holy Sacrament of the Eucharist was so spread and taught throughout the universal Church and unanimously professed by all the faithful, that when, five centuries ago, Berengarius presumed to deny this dogma, asserting that the Eucharist was only a sign, he was unanimously condemned in the Council of Vercelli, which Leo IX had immediately convoked, whereupon he himself anathematised his error.

Relapsing, however, into the same wicked folly, he was condemned by three different Councils, convened, one at Tours, the other two at Rome; of the two latter, one was summoned by Pope Nicholas II, the other by Pope Gregory VIII. The General Council of Lateran, held under Innocent III, further ratified the sentence. Finally, this truth was more clearly defined and established in the Councils of Florence and Trent.

Two Great Benefits of Proving the Real Presence

If, then, pastors will carefully explain these particulars, they will be able, while ignoring those who are blinded by error and hate nothing more than the light of truth, to strengthen the weak and administer joy and consolation to the pious, all the more as the faithful cannot doubt that this dogma is numbered among the Articles of faith.

Faith Is Strengthened

Believing and confessing, as they do, that the power of God is supreme over all things, they must also believe that His omnipotence can accomplish the great work which we admire and adore in the Sacrament of the Eucharist. And again since they believe the Holy Catholic Church, they must necessarily believe that the true doctrine of this Sacrament is that which we have set forth.

The Soul Is Gladdened

Nothing contributes more to the spiritual joy and advantage of pious persons than the contemplation of the exalted dignity of this most august Sacrament. In the first place they learn how great is the perfection of the Gospel Dispensation, under which we enjoy the reality of that which under the Mosaic Law was only shadowed forth by types and figures. Hence, St. Denis divinely says that our Church is midway between the Synagogue and the heavenly Jerusalem, and consequently participates of the nature of both. Certainly, then, the faithful can never sufficiently admire the perfection of holy Church and her exalted glory which seems to be removed only by one degree from the bliss of heaven. In common with the inhabitants of heaven, we too possess Christ, God and man, present with us. They are raised a degree above us, inasmuch as they are present with Christ and enjoy the Beatific Vision; while we, with a firm and unwavering faith, adore the Divine Majesty present with us, not, it is true, in a manner visible to mortal eye, but hidden by a miracle of power under the veil of the sacred mysteries.

Furthermore, the faithful experience in this Sacrament the most perfect love of Christ our Saviour. It became the goodness of the Saviour not to withdraw from us that nature which He assumed from us, but to desire, as far as possible, to remain among us so that at all times He might be seen to verify the words: *My delight is to be with the children of men.*

Meaning of the Real Presence

Christ Whole and Entire Is Present in The Eucharist

Here the pastor should explain that in this Sacrament are contained not only the true Body of Christ and all the constituents of a true body, such as bones and sinews, but also Christ whole and entire. He should point out that the word Christ designates the God-man, that is to say, one Person in whom are united the divine and human natures; that the Holy Eucharist, therefore, contains both, and whatever is included in the idea of both, the Divinity and humanity whole and entire, consisting of the soul, all the parts of the Body and the Blood, all of which must be believed to be in this Sacrament. In heaven the whole humanity is united to the Divinity in one hypostasis, or Person; hence it would be impious, to suppose that the Body of Christ, which is contained in the Sacrament, is separated from His Divinity.

Presence in Virtue of the Sacrament and In Virtue of Concomitance

Pastors, however, should not fail to observe that in this Sacrament not all these things are contained after the same manner, or by the same power. Some things, we say, are present in virtue of the consecration; for as the words of consecration effect what they signify, sacred writers usually say that whatever the form expresses, is contained in the Sacrament *by virtue of the Sacrament*. Hence, could we suppose any one thing to be entirely separated from the rest, the Sacrament, they teach, would be found to contain solely what the form expresses and nothing more.

On the other hand, some things are contained in the Sacrament because they are united to those which are expressed in the form. For instance, the words *This is My Body*, which comprise the form used to consecrate the bread, signify the Body of the Lord, and hence the Body itself of Christ the Lord is contained in the Eucharist by virtue of the Sacrament. Since, however, to Christ's Body are united His Blood, His soul, and His Divinity, all of these also must be found to coexist in the Sacrament; not, however, by virtue of the consecration, but by virtue of the union that subsists between them and His body. All these are said to be in the Eucharist *by virtue of concomitance*. Hence, it is clear that Christ, whole and entire, is contained in the Sacrament; for when two things are actually united, where one is, the other must also be.

Christ Whole and Entire Present Under Each Species

Hence, it also follows that Christ is so contained, whole and entire, under either species, that, as under the species of bread are contained not only the Body, but also the Blood and Christ entire; so in like manner, under the species of wine are truly contained not only the Blood, but also the Body and Christ entire.

But although these are matters on which the faithful cannot entertain a doubt, it was nevertheless wisely ordained that two distinct consecrations should take place. First, because they represent in a more lively manner the Passion of our Lord, in which His Blood was separated from His Body; and hence in the form of consecration we commemorate the shedding of His Blood. Secondly, since the Sacrament is to be used by us as the food and nourishment of our souls, it was most appropriate that it should be instituted as food and drink, two things which obviously constitute the complete sustenance of the (human) body.

Christ Whole and Entire Present in Every Part of Each Species

Nor should it be forgotten that Christ, whole and entire, is contained not only under either species, but also in each particle of either species. *Each*, says St. Augustine, *receives Christ the Lord, and He is entire in each portion. He is not diminished by being given to many, but gives Himself whole and entire to each.*

This is also an obvious inference from the narrative of the Evangelists. It is not to be supposed that our Lord consecrated the bread used at the Last Supper in separate parts, applying the form particularly to each, but that all the bread then used for the sacred mysteries was consecrated at the same time and with the same form, and in a quantity sufficient for all the Apostles. That the consecration of the chalice was performed in this manner, is clear from these words of the Saviour: *Take and divide it among you.*

What has hitherto been said is intended to enable pastors to show that the true Body and Blood of Christ are contained in the Sacrament of the Eucharist.

The Mystery of Transubstantiation

The next point to be explained is that the substance of the bread and wine does not continue to exist in the Sacrament after consecration. This truth, although well calculated to excite our profound admiration, is yet a necessary consequence from what has been already established.

Proof from the Dogma of the Real Presence

If, after consecration, the true Body of Christ is present under the species of bread and wine, since it was not there before, it must have become present either by change of place, or by creation, or by the change of some other thing into it. It cannot be rendered present by change of place, because it would then cease to be in heaven; for whatever is moved must necessarily cease to occupy the place from which it is moved. Still less can we suppose the Body of Christ to be rendered present by creation; nay, the very idea is inconceivable. In order that the Body of our Lord be present in the Sacrament, it remains, therefore, that it be rendered present by the change of the bread into it. Wherefore it is necessary that none of the substance of the bread remain.

Proof from the Councils

Hence, our predecessors in the faith, the Fathers of the General Councils of Lateran and of Florence, confirmed by solemn decrees the truth of this dogma. In the Council of Trent it was still more fully defined in these words: If any one shall say that in the most Holy Sacrament of the Eucharist the substance of the bread and wine remains, together with the Body and Blood of our Lord Jesus Christ, let him be anathema.

Proof from Scripture

The doctrine thus defined is a natural inference from the words of Scripture. When instituting this Sacrament, our Lord Himself said: *This is My Body.* The word *this* expresses the entire substance of the thing present; and therefore if the substance of the bread remained, our Lord could not have truly said: *This is My Body.*

In St. John Christ the Lord also says: *The bread that I will give is My Flesh, for the life of the world.* The bread which He promises to give, He here declares to be His Flesh. A little after He adds: *Unless you eat the Flesh of the son of man, and drink His Blood, you shall not have life in you. And again: My Flesh is meat indeed, and My Blood is drink indeed.* Since, therefore, in terms so clear and so explicit, He calls His Flesh bread and *meat indeed*, and His Blood *drink indeed*, He gives us sufficiently to understand that none of the substance of the bread and wine remains in the Sacrament.

Proof from the Fathers

Whoever turns over the pages of the holy Fathers will easily perceive that on this doctrine (of transubstantiation) they have been at all times unanimous. St. Ambrose says: *You say, perhaps, "this bread is no other than what is used for common food." True, before consecration it is bread; but no sooner are the words of consecration pronounced than from bread it becomes the Flesh of Christ.* To prove this position more clearly, he elucidates it by a variety of comparisons and examples. In another place, when explaining these words of the Psalmist, *Whatsoever the Lord pleased he hath done in heaven and on earth,* St. Ambrose says: *Although the species of bread and wine are visible, yet we must believe that after consecration, the Body and Blood of Christ are alone there.* Explaining the same doctrine almost in the same words, St. Hilary says that although externally it appear bread and wine, yet in reality it is the Body and Blood of the Lord.

Why the Eucharist is Called Bread after Consecration

Here pastors should observe that we should not at all be surprised, if, even after consecration, the Eucharist is sometimes called bread. It is so called, first because it retains the appearance of bread, and secondly because it keeps the natural quality of bread, which is to support and nourish the body.

Moreover, such phraseology is in perfect accordance with the usage of the Holy Scriptures, which call things by what they appear to be, as may be seen from the words of Genesis which say that Abraham saw three men, when in reality he saw three Angels. In like manner the two Angels who appeared to the Apostles after the Ascension of Christ the Lord into heaven, are called not Angels, but men.

The Meaning of Transubstantiation

To explain this mystery is extremely difficult. The pastor, however, should endeavour to instruct those who are more advanced in the knowledge of divine things on the manner of this admirable change. As for those who are yet weak in faith, they might possibly be overwhelmed by its greatness.

Transubstantiation a Total Conversion

This conversion, then, is so effected that the whole substance of the bread is changed by the power of God into the whole substance of the Body of Christ, and the whole substance of the wine into the whole substance of His Blood, and this, without any change in our Lord Himself. He is neither begotten, nor changed, not increased, but remains entire in His substance.

This sublime mystery St. Ambrose thus declares: *You see how efficacious are the words of Christ. If the word of the Lord Jesus is so powerful as to summon into existence that which did not exist, namely the world, how much more powerful is His word to change into something else that which already has existence?*

Many other ancient and most authoritative Fathers have written to the same effect. *We faithfully confess*, says St. Augustine, *that before consecration it is bread and wine, the product of nature; but after consecration it is the Body and Blood of Christ, consecrated by the blessing. The body*, says Damascene, *is truly united to the Divinity, that Body which was derived from the virgin; not that the Body thus derived descends from heaven, but that the bread and wine are changed into the Body and Blood of Christ.*

This admirable change, as the Council of Trent teaches, the Holy Catholic Church most appropriately expresses by the word *transubstantiation*. Since natural changes are rightly called *transformations*, because they involve a change of form; so likewise our predecessors in the faith wisely and appropriately introduced the term transubstantiation, in order to signify that in the Sacrament of the Eucharist the whole substance of one thing passes into the whole substance of another.

According to the admonition so frequently repeated by the holy Fathers, the faithful are to be admonished against curious searching into the manner in which this change is effected. It defies the powers of conception; nor can we find any example of it in natural transmutations, or even in the very work of creation. That such a change takes place must be recognised by faith; how it takes place we must not curiously inquire.

No less of caution should be observed by pastors in explaining the mysterious manner in which the Body of our Lord is contained whole and entire under the least particle of the bread. Indeed, discussions of this kind should scarcely ever be entered upon. Should Christian charity, however, require a departure from this rule, the pastor should remember first of all to prepare and fortify his hearers by reminding them that *no word shall be impossible with God.*

A Consequence of Transubstantiation

The pastor should next teach that our Lord is not in the Sacrament as in a place. Place regards things only inasmuch as they have magnitude. Now we do not say that Christ is in the Sacrament inasmuch as He is great or small, terms which belong to quantity, but inasmuch as He is a substance. The substance of the bread is changed into the substance of Christ, not into magnitude or quantity; and substance, it will be acknowledged by all, is contained in a small as well as in a large space. The substance of air, for instance, and its entire nature must be present under a small as well as a large quantity, and likewise the entire nature of water must be present no less in a glass than in a river. Since, then, the Body of our Lord succeeds to the substance of the bread, we must confess it to be in the Sacrament after the same manner as the substance of the bread was before consecration; whether the substance of the bread was present in greater or less quantity is a matter of entire indifference.

The Mystery of the Accidents without a Subject

We now come to the third great and wondrous effect of this Sacrament, namely, the existence of the species of bread and wine without a subject.

Proof from the Preceding Dogmas

What has been said in explanation of the two preceding points must facilitate for pastors the exposition of this truth. For, since we have already proved that the Body and Blood of our Lord are really and truly contained in the Sacrament, to the entire exclusion of the substance of the bread and wine, and since the accidents of bread and wine cannot inhere in the Body and Blood of Christ, it remains that, contrary to physical laws, they must subsist of themselves, inhering in no subject.

Proof from the Teaching of the Church

This has been at all times the uniform doctrine of the Catholic Church; and it can be easily established by the same authorities which, as we have already proved, make it plain that the substance of the bread and wine ceases to exist in the Eucharist.

Advantages of This Mystery

Nothing more becomes the piety of the faithful than, omitting all curious questionings, to revere and adore the majesty of this august Sacrament, and to recognize the wisdom of God in commanding that these holy mysteries should be administered under the species of bread and wine. For since it is most revolting to human nature to eat human flesh or drink human blood, therefore God in His infinite wisdom has established the administration of the Body and Blood of Christ under the forms of bread and wine, which are the ordinary and agreeable food of man.

There are two further advantages: first, it prevents the calumnious reproaches of the unbeliever, from which the eating of our Lord under His visible form could not easily be defended; secondly, the receiving Him under a form in which He is impervious to the senses avails much for increasing our faith. For faith, as the well known saying of St. Gregory declares, *has no merit in those things which fall under the proof of reason.*

The doctrines treated above should be explained with great caution, according to the capacity of the hearers and the necessities of the times.

The Effects of the Eucharist

But with regard to the admirable virtue and fruits of this Sacrament, there is no class of the faithful to whom a knowledge of them is not most necessary. For all that has been said at such length on this Sacrament has principally for its object, to make the faithful sensible of the advantages of the Eucharist. As, however, no language can convey an adequate idea of its utility and fruits, pastors must be content to treat of one or two points, in order to show what an abundance and profusion of all goods are contained in those sacred mysteries.

The Eucharist Contains Christ and is the Food of the Soul

This they will in some degree accomplish, if, having explained the efficacy and nature of all the Sacraments, they compare the Eucharist to a fountain, the other Sacraments to rivulets. For the Holy Eucharist is truly and necessarily to be called the fountain of all graces, containing, as it does, after an admirable manner, the fountain itself of celestial gifts and graces, and the author of all the Sacraments, Christ our Lord, from whom, as from its source, is derived whatever of goodness and perfection the other Sacraments possess. From this (comparison), therefore, we may easily infer what most ample gifts of divine grace are bestowed on us by this Sacrament.

It will also be useful to consider attentively the nature of bread and wine, which are the symbols of this Sacrament. For what bread and wine are to the body, the Eucharist is to the health and delight of the soul, but in a higher and better way. This Sacrament is not, like bread and wine, changed into our substance; but we are, in some wise, changed into its nature, so that we may well apply here the words of St. Augustine: *I am the food of the grown. Grow and thou shalt eat Me; nor shalt thou change Me into thee, as thy bodily food, but thou shalt be changed into Me.*

The Eucharist Gives Grace

If, then, *grace and truth came by Jesus Christ*, they must surely be poured into the soul which receives with purity and holiness Him who said of Himself: *He that eateth My Flesh and drinketh My Blood abideth in me and I in him.* Those who receive this Sacrament piously and fervently must, beyond all doubt, so receive the Son of God into their souls as to be ingrafted as living members on His Body. For it is written: *He that eateth Me, the same also shall live by Me*; also: *The bread which I will give is My Flesh for the life of the world.* Explaining this passage, St. Cyril says: *The Word of God, uniting Himself to His own Flesh, imparted to it a vivifying power: it became Him, therefore, to unite Himself to our bodies in a wonderful manner, through His sacred Flesh and precious Blood, which we receive in the bread and wine, consecrated by His vivifying benediction.*

The Grace of the Eucharist Sustains

When it is said that the Eucharist imparts grace, pastors must admonish that this does not mean that the state of grace is not required for a profitable reception of this Sacrament. For as natural food can be of no use to the dead, so in like manner the sacred mysteries can evidently be of no avail to a soul which lives not by the spirit. Hence, this Sacrament has been instituted under the forms of bread and wine to signify that the object of its institution is not to recall the soul to life, but to preserve its life.

The reason, then, for saying that this Sacrament imparts grace, is that even the first grace, with which all should be clothed before they presume to approach the Holy Eucharist, *lest they eat and drink judgment to themselves*, is given to none unless they receive in wish and desire this very Sacrament. For the Eucharist is the end of all the Sacraments, and the symbol of unity and brotherhood in the Church, outside which none can attain grace.

The Grace of the Eucharist Invigorates and Delights

Again, just as the body is not only supported but also increased by natural food, from which the taste every day derives new relish and pleasure; so also is the soul not only sustained but invigorated by feasting on the food of the Eucharist, which gives to the spirit an increasing zest for heavenly things. Most truly and fitly therefore do we say that grace is imparted by this Sacrament, for it may be justly compared to the manna *having in it the sweetness of every taste.*

The Eucharist Remits Venial Sins

It cannot be doubted that by the Eucharist are remitted and pardoned lighter sins, commonly called venial. Whatever the soul has lost through the fire of passion, by falling into some slight offence, all this the Eucharist, cancelling those lesser faults, repairs, in the same way not to depart from the illustration already adduced as natural food gradually restores and repairs the daily waste caused by the force of the vital heat within us. Justly, therefore, has St. Ambrose said of this heavenly Sacrament: *That daily bread is taken as a remedy for daily infirmity.* But these things are to be understood of those sins for which no actual affection is retained.

The Eucharist Strengthens Against Temptation

There is, furthermore, such a power in the sacred mysteries as to preserve us pure and unsullied from sin, keep us safe from the assaults of temptation, and, as by some heavenly medicine, prepare the soul against the easy approach and infection of virulent and deadly disease. Hence, as St. Cyprian records, when the faithful were formerly hurried in multitudes by tyrants to torments and death, because they confessed the name of Christ, it was an ancient usage in the Catholic Church to give them, by the hands of the Bishop, the Sacrament of the Body and Blood of our Lord, lest perhaps overcome by the severity of their sufferings, they should fail in the fight for salvation.

It also restrains and represses the lusts of the flesh, for while it inflames the soul more ardently with the fire of charity, it of necessity extinguishes the ardour of concupiscence.

The Eucharist Facilitates the Attainment of Eternal Life

Finally, to comprise all the advantages and blessings of this Sacrament in one word, it must be taught that the Holy Eucharist is most efficacious towards the attainment of eternal glory. For it is written: *He that eateth My Flesh, and drinketh My Blood, hath everlasting life, and I will raise him up on the last day.* That is to say, by the grace of this Sacrament men enjoy the greatest peace and tranquillity of conscience during the present life; and, when the hour of departing from this world shall have arrived, like Elias, who in the strength of the bread baked on the hearth, walked to Horeb, the mount of God, they, too, invigorated by the strengthening influence of this (heavenly food), will ascend to unfading glory and bliss.

How the Effects of the Eucharist May be Developed and Illustrated

All these matters will be most fully expounded by pastors, if they but dwell or the sixth chapter of St. John, in which are developed the manifold effects of this Sacrament. Or again, glancing at the admirable actions of Christ our Lord, they may show that if those who received Him beneath their roof during His mortal life, or were restored to health by touching His vesture or the hem of His garment, were justly and deservedly deemed most blessed, how much more fortunate and happy we, into whose soul, resplendent as He is with unfading glory, He disdains not to enter, to heal all its wounds, to adorn it with His choicest gifts, and unite it to Himself.

Recipient of the Eucharist

Threefold Manner of Communicating

That the faithful may learn to be zealous for the better gifts, they must be shown who can obtain these abundant fruits from the Holy Eucharist, must be reminded that there is not only one way of communicating. Wisely and rightly, then, did our predecessors in the faith, as we read in the Council of Trent, distinguish three ways of receiving this Sacrament.

Some receive it sacramentally only. Such are those sinners who do not fear to approach the holy mysteries with polluted lips and heart, who, as the Apostle says, eat and drink the Lord's body unworthily. Of this class of communicants St. Augustine says: *He who dwells not in Christ, and in whom Christ dwells not, most certainly does not eat spiritually His flesh, although carnally and visibly he press with his teeth the Sacrament of His Flesh and Blood.* Those, therefore, who receive the sacred mysteries with such a disposition, not only obtain no fruit therefrom, but, as the Apostle himself testifies, *eat and drink judgment to themselves.*

Others are said to receive the Eucharist in spirit only. They are those who, inflamed with a lively faith which worketh by charity, partake in wish and desire of that celestial bread offered to them, from which they receive, if not the entire, at least very great fruits.

Lastly, there are some who receive the Holy Eucharist both sacramentally and spiritually, those who, according to the teaching of the Apostle, having first proved themselves and having approached this divine banquet adorned with the nuptial garment, derive from the Eucharist those most abundant fruits which we have already described. Hence, it is clear that those who, having it in their power to receive with fitting preparation the Sacrament of the body of the Lord, are yet satisfied with a spiritual Communion only, deprive themselves of the greatest and most heavenly advantages.

Necessity of Previous Preparation for Communion

We now come to point out the manner in which the faithful should be previously prepared for sacramental Communion. To demonstrate the great necessity of this previous preparation, the example of the Saviour should be adduced. Before He gave to His Apostles the Sacrament of His precious Body and Blood, although they were already clean, He washed their feet to show that we must use extreme diligence before Holy Communion in order to approach it with the greatest purity and innocence of soul.

In the next place, the faithful are to understand that as he who approaches thus prepared and disposed is adorned with the most ample gifts of heavenly grace; so, on the contrary, he who approaches without this preparation not only derives from it no advantage, but even incurs the greatest misfortune and loss. It is characteristic of the best and most salutary things that, if seasonably made use of, they are productive of the greatest benefit; but if employed out of time, they prove most pernicious and destructive. It cannot, therefore, excite out surprise that the great and exalted gifts of God; when received into a soul properly disposed, are of the greatest assistance towards the attainment of salvation; while to those who receive them unworthily, they bring with them eternal death.

Of this the Ark of the Lord affords a convincing illustration. The people of Israel possessed nothing more precious and it was to them the source of innumerable blessings from God; but when the Philistines carried it away, it brought on them a most destructive plague and the heaviest calamities, together with eternal disgrace.

Thus, also food when received from the mouth into a healthy stomach nourishes and supports the body; but when received into an indisposed stomach, causes grave disorders.

Preparation of Soul

The first preparation, then, which the faithful should make, is to distinguish table from table, this sacred table from profane tables, this celestial bread from common bread. This we do when we firmly believe that there is truly present the Body and Blood of the Lord, of Him whom the Angels adore in heaven, *at whose nod the pillars of heaven fear and tremble*, of whose glory the heavens and the earth are full. This is to discern the Body of the Lord in accordance with the admonition of the Apostle. We should venerate the greatness of the mystery rather than too curiously investigate its truth by idle inquiry.

Another very necessary preparation is to ask ourselves if we are at peace with and sincerely love our neighbor. *If, therefore, thou offerest thy gift at the altar, and there rememberest that thy brother hath anything against thee, leave there thy offering before the altar, and go first to be reconciled to thy brother, and then coming thou shalt offer thy gift.*

We should, in the next place, carefully examine whether our consciences be defiled by mortal sin, which has to be repented of, in order that it may be blotted out before Communion by the remedy of contrition and confession. The Council of Trent has defined that no one conscious of mortal sin and having an opportunity of going to confession, however contrite he may deem himself, is to approach the Holy Eucharist until he has been purified by sacramental confession.

We should also reflect in the silence of our own hearts how unworthy we are that the Lord should bestow on us this divine gift, and with the centurion of whom our Lord declared that he found *not so great faith in Israel*, we should exclaim from our hearts: *Lord, I am not worthy that Thou shouldst enter under my roof.*

We should also put the question to ourselves whether we can truly say with Peter: Lord, thou knowest that I love Thee, and should recollect that he who sat down at the banquet of the Lord without a wedding garment was cast into a dark dungeon and condemned to eternal torments.

Preparation of Body

Our preparation should not, however, be confined to the soul; it should also extend to the body. We are to approach the Holy Table fasting, having neither eaten nor drunk anything at least from the preceding midnight until the moment of Communion.

The dignity of so great a Sacrament also demands that married persons abstain from the marriage debt for some days previous to Communion. This observance is recommended by the example of David, who, when about to receive the show-bread from the hands of the priest, declared that he and his servants had been *clean from women for three days*.

The above are the principal things to be done by the faithful preparatory to receiving the sacred mysteries with profit; and to these heads may be reduced whatever other things may seem desirable by way of preparation.

The Obligation of Communion

How Often Must Communion Be Received?

Lest any be kept away from Communion by the fear that the requisite preparation is too hard and laborious, the faithful are frequently to be reminded that they are all bound to receive the Holy Eucharist. Furthermore, the Church has decreed that whoever neglects to approach Holy Communion once a year, at Easter, is liable to sentence of excommunication.

The Church Desires the Faithful to Communicate Daily

However, let not the faithful imagine that it is enough to receive the Body of the Lord once a year only, in obedience to the decree of the Church. They should approach oftener; but whether monthly, weekly, or daily, cannot be decided by any fixed universal rule. St. Augustine, however, lays down a most certain norm: *Live in such a manner as to be able to receive every day.*

It will therefore be the duty of the pastor frequently to admonish the faithful that, as they deem it necessary to afford daily nutriment to the body, they should also feel solicitous to feed and nourish the soul every day with this heavenly food. It is clear that the soul stands not less in need of spiritual, than the body of corporal food. Here it will be found most useful to recall the inestimable and divine advantages which, as we have already shown, flow from sacramental Communion. It will be well also to refer to the manna, which was a figure (of this Sacrament), and which refreshed the bodily powers every day. The Fathers who earnestly recommended the frequent reception of this Sacrament may also be cited. The words of St. Augustine, *Thou sinnest daily, receive daily*, express not his opinion only, but that of all the Fathers who have written on the subject, as anyone may easily discover who will carefully read them.

That there was a time when the faithful approached Holy Communion every day we learn from the Acts of the Apostles. All who then professed the faith of Christ burned with such true and sincere charity that, devoting themselves to prayer and other works of piety, they were found prepared to communicate daily. This devout practice, which seems to have been interrupted for a time, was again partially revived by the holy Pope and martyr Anacletus, who commanded that all the ministers who assisted at the Sacrifice of the Mass should communicate an ordinance, as the Pontiff declares, of Apostolic institution. It was also for a long time the practice of the Church that, as soon as the Sacrifice was complete, and when the priest himself had communicated, he turned to the congregation and invited the faithful to the Holy Table in these words: *Come, brethren, and receive Communion*; and thereupon those who were prepared, advanced to receive the holy mysteries with the most fervent devotion.

The Church Commands; The Faithful to Communicate Once a Year

But subsequently, when charity and devotion had grown so cold that the faithful very seldom approached Communion, it was decreed by Pope Fabian, that all should communicate thrice every year, at Christmas, at Easter, and at Pentecost. This decree was afterwards confirmed by many Councils, particularly by the first of Agde.

Such at length was the decay of piety that not only was this holy and salutary law unobserved, but Communion was deferred for years. The Council of Lateran, therefore, decreed that all the faithful should receive the sacred Body of the Lord, at least once a year, at Easter, and that neglect of this duty should be chastised by exclusion from the society of the faithful.

Who Are Obliged by the Law of Communion

But although this law, sanctioned by the authority of God and of His Church, concerns all the faithful, it should be taught that it does not extend to those who on account of their tender age have not attained the use of reason. For these are not able to distinguish the Holy Eucharist from common and ordinary bread and cannot bring with them to this Sacrament piety and devotion. Furthermore (to extend the precept to them) would appear inconsistent with the ordinance of our Lord, for He said: *Take and eat* words which cannot apply to infants, who are evidently incapable of taking and eating.

In some places, it is true, an ancient practice prevailed of giving the Holy Eucharist even to infants; but, for the reasons already assigned, and for other reasons in keeping with Christian piety, this practice has been long discontinued by authority of the Church.

With regard to the age at which children should be given the holy mysteries, this the parents and confessor can best determine. To them it belongs to inquire and to ascertain from the children themselves whether they have some knowledge of this admirable Sacrament and whether they desire to receive it.

Communion must not be given to persons who are insane and incapable of devotion. However, according to the decree of the Council of Carthage, it may be administered to them at the close of life, provided they have shown, before losing their minds, a pious and religious disposition, and no danger, arising from the state of the stomach or other inconvenience or disrespect, is likely.

The Rite of Administering Communion

As to the rite to be observed in communicating, pastors should teach that the law of the holy Church forbids Communion under both kinds to anyone but the officiating priests, without the authority of the Church itself.

Christ the Lord, it is true, as has been explained by the Council of Trent, instituted and delivered to His Apostles at His Last Supper this most sublime Sacrament under the species of bread and wine; but it does not follow that by doing so our Lord and Saviour established a law ordering its administration to all the faithful under both species. For speaking of this Sacrament, He Himself frequently mentions it under one kind only, as, for instance, when He says: *If any man eat of this bread, he shall live for ever*, and: *The bread that I will give is My*

Flesh for the life of the world, and: He that eateth this bread shall live for ever.

Why the Celebrant Alone Receives Under Both Species

It is clear that the Church was influenced by numerous and most cogent reasons, not only to approve, but also to confirm by authority of its decree, the general practice of communicating under one species. In the first place, the greatest caution was necessary to avoid spilling the Blood of the Lord on the ground, a thing that seemed not easily to be avoided, if the chalice were administered in a large assemblage of the people.

In the next place, whereas the Holy Eucharist ought to be in readiness for the sick, it was very much to be apprehended, were the species of wine to remain long unconsumed, that it might turn acid.

Besides, there are many who cannot at all bear the taste or even the smell of wine. Lest, therefore, what is intended for the spiritual health should prove hurtful to the health of the body, it has been most prudently provided by the Church that it should be administered to the people under the species of bread only.

We may also further observe that in many countries wine is extremely scarce; nor can it, moreover, be brought from elsewhere without incurring very heavy expenses and encountering very tedious and difficult journeys.

Finally, a most important reason was the necessity of opposing the heresy of those who denied that Christ, whole and entire, is contained under either species, and asserted that the Body is contained under the species of bread without the Blood, and the Blood under the species of wine without the Body. In order, therefore, to place more clearly before the eyes of all the truth of the Catholic faith, Communion under one kind, that is, under the species of bread, was most wisely introduced.

There are also other reasons, collected by those who have treated on this subject, and which, if it shall appear necessary, can be brought forward by pastors.

The Minister of the Eucharist

To omit nothing doctrinal on this Sacrament, we now come to speak of its minister, a point, however, on which scarcely anyone can be ignorant.

Only Priests Have Power to Consecrate and Administer the Eucharist

It must be taught, then, that to priests alone has been given power to consecrate and administer to the faithful, the Holy Eucharist. That this has been the unvarying practice of the Church, that the faithful should receive the Sacrament from the priests, and that the officiating priests should communicate themselves, has been explained by the holy Council of Trent, which has also shown that this practice, as having proceeded from Apostolic tradition, is to be religiously retained, particularly as Christ the Lord has left us an illustrious example thereof, having consecrated His own most sacred Body, and given it to the Apostles with His own hands.

The Laity Prohibited to Touch the Sacred Vessels

To safeguard in every possible way the dignity of so august a Sacrament, not only is the power of its administration entrusted exclusively to priests, but the Church has also prohibited by law any but consecrated persons, unless some case of great necessity intervene, to dare handle or touch the sacred vessels, the linen, or other instruments necessary to its completion.

Priests themselves and the rest of the faithful may hence understand how great should be the piety and holiness of those who approach to consecrate, administer or receive the Eucharist.

The Unworthiness of the Minister Does Not Invalidate the Sacrament

What, however, has been already said of the other Sacraments, holds good also with regard to the Sacrament of the Eucharist; namely, that a Sacrament is validly administered even by the wicked, provided all the essentials have been duly observed. For we are to believe that all these depend not on the merit of the minister, but are operated by the virtue and power of Christ our Lord.

These are the things necessary to be explained regarding the Eucharist as a Sacrament.

The Eucharist as a Sacrifice

We must now proceed to explain its nature as a Sacrifice, that pastors may understand what are the principal instructions which they ought to impart to the faithful on Sundays and holy days, regarding this mystery in conformity with the decree of the holy Council (of Trent).

Importance of Instruction on the Mass

This Sacrament is not only a treasure of heavenly riches, which if turned to good account will obtain for us the grace and love of God; but it also possesses a peculiar character, by which we are enabled to make some return to God for the immense benefits bestowed upon us.

How grateful and acceptable to God is this victim, if duly and legitimately immolated, is inferred from the following consideration. Of the sacrifices of the Old Law it is written: *Sacrifice and oblation thou wouldst not*; and again: *If thou hadst desired sacrifice, I would indeed have given it: with burnt offerings thou wilt not be delighted.* Now if these were so pleasing in the Lord's sight that, as the Scripture testifies, from them God smelled a sweet savour, that is to say, they were grateful and acceptable to Him; what have we not to hope from that Sacrifice in which is immolated and offered He Himself of whom a voice from heaven twice proclaimed: *This is My beloved Son, in whom I am well pleased.*

This mystery, therefore, pastors should carefully explain, so that when the faithful are assembled at the celebration of divine service, they may learn to meditate with attention and devotion on the sacred things at which they are present.

Distinction of Sacrament and Sacrifice

They should teach, then, in the first place, that the Eucharist was instituted by Christ for two purposes: one, that it might be the heavenly food of our souls, enabling us to support and preserve spiritual life; and the other, that the Church might have a perpetual Sacrifice, by which our sins might be expiated, and our heavenly Father, oftentimes grievously offended by our crimes, might be turned away from wrath to mercy, from the severity of just chastisement to clemency. Of this thing we may observe a type and resemblance in the Paschal lamb, which was wont to be offered and eaten by the children of Israel as a sacrament and a sacrifice.

Nor could our Saviour, when about to offer Himself to God the Father on the altar of the Cross, have given any more illustrious indication of His unbounded love towards us than by bequeathing to us a visible Sacrifice, by which that bloody Sacrifice, which was soon after to be offered once on the Cross, would be renewed, and its memory daily celebrated with the greatest utility, unto the consummation of ages by the Church diffused throughout the world.

But (between the Eucharist as a Sacrament and a Sacrifice) the difference is very great; for as a Sacrament it is perfected by consecration; as a Sacrifice, all its force consists in its oblation. When, therefore, kept in a pyx, or borne to the sick, it is a Sacrament, not a Sacrifice. As a Sacrament also, it is to them that receive it a source of merit, and brings with it all those advantages which have been already mentioned; but as a Sacrifice, it is not only a source of merit, but also of satisfaction. For as, in His Passion, Christ the Lord merited and satisfied for us; so also those who offer this Sacrifice, by which they communicate with us, merit the fruit of His Passion, and satisfy.

The Mass Is a True Sacrifice

Proof from the Council of Trent

With regard to the institution of this Sacrifice, the holy Council of Trent has left no room for doubt, by declaring that it was instituted by our Lord at His Last Supper; while it condemns under anathema all those who assert that in it is not offered to God a true and proper Sacrifice; or that to offer means nothing else than that Christ is given as our spiritual food.

Nor did (the Council) omit carefully to explain that to God alone is offered this Sacrifice. For although the Church sometimes offers Masses in honour and in memory of the Saints, yet she teaches that the Sacrifice is offered, not to them, but to God alone, who has crowned the Saints with immortal glory. Hence, the priest never says: *I offer Sacrifice to thee Peter, or to thee Paul*; but, while he offers Sacrifice to God alone, he renders Him thanks for the signal victory won by the blessed martyrs, and thus implores their patronage, that they, whose memory we celebrate on earth, may vouchsafe to intercede for us in heaven."

Proof from Scripture

This doctrine, handed down by the Catholic Church, concerning the truth of this Sacrifice, she received from the words of our Lord, when, on that last night, committing to His Apostles these same sacred mysteries, He said: *Do this for a commemoration of Me*; for then, as was defined by the holy Council, He ordained them priests, and commanded that they and their successors in the priestly office, should immolate and offer His body.

Of this the words of the Apostle to the Corinthians also afford a sufficient proof: *You cannot drink the chalice of the Lord, and the chalice of devils: you cannot be partakers of the table of the Lord and of the table of devils.* As then by the table of devils must be understood the altar on which sacrifice was offered to them; so also if the conclusion proposed to Himself by the Apostle is to be legitimately drawn *by the table of the Lord* can be understood nothing else than the altar on which Sacrifice was offered to the Lord.

Should we look for figures and prophecies of this Sacrifice in the Old Testament, in the first place Malachy most clearly prophesied thereof in these words: *From the rising of the sun even to the going down, My name is great among the Gentiles, and in every place there is sacrifice, and there is offered to My name a clean oblation: for My name is great among the Gentiles, saith the Lord of hosts.*

Moreover, this victim was foretold, as well before as after the promulgation of the Law, by various kinds of sacrifices; for this victim alone, as the perfection and completion of all, comprises all the blessings which were signified by the other sacrifices. In nothing, however, do we behold a more lively image of the Eucharistic Sacrifice than in that of Melchisedech; for the Saviour Himself offered to God the Father, at His Last Supper, His Body and Blood, under the appearances of bread and wine, declaring that He was constituted a priest for ever, after the order of Melchisedech.

Excellence of the Mass

The Mass is the Same *Sacrifice* as That of the Cross

We therefore confess that the Sacrifice of the Mass is and ought to be considered one and the same Sacrifice as that of the Cross, for the victim is one and the same, namely, Christ our Lord, who offered Himself, once only, a bloody Sacrifice on the altar of the Cross. The bloody and unbloody victim are not two, but one victim only, whose Sacrifice is daily renewed in the Eucharist, in obedience to the command of our Lord: *Do this for a commemoration of Me.*

The priest is also one and the same, Christ the Lord; for the ministers who offer Sacrifice, consecrate the holy mysteries, not in their own person, but in that of Christ, as the words of consecration itself show, for the priest does not say: *This is the Body of Christ*, but, *This is My Body*; and thus, acting in the Person of Christ the Lord, he changes the substance of the bread and wine into the true substance of His Body and Blood.

The Mass a Sacrifice of Praise, Thanksgiving and Propitiation

This being the case, it must be taught without any hesitation that, as the holy Council (of Trent) has also) explained, the sacred and holy Sacrifice of the Mass is not a Sacrifice of praise and thanksgiving only, or a mere commemoration of the Sacrifice performed on the cross, but also truly a propitiatory Sacrifice, by which God is appeased and rendered propitious to us. If, therefore, with a pure heart, a lively faith, and affected with an inward sorrow for our transgressions, we immolate and offer this most holy victim, we shall, without doubt, obtain mercy from the Lord, and grace in time of need; for so delighted is the Lord with the door of this victim that, bestowing on us the gift of grace and repentance, He pardons our sins. Hence, this usual prayer of the Church: *As often as the commemoration of this victim is celebrated, so often is the work of our salvation being done*; that is to say, through this unbloody Sacrifice flow to us the most plenteous fruits of that bloody victim.

The Mass Profits both the Living and the Dead

Pastors should next teach that such is the efficacy of this Sacrifice that its benefits extend not only to the celebrant and communicant, but to all the faithful, whether living with us on earth, or already numbered with those who are dead in the Lord, but whose sins have not yet been fully expiated. For, according to the most authentic Apostolic tradition, it is not less available when offered for them, than when offered for the sins of the living, their punishments, satisfactions, calamities, and difficulties of every sort.

It is hence easy to perceive, that all Masses, as being conducive to the common interest and salvation of all the faithful, are to be considered common to all.

The Rites and Ceremonies of the Mass

The Sacrifice (of the Mass) is celebrated with many solemn rites and ceremonies, none of which should be deemed useless or superfluous. On the contrary, all of them tend to display the majesty of this august Sacrifice, and to excite the faithful when beholding these saving mysteries, to contemplate the divine things which lie concealed in the Eucharistic Sacrifice. On these rites and ceremonies we shall not dwell, since they require a more lengthy exposition than is compatible with the nature of the present work; moreover priests can easily consult on the subject some of the many booklets and works that have been written by pious and learned men.

What has been said so far will, with the divine assistance, be found sufficient to explain the principal things which regard the Holy Eucharist both as a Sacrament and Sacrifice.

Quo Primum—
Papal Bull Establishing the Tridentine Rite

Apostolic Constitution of
His Holiness Pope Saint Pius V
July 13, 1570

To Our Venerable Brethren: the Patriarchs, Primates, Archbishops, Bishops, and other Local Ordinaries in Peace and Communion with the Apostolic See—Venerable Brethren, health and Apostolic Benediction!

From the very first, upon Our elevation to the chief Apostleship, We gladly turned our mind and energies and directed all out thoughts to those matters which concerned the preservation of a pure liturgy, and We strove with God's help, by every means in our power, to accomplish this purpose. For, besides other decrees of the sacred Council of Trent, there were stipulations for Us to revise and re-edit the sacred books: the Catechism, the Missal, and the Breviary. With the Catechism published for the instruction of the faithful, by God's help, and the Breviary thoroughly revised for the worthy praise of God, in order that the Missal and Breviary may be in perfect harmony, as fitting and proper—for its most becoming that there be in the Church only one appropriate manner of reciting the Psalms and only one rite for the celebration of Mass—We deemed it necessary to give our immediate attention to what still remained to be done, *viz*, the re-editing of the Missal as soon as possible.

Hence, We decided to entrust this work to learned men of our selection. They very carefully collated all their work with the ancient codices in Our Vatican Library and with reliable, preserved, or emended codices from elsewhere. Besides this, these men consulted the works of ancient and approved authors concerning the same sacred rites; and thus they have restored the Missal itself to the original form and rite of the holy Fathers. When this work has been gone over numerous times and further emended, after serious study and reflection, We commanded that the finished product be printed and published as soon as possible, so that all might enjoy the fruits of this labor; and thus, priests would know which prayers to use and which rites and ceremonies they were required to observe from now on in the celebration of Masses.

Let all everywhere adopt and observe what has been handed down by the Holy Roman Church, the Mother and Teacher of the other churches, and let Masses not be sung or read according to any other formula than that of this Missal published by Us. This ordinance applies, henceforth, now, and forever, throughout all the provinces of the Christian world, to all patriarchs, cathedral churches, collegiate and parish churches, be they secular or religious, both of men and of women—even of military orders—and of churches or chapels without a specific congregation in which conventual Masses are sung aloud in choir or read privately in accord with the rites and customs of the Roman Church. This Missal is to be used by all churches, even by those which in their authorization are made exempt, whether by Apostolic indult, custom, or privilege, or even if by oath or official confirmation of the Holy See, or have their rights and faculties guaranteed to them by any other manner whatsoever.

This new rite alone is to be used unless approval of the practice of saying Mass differently was given at the very time of the institution and confirmation of the church by Apostolic See at least 200 years ago, or unless there has prevailed a custom of a similar kind which has been continuously followed for a period of not less than 200 years, in which most cases We in no wise rescind their above-mentioned prerogative or custom. However, if this Missal, which we have seen fit to publish, be more agreeable to these latter, We grant them permission to celebrate Mass according to its rite, provided they have the consent of their bishop or prelate or of their whole Chapter, everything else to the contrary notwithstanding. All other of the churches referred to above, however, are hereby denied the use of other missals, which are to be discontinued entirely and absolutely; whereas, by this present Constitution, which will be valid henceforth, now, and forever, We order and enjoin that nothing must be added to Our recently published Missal, nothing omitted from it, nor anything whatsoever be changed within it under the penalty of Our displeasure.

We specifically command each and every patriarch, administrator, and all other persons or whatever ecclesiastical dignity they may be, be they even cardinals of the Holy Roman Church, or possessed of any other rank or pre-eminence, and We order them in virtue of holy obedience to chant or to read the Mass according to the rite and manner and norm herewith laid down by Us and, hereafter, to discontinue and completely discard all other rubrics and rites of other missals, however ancient, which they have customarily followed; and they must not in celebrating Mass presume to introduce any ceremonies or recite any prayers other than those contained in this Missal.

Furthermore, by these presents [this law], in virtue of Our Apostolic authority, We grant and concede in perpetuity that, for the chanting or reading of the Mass in any church whatsoever, this Missal is hereafter to be followed absolutely, without any scruple of conscience or fear of incurring any penalty, judgment, or censure, and may freely and lawfully be used. Nor are superiors, administrators, canons, chaplains, and other secular priests, or religious, of whatever title designated, obliged to celebrate the Mass otherwise than as enjoined by Us. We likewise declare and ordain that no one whosoever is forced or coerced to alter this Missal, and that this present document cannot be revoked or modified, but remain always valid and retain its full force notwithstanding the previous constitutions and decrees of the Holy See, as well as any general or special constitutions or edicts of provincial or synodal councils, and notwithstanding the practice and custom of the aforesaid churches, established by long and immemorial prescription—except, however, if more than two hundred years' standing.

It is Our will, therefore, and by the same authority, We decree that, after We publish this constitution and the edition of the Missal, the priests of the Roman Curia are, after thirty days, obliged to chant or read the Mass according to it; all others south of the Alps, after three months; and those beyond the Alps either within six months or whenever the Missal is available for sale. Wherefore, in order that the Missal be preserved incorrupt throughout the whole world and kept free of flaws and errors, the penalty for nonobservance for printers, whether mediately or immediately subject to Our dominion, and that of the Holy Roman Church, will be the forfeiting of their books and a fine of one hundred gold ducats, payable ipso facto to the Apostolic Treasury. Further, as for those located in other parts of the world, the penalty is excommunication *latae sententiae*, and such other penalties as may in Our judgment be imposed; and We decree by this law that they must not dare or presume either to print or to publish or to sell, or in any way to accept books of this nature without Our approval and consent, or without the express consent of the Apostolic Commissaries of those places, who will be appointed by Us. Said printer must receive a standard Missal and agree faithfully with it and in no wise vary from the Roman Missal of the large type (*secundum magnum impressionem*).

Accordingly, since it would be difficult for this present pronouncement to be sent to all parts of the Christian world and simultaneously come to light everywhere, We direct that it be, as usual, posted and published at the doors of the Basilica of the Prince of the Apostles, also at the Apostolic Chancery, and on the street at Campo Flora; furthermore, We direct that printed copies of this same edict signed by a notary public and made official by an ecclesiastical dignitary possess the same indubitable validity everywhere and in every nation, as if Our manuscript were shown there. Therefore, no one whosoever is permitted to alter this notice of Our permission, statute, ordinance, command, precept, grant, indult, declaration, will, decree, and prohibition. Should know that he will incur the wrath of Almighty God and of the Blessed Apostles Peter and Paul.

Given at St. Peter's in the year of the Lord's Incarnation, 1570, on the 14th of July of the Fifth year of Our Pontificate.

"Thoughts on Alterations in the Liturgy Respectfully Submitted to the Clergy"

John Henry Cardinal Newman
September 9, 1833

Attempts are making to get the Liturgy altered. My dear Brethren, I beseech you consider with me whether you ought not to resist the alteration of even one jot or tittle of it. Though you would in your own private judgments wish to have this or that phrase or arrangement amended, is this a time to concede one tittle?

Why do I say this? Because, though most of you would wish some immaterial points altered, yet not many of you agree in those points, and not many of you agree what is and what is not immaterial. If all your respective emendations are taken, the alterations in the Services will be extensive; and though each will gain something he wishes, he will lose more from those alterations which he did not wish. Tell me, are the present imperfections (as they seem to each) of such a nature, and so many, that their removal will compensate for the recasting of much which each thinks to be no imperfection, or rather an excellence?

There are persons who wish the Marriage Service emended: there are others who would be indignant at the changes proposed. There are some who wish the Consecration Prayer in the Holy Sacrament to be what it was in King Edward's first book; there are others who think this would be an approach to Popery.* There are some who wish the imprecatory Psalms omitted; there are others who would lament this omission as savoring of the shallow and detestable liberalism of the day. There are some who wish the Services shortened; there are others who think we should have far more Services, and more frequent attendance at public worship than we have.

How few would be pleased by *any given* alterations; and how many

---

* Ed. Note: Newman penned these words while still an Anglican. He converted twelve years later, on October 9, 1845.

pained! But once begin altering, and there will he no reason or justice in stopping, till the criticisms of all parties are satisfied. Thus, will not the Liturgy be in the evil case described in the well-known story of the picture subjected by the artist to the observations of passersby? And, even to speak at present of comparatively immaterial alterations. I mean such as do not infringe upon the doctrines of the Prayer Book, will not it even with these be a changed book, and will not that new book be for certain an inconsistent one, the alterations being made, not on principle, but upon chance objections urged from various quarters?

But this is not all. A taste for criticism grows upon the mind. When we begin to examine and take to pieces, our judgment becomes perplexed, and our feelings unsettled. I do not know whether others feel this to the same extent, but for myself, I confess there are few parts of the Service that I could not disturb myself about, and feel fastidious at, if I allowed my mind in this abuse of reason. First, e.g., I might object to the opening sentences; "they are not evangelical enough; CHRIST is not mentioned in them; they are principally from the Old Testament." Then I should criticise the exhortation, as having too many words, and as antiquated in style. I might find it hard to speak against the Confession; but "the Absolution." it might be said, "is not strong enough; it is a mere declaration, not an announcement of pardon to those who have confessed." And so on.

Now I think this unsettling of the mind a frightful thing; both to ourselves, and more so to our flocks. They have long regarded the Prayer Book with reverence as the say of their faith and devotion. The weaker sort it will make skeptical: the better it will offend and pain. Take, e.g., an alteration which some have offered in the Creed, to omit or otherwise word the clause. "He descended into Hell." Is it no comfort for mourners to be told that CHRIST Himself has been in that unseen state, or Paradise, which is the allotted place of sojourn for departed spirits? Is it not very easy to explain the ambiguous word? Is it any great harm if it is misunderstood, and is it not very difficult to find any substitute for it in harmony with the composition of the Creed? I suspect we should find the best men in the number of those who would retain it as it is. On the other hand, will not the unstable learn from us the habit of criticising what they should never think of but as a divine voice supplied by the Church for their need?

But as regards ourselves, the Clergy, what will be the effect of this temper of innovation in us? We have the power to bring about changes in the Liturgy; shall we not exert it? Have we any security, if we once begin, that we shall ever end? Shall not we pass from non-essentials to essentials? And then, on looking back after the mischief is done, what excuse shall we be able to make for ourselves for having encouraged such proceedings at first? Were there grievous errors in the Prayer Book, something might be said for beginning, but who can point out any? Cannot we very well *bear* things as they are? Does any part of it seriously disquiet us? No—we have before now freely given our testimony to its accordance with Scripture.

But it may be said that "we must conciliate an outcry which is made; that some alteration is demanded." By whom? No one can tell who cries, or who can be conciliated. Some of the laity, I suppose, now consider this carefully. Who are these lay persons? Are they serious men and are their consciences involuntarily hurt by the things they wish altered? Are they not rather the men you meet in company, worldly men, with little personal religion, of lax conversation and lax professed principles, who sometimes perhaps come to Church, and then are wearied and disgusted? Is it not so? You have been dining, perhaps, with a wealthy neighbor, or fall in with this great Statesman, or that noble Land-holder, who considers the Church two centuries behind the world, and expresses to you wonder that its enlightened members do nothing to improve it. And then you get ashamed, and are betrayed into admissions which sober reason disapproves. You consider, too, that it is a great pity so estimable or so influential a man should be disaffected to the Church; and you go away with a vague notion that something must be done to conciliate such persons. Is this to bear about you the solemn office of a GUIDE and TEACHER in Israel, or *to follow a lead?*

But consider what are the concessions which would conciliate such men. Would immaterial alterations? Do you really think they care one jot about the verbal or other changes which some recommend, and others are disposed to grant whether "the unseen state" is substituted for "hell," "condemnation" for "damnation." or the order of Sunday Lessons is remodeled? No. they dislike the *doctrine* of the Liturgy. These men of the world do not like the anathemas of the Athanasian Creed, and other such peculiarities of our Services. But even were the alterations, which would please them, small, are they the persons whom it is of use, whom it is becoming to conciliate by going out of our way?

I need not go on to speak against doctrinal alterations, because most thinking men are sufficiently averse to them. But, I earnestly beg you to consider whether we must not come to them if we once begin. For by altering immaterials, we merely *raise* without *gratifying* the desire of correcting; we excite the craving, but withhold the food. And it should be observed, that the changes called immaterial often contain in themselves the germ of some principle, of which they are thus the introduction, e.g., if we were to leave out the imprecatory Psalms, we certainly countenance the notion of the day, that love and love only is in the Gospel the character of ALMIGHTY GOD and the duty of regenerate man; whereas the Gospel, rightly understood, shows His Infinite Holiness and Justice as well as His Infinite Love; and it enjoins on men the duties of zeal towards Him, hatred of sin, and separation from sinners, as well as that of kindness and charity.

To the above observations it may be answered, that changes have formerly been made in the Services without leading to the issue I am predicting now; and therefore they may be safely made again. But, waiving all other remarks in answer to this argument, is not this enough, *viz.* that there *is* peril? No one will deny that the rage of the day is for concession. Have we not already granted (political) points, without stopping the course of innovation? This is a fact. Now, is it worthwhile even to *risk* fearful changes merely to gain petty improvements, allowing those which are proposed to be such?

We know not what is to come upon us; but the writer for one will try so to acquit himself now, that if any irremediable calamity befalls the Church, he may not have to vex himself with the recollections of silence on his part and indifference, when he might have been up and alive. There was a time when he. as well as others, might feel the wish, or rather the temptation, of steering a middle course between parties; but if so, a more close attention to passing events has cured his infirmity. In a day like this there are but two sides, zeal and persecution, the Church and the world; and those who attempt to occupy the ground between them, at best will lose their labor, but probably will be drawn back to the latter. Be practical, I respectfully urge you; do not attempt impossibilities; sail not as if in pleasure boats upon a troubled sea. Not a word falls to the ground, in a time like this. Speculations about ecclesiastical improvements which might he innocent at other times, have a strength of mischief now. They are recalled before he who utters them understands that he has committed himself.

Be prepared then for petitioning against any alterations in the Prayer Book which may be proposed. And, should you see that our Fathers the Bishops seem to countenance them, petition still. Petition *them.* They will thank you for such a proceeding. *They do not wish these alterations;* but how can they resist them without the support of their Clergy? They consent to them (if they do) partly from the notion that they are thus pleasing you. Undeceive them. They will be rejoiced to hear that you are as unwilling to receive them as they are. However, if after all there be persons determined to allow some alterations, then let them quickly make up their minds *how far* they will go. They think it easier to draw the line elsewhere, than as things now exist. Let them point out the limit of their concessions now; and let them keep to it then; and (if they can do this) I will say that, though they are not as wise as they might have been, they are at least firm, and have at last come right.

From *Prayers And Ceremonies of The Mass; or, Moral, Doctrinal, and Liturgical Explanations of the Prayers and Ceremonies of the Mass*

The Very Rev. John T. Sullivan, V. G., 1870

It is affirmed that [the disciplinary legislation by which the Church has required her pastors to use the Latin language in the sacred liturgy] is unreasonable in itself, and, in its consequences, injurious to the people. We, on the contrary, maintain that she had and still has good reasons for deciding that it is inexpedient to use the vernacular tongue in the Mass. The Church adopted the Latin as the language of her liturgy at a time when that language was spoken by the greatest part of the civilized world the Roman Empire. She continued to use it, even when the Latin ceased to be a living, spoken language, for the following good reasons:

1. She considers a language no longer under going changes as best suited for the celebration of mysteries and the administration of sacraments in which the faith that changeth not is conveyed.

2. The preservation of a common language in our common service, tends to preserve and strengthen the extended union of her holy brotherhood.

3. It enables her clergy to officiate at every altar, and makes her laity find a home in every church of her communion.

4. All tongues and tribes and nations are thus united together, and become one people, adoring one common Father, grateful to one common Redeemer, and beseeching sanctification from one Holy Spirit.

5. Moreover, this salutary discipline unites ages as it binds nations, for the liturgy which we use has descended to us from the primitive days of our religion. The very words in which an Ambrose and an Augustine officiated, whose substance they received from apostolic men, being now repeated at our altars.

We further maintain that no injury is done the people, for whatever the officiating minister at the altar says in the Latin language, they may possess in their own tongue faithful translations of the liturgy, and books with appropriate prayers, being allowed by the Church.

The Liturgical Language

Peter C. Yorke, S. T. D.
The Roman Liturgy 1897

38. **Languages.** The language which a people naturally uses is called its "vernacular," or "mother tongue." Thus, French is the vernacular of the French people, and German the vernacular of the German. A "living language" is one in common use by ordinary persons. A "dead language" is one that has ceased to be spoken among the people, though preserved in books and still studied. An "acquired language" is a dead or a living speech that is acquired by study. To the vast majority of the people of the United States, English is their vernacular or mother tongue; to immigrants from non-English-speaking countries English is an acquired language. When we speak of the learned languages we usually mean Latin, Greek, and Hebrew.

39. The Ancient Vernaculars. The dead languages, of course, were originally living. At the beginning of the Christian era, Latin and Greek were in vigorous life all over the Roman Empire. Latin prevailed in the West; Greek in the East. In the greater part of these territories both Latin and Greek were acquired languages. The old vernaculars still lived on, but Latin and Greek were used in governmental business, in commerce, in literature, in religion. In the West the old vernaculars, chiefly of the Celtic and Germanic stocks, were forced into the remoter regions or died out altogether when Rome conquered their homelands.

When we say a language dies we do not mean that it leaves no trace behind it. Usually, in dying it also kills the acquired language and produces a new tongue.

Thus, when Latin died in Europe, new languages took its place, such as Italian, Spanish, French; and these differ from one another mainly by the effect the old vernaculars had on the speech of the conqueror. In the East, however, Latin failed to make much headway against the Greek; on the contrary, the Greek culture conquered the Latin, and in Rome, at any rate, Greek was as familiar as the ancient vernacular. In the East, Greek itself was confronted by two far more ancient civilizations. In Asia, it had to face the Semitic dialects of the great Assyrian and Babylonian Empire, and in Egypt the immemorial tongue of the Pharaos. Hence, we may say, in general, that when the

Church began her work, Latin and Greek were the common tongues of the West, Greek and Syriac the common tongues of Western Asia, and Greek and Egyptian the common tongues of Eastern Africa.

40. The Vernacular in the Liturgy. In the time of our Lord the ancient Hebrew had become a dead language, and, though it was used in the Temple and the synagogue, Syriac and Greek were languages of the ordinary intercourse. When the Apostles began to preach to the people they did not take over the Hebrew language, with the exception of a few words, but they used the various vernaculars. In the same way, the common tongue was used in the Liturgy. Now, as we said, there were three great centers whence the liturgies spread, namely, Antioch, Alexandria, and Rome, and we find that the chief languages used in public prayer and sacrifice, are for the first Greek and Syriac, as Antioch, while a Greek city, was the Seagate of all Syria, both Eastern and Western. Alexandria bore the same relation to Egypt, and we find the Liturgy of St. Mark in Greek and Coptic, that is, the language of the hieroglyphics written in Greek characters. While in Rome, the Latin language resumed exclusive sway as the shifting of the center of gravity of the empire to the Bosphorus retired the Greek to its ancient limits. When the Germanic and Slavonic nations poured in on the empire, and were gradually converted to Christianity, the East and the West developed two different policies in dealing with their languages. As a general rule, the East translated the Liturgy into the vernaculars of the new nations, while the peoples evangelized from the West were content to adopt the language of Rome in their public worship. Thus, it came to pass that Slavonic tribes, such as the Russians, who received Christianity from Constantinople, use Slavonic in their liturgy, while other Slavonic tribes, such as the Poles, who were converted under Roman influence, use Latin. In the same way, the Abyssinians, who received the faith from Alexandria, use Ethiopic, and the Irish, who received the faith from Rome, use Latin.

41. The Modern Languages. From what has been said of dead languages, it is easily understood that the languages we speak now are new growths. As a matter of fact, languages are constantly changing. If you read the English written two hundred years ago, you will notice at once that, while you understand it perfectly, there is something unfamiliar about it; if you go back two hundred years farther, you will need a glossary, and the phrases will often be quite unintelligible. Read the English of a thousand years ago, and you are face to face with another language that has to be studied as you study German today. What is true of English is true in greater or less degree of all the other modern tongues. The result has been that even in countries like Russia, where the Liturgy was translated into the vernacular, the Church Russian is as strange to the Russian speaker of our time as Latin is to a Frenchman or a Spaniard.

42. Latin an Emphasis of Doctrine. It may be asked why does not the Church now translate the Liturgy into the vernacular or vulgar tongue? There are many reasons, but so far as the Latin Liturgy is concerned the chief is that the use of Latin has become an emphasis of doctrine. In the sixteenth century there came the great revolution known as Protestantism. One of the leading doctrines of that heresy struck at the public officers of the Church. Protestants denied the right of the officers of the Church to choose other officers according to the words of Christ, "Ye have not chosen Me, but I have chosen you." Hence, the ministers were not sent out to bring the people into the Church, but the people had the right to choose their own ministers, who, like the civil officers, had power only as long as they represented the people. Again, the Protestants denied the existence of a sacrifice in the Church, and of course with the sacrifice went the altar and the priest. All divine service was therefore merely public prayer, and all the people were equally qualified to perform it. Hence, it was necessary that the divine worship should be performed in a language which all understood, and hence it is that all the Protestant sects hold service in the language used by the congregation. Their minister has no power or authority whatsoever. He is merely one of the congregation set aside for convenience sake to lead in prayer, just as a man is set aside for convenience sake to ring the bells or play the organ. As we have already seen, the Catholic doctrine is the very opposite of the Protestant teaching. All men are born into civil society. By the very fact that they exist they must exist in some government. Hence, it is that they all have a right in the government, and as a matter of fact exercise that right in a greater or less degree. But men are not born into the Church. They are brought into it either early or late in life. Hence, before there was a Christian people there were ministers sent out to form a Christian people. This is the commission Christ gave His Apostles to go out, not in the name of the people, but to the people in His Name, and to make disciples of them all, without distinction of race or color or condition. Hence, the mission or authority of the public official in the Catholic Church does not come from the people, but from Christ through the Apostles and the subsequent succession of public officials. This is what is called the Apostolic Succession. In order, therefore, to emphasize the fact that the public official is a public official in her sight, even though the people do not choose him, and that public prayer is public prayer, even when offered alone by the proper officer, the Church insisted on retaining Latin in her services. This language, not known to the people, marked in the clearest way that it was not they but the properly constituted officer who was offering the public prayer. Moreover, the sacrifice was continued in Latin to show that it was the priest who offered the sacrifice, and that he offered it not because he derived his authority from the people, but because by the Apostolic Succession he had received a share of the Priesthood of Jesus Christ. Latin then became, as it were, a barrier or dividing line between priest and people an emphasis on the doctrine not only of the sacrificial character of the Mass, but also of the public character of the ministers of religion.

LATIN IN THE MASS.

43. Latin a Symbol of Unity. Besides being an emphasis of the true teaching concerning the nature of public worship, Latin is also a symbol of the unity of the Church. As at the tower of Babel the confusion of tongues marked the dispersion of the nations, so in the Church unity of speech is a lesson that Christ has joined all men in the bonds of brotherhood. The use of Latin thus connects us with our fathers in the faith. It is a heritage from the days of old and a memorial of the time when in the Western world there was only one faith and one tongue. A Catholic hears Mass in the same familiar accents in Europe, in America, in China, in the Islands of the Sea. He is at home in every land, and nowhere does the worship seem strange to him.

Thus, like the Communion of Saints, our liturgical language binds together ages and countries the most remote and is a visible sign to all of the unity of the Church of Christ.

44. Advantages of Latin. Moreover, Latin has this great advantage that it never changes. Spoken languages, on the contrary, are never fixed, but the words and phrases in them are always taking on new meanings. Hence, a Liturgy in the spoken language sometimes becomes unintelligible and often positively misleading. Thus, for example, a prayer which is said during the Mass formerly began "Prevent, we beseech Thee, Lord, our actions by Thy Holy Inspiration."

Then the meaning was, "Further our actions," or "Go before our actions." Now, however, it means the very opposite, "Stop our actions." So, too, the Psalms which are read in Protestant churches are now almost unintelligible to the uneducated even in English, not only on account of their subject, but on account of the words used. From these disadvantages Latin is free. There is no danger of irreverence from ridiculous or evil meanings attributed to words, but the whole service is conducted with a decency and a majesty which can be gained only by the use of a language so stately and so full-sounding as the Latin.

"We all know that when a piece of our silver money has for a long time been fulfilling its part as pale and common drudge tween man and man, whatever it had, at first, of sharper outline and livelier impress is in the end nearly or altogether worn away. So it is with words, above all with words of theology and science. These, getting into general use, and passing often from mouth to mouth, lose the image and superscription which they had, before they descended from the school to the market-place, from the pulpit to the street. Being now caught up by those who understood imperfectly and thus incorrectly their true value, who will not be at the pains of learning what that is, or who are incapable of so doing, they are obliged to accommodate themselves to the lower sphere in which they circulate, by laying aside much of the precision and accuracy and fullness which once they had; they become feebler, shallower, more indistinct, till in the end, as true and adequate exponents of thought or feeling, they cease to be of any service at all." (*French, English Past and Present*)

45. Disadvantages of Latin. The only objection which can be made against Latin is that it is not "understanded of the people." This disadvantage is well known by those in authority in the Church; still, though the question was discussed, it was considered more advisable to keep to the Latin. We have seen Latin is not necessary for the essence of public worship; other languages are used, and any language might be employed. But we have seen, too, that it is not necessary for the essence of public worship that the people should understand. The reasons, therefore, for its continuance or discontinuance by the proper authorities are reasons of advantage. Is it more useful to keep Latin or to adopt the vulgar tongue? As we have said, this question was debated, and the Council of Trent decided in favor of Latin. The utility of Latin in being an Emphasis of Doctrine, a symbol of unity, and a conservator of dignity was considered greater than the utility of a language in common use. This decision was reached the more readily because the Latin service is not so unintelligible as some would make it out to be. In the first place, Catholics, who are familiar with it from childhood, grow into its spirit and unconsciously imbibe its meaning. In the second place, books in which the prayers are translated and the ceremonies explained are plenty and cheap. In the third place, the Council of Trent has ordered frequent oral instructions on the nature of the Liturgy for those who cannot find time or occasion for studying books. Hence, it is a fact of experience that if we take a Protestant and a Catholic from the same walk of life, with the same advantages, the same education, the Catholic can give a fuller and better account of the services of his Church, though they are in Latin, than the Protestant can of the observances of his own sect, though all is in English. The reason is that in the Catholic Church everything teaches. The ceremonies, the vestments, the altar, the pictures, the statues, all teach through the eye far more quickly and far more thoroughly than mere words can teach through the ear.

"Although the Mass containeth much instruction for the faithful people, nevertheless it hath not seemed good to the fathers that it should be celebrated in all places in the vulgar tongue. Wherefore, retaining everywhere the ancient rite of each Church which hath been approved by the Roman Church, the mother and mistress of all churches, lest the sheep of Christ should be a-hungered and the little children should ask for bread and no man should break it unto them: the holy synod doth command pastors and them who have the cure of souls to explain frequently either in person or by deputy during the celebration of the Mass some particular of those things which are read in the Mass; and especially on Sundays and festivals to publish among other subjects some mystery of this most holy sacrifice." (*Council of Trent*)

46. Our Personal Debt of Honor. When the Council of Trent ordered frequent explanations of the Mass in Church, books were not as cheap and as plenty as they are now, neither was popular education so widely spread. In our conditions, it is possible for practically all Catholics to study and understand what is done at the altar if they have the good will. Of course, we can hear Mass without a book at all or while saying the beads, and perhaps hear it more profitably than some who can give an account of every point in the service; but, as we can see from the official declaration of the Church in the Council of Trent, it is her wish that all her children should by instruction and knowledge have access to the spiritual treasures that lie hid in the mystery of the Mass. Catholics, therefore, who are receiving a Catholic education are under a special obligation of honor to acquire this familiarity with the chief action of their religion. Especially students who are pursuing the higher studies should deem it their dearest privilege to be able to enter in spirit into this Holy of Holies. Those who are studying Latin may, even towards the end of their first year, be able to follow the priest in the general order of the Mass in a Latin Missal. Those who are not learning Latin will find English translations of the Missal easy to procure at a reasonable price. Gradually, the prayers of the Liturgy will become as familiar to them as those they learned at their mother's knee, and they will be brought into close and intimate communion with our blessed Lord, who in this wonderful rite has left us the memorial of His love.

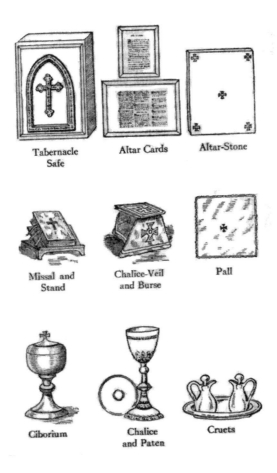

Tabernacle Safe Altar Cards Altar-Stone

Missal and Stand Chalice-Veil and Burse Pall

Ciborium Chalice and Paten Cruets

Excerpt from *Jesus in the Eucharist*

Very Rev. W. J. Kelly, V. F., 1903

Latin is the liturgical language of the Church in all the countries of the Western Hemisphere; but in the Eastern Hemisphere Greek is used, and also Syro-Chaldaic. Latin and Greek were the prevalent languages at the time of the establishment of Christianity, and when they ceased to be vernacular the Church continued to use them. The Jewish Sanhedrin did the same under similar circumstances. During the Babylonian captivity Syro-Chaldaic became the language of the Jewish people, and the primitive Hebrew quite died out of common usage; but, in spite of this fact, Hebrew was retained in the public services of the Temple and synagogues, even when its meaning had become quite unknown to the people in general. If this practice had been reprehensible, doubtless Our Lord would have found fault with it, for He attended Divine service in the Temple and in the synagogues.

Latin was the language in which the Church first worshipped when she established herself in the Roman Empire, and in it the early martyrs, saints, and Fathers gave expression, with the greatest force and beauty, to their Christian belief and feelings. What more natural, therefore, than that the Church should have retained this language, carrying it everywhere with her, and carefully making use of the same words from age to age to express exactly the same ideas, so that everywhere and always there might be identity of faith and worship?

As the Church is Catholic that is to say, Universal, and, therefore, embraces all nations, and has everywhere the same faith, sacraments, and sacrifice, it is necessary that she should make use of a language that is characterized by unity and universality, and such a language is Latin, which is universally the language of the learned, and is immutable. The Church has need of a language that is unchanging, like her teaching and her Divine Founder, who is yesterday, and to-day, and the same for ever.

As all are aware, living languages change, words become obsolete,† or acquire different meanings, whereas a dead language, such as the

---

† How many words in Wyckliffe's translation of St. John's Gospel, or in Chaucer's Canterbury Tales, are now unintelligible to the ordinary reader!

Latin, changes not. Its words have a recognised and constant meaning, and hence, as time passes, there is no danger of error creeping in through misconception of words and phrases. Besides, it frequently happens that the words of one language cannot express the full force of certain phrases in another tongue, so that, if in different countries Mass were celebrated in different languages, it would be difficult to preserve an identity of sense. Add to this the practical impossibility of preventing errors arising from changes in the vernacular, and we have sufficient reason for the retention of Latin by the Church in her Ritual and Liturgy. By doing so she has secured them from error, and has preserved untainted the principal channels of tradition. Not only would there be danger to faith, but many other inconveniences would ensue if the Church were to use in her public worship a language which is ever changing and which might grow obsolete.

She has existed in practically every part of the world for many centuries. The languages and dialects of her children are to be numbered by hundreds, and they have been changing age after age. How, then, would it have been possible for her to have kept up, during all those centuries, the work of translating and re-translating her liturgical books, so as to adapt them to the vernacular of her children scattered over the whole earth, from Alaska to Manchuria, from Greenland's icy mountains to Africa's torrid zones?

Even if it were possible to give a vernacular ritual to each nation and tribe the gain would be a doubtful one; whereas the use of a common language has many advantages. It enables the Catholic, wherever he may be, to feel at home at the public services of the Church. If miners of a dozen nationalities attend Mass in the Catholic church at Klondyke, each one is able to assist at it as if he were in his own native place. Thus, it is evident that having the Mass in Latin is a great boon to all Catholics who travel for pleasure or business, and it is of especial benefit to priests, who are able to say Mass in any country in which they may find themselves.

In this language are enshrined the treasures of Christian and heathen literature, and in obliging her priests to learn Latin the Church enables them to have access not only to the writings of the Fathers and Doctors of the Church, to the ancient Liturgies, to Canon and Civil Law, but also to the writings, sacred and profane, of innumerable learned authors of every age and country.

Moreover, by this means the Church has maintained a medium of communication between every part of Christendom, in correspondence, in travelling, in the assembling of general councils; thus keeping in touch with the faithful of all parts of the world, and holding her children of all nations attached to the centre of Christian unity. As the Powers in their diplomatic dealings with one another make use of a common language, so obviously it is necessary that the Church should have a common language for the transaction of her general affairs, since she has to treat with people of every nationality.

Hence, Latin has been wisely retained by the Church, because it was necessary for the general good of the Church. It is the best-known language of the world, and, by its constant use in the Church, it has become, to some extent, familiar even to the unlearned. In many Catholic prayer-books the Mass is to be found in full, with a verbatim translation in the vernacular, and all of them contain devotions for the Mass, which are a series of prayers corresponding with every part of the Liturgy. This is true, not only of England, but of all countries, and it has always been so.

Apart from all these reasons, the objection to the use of Latin in the Mass loses all its force if it be allowed that the Mass is not a mere form of devotion, but a sacrifice in which the priest, as minister of Christ, mediates between God and the people.

As [St. Robert] Bellarmine remarks, the oblation of the Mass consists more in the act which is performed than in the words; for, without offering Him in words, the very action by which the Victim, Jesus Christ, is presented on the altar is a true oblation. For the consecration, the words are, indeed, necessary; but these are said, not to instruct the people, but to offer the sacrifice. Even the words of oblation are directed, not to the people, but to God, who understands every language.

This fact also justifies the practice of saying the most sacred parts of the Mass in secret. The custom is a very old one, for its observance is directed in the liturgies of St. John Chrysostom and St. Basil.

That it was observed in the Latin Church in the beginning of the fifth century is certain from the fact that it is mentioned by Pope Innocent I. in his letter to the Bishop of Eugubium. It owed its origin, doubtless, to a profound reverence for the sacredness of the mysteries that were being celebrated, and for this reason, and on account also of its antiquity, it was approved by the Council of Trent.

It must not be imagined that Catholics are at all adverse to this custom, or that it prevents them from joining in the holy sacrifice in a less intelligent manner. Even if, as sometimes happens in large churches, they are unable, not only to hear, but even to see, the celebrant, they are, nevertheless, able by long experience and the ringing of the altar bell to follow the course of the Mass as well as if they saw and heard everything that was taking place.

If those who assisted at Mass were required to listen to every word of it, the strain would be very great on the priest, it would be impossible for a large concourse of people to assist at the same Mass, and not more than one priest could celebrate at the same time in the same church.

The ceremonies used in the celebration of Mass are, above all, a source of perplexity and of scandal to many non-Catholics; but this perplexity and scandal merely result from a want of comprehension of the things of faith, and is one of the sad legacies bequeathed by the moral revolutionists of the sixteenth century. There is no doubt at all that the ceremonies employed by the Church in the celebration of Mass are of great antiquity, and some of them, as the Council of Trent testified, go back to the time of the Apostles.

It is urged by anti-ritualists that they are unscriptural, but this is a weak objection, for, as many writers have shown, the Church has ample authority in the New Testament for the employment of ceremonial in her worship. Besides, the New Testament was not written as a formal treatise on Christian faith and discipline, and it omits much that can only be supplied by Christian tradition.

Under the Old Law the rites used in the Jewish sacrifices were fully and explicitly revealed by God, because these rites were merely prophetic and typical. Under the New Dispensation God left the inception and development of ceremonial to His Church as was fitting, for, according to the promise of her Divine Founder, she was ever to be animated by the Spirit of God. It was, in fact, necessary that the Church which was to last forever, and have a world-wide expansion, should have a creative power as regards ritual, so that she might adapt her services to the circumstances in which she might find herself.

As the Mass is the highest worship that can be paid to God, it is fitting that it should be celebrated with the utmost solemnity, and the Church does so, when she can, out of love for God and consideration for her children. The ceremonies she employs serve the purpose of exciting the devotion of the faithful and of keeping their attention fixed upon the great act that is being performed. By impressing the senses, she seeks to raise their souls above the things of sense, and to inspire awe and reverence for the sacred mystery at which they are privileged to assist. The altar, blazing with lights and beautiful with flowers; the rich vestments of the sacred ministers; the incense and solemn music all these things help to touch the heart and to raise the mind of the worshipper to the contemplation of that Divine Presence veiled under the humble form of bread.

What reliance, says Chateaubriand, should not be placed in men who receive their God amidst ceremonies calculated to awe the imagination and to move the heart? An altar sparkling with gold and blazing with the light of a hundred tapers, and a temple resounding with tones of solemn and sacred harmony! The imagination is subdued, the senses are melted, the attention is fixed, while each incorporates with his own flesh and blood the Flesh and Blood of His God, amidst a still and breathless silence. Who after such a scene would presume to commit a sin, or even conceive the first thoughts of voluntary transgression? (*Genie du Christianisme*).

If a solemn Mass could give rise to such thoughts as these in the mind of an infidel, what must be its effect on the man of faith? And who, then, will venture to say that such means of elevating the mind can be displeasing to Him who has imparted to this world in which we live a splendour which serves to raise our minds to the Source of all good and beauty?

It is objected that all this ceremonial makes our worship a sensuous worship, but this is very far from the truth. The non-Catholic who may assist at solemn Mass gives his whole attention to what he sees and hears, but it is not so with the Catholic worshipper. Instead of dwelling on the music and ceremonies, or being distracted by them, he is by their instrumentality lifted above the corroding cares of everyday life, and placed in spirit at the feet of his Lord, whom he believes to be present before his eyes, or hidden away in the tabernacle. Whether, says Marshall, he assists at the holy sacrifice, which constitutes the chief act of his religion, or at any other of the Divine offices which attract him with irresistible power to the house of prayer, his eye and heart are fixed, not on sensible objects, but on that awful Presence which at one time is veiled in the tabernacle, at another manifested to the gaze of the faithful. Vestments, music, and incense, whatever meets the eye or ear, he hardly notes, for there is something there which speaks to the soul and taxes all its powers. Let the accompanying ceremonial be meagre or imposing, it is with the mind of a Christian, not an artist, that he marks its presence.

All he asks is that it shall not distract him; the rest, in the presence of those stupendous mysteries, is of little import. Like Mary and Salome, he is thinking of the Body which he has come to adore, not of the "sweet spices" which he has brought to anoint it. He provides, indeed, out of reverent love, the "fine linen," the "myrrh and aloes," and whatsoever else his devotion may inspire or the Church appoint, for in this august action she leaves nothing to human caprice or invention; but all these accessories of his worship, from the least to the greatest the clouds of incense, the blazing lights, the swelling choir, and the jewelled robes have no worth and no significance but as offerings to Him who gives them all their value by deigning to accept them.‡

As this eloquent writer points out, all this ceremonial is prompted by the love of God. The splendour of ceremony with which the Church celebrates Mass, when she has the means to do so, arises from her unhesitating belief in the presence of her Divine Lord on the altar and the desire to make a fitting acknowledgment of His condescension in being thus present. All the pomp, the genuflections, the reverences, come naturally to those who are animated with a vivid faith in the Real Presence. The feelings that dominate a Catholic are truly and beautifully expressed in the following passage from Lavater: *He doth not know Thee, O Jesus Christ, who dishonoureth even Thy shadow. I honour all things where I find the intention of honouring Thee.*

I will love them because of Thee. What, then, do I behold here? What do I hear in this place? Does nothing under these majestic vaults speak to me of Thee? This cross, this golden image, is it not made for Thy honour? The censer which waves round the priests; the *Gloria* sung in choirs; the peaceful light of the perpetual lamp; these lighted tapers all is done for Thee. Why is the Host elevated, if it be not to honour Thee, O Jesus Christ, who art dead for love of us? Because It is no more, and Thou art It, the believing Church bends the knee. It is in Thy honour alone that these children, early instructed, make the sign of the Cross; that their tongues sing Thy praise; and that they strike their breasts thrice with their hands. It is for love of Thee, O Jesus Christ, that one kisses the spot which bears Thy adorable Blood. For Thee the child who serves sounds the little bell and does all that

---

‡ *Christian Missions*, T. W. Marshall.

he does. The riches collected from distant countries, the magnificence of chasubles all that has relation to Thee. Why are the walls and the high altar of marble clothed with tapestry on the day of the Blessed Sacrament? For whom do they make a road of flowers? For whom are these banners embroidered? When the *Ave Maria* sounds, is it not for Thee? Matins, vespers, prime, and nones are they not consecrated to Thee? These bells within a thousand towers, purchased with the gold of whole cities do they not bear Thy image cast in the very mold? Is it not for Thee that they send forth their solemn tone? It is under Thy protection, O Jesus Christ, that every man places himself who loves solitude, chastity, and poverty. Without Thee the orders of St. Benedict and St. Bernard would not have been founded. The cloister, the tonsure, the breviary, and the chaplet render testimony of Thee. O delightful rapture, Jesus Christ, for Thy disciple to trace the marks of Thy finger when the eyes of the world see them not! O joy ineffable, for souls devoted to Thee to behold in caves and in rocks, in every crucifix placed upon hills and on the highways, Thy seal and that of Thy love! Who will not rejoice in the honours of which Thou art the object and the soul? Who will not shed tears in hearing the words, "Jesus Christ be praised"? O the hypocrite who knoweth that name and answereth not with joy, "Amen!" who saith not, with an intense transport, "Jesus be blessed for eternity!"

It is a true and laudable instinct that prompts us to make much of our Generals and soldiers who have fought our battles, and the same instinct has prompted, under God's guidance, the ceremonial of the Mass. It is in great measure the outcome of a desire to make up to the Lord of all things for His sufferings and humiliations, and, above all, for the wondrous love which prompts Him to remain with His Church under the Sacramental veils. The human heart is moved to give expression to its natural instincts of compensation and reparation, and these instincts supply the key to that magnificence of ceremonial which is to be found in the rich churches and cathedrals of Catholic countries.

Like the wise men of old at the crib of Bethlehem, the Church prostrates herself before her Saviour and pours out her treasures, all that she has of good or beautiful, at His feet, seeking in her fond love to enrich Him who has made Himself poor for love of man. Because He humbled Himself becoming obedient unto death, even the death of the Cross the Church does what in her lies to glorify Him, and pays Him, in His Sacramental state, a homage such as the mightiest of monarchs have never dreamed of exacting from their subjects. And shall we blame her for this affectionate worship? On the contrary, those who would do so should pause to consider whether they are not, perhaps, associating themselves with Judas, who blamed the Magdalen for pouring precious ointment on her Saviour's feet, or with those who wished the Lord to restrain the people from giving Him a royal welcome on His entry into Jerusalem.

The Language of The Mass

M. Gavin, S. J.
The Sacrifice of the Mass:
An Explanation of its Doctrine, Rubrics and Prayers,
Published in London, 1903

THE Church's services may be classed under two heads: liturgical and extra-liturgical. By liturgical services I mean here pre-eminently the Holy Mass, and next the Office recited by priests and monks, also all services in the Roman Missal, Breviary, Pontifical, and Ritual. Such services are official. By extra-liturgical services are meant the additional hymns, prayers, and devotions found in popular manuals and approved by the Bishop of the diocese. Liturgical services are prescribed and regulated by the Holy See alone; they are the same everywhere, at least in the Western Church, and continue through the centuries substantially unchanged. Extra-liturgical services are subject to the revision, direction, and approval of the Ordinary: they differ much at different times and in different countries.

The extra-liturgical services are wont to be in the vernacular of the country where they are in use, but the liturgical services are always in Latin in the Churches of the Western rite. We say of the Western rite, for, strictly speaking, the Church has no language distinctively her own. If at this moment she obliges all her priests in the Western Church to celebrate Mass in Latin, she likewise requires those clergy of her communion who follow the Oriental rite, to use Greek and Syriac, Coptic and Slavonic. In p. 52 of the *Catholic Directory for 1903* for Great Britain, under the general heading of the Oriental rite, we have some twelve rites with six different languages prescribed for the Holy Sacrifice. The Church, then, cannot be said to use any one language to the exclusion of all the rest.

But the fact remains, that Latin is the most widely diffused of all ritual languages, and it is of obligation in the liturgical services of the Western Church. Non-Catholics occasionally, and also some ill-instructed Catholics, clamour for the vernacular in Mass. Can the

Pope allow Mass to be said in the vernacular of any country? Most unquestionably he can. He cannot change a single point of doctrine, or any essential point of the discipline which our Lord Himself established. But the choice of a liturgical language falls under neither of these categories. It is a matter of mere ecclesiastical law, and he can make or unmake laws which help or impede the Church's work on earth. With regard to the use of the Latin language, the Council of Trent declares (Sess. xxii. ch. 8, on the *Sacrifice of the Mass*, Denzinger, 823), that the Fathers thought it inexpedient to have Mass said everywhere in the vernacular; and in the ninth canon the Council condemns those who maintain that Mass ought only to be celebrated in the vulgar tongue. (Denzinger, 833) The Church's authoritative teaching then, as declared by the Fathers of Trent, was comprised in these two points: (1) that it was inexpedient to say Mass everywhere in the vernacular, (2) that it was not lawful for a Catholic to hold that Mass should be said only in the vulgar tongue. It is hardly possible for the voice of authority to speak with more studied moderation.

For well-nigh two thousand years the Church has been using Latin in that rite which counts far more members than all others together. It remains for us to give the reasons which justify her in adopting and retaining that language. It is not denied that the Apostles not only preached but celebrated the sacred rites in the vernacular. It is not maintained that St. Peter used Latin in the Church services. He may have done so; but that is all we can say, for at that time in Rome there was a Greek-speaking community. The New Testament (except perhaps St. Matthew and the Epistle to the Hebrews) was written in Greek, and this fact seems to show that the educated and influential members of the Church were more familiar with Greek than Latin. It is also probable that in the West the first missionaries spoke mainly Greek, which was the language of the educated class throughout Europe. The Greek inscriptions on the tombs of Popes Fabian (251), Lucius (252), and Eutychianus (275), prove that Greek was the official language of the Holy See at that time, as De Rossi, a great authority on the subject, points out. We may perhaps take the conversion of Constantine (325), as about the date when Greek ceased to be the language of the Church in Rome. Survivals of the days when Greek was used in the Liturgy of the Roman Church, may be seen in the *Kyrie Eleison* said at all Masses, in the *Trisagion* on Good Friday, *Agios o Theos, Agios ischyros, Agios athanatos, eleison imas*; and in the singing of the Epistle and Gospel in Latin and Greek during the

Pope's Solemn High Mass at St. Peter's. (See *Dictionary of Christian Antiquities*, by Cheetham and Smith, p. 1,016, London, 1875)

When, however, Roman Christianity was first preached, Latin was rapidly becoming the common tongue of a large portion of Western Europe. St. Augustine (353-430) in his City of God, tells us that Rome imposed her language on the subject-races. Latin was commonly spoken in the Roman colony of Africa, and St. Augustine says he learnt Latin in the nursery. Gaul and Spain after their subjugation by Rome adopted Latin, and the upper classes knew something of it even in distant Britain. The Roman officials are said to have spoken Latin throughout the Western Empire. There is no evidence of vernacular services in Britain or in Ireland, where St. Patrick (373 AD) and his followers preached the Gospel. It is most natural to suppose that the missionaries would have employed the language familiar to them in the Liturgy of Rome. In a service so sacred as the Mass, where every word is of importance, the missionaries would naturally use the language in which its prayers were learnt by heart. For Mass in those early times was probably said from memory. The Canon was probably not written before the fifth century, and it is admitted that the Liturgies which bore the names of SS. Peter, James, and Mark, were not written by them. (Le Brun, *Explication de la Messe*, vol. ii. p. 14, Paris, 1726) That the Latin of the Church's Liturgy was not "understanded of the people," seems scarcely doubtful. If at this day in Italy the peasantry speak several dialects mutually unintelligible, is it likely that the Latin of Pope Leo I (440-460), or Gregory the Great (590-604), was understood by the uneducated classes? What was true of Italy was more likely to be true of Africa, Gaul, and Spain; of England and of Ireland. There was nothing to prevent the missionaries from teaching the people in their own tongue the great truths of the faith, or from instructing them in the august mysteries of the Adorable Sacrifice, while they reserved for the Mass and other Offices the Latin idiom, which with Hebrew and Greek, the three languages used in the inscription upon the Cross of Calvary, must have possessed a sacred character in their eyes.

A further question may be asked, Why has Latin been retained all these centuries as the official language of the Church? Various reasons may be adduced. Latin amongst other tongues is distinguished by its dignity, gravity, clearness, and precision. The ear is naturally struck by the majesty of its sentences and the harmony of its cadences. Latin has, moreover, the great advantage of being readily pronounced even by those who never studied it. Music is of obligation in many Church services, and Latin lends itself easily to the solemn chants of the Church's liturgy. Even the poor people, as we call them, not merely in Catholic countries but in England, sing many of the Latin hymns by heart.

A much higher reason is found in the mission of the Church on earth. She is not limited to country or race. She is not the English Church nor the Russian. She is Catholic or universal. She is for "all nations and every creature." One language in her liturgy is a distinct help to unity of worship. Wherever Catholics go, they kneel before the same altar and hear the same prayers in a common language.

But the strongest reason of all in retaining Latin in a liturgical service, is the Church's zeal for teaching and preserving the faith. According to a theological maxim her prayer is the rule of her belief. Like her Divine Master of old, she opens her mouth to pray, and in her prayer she teaches the multitude. The *Gloria Patri* teaches and enforces the mystery of the Trinity; the Church's exorcisms over catechumens before Baptism imply the doctrine of original sin; the necessity of grace to make an action supernatural and worthy of eternal reward is inculcated constantly in her public supplications; her prayers for the dead from earliest ages set forth her teaching on Purgatory. Apart from the Creed, an epitome of Catholic belief said at Mass on Sundays, holidays, and all great festivals, the Church during the Holy Sacrifice proclaims the following doctrines the Unity and Trinity of God; the Incarnation and Redemption of Christ; His blessed Passion, Resurrection, and glorious Ascension; the perpetual virginity of our Lady; the intercession of angels and saints; the veneration due to relics; the Sacrament of Holy Orders; the reality and necessity of sacrifice; the Real Presence of Christ in the Eucharist under both kinds; the efficacy of prayer and Mass for the dead, and the existence of Purgatory. The truths of faith are necessarily expressed in words, and it is important that the language in which they are expressed should always remain the same, both as regards the words, and even more as regards their meaning. A vernacular being essentially a living language fluctuates, while an ancient tongue like the Latin is fixed and stable in its character. The latter is much better adapted to the exact expression of the Church's doctrine and rites in these liturgical forms which play so large a part in handing down to successive generations the revelation of God.

Let us now consider the views of those who assert that the Mass should be conducted in a language "understanded of the people." The objection wherever found, implies an unconscious ignorance of the true nature of the Holy Sacrifice. Mass is not merely a prayer, in which the faithful join, as they take part in a litany. Mass is the public official act of service which is said in the name of the Church for the living and the dead. Mass is offered, not by any one, but by a man on whom a great Sacrament has been conferred to enable him to convert bread and wine into the Body and Blood of our Lord. This official act is always public, because offered in the name of the Church. A private Mass, strictly speaking, does not exist. Mass in a hermit's cell without a server is a magnificent act of public worship offered by the Church to God "for all faithful Christians, living and dead." The people do join in the Mass, but they cannot offer sacrifice in the same manner as the priest. They are bound to be present at Mass on Sundays and holidays. There is, however, no obligation to follow the Mass prayers. The poor man, saying his beads, most certainly fulfils his obligation of hearing Mass. Is it not strange, too, that there should be this cry in favour of the vernacular, when half the Mass, and that the more important, is said in secret, and is inaudible to the congregation?

But an interesting historical incident shows the Church's mind as to the kind of language appropriate for the solemn services of the Mass. Early in the sixteenth century, Father Couplet, the Procurator General of the Jesuit Missions in China, on behalf of the missionaries, petitioned for leave from Paul V to say Mass and Office in Chinese, and to use the same language in administering the Sacraments. Here is the answer of the Holy Inquisition on March 26th, 1611, as given in Le Brim. (Vol. ii. p. 241, with addition xiv. Paris, 1726)

> *Feria quinta die 26 Martii, 1611. In generali Congregatione Sanctse Romance, et universalis Inquisitionis habita in Palatio Apostolico apud Sanctum Petrum coram Sanctissimo Domino nostro Paulo V. . . . Item permisit Sanctitas sua iisdem Patribus, ut possint transferre sacra Biblia in Linguam Sinarum, non tamen vulgarem, sed eruditam et litteratorum propriam, illisque sic translates uti, et simul mandat ut in translatione Bibliorum, adhibeant summam et exquisitam diligentiam, et translatio fidelissima sit, ac in eadem lingua Sinarum possint a Sinis celebrari divina officia Missarum et Horarum Canonicarum. Denique permisit ut in*

eadem lingua erudita Sinarum, possint a Sinis Sacramenta ministrari, et aliae Ecclesiae functiones peragi.

In a General Congregation of the Holy Roman and Universal Inquisition held in the Apostolic Palace at St. Peter's in the presence of our most holy Lord Paul V. . . . His Holiness like wise gave leave to the Fathers to translate the holy books of the Bible into the Chinese language, not into the language of the people, but into the learned language distinctive of educated men, and to make use of these books thus translated; at the same time (Paul V) commands that in the translation of the Bible the Fathers show every conceivable care and that the translation be most faithful, and he gives leave for the Divine service of the Mass and of the Canonical Hours to be said by the Chinese missionaries in the same Chinese language. Finally, he gave leave for the Sacraments and other Ecclesiastical rites to be administered by Chinese missionaries in the same classical Chinese language.

The Holy Office in reply drew a distinction between the popular Chinese (*lingua vulgaris*) as now spoken by that people and the Chinese spoken by the learned and literary class. Leave was given to the Jesuit missionaries to translate Bible and liturgy into the latter (*eruditam et littevatovum propriam*), not into the former (*noti tamen vulgarem*). A Chinese scholar explains to me the point of this distinction. The Chinese of the people is a fluctuating language, comparable in this respect with the vernacular tongues of European nations. The learned Chinese, or if we may be allowed the expression, the classical Chinese, is a language of ancient origin, going back to the time of Confucius (B.C. 500), stable in its forms and in the meanings attached to them, and bearing the same relation to modern Chinese, as ancient Latin to modern Italian.

It has been stated in an earlier part of this article that six different languages are at the present moment in the East sanctioned by the Holy See in the celebration of Mass. Not one of these languages, so I am assured by an Oriental scholar, is the vernacular of the country. To take two familiar instances. In the Russian liturgy the language is not modern Russian but Slavonic of the time of St. Cyril and St. Methodius in the ninth century. Mass in Coptic is less understood than Mass in Latin; not only has Coptic no affinity with the Arabic spoken by the people, but many of the Coptic priests can hardly read the Coptic Missal. Here is the case of a language unintelligible not only to the people but even to the priests, still kept in the liturgy with the sanction of authority. It can hardly be asserted that the Church favours the vernacular in her liturgy.

Lastly: if the Church's liturgy is to be said in the vernacular, where shall we end? The people may then fairly claim Mass in their local dialects which may be described as their vernacular. We must have at least two liturgies in Italy and France. For the Piedmontese peasant cannot understand the language of an educated Italian, and the rustics in the South of France cannot follow the polished French of Paris. High German and Low German are widely apart, Belgium will ask for Mass in French and in Flemish, Ireland will insist on Mass in English and Irish. No thoughtful man can suppose that a multiplication of liturgies can do else than diminish the reverence of the faithful for the adorable Sacrifice of the Altar.

Cassock   Amice   Alb

Cincture   Maniple and Stole   Chasuble

Tunic or   Humeral   Cope
Dalmatic   Veil

Tra le Sollecitudini:
Instruction on Sacred Music

Pope St. Pius X
Encyclical of November 22, 1903

Papal Letter to the Cardinal Vicar of Rome—December 8, 1903

Among the cares of the pastoral office, not only of this Supreme Chair, which We, though unworthy, occupy through the inscrutable dispositions of Providence, but of every local church, a leading one is without question that of maintaining and promoting the decorum of the House of God in which the august mysteries of religion are celebrated, and where the Christian people assemble to receive the grace of the Sacraments, to assist at the Holy Sacrifice of the Altar, to adore the most august Sacrament of the Lord's Body, and to unite in the common prayer of the Church in the public and solemn liturgical offices. Nothing should have place, therefore, in the temple calculated to disturb or even merely to diminish the piety and devotion of the faithful, nothing that may give reasonable cause for disgust or scandal, nothing, above all, which directly offends the decorum and sanctity of the sacred functions and is thus unworthy of the House of Prayer and of the Majesty of God. We do not touch separately on the abuses in this matter which may arise. Today Our attention is directed to one of the most common of them, one of the most difficult to eradicate, and the existence of which is sometimes to be deplored in places where everything else is deserving of the highest praise—the beauty and sumptuousness of the temple, the splendor and the accurate performance of the ceremonies, the attendance of the clergy, the gravity and piety of the officiating ministers. Such is the abuse affecting sacred chant and music. And indeed, whether it is owing to the very nature of this art, fluctuating and variable as it is in itself, or to the succeeding changes in tastes and habits with the course of time, or to the fatal influence exercised on sacred art by profane and theatrical art, or to the pleasure that music directly produces, and that is not always easily contained within the right limits, or finally to the many prejudices on the matter, so lightly introduced and so tenaciously maintained even among responsible and pious persons, the fact remains that there is a general tendency to deviate from the right rule, prescribed by the end for which art is admitted to the service of public worship and which is set forth very clearly in the ecclesiastical Canons, in the Ordinances of the General and Provincial Councils, in the prescriptions which have at various times emanated from the Sacred Roman Congregations, and from Our Predecessors the Sovereign Pontiffs.

It is with real satisfaction that We acknowledge the large amount of good that has been effected in this respect during the last decade in this Our fostering city of Rome, and in many churches in Our country, but in a more especial way among some nations in which illustrious men, full of zeal for the worship of God, have, with the approval of the Holy See and under the direction of the Bishops, united in flourishing Societies and restored sacred music to the fullest honor in all their churches and chapels. Still the good work that has been done is very far indeed from being common to all, and when We consult Our own personal experience and take into account the great number of complaints that have reached Us during the short time that has elapsed since it pleased the Lord to elevate Our humility to the supreme summit of the Roman Pontificate, We consider it Our first duty, without further delay, to raise Our voice at once in reproof and condemnation of all that is seen to be out of harmony with the right rule above indicated, in the functions of public worship and in the performance of the ecclesiastical offices. Filled as We are with a most ardent desire to see the true Christian spirit flourish in every respect and be preserved by all the faithful, We deem it necessary to provide before anything else for the sanctity and dignity of the temple, in which the faithful assemble for no other object than that of acquiring this spirit from its foremost and indispensable font, which is the active participation in the most holy mysteries and in the public and solemn prayer of the Church. And it is vain to hope that the blessing of heaven will descend abundantly upon us, when our homage to the Most High, instead of ascending in the odor of sweetness, puts into the hand of the Lord the scourges wherewith of old the Divine Redeemer drove the unworthy profaners from the Temple.

Hence, in order that no one for the future may be able to plead in excuse that he did not clearly understand his duty and that all vagueness may be eliminated from the interpretation of matters which have already been commanded, We have deemed it expedient to point out briefly the principles regulating sacred music in the functions of public worship, and to gather together in a general survey the principal prescriptions of the Church against the more common abuses in this subject. We do therefore publish, *motu proprio* and with certain knowledge, Our present Instruction to which, as to a juridical code of sacred music (*quasi a codice giuridice della musica sacra*), We will with the fullness of Our Apostolic Authority that the force of law be given, and We do by Our present handwriting impose its scrupulous observance on all.

Instruction on Sacred Music

I General principles

1. Sacred music, being a complementary part of the solemn liturgy, participates in the general scope of the liturgy, which is the glory of God and the sanctification and edification of the faithful. It contributes to the decorum and the splendor of the ecclesiastical ceremonies, and since its principal office is to clothe with suitable melody the liturgical text proposed for the understanding of the faithful, its proper aim is to add greater efficacy to the text, in order that through it the faithful may be the more easily moved to devotion and better disposed for the reception of the fruits of grace belonging to the celebration of the most holy mysteries.

2. Sacred music should consequently possess, in the highest degree, the qualities proper to the liturgy, and in particular sanctity and goodness of form, which will spontaneously produce the final quality of universality.

It must be holy, and must, therefore, exclude all profanity not only in itself, but in the manner in which it is presented by those who execute it.

It must be true art, for otherwise it will be impossible for it to exercise on the minds of those who listen to it that efficacy which the Church aims at obtaining in admitting into her liturgy the art of musical sounds.

But it must, at the same time, be universal in the sense that while every nation is permitted to admit into its ecclesiastical compositions those special forms which may be said to constitute its native music, still these forms must be subordinated in such a manner to the general characteristics of sacred music that nobody of any nation may receive an impression other than good on hearing them.

II. The different kinds of sacred music

3. These qualities are to be found, in the highest degree, in Gregorian Chant, which is, consequently the Chant proper to the Roman Church, the only chant she has inherited from the ancient fathers, which she has jealously guarded for centuries in her liturgical codices, which she directly proposes to the faithful as her own, which she prescribes exclusively for some parts of the liturgy, and which the most recent studies have so happily restored to their integrity and purity.

On these grounds Gregorian Chant has always been regarded as the supreme model for sacred music, so that it is fully legitimate to lay down the following rule: the more closely a composition for church approaches in its movement, inspiration and savor the Gregorian form, the more sacred and liturgical it becomes; and the more out of harmony it is with that supreme model, the less worthy it is of the temple.

The ancient traditional Gregorian Chant must, therefore, in a large measure be restored to the functions of public worship, and the fact must be accepted by all that an ecclesiastical function loses none of its solemnity when accompanied by this music alone.

Special efforts are to be made to restore the use of the Gregorian Chant by the people, so that the faithful may again take a more active part in the ecclesiastical offices, as was the case in ancient times.

4. The above-mentioned qualities are also possessed in an excellent degree by Classic Polyphony, especially of the Roman School, which reached its greatest perfection in the fifteenth century, owing to the works of Pierluigi da Palestrina, and continued subsequently to produce compositions of excellent quality from a liturgical and musical standpoint. Classic Polyphony agrees admirably with Gregorian Chant, the supreme model of all sacred music, and hence it has been found worthy of a place side by side with Gregorian Chant, in the more solemn functions of the Church, such as those of the

Pontifical Chapel. This, too, must therefore be restored largely in ecclesiastical functions, especially in the more important basilicas, in cathedrals, and in the churches and chapels of seminaries and other ecclesiastical institutions in which the necessary means are usually not lacking.

5. The Church has always recognized and favored the progress of the arts, admitting to the service of religion everything good and beautiful discovered by genius in the course of ages—always, however, with due regard to the liturgical laws. Consequently modern music is also admitted to the Church, since it, too, furnishes compositions of such excellence, sobriety, and gravity, that they are in no way unworthy of the liturgical functions.

Still, since modern music has risen mainly to serve profane uses, greater care must be taken with regard to it, in order that the musical compositions of modern style which are admitted in the Church may contain nothing profane, be free from reminiscences of motifs adopted in the theaters, and be not fashioned even in their external forms after the manner of profane pieces.

6. Among the different kinds of modern music, that which appears less suitable for accompanying the functions of public worship is the theatrical style, which was in the greatest vogue, especially in Italy, during the last century. This of its very nature is diametrically opposed to Gregorian Chant and classic polyphony, and therefore to the most important law of all good sacred music. Besides the intrinsic structure, the rhythm and what is known as the conventionalism of this style adapt themselves but badly to the requirements of true liturgical music.

III. The liturgical text

7. The language proper to the Roman Church is Latin. Hence, it is forbidden to sing anything whatever in the vernacular in solemn liturgical functions—much more to sing in the vernacular the variable or common parts of the Mass and Office.

8. As the texts that may be rendered in music, and the order in which they are to be rendered, are determined for every liturgical function, it is not lawful to confuse this order or to change the prescribed texts for others selected at will, or to omit them either entirely or even in part, unless when the rubrics allow that some versicles of the text be supplied with the organ, while these versicles are simply recited in the choir. However, it is permissible, according to the custom of the Roman Church, to sing a motet to the Blessed Sacrament after the

Benedictus in a solemn Mass. It is also permitted, after the Offertory prescribed for the mass has been sung, to execute during the time that remains a brief motet to words approved by the Church.

9. The liturgical text must be sung as it is in the books, without alteration or inversion of the words, without undue repetition, without breaking syllables, and always in a manner intelligible to the faithful who listen.

IV. External form of the sacred compositions

10. The different parts of the Mass and the Office must retain, even musically, that particular concept and form which ecclesiastical tradition has assigned to them, and which is admirably brought out by Gregorian Chant. The method of composing an *introit*, a gradual, an antiphon, a psalm, a hymn, a *Gloria in excelsis*, etc., must therefore be distinct from one another.

11. In particular the following rules are to be observed:

(a) The *Kyrie, Gloria, Credo*, etc., of the Mass must preserve the unity of composition proper to the text. It is not lawful, therefore, to compose them in separate movements, in such a way that each of these movements form a complete composition in itself, and be capable of being detached from the rest and substituted by another.

(b) In the office of Vespers it should be the rule to follow the *Caeremoniale Episcoporum*, which prescribes Gregorian Chant for the psalmody and permits figured music for the versicles of the *Gloria Patri* and the hymn.

It will nevertheless be lawful on greater solemnities to alternate the Gregorian Chant of the choir with the so called *falsi-bordoni* or with verses similarly composed in a proper manner.

It is also permissible occasionally to render single psalms in their entirety in music, provided the form proper to psalmody be preserved in such compositions; that is to say, provided the singers seem to be psalmodising among themselves, either with new motifs or with those taken from Gregorian Chant or based upon it.

The psalms known as *di concerto* are therefore forever excluded and prohibited.

(c) In the hymns of the Church the traditional form of the hymn is preserved. It is not lawful, therefore, to compose, for instance, a *Tantum ergo* in such wise that the first strophe presents a romanza, a *cavatina*, an *adagio* and the *Genitori an allegro*.

(d) The antiphons of the Vespers must be as a rule rendered with the Gregorian melody proper to each. Should they, however, in some special case be sung in figured music, they must never have either the form of a concert melody or the fullness of a *motet* or a *cantata*.

V. The singers

12. With the exception of the melodies proper to the celebrant at the altar and to the ministers, which must be always sung in Gregorian Chant, and without accompaniment of the organ, all the rest of the liturgical chant belongs to the choir of levites, and, therefore, singers in the church, even when they are laymen, are really taking the place of the ecclesiastical choir. Hence, the music rendered by them must, at least for the greater part, retain the character of choral music.

By this it is not to be understood that solos are entirely excluded. But solo singing should never predominate to such an extent as to have the greater part of the liturgical chant executed in that manner; the solo phrase should have the character or hint of a melodic projection (*spunto*), and be strictly bound up with the rest of the choral composition.

13. On the same principle it follows that singers in church have a real liturgical office, and that therefore women, being incapable of exercising such office, cannot be admitted to form part of the choir. Whenever, then, it is desired to employ the acute voices of sopranos and contraltos, these parts must be taken by boys, according to the most ancient usage of the Church.

14. Finally, only men of known piety and probity of life are to be admitted to form part of the choir of a church, and these men should by their modest and devout bearing during the liturgical functions show that they are worthy of the holy office they exercise. It will also be fitting that singers while singing in church wear the ecclesiastical habit and surplice, and that they be hidden behind gratings when the choir is excessively open to the public gaze.

VI. Organ and instruments

15. Although the music proper to the Church is purely vocal music, music with the accompaniment of the organ is also permitted. In some special cases, within due limits and with proper safeguards, other instruments may be allowed, but never without the special permission of the Ordinary, according to prescriptions of the *Caeremoniale Episcoporum*.

16. As the singing should always have the principal place, the organ or other instruments should merely sustain and never oppress it.

17. It is not permitted to have the chant preceded by long preludes or to interrupt it with intermezzo pieces.

18. The sound of the organ as an accompaniment to the chant in preludes, interludes, and the like must be not only governed by the special nature of the instrument, but must participate in all the qualities proper to sacred music as above enumerated.

19. The employment of the piano is forbidden in church, as is also that of noisy or frivolous instruments such as drums, cymbals, bells, and the like.

20. It is strictly forbidden to have bands play in church, and only in special cases with the consent of the Ordinary will it be permissible to admit wind instruments, limited in number, judiciously used, and proportioned to the size of the place provided the composition and accompaniment be written in grave and suitable style, and conform in all respects to that proper to the organ.

21. In processions outside the church the Ordinary may give permission for a band, provided no profane pieces be executed. It would be desirable in such cases that the band confine itself to accompanying some spiritual canticle sung in Latin or in the vernacular by the singers and the pious associations which take part in the procession.

VII. The length of the liturgical chant

22. It is not lawful to keep the priest at the altar waiting on account of the chant or the music for a length of time not allowed by the liturgy. According to the ecclesiastical prescriptions the *Sanctus* of the Mass should be over before the elevation, and therefore the priest must here have regard for the singers. The *Gloria* and the *Credo* ought, according to the Gregorian tradition, to be relatively short.

23. In general it must be considered a very grave abuse when the liturgy in ecclesiastical functions is made to appear secondary to and in a manner at the service of the music, for the music is merely a part of the liturgy and its humble handmaid.

VIII. Principal means

24. For the exact execution of what has been herein laid down, the Bishops, if they have not already done so, are to institute in their dioceses a special Commission composed of persons really competent

in sacred music, and to this Commission let them entrust in the manner they find most suitable the task of watching over the music executed in their churches. Nor are they to see merely that the music is good in itself, but also that it is adapted to the powers of the singers and be always well executed.

25. In seminaries of clerics and in ecclesiastical institutions let the above-mentioned traditional Gregorian Chant be cultivated by all with diligence and love, according to the Tridentine prescriptions, and let the superiors be liberal of encouragement and praise toward their young subjects. In like manner let a *Schola Cantorum* be established, whenever possible, among the clerics for the execution of sacred polyphony and of good liturgical music.

26. In the ordinary lessons of Liturgy, Morals, and Canon Law given to the students of theology, let care be taken to touch on those points which regard more directly the principles and laws of sacred music, and let an attempt be made to complete the doctrine with some particular instruction in the aesthetic side of sacred art, so that the clerics may not leave the seminary ignorant of all those subjects so necessary to a full ecclesiastical education.

27. Let care be taken to restore, at least in the principal churches, the ancient *Scholae Cantorum*, as has been done with excellent fruit in a great many places. It is not difficult for a zealous clergy to institute such Scholae even in smaller churches and country parishes—nay, in these last the pastors will find a very easy means of gathering around them both children and adults, to their own profit and the edification of the people.

28. Let efforts be made to support and promote, in the best way possible, the higher schools of sacred music where these already exist, and to help in founding them where they do not. It is of the utmost importance that the Church herself provide for the instruction of her choirmasters, organists, and singers, according to the true principles of sacred art.

IX. Conclusion

29. Finally, it is recommended to choirmasters, singers, members of the clergy, superiors of seminaries, ecclesiastical institutions, and religious communities, parish priests and rectors of churches, canons of collegiate churches and cathedrals, and, above all, to the diocesan ordinaries to favor with all zeal these prudent reforms, long desired and demanded with united voice by all; so that the authority of the

Church, which herself has repeatedly proposed them, and now inculcates them, may not fall into contempt.

Given from Our Apostolic Palace at the Vatican, on the day of the Virgin and martyr, Saint Cecilia, November 22, 1903, in the first year of Our Pontificate.

Pius X, Pope

The Liturgy of the Mass

Fr. Adrian Fortescue
The Catholic Encyclopedia of 1913

The Mass is the complex of prayers and ceremonies that make up the service of the Eucharist in the Latin rites. As in the case of all liturgical terms the name is less old than the thing. From the time of the first preaching of the Christian Faith in the West, as everywhere, the Holy Eucharist was celebrated as Christ had instituted it at the Last Supper, according to His command, in memory of Him. But it was not till long afterwards that the late Latin name *Missa*, used at first in a vaguer sense, became the technical and almost exclusive name for this service.

In the first period, while Greek was still the Christian language at Rome, we find the usual Greek names used there, as in the East. The commonest was *Eucharistia*, used both for the consecrated bread and wine and for the whole service. Clement of Rome (d. about 101) uses the verbal form still in its general sense of "giving thanks," but also in connection with the Liturgy (I Clem., *Ad Cor.*, xxxviii, 4: *kata panta eucharistein auto*). The other chief witness for the earliest Roman Liturgy, Justin Martyr (d. c. 167), speaks of eucharist in both senses repeatedly (Apol., I, lxv, 3, 5; lxvi, 1; lxvii, 5). After him the word is always used, and passes into Latin (*eucharistia*) as soon as there is a Latin Christian Literature [Tertullian (d. c. 220), "*De pr scr.*," xxxvi, in P.L., II, 50; St. Cyprian (d. 258), *Ep., liv*, etc.]. It remains the normal name for the sacrament throughout Catholic theology, but is gradually superseded by *Missa* for the whole rite. Clement calls the service *Leitourgia* (1 Corinthians 40:2, 5; 41:1) and *prosphora* (*ibid*, 2, 4), with, however, a shade of different meaning ("rite," "oblation"). These and the other usual Greek names (*klasis artou* in the Catacombs; *koinonia, synaxis, syneleusis* in Justin, "I Apol.," lxvii, 3), with their not yet strictly technical connotation, are used during the first two centuries in the West as in the East. With the use of the Latin language in the third century came first translations of the Greek terms. While *eucharistia* is very common, we find also its translation *gratiarum actio* (Tertullian, "*Adv. Marcionem*," I, xxiii, in P.L., II, 274); *benedictio* (=*eulogia*) occurs too (*ibid*, III, xxii; "*De idolol.*," xxii); *sacrificium*, generally with an attribute (*divina sacrificia, novum sacrificium, sacrificia Dei*), is a favourite expression of St. Cyprian (Ep. liv, 3; *"De orat. dom.,"* iv; *"Test. adv. Iud.,"* I, xvi; Ep. xxxiv, 3; lxiii, 15, etc.). We find also *Solemnia* (Cypr., *"De lapsis,"* xxv), *"Dominica solemnia"* (Tert., *"De fuga,"* xiv), *Prex, Oblatio, Coena Domini* (Tert., *"Ad uxor.,"* II, iv, in P.L., I, 1294), *Spirituale ac coeleste sacramentum* (Cypr., Ep., lxiii, 13), *Dominicum* (Cypr., *"De opere et eleem.,"* xv; Ep. lxiii, 16), *Officium* (Tertullian, *"De orat.,"* xiv), even *Passio* (Cypr., Ep. xlii), and other expressions that are rather descriptions than technical names.

All these were destined to be supplanted in the West by the classical name *Missa*. The first certain use of it is by St. Ambrose (d. 397). He writes to his sister Marcellina describing the troubles of the Arians in the years 385 and 386, when the soldiers were sent to break up the service in his church: "The next day (it was a Sunday) after the lessons and the tract, having dismissed the catechumens, I explained the creed [*symbolum tradebam*] to some of the competents [people about to be baptized] in the baptistry of the basilica. There I was told suddenly that they had sent soldiers to the Portiana basilica. . . . But I remained at my place and began to say Mass [*missam facere coepi*]. While I offer [*dum ofero*], I hear that a certain Castulus has been seized by the people" (Ep., I, xx, 4-5). It will be noticed that *missa* here means the Eucharistic Service proper, the Liturgy of the Faithful only, and does not include that of the Catechumens. Ambrose uses the word as one in common use and well known. There is another, still earlier, but very doubtfully authentic instance of the word in a letter of Pope Pius I (from c. 142 to c. 157): "Euprepia has handed over possession of her house to the poor, where . . . we make Masses with our poor" (*cum pauperibus nostris . . . missas agimus"*—Pii I, Ep. I, in Galland, *"Bibl. vet. patrum,"* Venice, 1765, I, 672). The authenticity of the letter, however, is very doubtful. If *Missa* really occurred in the second century in the sense it now has, it would be surprising that it never occurs in the third. We may consider St. Ambrose as the earliest certain authority for it.

From the fourth century the term becomes more and more common. For a time it occurs nearly always in the sense of dismissal. St. Augustine (d. 430) says: "After the sermon the dismissal of the catechumens takes place" (*post sermonem fit missa catechumenorum*—Serm., xlix, 8, in P.L., XXXVIII, 324). The Synod of Lérida in Spain (524) declares that people guilty of incest may be admitted to church *"usque ad missam catechumenorum,"* that is, till the catechumens are dismissed (Can., iv, Hefele-Leclercq, *"Hist. des*

Conciles," II, 1064). The same expression occurs in the Synod of Valencia at about the same time (Can., i, *ibid*, 1067), in Hincmar of Reims (d. 882) ("*Opusc. LV capitul.*," xxiv, in P.L., CXXVI, 380), etc. Etheria (fourth century) calls the whole service, or the Liturgy of the Faithful, *missa* constantly ("*Peregr. Silviæ*," e.g., xxiv, 11, *Benedicit fideles et fit missa*, etc.). So also Innocent I (401-17) in Ep., xvii, 5, P.L., XX, 535, Leo I (440-61), in Ep., ix, 2, P.L., LIV, 627. Although from the beginning the word *Missa* usually means the Eucharistic Service or some part of it, we find it used occasionally for other ecclesiastical offices too. In St. Benedict's (d. 543) Rule *fiant missae* is used for the dismissal at the end of the canonical hours (chap., xvii, *passim*). In the Leonine Sacramentary, the word in its present sense is supposed throughout. The title, "*Item alia*," at the head of each Mass means "*Item alia missa.*" The Gelasian book (sixth or seventh cent. Cf. *ibid*) supplies the word: "*Item alia missa*," "*Missa Chrismatis*," "*Orationes ad missa* [sic] *in natale Sanctorum*," and so on throughout. From that time it becomes the regular, practically exclusive, name for the Holy Liturgy in the Roman and Gallican Rites.

The origin and first meaning of the word, once much discussed, is not really doubtful. We may dismiss at once such fanciful explanations as that *missa* is the Hebrew *missah* ("oblation"—so Reuchlin and Luther), or the Greek *myesis* ("initiation"), or the German *Mess* ("assembly," "market"). Nor is it the participle feminine of *mittere*, with a noun understood ("*oblatio missa ad Deum*," "*congregatio missa*," i.e., *dimissa*—so Diez, "*Etymol. Wörterbuch der roman. Sprachen*," 212, and others). It is a substantive of a late form for *missio*. There are many parallels in medieval Latin, *collecta, ingressa, confessa, accessa, ascensa*—all for forms in -io. It does not mean an offering (*mittere*, in the sense of handing over to God), but the dismissal of the people, as in the versicle: "*Ite missa est*" (Go, the dismissal is made). It may seem strange that this unessential detail should have given its name to the whole service. But there are many similar cases in liturgical language. Communion, confession, breviary are none of them names that express the essential character of what they denote. In the case of the word *missa* we can trace the development of its meaning step by step. We have seen it used by St. Augustine, synods of the sixth century, and Hincmar of Reims for "dismissal." *Missa Catechumenorum* means the dismissal of the catechumens. It appears that *missa fit* or *missa est* was the regular formula for sending people away at the end of a trial or legal process. Avitus of Vienne (d. 523) says: "In churches and palaces or law-courts the dismissal is proclaimed to be made [*missa pronuntiatur*], when the people are dismissed from their attendance" (Ep. i). So also St. Isidore of Seville: "At the time of the sacrifice the dismissal is [*missa tempore sacrificii est*] when the catechumens are sent out, as the deacon cries: If any one of the catechumens remain, let him go out: and thence it is the dismissal [*et inde missa*]" ("*Etymol.*," VI, xix, in P.L., LXXXII, 252). As there was a dismissal of the catechumens at the end of the first part of the service, so was there a dismissal of the faithful (the baptized) after the Communion. There were, then, a *missa catechumenorum* and a *missa fidelium*, both, at first, in the sense of dismissals only. So Florus Diaconus (d. 860): "*Missa* is understood as nothing but *dimissio*, that is, *absolutio*, which the deacon pronounces when the people are dismissed from the solemn service. The deacon cried out and the catechumens were sent [*mittebantur*], that is, were dismissed outside [*id est, dimittebantur foras*]. So the *missa caechumenorum* was made before the action of the Sacrament (i.e., before the *Canon Actionis*), the *missa fidelium* is made"—note the difference of tense; in Florus's time the dismissal of the catechumens had ceased to be practised—"after the consecration and communion" [*post confectionem et participationem*] (P.L., CXIX 72).

How the word gradually changed its meaning from dismissal to the whole service, up to and including the dismissal, is not difficult to understand. In the texts quoted we see already the foundation of such a change. To stay till the *missa catechumenorum* is easily modified into: to stay for, or during, the *missa catechumenorum*. So we find these two *missae* used for the two halves of the Liturgy. Ivo of Chartres (d. 1116) has forgotten the original meaning, and writes: "Those who heard the *missa catechumenorum* evaded the *missa sacramentorum*" (Ep. ccxix, in P.L., CLXII, 224). The two parts are then called by these two names; as the discipline of the catechumenate is gradually forgotten, and there remains only one connected service, it is called by the long familiar name *missa*, without further qualification. We find, however, through the Middle Ages the plural *miss, missarum solemnia*, as well as *missae sacramentum* and such modified expressions also. Occasionally the word is transferred to the feast-day. The feast of St. Martin, for instance, is called *Missa S. Martini*. It is from this use that the German *Mess, Messtag*, and so on are derived. The day and place of a local feast was the occasion of a market (for all this see Rottmanner, *op. cit.*, in bibliography below). *Kirmess* (Flemish *Kermis*, Fr. *kermesse*) is *Kirch-mess*, the anniversary of the dedication of a church, the occasion of a fair. The Latin *missa* is modified in all Western languages (It. *messa*, Sp. *misa*, Fr. *messe*, Germ. *Messe*, etc.). The English form before the Conquest was *maesse*, then Middle Engl. *messe, masse*—" It nedith not to speke of the masse ne the seruise that thei hadde that day" ("Merlin" in the Early Engl. Text Soc., II, 375)—"And whan our parish masse was done" ("Sir Cauline," Child's Ballads, III, 175). It also existed as a verb: "to mass" was to say mass; "massing-priest" was a common term of abuse at the Reformation.

It should be noted that the name Mass (*missa*) applies to the Eucharistic service in the Latin rites only. Neither in Latin nor in Greek has it ever been applied to any Eastern rite. For them the corresponding word is Liturgy (*liturgia*). It is a mistake that leads to confusion, and a scientific inexactitude, to speak of any Eastern Liturgy as a Mass.

The origin of the Mass

The Western Mass, like all Liturgies, begins, of course, with the Last Supper. What Christ then did, repeated as he commanded in memory of Him, is the nucleus of the Mass. As soon as the Faith was brought to the West the Holy Eucharist was celebrated here, as in the East. At first the language used was Greek. Out of that earliest Liturgy, the language being changed to Latin, developed the two great parent rites of the West, the Roman and the Gallican. Of these two the Gallican Mass may be traced without difficulty. It is so plainly Antiochene in its structure, in the very text of many of its prayers, that we are safe in accounting for it as a translated form of the Liturgy of Jerusalem-Antioch, brought to the West at about the time when the more or less fluid universal Liturgy of the first three centuries gave place to different fixed rites. The origin of the Roman Mass, on the other hand, is a most difficult question, We have here two fixed and certain data: the Liturgy in Greek described by St. Justin Martyr (d. c. 165), which is that of the Church of Rome in the second century, and, at the other end of the development, the Liturgy of the first Roman Sacramentaries in Latin, in about the sixth century. The two are very different. Justin's account represents a rite of what we should now call an Eastern type, corresponding with remarkable exactness to that of the Apostolic Constitutions. The Leonine and Gelasian Sacramentaries show us what is practically our present Roman Mass. How did the service change from the one to the other? It is one of the chief difficulties in the history of liturgy. During the last few years, especially, all manner of solutions and combinations have been proposed. We will first note some points that arecertain, that may serve as landmarks in an investigation.

Justin Martyr, Clement of Rome, Hippolytus (d. 235), and Novatian (c. 250) all agree in the Liturgies they describe, though the evidence of the last two is scanty (Probst, *"Liturgie der drei ersten christl. Jahrhdte;"* Drews, *"Untersuchungen über die sogen. clement. Liturgie"*). Justin gives us the fullest Liturgical description of any Father of the first three centuries (Apol. I, lxv, lxvi). He describes how the Holy Eucharist was celebrated at Rome in the middle of the second century; his account is the necessary point of departure, one end of a chain whose intermediate links are hidden. We have hardly any knowledge at all of what developments the Roman Rite went through during the third and fourth centuries. This is the mysterious time where conjecture may, and does, run riot. By the fifth century we come back to comparatively firm ground, after a radical change. At this time we have the fragment in Pseudo-Ambrose, *"De sacramentis"* (about 400. Cf. P.L., XVI, 443), and the letter of Pope Innocent I (401-17) to Decentius of Eugubium (P.L., XX, 553). In these documents we see that the Roman Liturgy is said in Latin and has already become in essence the rite we still use. A few indications of the end of the fourth century agree with this. A little later we come to the earliest Sacramentaries (Leonine, fifth or sixth century; Gelasian, sixth or seventh century) and from then the history of the Roman Mass is fairly clear. The fifth and sixth centuries therefore show us the other end of the chain. For the interval between the second and fifth centuries, during which the great change took place, although we know so little about Rome itself, we have valuable data from Africa. There is every reason to believe that in liturgical matters the Church of Africa followed Rome closely. We can supply much of what we wish to know about Rome from the African Fathers of the third century, Tertullian (d. c. 220), St. Cyprian (d. 258), the Acts of St. Perpetua and St. Felicitas (203), St. Augustine (d. 430) (see Cabrol, *"Dictionnaire d' archéologie,"* I, 591-657). The question of the change of language from Greek to Latin is less important than if might seem. It came about naturally when Greek ceased to be the usual language of the Roman Christians. Pope Victor I (190-202), an African, seems to have been the first to use Latin at Rome, Novatian writes in Latin. By the second half of the third century the usual liturgical language at Rome seems to have been Latin (Kattenbusch, *"Symbolik,"* II, 331), though fragments of Greek remained for many centuries. Other writers think that Latin was not finally adopted till the end of the fourth century (Probst, *"Die abendländ. Messe,"* 5;

Rietschel, "*Lehrbuch der Liturgik*," I, 337). No doubt, for a time both languages were used. The question is discussed at length in C. P. Caspari, "*Quellen zur Gesch. des Taufsymbols u. der Glaubensregel*" (Christiania, 1879), III, 267 sq. The Creed was sometimes said in Greek, some psalms were sung in that language, the lessons on Holy Saturday were read in Greek and Latin as late as the eighth century (*Ordo Rom.*, I, P.L., LXXVIII, 966-68, 955). There are still such fragments of Greek ("*Kyrie eleison*," "*Agios O Theos*") in the Roman Mass. But a change of language does not involve a change of rite. Novatian's Latin allusions to the Eucharistic prayer agree very well with those of Clement of Rome in Greek, and with the Greek forms in Apost. Const., VIII (Drews, *op. cit.*, 107-22). The Africans, Tertullian, St. Cyprian, etc., who write Latin, describe a rite very closely related to that of Justin and the Apostolic Constitutions (Probst, *op. cit.*, 183-206; 215-30). The Gallican Rite, as in Germanus of Paris (Duchesne, "*Origines du Culte*," 180-217), shows how Eastern—how "Greek"—a Latin Liturgy can be. We must then conceive the change of language in the third century as a detail that did not much affect the development of the rite. No doubt the use of Latin was a factor in the Roman tendency to shorten the prayers, leave out whatever seemed redundant in formulas, and abridge the whole service. Latin is naturally terse, compared with the rhetorical abundance of Greek. This difference is one of the most obvious distinctions between the Roman and the Eastern Rites.

If we may suppose that during the first three centuries there was a common Liturgy throughout Christendom, variable, no doubt, in details, but uniform in all its main points, which common Liturgy is represented by that of the eighth book of the Apostolic Constitutions, we have in that the origin of the Roman Mass as of all other liturgies. There are, indeed, special reasons for supposing that this type of liturgy was used at Rome. The chief authorities for it (Clement, Justin, Hippolytus, Novatian) are all Roman. Moreover, even the present Roman Rite, in spite of later modifications, retains certain elements that resemble those of the Apost. Const. Liturgy remarkably. For instance, at Rome there neither is nor has been a public Offertory prayer. The "*Oremus*" said just before the Offertory is the fragment of quite another thing, the old prayers of the faithful, of which we still have a specimen in the series of collects on Good Friday. The Offertory is made in silence while the choir sings part of a psalm. Meanwhile, the celebrant says private Offertory prayers which in the old form of the Mass are the Secrets only. The older Secrets are true Offertory prayers. In the Byzantine Rite, on the other hand, the gifts are prepared beforehand, brought up with the singing of the *Cherubikon*, and offered at the altar by a public *Synapte* of deacon and people, and a prayer once sung aloud by the celebrant (now only the *Ekphonesis* is sung aloud). The Roman custom of a silent offertory with private prayer is that of the Liturgy of the Apostolic Constitutions. Here too the rubric says only: "The deacons bring the gifts to the bishop at the altar" (VIII, xii, 3) and "The Bishop, praying by himself [*kath heauton*, "silently"] with the priests . . ." (VIII, xii, 4). No doubt in this case, too, a psalm was sung meanwhile, which would account for the unique instance of silent prayer. The Apostolic Constitutions order that at this point the deacons should wave fans over the oblation (a practical precaution to keep away insects, VIII, xii, 3); this, too, was done at Rome down to the fourteenth century (Martène, "*De antiquis eccl. ritibus*," Antwerp, 1763, I, 145). The Roman Mass, like the Apostolic Constitutions (VIII, xi, 12), has a washing of hands just before the Offertory. It once had a kiss of peace before the Preface. Pope Innocent I, in his letter to Decentius of Eugubium (416), remarks on this older custom of placing it *ante confecta mysteria* (before the Eucharistic prayer—P.L., XX, 553). That is its place in the Apost. Const. (VIII, xi, 9). After the Lord's Prayer, at Rome, during the fraction, the celebrant sings: "*Pax Domini sit semper vobiscum.*" It seems that this was the place to which the kiss of peace was first moved (as in Innocent I's letter). This greeting, unique in the Roman Rite, occurs again only in the Apostolic Constitutions (*he eirene tou theou meta panton hymon*). Here it comes twice: after the Intercession (VIII, xiii, 1) and at the kiss of peace (VIII, xi, 8). The two Roman prayers after the Communion, the Postcommunion, and the *Oratio super populum* (*ad populum* in the Gelasian Sacramentary) correspond to the two prayers, first a thanksgiving, then a prayer over the people, in Apost. Const., VIII, xv, 1-5 and 7-9.

There is an interesting deduction that may be made from the present Roman Preface. A number of Prefaces introduce the reference to the angels (who sing the *Sanctus*) by the *form et ideo*. In many cases it is not clear to what this *ideo* refers. Like the *igitur* at the beginning of the Canon, it does not seem justified by what precedes. May we conjecture that something has been left out? The beginning of the Eucharistic prayer in the Apost. Const., VIII, xii, 6-27 (the part before the *Sanctus*, our Preface, it is to be found in Brightman, "Liturgies, Eastern and Western," I, Oxford, 1896, 14-18), is much longer, and enumerates at length the benefits of creation and various events of the Old Law. The angels are mentioned twice, at the beginning as the first creatures and then again at the end abruptly, without connection with what has preceded in order to introduce the *Sanctus*. The shortness of the Roman Prefaces seems to make it certain that they have been curtailed. All the other rites begin the Eucharistic prayer (after the formula: "Let us give thanks") with a long thanksgiving for the various benefits of God, which are enumerated. We know, too, how much of the development of the Roman Mass is due to a tendency to abridge the older prayers. If then we suppose that the Roman Preface is such an abridgement of that in the Apost. Const., with the details of the Creation and Old Testament history left out, we can account for the *ideo*. The two references to the angels in the older prayer have met and coalesced. The *ideo* refers to the omitted list of benefits, of which the angels, too, have their share. The parallel between the orders of angels in both liturgies is exact:

ROMAN MISSAL:

. . . . *cum Angelis*

et Archangelis, cum Thronis

et Dominationibus, cumque

omni militia cœlestis exercitus

. . . . *sine fine dicentes.*

APOSTOLIC CONSTITUTIONS:

. . . . *stratiai aggelon,*

archallelon, ... *thronon,*

kyrioteton, ...

. . . . *stration*

aionion, ...

legonta akatapaustos.

Another parallel is in the old forms of the "*Hanc igitur*" prayer. Baumstark ("*Liturgia romana,*" 102-07) has found two early Roman forms of this prayer in Sacramentaries at Vauclair and Rouen, already published by Martène ("*Voyage littéraire,*" Paris, 1724, 40) and Delisle (in Ebner, "*Iteritalicum,*" 417), in which it is much longer and has plainly the nature of an Intercession, such as we find in the Eastern rites at the end of the *Anaphora*. The form is: "*Hanc igitur oblationem servitutis nostræ sed et cunctæ familiæ tuæ, quæsumus Domine placatus accipias, quam tibi devoto offerimus corde pro pace et caritate et unitate sanctæ ecclesiæ, pro fide catholica . . . pro sacerdotibus et omni gradu ecclesiæ, pro regibus . . .*" (Therefore, O Lord, we beseech Thee, be pleased to accept this offering of our service and of all Thy household, which we offer Thee with devout heart for the peace, charity, and unity of Holy Church, for the Catholic Faith . . . for the priests and every order of the Church, for kings . . .) and so on, enumerating a complete list of people for whom prayer is said. Baumstark prints these clauses parallel with those of the Intercession in various Eastern rites; most of them may be found in that of the Apost. Const. (VIII, xii, 40-50, and xiii, 3-9). This, then, supplies another missing element in the Mass. Eventually the clauses enumerating the petitions were suppressed, no doubt because they were thought to be a useless reduplication of the prayers "*Te igitur,*" "*Communicantes,*" and the two *Mementos* (Baumstark, op. cit., 107), and the introduction of this Intercession (*Hanc igitur . . . placatus accipias*) was joined to what seems to have once been part of a prayer for the dead (*diesque nostros in tua pace disponas,* etc.).

We still have a faint echo of the old Intercession in the clause about the newly-baptized interpolated into the "*Hanc igitur*" at Easter and Whitsuntide. The beginning of the prayer has a parallel in Apost. Const., VIII, xiii, 3 (the beginning of the deacon's Litany of Intercession). Drews thinks that the form quoted by Baumstark, with its clauses all beginning pro, was spoken by the deacon as a litany, like the clauses in Apost. Const. beginning hyper (*Untersuchungen über die sog. clem. Lit.,* 139). The prayer containing the words of Institution in the Roman Mass (*Qui pridie . . in mei memoriam facietis*) has just the constructions and epithets of the corresponding text in Apost. Const., VIII, xii, 36-37. All this and many more parallels between the Mass and the Apost. Const. Liturgy may be studied in Drews (*op. cit.*). It is true that we can find parallel passages with other liturgies too, notably with that of Jerusalem (St. James). There are several forms that correspond to those of the Egyptian Rite, such as the Roman "*de tuis donis ac datis*" in the "*Unde et memores*" (St. Mark: *ek ton son doron*; Brightman, "Eastern Liturgies," p. 133, 1. 30); "*offerimus præclaræ maiestati tuæ de tuis donis ac datis,*" is found exactly in the Coptic form ("before thine holy glory we have set thine own gift of thine own," *ibid,* p. 178, 1. 15). But this does not mean merely that there are parallel passages between any two rites.

The similarities of the Apost. Const. are far more obvious than those of any other. The Roman Mass, even apart from the testimony of Justin Martyr, Clement, Hippolytus, Novatian, still bears evidence of its development from a type of liturgy of which that of the Apostolic Constitutions is the only perfect surviving specimen. There is reason to believe, moreover, that it has since been influenced both from Jerusalem-Antioch and Alexandria, though many of the forms common to it and these two may be survivals of that original, universal fluid rite which have not been preserved in the Apost. Const. It must always be remembered that no one maintains that the Apost. Const. Liturgy is word for word the primitive universal Liturgy. The thesis defended by Probst, Drews, Kattenbusch, Baumstark, and others is that there was a comparatively vague and fluid rite of which the Apost. Const. have preserved for us a specimen.

But between this original Roman Rite (which we can study only in the Apost. Const.) and the Mass as it emerges in the first sacramentaries (sixth to seventh century) there is a great change. Much of this change is accounted for by the Roman tendency to shorten. The Apost, Const. has five lessons; Rome has generally only two or three. At Rome the prayers of the faithful after the expulsion of the catechumens and the Intercession at the end of the Canon have gone. Both no doubt were considered superfluous since there is a series of petitions of the same nature in the Canon. But both have left traces. We still say *Oremus* before the Offertory, where the prayers of the faithful once stood, and still have these prayers on Good Friday in the collects. And the "*Hanc Igitur*" is a fragment of the Intercession. The first great change that separates Rome from all the Eastern rites is the influence of the ecclesiastical year. The Eastern liturgies remain always the same except for the lessons, *Prokeimenon* (Gradual-verse), and one or two other slight modifications. On the other hand the Roman Mass is profoundly affected throughout by the season or feast on which it is said. Probst's theory was that this change was made by Pope Damasus (366-84; "*Liturgie des vierten Jahrh,*" pp. 448-72). This idea is now abandoned (Funk in "*Tübinger Quartalschrift,*" 1894, pp. 683 sq.). Indeed, we have the authority of Pope Vigilius (540-55) for the fact that in the sixth century the order of the Mass was still hardly affected by the calendar ("*Ep. ad Eutherium*" in P.L., LXIX, 18). The influence of the ecclesiastical year must have been gradual. The lessons were of course always varied, and a growing tendency to refer to the feast or season in the prayers, Preface, and even in the Canon, brought about the present state of things, already in full force in the Leonine Sacramentary. That Damasus was one of the popes who modified the old rite seems, however, certain. St. Gregory I (590-604) says he introduced the use of the Hebrew *Alleluia* from Jerusalem (*"Ep. ad Ioh. Syracus."* in P.L., LXXVII, 956). It was under Damasus that the Vulgate became the official Roman version of the Bible used in the Liturgy; a constant tradition ascribes to Damasus's friend St. Jerome (d. 420) the arrangement of the Roman Lectionary. Msgr. Duchesne thinks that the Canon was arranged by this pope (*Origines du Culte*, 168-69). A curious error of a Roman theologian of Damasus's time, who identified Melchisedech with the Holy Ghost, incidentally shows us one prayer of our Mass as existing then, namely the *"Supra quæ"* with its allusion to *"summus sacerdos tuus Melchisedech"* (*"Quæst. V. et N. Test."* in P.L., XXXV, 2329).

The Mass from the fifth to the seventh century

By about the fifth century we begin to see more clearly. Two documents of this time give us fairly large fragments of the Roman Mass. Innocent I (401-17), in his letter to Decentius of Eugubium (about 416; P.L., XX, 553), alludes to many features of the Mass. We notice that these important changes have already been made: the kiss of peace has been moved from the beginning of the Mass of the Faithful to after the Consecration, the Commemoration of the Living and Dead is made in the Canon, and there are no longer prayers of the faithful before the Offertory. Rietschel (*Lehrbuch der Liturgik*, I, 340-1) thinks that the Invocation of the Holy Ghost has already disappeared from the Mass. Innocent does not mention it, but we have evidence of it at a later date under Gelasius I (492-6:). Rietschel (*loc. cit.*) also thinks that there was a dogmatic reason for these changes, to emphasize the sacrificial idea. We notice especially that in Innocent's time the prayer of Intercession follows the Consecration. The author of the treatise *"De Sacramentis"* (wrongly attributed to St. Ambrose, in P.L., XVI, 418 sq.) says that he will explain the Roman Use, and proceeds to quote a great part of the Canon. From this document we can reconstruct the following scheme: The Mass of the Catechumens is still distinct from that of the faithful, at least in theory. The people sing *"Introibo ad altare Dei"* as the celebrant and his ministers approach the altar (the *Introit*). Then follow lessons from Scripture, chants (Graduals), and a sermon (the Catechumens Mass). The people still make the Offertory of bread and wine. The Preface and *Sanctus* follow (*laus Deo defertur*), then the prayer of Intercession (*oratione petitur pro populo, pro regibus, pro ceteris*) and the Consecration by the words of Institution (*ut conficitur ven. sacramentum . . . utitur sermonibus Christi*). From this point (*Fac nobis hanc oblationem ascriptam, ratam, rationabilem . . .*) the text of the Canon is quoted. Then come the Anamnesis (*Ergo memores . . .*), joined to it the prayer of oblation (*offerimus tibi hanc immaculatam hostiam . . .*), i.e. practically our "*Supra quæ*" prayer, and the Communion with the form: "*Corpus Christi, R. Amen,*" during which Ps. xxii is sung. At the end the Lord's Prayer is said.

In the "*De Sacramentis*" then, the Intercession comes before the Consecration, whereas in Innocent's letter it came after. This transposition should be noted as one of the most important features in the development of the Mass. The "*Liber Pontificalis*" (ed. Duchesne, Paris, 1886-92) contains a number of statements about changes in and additions to the Mass made by various popes, as for instance that Leo I (440-61) added the words "*sanctum sacrificium, immaculatam hostiam*" to the prayer "*Supra quæ,*" that Sergius I (687-701) introduced the *Agnus Dei*, and so on. These must be received with caution; the whole book still needs critical examination. In the case of the *Agnus Dei* the statement is made doubtful by the fact that it is found in the Gregorian Sacramentary (whose date, however, is again doubtful). A constant tradition ascribes some great influence on the Mass to Gelasius I (492-6). Gennadius (*De vir. illustr.* xciv) says he composed a sacramentary; the *Liber Pontificalis* speaks of his liturgical work, and there must be some basis for the way in which his name is attached to the famous Gelasian Sacramentay. What exactly Gelasius did is less easy to determine.

We come now to the end of a period at the reign of St. Gregory I (590-604). Gregory knew the Mass practically as we still have it. There have been additions and changes since his time, but none to compare with the complete recasting of the Canon that took place before him. At least as far as the Canon is concerned, Gregory may be considered as having put the last touches to it. His biographer, John the Deacon, says that he "collected the Sacramentary of Gelasius in one book, leaving out much, changing little, adding something for the exposition of the Gospels" (*Vita S. Greg.*, II, xvii). He moved the Our Father from the end of the Mass to before the Communion, as he says in his letter to John of Syracuse: "We say the Lord's Prayer immediately after the Canon [*max post precem*] . . . It seems to me very unsuitable that we should say the Canon [*prex*] which an unknown scholar composed [*quam scholasticus composuerat*] over the oblation and that we should not say the prayer handed down by our Redeemer Himself over His Body and Blood" (P.L., LXXVII, 956). He is also credited with the addition: *"diesque nostros, etc."* to the "Hanc igitur." Benedict XIV says that "no pope has added to, or changed the Canon since St. Gregory" (*De SS. Missæ sacrificio*, p. 162). There has been an important change since, the partial amalgamation of the old Roman Rite with Gallican features; but this hardly affects the Canon. We may say safely that a modern Latin Catholic who could be carried back to Rome in the early seventh century would—while missing some features to which he is accustomed—find himself on the whole quite at home with the service he saw there.

This brings us back to the most difficult question: Why and when was the Roman Liturgy changed from what we see in Justin Martyr to that of Gregory I? The change is radical, especially as regards the most important element of the Mass, the Canon. The modifications in the earlier part, the smaller number of lessons, the omission of the prayers for and expulsion of the catechumens, of the prayers of the faithful before the Offertory and so on, may be accounted for easily as a result of the characteristic Roman tendency to shorten the service and leave out what had become superfluous. The influence of the calendar has already been noticed. But there remains the great question of the arrangement of the Canon. That the order of the prayers that make up the Canon is a cardinal difficulty is admitted by every one. The old attempts to justify their present order by symbolic or mystic reasons have now been given up. The Roman Canon as it stands is recognized as a problem of great difficulty. It differs fundamentally from the Anaphora of any Eastern rite and from the Gallican Canon. Whereas in the Antiochene family of liturgies (including that of Gaul) the great Intercession follows the Consecration, which comes at once after the *Sanctus*, and in the Alexandrine class the Intercession is said during what we should call the Preface before the *Sanctus*, in the Roman Rite the Intercession is scattered throughout the Canon, partly before and partly after the Consecration. We may add to this the other difficulty, the omission at Rome of any kind of clear Invocation of the Holy Ghost (*Epiklesis*). Paul Drews has tried to solve this question. His theory is that the Roman Mass, starting from the primitive vaguer rite (practically that of the Apostolic Constitutions), at first followed the development of Jerusalem-Antioch, and was for a time very similar to the Liturgy of St. James. Then it was recast to bring if nearer to Alexandria. This change was made probably by Gelasius I under the influence of his guest, John Talaia of Alexandria. . . . Here we need only add that if has received in the main the support of F.X. Funk (who at first opposed it; see *"Histor. Jahrbuch der Görresgesellschaft,"* 1903, pp. 62, 283; but see also his *"Kirchengesch. Abhandlungen,"* III, Paderborn, 1907, pp. 85-134, in which he will not admit that he has altogether changed his mind), A. Baumstark (*"Liturgia romana e Liturgla dell' Esarcato,"* Rome, 1904), and G. Rauschen (*"Eucharistie und Bussakrament,"* Freiburg, 1908, p. 86). But other theories have been suggested. Baumstark does not follow Drews in the details. He conceives (*op. cit.*) the original Canon as consisting of a Preface in which God is thanked for the benefits of creation; the *Sanctus* interrupts the prayers, which then continue (*Vere Sanctus*) with a prayer (now disappeared) thanking God for Redemption and so coming to the Institution (*Pridie autem quam pateretur . . .*). Then follow the Anamnesis (*Unde et memores*), the *"Supra quæ,"* the *"Te igitur,"* joined to an *Epiklesis* after the words *"hæc sancta sacrificia illibata."* Then the Intercession (*In primis quæ tibi offerimus . . .*), *"Memento vivorum," "Communicantes," "Memento defunctorum"* (*Nos quoque peccatores . . . intra sanctorum tuorum consortium non æstimator meriti sed veniæ quæsumus largitor admitte, per Christum Dominum nostrum*).

This order then (according to Baumstark) was dislocated by the insertion of new elements, the *"Hanc Igitur," "Quam oblationem," "Supra quæ"* and *"Supplices,"* the list of saints in the *"Nobis quoque,"* all of which prayers were in some sort reduplications of what was already contained in the Canon. They represent a mixed influence of Antioch and Alexandria, which last reached Rome through Aquilea and Ravenna, where there was once a rite of the Alexandrine type. St. Leo I began to make these changes; Gregory I finished the process and finally recast the Canon in the form if still has. It will be seen that Baumstark's theory agrees with that of Drews in the main issue—that at Rome originally the whole Intercession followed the Canon. Dom Cagin (*Paléographie musicale*, V, 80 sq.) and Dom Cabrol (*Origines liturgiques*, 354 sq.) propose an entirely different theory. So far it has been admitted on all sides that the Roman and Gallican rites belong to different classes; the Gallican Rite approaches that of Antioch very closely, the origin of the Roman one being the great problem. Cagin's idea is that all that must be reversed, the Gallican Rite has no connection at all with Antioch or any Eastern Liturgy; it is in its origin the same rite as the Roman. Rome changed this earlier form about the sixth or seventh century. Before that the order at Rome was: Secrets, Preface, *Sanctus*, *"Te igitur;"* then *"Hanc igitur," "Quam oblationem," "Qui pridie"* (these three prayers correspond to the Gallican Post-*Sanctus*). Then followed a group like the Gallican Post

Pridie, namely *"Unde et memores," "Offerimus praeclaræ," "Supra guæ," "Supplices," "Per eundem Christum* etc.," *"Per quem hæc omnia,"* and the Fraction. Then came the Lord's Prayer with its embolism, of which the *"Nobis quoque"* was a part. The two *Mementos* were originally before the Preface. Dom Cagin has certainly pointed out a number of points in which Rome and Gaul (that is all the Western rites) stand together as opposed to the East. Such points are the changes caused by the calendar, the introduction of the Institution by the words *"Qui pridie,"* whereas all Eastern Liturgies have the form "In the night in which he was betrayed." Moreover the place of the kiss of peace (in Gaul before the Preface) cannot be quoted as a difference between Rome and Gaul, since, as we have seen it stood originally in that place at Rome too. The Gallican diptychs come before the Preface; but no one knows for certain where they were said originally at Rome. Cagin puts them in the same place in the earlier Roman Mass. His theory may be studied further in Dom Cabrol's *"Origines liturgiques,"* where if is very clearly set out (pp. 353-64). Msgr. Duchesne has attacked it vigorously and not without effect in the *"Revue d'histoire et de litérature ecclésiastiques"* (1900), pp. 31 sq. Mr. Edmund Bishop criticizes the German theories (Drews, Baumstark, etc.), and implies in general terms that the whole question of the grouping of liturgies will have to be reconsidered on a new basis, that of the form of the words of Institution (Appendix to Dom R. Connolly's *"Liturgical Homilies of Narsai"* in "Cambridge Texts and Studies," VIII, I, 1909). If is to be regretted that he has not told us plainly what position he means to defend, and that he is here again content with merely negative criticism. The other great question, that of the disappearance of the Roman *Epiklesis,* cannot be examined here. We will only add to what has been said in those articles that the view is growing that there was an Invocation of the Second Person of the Holy Trinity, an *Epiklesis* of the Logos, before there was one of the Holy Ghost. The *Anaphora* of Serapion (fourth century in Egypt) contains such an *Epiklesis* of the Logos only (in Funk, *"Didascalia,"* II, Paderborn, 1905, pp. 174-6). Mr. Bishop (in the above-named Appendix) thinks that the Invocation of the Holy Ghost did not arise till later (Cyril of Jerusalem, about 350, being the first witness for it), that Rome never had it, that her only *Epiklesis* was the *"Quam oblationem"* before the words of Institution. Against this we must set what seems to be the convincing evidence of Gelasius I's letter.

We have then as the conclusion of this paragraph that at Rome the Eucharistic prayer was fundamentally changed and recast at some uncertain period between the fourth and the sixth and seventh centuries. During the same time the prayers of the faithful before the Offertory disappeared, the kiss of peace was transferred to after the Consecration, and the *Epiklesis* was omitted or mutilated into our "*Supplices*" prayer. Of the various theories suggested to account for this it seems reasonable to say with Rauschen: "Although the question is by no means decided, nevertheless there is so much in favour of Drews's theory that for the present it must be considered the right one. We must then admit that between the years 400 and 500 a great transformation was made in the Roman Canon" (Euch. u. Bussakr., 86).

From the seventh century to modern times

After Gregory the Great (590-604) it is comparatively easy to follow the history of the Mass in the Roman Rite. We have now as documents first the three well-known sacramentaries. The oldest, called Leonine, exists in a seventh-century manuscript. Its composition is ascribed variously to the fifth, sixth, or seventh century. It is a fragment, wanting the Canon, but, as far as it goes, represents the Mass we know (without the later Gallican additions). Many of its collects, secrets, post-communions, and prefaces are still in use. The Gelasian book was written in the sixth, seventh, or eighth century (*ibid*); it is partly Gallicanized and was composed in the Frankish Kingdom. Here we have our Canon word for word. The third sacramentary, called Gregorian, is apparently the book sent by Pope Adrian I to Charlemagne probably between 781 and 791 (*ibid*). It contains additional Masses since Gregory's time and a set of supplements gradually incorporated into the original book, giving Frankish (i.e. older Roman and Gallican) additions. Dom Suitbert Bäumer ("*Ueber das sogen. Sacram. Gelasianum*" in the "*Histor. Jahrbuch*," 1893, pp. 241-301) and Mr. Edmund Bishop ("The Earliest Roman Massbook" in "Dublin Review," 1894, pp. 245-78) explain the development of the Roman Rite from the ninth to the eleventh century in this way: The (pure) Roman Sacramentary sent by Adrian to Charlemagne was ordered by the king to be used alone throughout the Frankish Kingdom. But the people were attached to their old use, which was partly Roman (Gelasian) and partly Gallican. So when the Gregorian book was copied they (notably Alcuin d. 804) added to it these Frankish supplements. Gradually the supplements became incorporated into the original book. So composed it came back to Rome (through the influence of the Carlovingian emperors) and became the "use of the Roman Church." The "*Missale Romanum*

Lateranense" of the eleventh century (ed. Azevedo, Rome, 1752) shows this fused rite complete as the only one in use at Rome. The Roman Mass has thus gone through this last change since Gregory the Great, a partial fusion with Gallican elements. According to Bäumer and Bishop the Gallican influence is noticeable chiefly in the variations for the course of the year. Their view is that Gregory had given the Mass more uniformity (since the time of the Leonine book), had brought it rather to the model of the unchanging Eastern liturgies. Its present variety for different days and seasons came back again with the mixed books later. Gallican influence is also seen in many dramatic and symbolic ceremonies foreign to the stern pure Roman Rite (see Bishop, "The Genius of the Roman Rite"). Such ceremonies are the blessing of candles, ashes, palms, much of the Holy Week ritual, etc.

The Roman Ordines, of which twelve were published by Mabillon in his "*Museum Italicum*" (others since by De Rossi and Duchesne), are valuable sources that supplement the sacramentaries. They are descriptions of ceremonial without the prayers (like the "*Cærimoniale Episcoporum*"), and extend from the eighth to the fourteenth or fifteenth centuries. The first (eighth century) and second (based on the first, with Frankish additions) are the most important. From these and the sacramentaries we can reconstruct the Mass at Rome in the eighth or ninth century. There were as yet no preparatory prayers said before the altar. The pope, attended by a great retinue of deacons, subdeacons, acolytes, and singers, entered while the *Introit* psalm was sung. After a prostration the *Kyrie eleison* was sung, as now with nine invocations; any other litany had disappeared. The *Gloria* followed on feasts. The pope sang the prayer of the day, two or three lessons followed, Interspersed with psalms. The prayers of the faithful had gone, leaving only the one word *Oremus* as a fragment. The people brought up the bread and wine while the Offertory psalm was sung; the gifts were arranged on the altar by the deacons. The Secret was said (at that time the only Offertory prayer) after the pope had washed his hands. The Preface, *Sanctus*, and all the Canon followed as now. A reference to the fruits of the earth led to the words "*per quem hæc omnia*" etc. Then came the Lord's Prayer, the Fraction with a complicated ceremony, the kiss of peace, the *Agnus Dei* (since Pope Sergius, 687-701), the Communion under both kinds, during which the Communion psalm was sung, the Post-Communion prayer, the dismissal, and the procession back to the sacristy (for a more detailed account see C. Atchley, "*Ordo Romanus Primus*," London, 1905; Duchesne, "*Origines du Culte chrétien*," vi).

It has been explained how this (mixed) Roman Rite gradually drove out the Gallican Use. By about the tenth or eleventh century the Roman Mass was practically the only one in use in the West. Then a few additions (none of them very important) were made to the Mass at different times. The Nicene Creed is an importation from Constantinople. It is said that in 1014 Emperor Henry II (1002-24) persuaded Pope Benedict VIII (1012-24) to add it after the Gospel (Berno of Reichenau, *"De quibusdam rebus ad Missæ offic,pertin.,"* ii), It had already been adopted in Spain, Gaul, and Germany. All the present ritual and the prayers said by the celebrant at the Offertory were introduced from France about the thirteenth century (*"Ordo Rom.* XIV," liii, is the first witness; P. L., LXXVIII, 1163-4); before that the secrets were the only Offertory prayers (*"Micrologus,"* xi, in P.L., CLI, 984). There was considerable variety as to these prayers throughout the Middle Ages until the revised Missal of Pius V (1570). The incensing of persons and things is again due to Gallican influence; It was not adopted at Rome till the eleventh or twelfth century (Micrologus, ix). Before that time incense was burned only during processions (the entrance and Gospel procession; see C. Atchley, *"Ordo Rom.* Primus," 17-18). The three prayers said by the celebrant before his communion are private devotions introduced gradually into the official text. Durandus (thirteenth century, *"Rationale,"* IV, liii) mentions the first (for peace); the Sarum Rite had instead another prayer addressed to God the Father (*"Deus Pater fons et origo totius bonitatis,"* ed. Burntisland, 625). Micrologus mentions only the second (*D. I. Chr. qui ex voluntate Patris*), but says that many other private prayers were said at this place (xviii). Here too there was great diversity through the Middle Ages till Pius V's Missal. The latest additions to the Mass are its present beginning and end. The psalm *"Iudica me,"* the Confession, and the other prayers said at the foot of the altar, are all part of the celebrant's preparation, once said (with many other psalms and prayers) in the sacristy, as the *"Præparatio ad Missam"* in the Missal now is. There was great diversity as to this preparation till Pius V established our modern rule of saying so much only before the altar. In the same way all that follows the *"Ite missa est"* is an afterthought, part of the thanksgiving, not formally admitted till Pius V.

We have thus accounted for all the elements of the Mass. The next stage of its development is the growth of numerous local varieties of the Roman Mass in the Middle Ages. These medieval rites (Paris, Rouen, Trier, Sarum, and so on all over Western Europe) are simply exuberant local modifications of the old Roman rite. The same applies to the particular uses of various religious orders (Carthusians, Dominicans, Carmelites, etc.). None of these deserves to be called even a derived rite; their changes are only ornate additions and amplifications; though certain special points, such as the Dominican preparation of the offering before the Mass begins, represent more Gallican influence. The Milanese and Mozarabic liturgies stand on quite a different footing; they are the descendants of a really different rite—the original Gallican—though they too have been considerably Romanized.

Meanwhile, the Mass was developing in other ways also. During the first centuries it had been a common custom for a number of priests to concelebrate; standing around their bishop, they joined in his prayers and consecrated the oblation with him. This is still common in the Eastern rites. In the West it had become rare by the thirteenth century. St. Thomas Aquinas (d. 1274) discusses the question, "Whether several priests can consecrate one and the same host" (*Summa Theol.*, III, Q. lxxxii, a. 2). He answers of course that they can, but quotes as an example only the case of ordination. In this case only has the practice been preserved. At the ordination of priests and bishops all the ordained concelebrate with the ordainer. In other cases concelebration was in the early Middle Ages replaced by separate private celebrations. No doubt the custom of offering each Mass for a special intention helped to bring about this change. The separate celebrations then involved the building of many altars in one church and the reduction of the ritual to the simplest possible form. The deacon and subdeacon were in this case dispensed with; the celebrant took their part as well as his own. One server took the part of the choir and of all the other ministers, everything was said instead of being sung, the incense and kiss of peace were omitted. So we have the well-known rite of low Mass (*missa privata*). This then reacted on high Mass (*missa solemnis*), so that at high Mass too the celebrant himself recites everything, even though it be also sung by the deacon, subdeacon, or choir.

The custom of the intention of the Mass further led to Mass being said every day by each priest. But this has by no means been uniformly carried out. On the one hand, we hear of an abuse of the same priest saying Mass several times in the day, which medieval councils constantly forbid. Again, many most pious priests did not celebrate daily. Bossuet (d. 1704), for instance, said Mass only on Sundays, Feasts, every day in Lent, and at other times when a special ferial Mass is provided in the Missal. There is still no obligation for a priest to celebrate daily, though the custom is now very common. The Council of Trent desired that priests should celebrate at least on Sundays and solemn feasts (Sess. XXIII, cap. xiv). Celebration with no assistants at all (*missa solitaria*) has continually been forbidden, as by the Synod of Mainz in 813. Another abuse was the *missa bifaciata* or *trifaciata*, in which the celebrant said the first part, from the *Introit* to the Preface, several times over and then joined to all one Canon, in order to satisfy several intentions. This too was forbidden by medieval councils (Durandus, "*Rationale*," IV, i, 22). The *missa sicca* (dry Mass) was a common form of devotion used for funerals or marriages in the afternoon, when a real Mass could not be said. It consisted of all the Mass except the Offertory, Consecration and Communion (Durandus, *ibid*, 23). The *missa nautica* and *missa venatoria*, said at sea in rough weather and for hunters in a hurry, were kinds of dry Masses. In some monasteries each priest was obliged to say a dry Mass after the real (conventual) Mass. Cardinal Bona (*Rerum liturg. libr. duo*, I, xv) argues against the practice of saying dry Masses. Since the reform of Pius V it has gradually disappeared. The Mass of the Presanctified (*missa præsanctificatorum, leitourgia ton proegiasmenon*) is a very old custom described by the Quinisext Council (Second Trullan Synod, 692). It is a Service (not really a Mass at all) of Communion from an oblation consecrated at a previous Mass and reserved. It is used in the Byzantine Church on the week-days of Lent (except Saturdays); in the Roman Rite only on Good Friday.

Finally, came uniformity in the old Roman Rite and the abolition of nearly all the medieval variants. The Council of Trent considered the question and formed a commission to prepare a uniform Missal. Eventually the Missal was published by Pius V by the Bull "*Quo primum*" (still printed in it) of 13 July 1570.[**] That is really the last stage of the history of the Roman Mass. It is Pius V's Missal that is used throughout the Latin Church, except in a few cases where he allowed a modified use that had a prescription of at least two centuries. This exception saved the variants used by some religious orders and a few local rites as well as the Milanese and Mozarabic liturgies. Clement VIII (1604), Urban VIII (1634), and Leo XIII (1884) revised the book slightly in the rubrics and the texts of Scripture. Pius X has revised the chant (1908). But these revisions

---

[**] **Ed. Note:** Fortescue gives the date as July 13. Other sources cited in this volume provide July 14.

leave it still the Missal of Pius V. There has been since the early Middle Ages unceasing change in the sense of additions of masses for new feasts, the Missal now has a number of supplements that still grow, but liturgically these additions represent no real change. The new Masses are all built up exactly on the lines of the older ones.

We turn now to the present Roman Mass, without comparison the most important and widespread, as it is in many ways the most archaic service of the Holy Eucharist in Christendom.

The present Roman Mass

It is not the object of this paragraph to give instruction as to how the Roman Mass is celebrated. The very complicated rules of all kinds, the minute rubrics that must be obeyed by the celebrant and his ministers, all the details of coincidence and commemoration—these things, studied at length by students before they are ordained, must be sought in a book of ceremonial. . . . It will be sufficient here to give a general outline of the arrangement. The ritual of the Mass is affected by (1) the person who celebrates, (2) the day or the special occasion on which it is said, (3) the kind of Mass (high or low) celebrated. But in all cases the general scheme is the same. The normal ideal may be taken as high Mass sung by a priest on an ordinary Sunday or feast that has no exceptional feature.

Normally, Mass must be celebrated in a consecrated or blessed Church (private oratories or even rooms are allowed for special reasons: see Le Vavasseur, I, 200-4) and at a consecrated altar (or at least on a consecrated altar-stone), and may be celebrated on any day in the year except Good Friday (restrictions are made against private celebrations on Holy Saturday and in the case of private oratories for certain great feasts) at any time between dawn and midday. A priest may say only one Mass each day, except that on Christmas Day he may say three, and the first may (or rather, should) then be said immediately after midnight. In some countries (Spain and Portugal) a priest may also celebrate three times on All Souls' Day (2 November). Bishops may give leave to a priest to celebrate twice on Sundays and feasts of obligation, if otherwise the people could not fulfil their duty of hearing Mass. In cathedral and collegiate churches, as well as in those of religious orders who are bound to say the Canonical Hours every day publicly, there is a daily Mass corresponding to the Office and forming with it the complete cycle of the public worship of God. This official public Mass is called the conventual Mass; if possible it should be a high Mass, but, even if it be not, it always has some of the features of high Mass. The time for this conventual Mass on feasts and Sundays is after Terce has been said in choir. On Simples and feriæ the time is after Sext; on feriæ of Advent, Lent, on Vigils and Ember days after None. Votive Masses and the Requiem on All Souls' Day are said also after None; but ordinary requiems are said after Prime. The celebrant of Mass must be in the state of grace, fasting from midnight, free of irregularity and censure, and must observe all the rubrics and laws concerning the matter (azyme bread and pure wine), vestments, vessels, and ceremony.

The scheme of high Mass is this: the procession comes to the altar, consisting of thurifer, acolytes, master of ceremonies, subdeacon, deacon, and celebrant, all vested as the rubrics direct. First, the preparatory prayers are said at the foot of the altar; the altar is incensed, the celebrant reads at the south (*Epistle*) side the *Introit,* and *Kyrie.* Meanwhile, the choir sing the *Introit* and *Kyrie.* On days on which the "*Te Deum*" is said in the office, the celebrant intones the "*Gloria in excelsis,*" which is continued by the choir. Meanwhile, he, the deacon, and subdeacon recite it, after which they may sit down till the choir has finished. After the greeting "*Dominus vobiscum,* and its answer "*Et cum spiritu tuo,*" the celebrant chants the collect of the day, and after it as many more collects as are required either to commemorate other feasts or occasions, or are to be said by order of the bishop, or (on lesser days) are chosen by himself at his discretion from the collection in the Missal, according to the rubrics. The subdeacon chants the Epistle and the choir sings the Gradual. Both are read by the celebrant at the altar, according to the present law that he is also to recite whatever is sung by any one else. He blesses the incense, says the "*Munda Cor meum*" prayer, and reads the Gospel at the north (Gospel) side. Meanwhile, the deacon prepares to sing the Gospel. He goes in procession with the subdeacon, thurifer, and acolytes to a place on the north of the choir, and there chants it, the subdeacon holding the book, unless an ambo be used. If there is a sermon, if should be preached immediately after the Gospel. This is the traditional place for the homily, after the lessons (Justin Martyr, "I Apolog.," lxvii, 4). On Sundays and certain feasts the Creed is sung next, just as was the *Gloria.* At this point, before or after the Creed (which is a later introduction, as we have seen), ends in theory the Mass of the Catechumens. The celebrant at the middle of the altar chants "*Dominus vobiscum* and "*Oremus*"—the last remnant of the old prayers of the faithful. Then follows the Offertory. The bread is offered to God with the prayer "*Suscipe sancte Pater;*" the deacon pours wine into the chalice and the subdeacon water. The chalice is offered by the celebrant in the same way as the bread (*Offerimus tibi Domine*), after which the gifts, the altar, the celebrant, ministers, and people are all incensed. Meanwhile, the choir sings the Offertory. The celebrant washes his hands saying the *"Lavabo."* After another offertory prayer (*Suscipe sancta Trinitas*), and an address to the people (*Orate fratres*) with its answer, which is not sung (it is a late addition), the celebrant says the secrets, corresponding to the collects. The last secret ends with an *Ekphonesis* (*Per omnia sæcula sæculorum*). This is only a warning of what is coming. When prayers began to be said silently, it still remained necessary to mark their ending, that people might know what is going on. So the last clauses were said or sung aloud. This so-called *Ekphonesis* is much developed in the Eastern rites. In the Roman Mass there are three cases of it—always the words: *"Per omnia sæcula sæculorum,"* to which the choir answers "Amen." After the *Ekphonesis* of the Secret comes the dialogue, *"Sursum Corda,"* etc., used with slight variations in all rites, and so the beginning of the Eucharistic prayer which we call the Preface, no longer counted as part of the Canon. The choir sings and the celebrant says the *Sanctus*. Then follows the Canon, beginning *"Te Igitur"* and ending with an *ekphonesis* before the Lord's Prayer. . . . Lord's Prayer follows, introduced by a little clause (*Præceptis salutaribus moniti*) and followed by an embolism, said silently and ending with the third *ekphonesis*. The Fraction follows with the versicle *"Pax domini sit semper vobiscum,"* meant to introduce the kiss of peace. The choir sings the *Agnus Dei*, which is said by the celebrant together with the first Communion prayer, before he gives the kiss to the deacon. He then says the two other Communion prayers, and receives Communion under both kinds. The Communion of the people (now rare at high Mass) follows. Meanwhile, the choir sings the Communion. The chalice is purified and the post-Communions are sung, corresponding to the collects and secrets. Like the collects, they are introduced by the greeting *"Dominus vobiscum* and its answer, and said at the south side. After another greeting by the celebrant the deacon sings the dismissal. There still follow, however, three later additions, a blessing by the celebrant, a short prayer that God may be pleased with the sacrifice (*Placeat tibi*) and the Last Gospel, normally the beginning of St. John. The procession goes back to the sacristy.

This high Mass is the norm; it is only in the complete rite with deacon and subdeacon that the ceremonies can be understood. Thus, the rubrics of the Ordinary of the Mass always suppose that the Mass is high. Low Mass, said by a priest alone with one server, is a shortened and simplified form of the same thing. Its ritual can be explained only by a reference to high Mass. For instance, the celebrant goes over to the north side of the altar to read the Gospel, because that is the side to which the deacon goes in procession at high Mass; he turns round always by the right, because at high Mass he should not turn his back to the deacon and so on. A sung Mass (*Missa Cantata*) is a modern compromise. It is really a low Mass, since the essence of high Mass is not the music but the deacon and subdeacon. Only in churches which have no ordained person except one priest, and in which high Mass is thus impossible, is it allowed to celebrate the Mass (on Sundays and feasts) with most of the adornment borrowed from high Mass, with singing and (generally) with incense. The Sacred Congregation of Rites has on several occasions (9 June, 1884; 7 December, 1888) forbidden the use of incense at a *Missa Cantata*; nevertheless, exceptions have been made for several dioceses, and the custom of using it is generally tolerated (Le Vavasseur, op. cit., I, 514-5). In this case, too, the celebrant takes the part of deacon and subdeacon; there is no kiss of peace.

The ritual of the Mass is further affected by the dignity of the celebrant, whether bishop or only priest. There is something to be said for taking the pontifical Mass as the standard, and explaining that of the simple priest as a modified form, just as low Mass is a modified form of high Mass. On the other hand historically the case is not parallel throughout; some of the more elaborate pontifical ceremony is an after-thought, an adornment added later. Here it need only be said that the main difference of the pontifical Mass (apart from some special vestments) is that the bishop remains at his throne (except for the preparatory prayers at the altar steps and the incensing of the altar) till the Offertory; so in this case the change from the Mass of the Catechumens to that of the Faithful is still clearly marked. He also does not put on the maniple till after the preparatory prayers, again an archaic touch that marks them as being outside the original service. At low Mass the bishop's rank is marked only by a few unimportant details and by the later assumption of the maniple. Certain prelates, not bishops, use some pontifical ceremonies at Mass. The pope again has certain special ceremonies in his Mass, of which some represent remnants of older customs, of these we note especially that he makes his Communion seated on the throne and drinks the consecrated wine through a little tube called fistula.

Durandus (*Rationale*, IV, i) and all the symbolic authors distinguish various parts of the Mass according to mystic principles. Thus, it has four parts corresponding to the four kinds of prayer named in I Tim., ii, 1. It is an *Obsecratio* from the *Introit* to the Offertory, an *Oratio* from the Offertory to the *Pater Noster*, a *Postulatio* to the Communion, a *Gratiarum actio* from then to the end (Durandus, *ibid*). The Canon especially has been divided according to all manner of systems, some very ingenious. But the distinctions that are really important to the student of liturgy are, first the historic division between the Mass of the Catechumens and Mass of the Faithful, already explained, and then the great practical distinction between the changeable and unchangeable parts. The Mass consists of an unchanged framework into which at certain fixed points the variable prayers, lessons, and chants are fitted. The two elements are the Common and the Proper of the day (which, however, may again be taken from a common Mass provided for a number of similar occasions, as are the Commons of various classes of saints). The Common is the Ordinary of the Mass (*Ordinarium Missae*), now printed and inserted in the Missal between Holy Saturday and Easter Day. Every Mass is fitted into that scheme; to follow Mass one must first find that. In it occur rubrics directing that something is to be said or sung, which is not printed at this place. The first rubric of this kind occurs after the incensing at the beginning: "Then the Celebrant signing himself with the sign of the Cross begins the *Introit*." But no *Introit* follows. He must know what Mass he is to say and find the *Introit*, and all the other proper parts, under their heading among the large collection of masses that fill the book. These proper or variable parts are first the four chants of the choir, the *Introit*, Gradual (or tract, *Alleluia*, and perhaps after it a Sequence), Offertory, and Communion; then the lessons (Epistle, Gospel, sometimes Old Testament lessons too), then the prayers said by the celebrant (Collect, Secret, post-communion; often several of each to commemorate other feasts or days). By fitting these into their places in the Ordinary the whole Mass is put together. There are, however, two other elements that occupy an intermediate place between the Ordinary and the Proper. These are the Preface and a part of the Canon. We have now only eleven prefaces, ten special ones and a common preface. They do not then change sufficiently to be printed over and over again among the proper Masses, so all are inserted in the Ordinary; from them naturally the right one must be chosen according to the rubrics. In the same way, five great feasts have a special clause in the *Communicantes* prayer in the Canon, two (Easter and Whitsunday) have a special *"Hanc Igitur"* prayer, one day (Maundy Thursday) affects the *"Qui pridie"* form. These exceptions are printed after the corresponding prefaces; but Maundy Thursday, as it occurs only once, is to be found in the Proper of the day.

It is these parts of the Mass that vary, and, because of them, we speak of the Mass of such a day or of such a feast. To be able to find the Mass for any given day requires knowledge of a complicated set of rules. These rules are given in the rubrics at the beginning of the Missal. In outline the system is this. First, a Mass is provided for every day in the year, according to the seasons of the Church. Ordinary week days (feriæ) have the Mass of the preceding Sunday with certain regular changes; but feriæ of Lent, rogation and ember days, and vigils have special Masses. All this makes up the first part of the Missal called *Proprium de tempore*. The year is then overladen, as it were, by a great quantity of feasts of saints or of special events determined by the day of the month (these make up the *Proprium Sanctorum*). Nearly every day in the year is now a feast of some kind; often there are several on one day. There is then constantly coincidence (*concurrentia*) of several possible Masses on one day. There are cases in which two or more conventual Masses are said, one for each of the coinciding offices. Thus, on feriæ that have a special office, if a feast occurs as well, the Mass of the feast is said after Terce, that of the feria after None. If a feast falls on the Eve of Ascension Day there are three Conventual Masses—of the feast after Terce, of the Vigil after Sext, of Rogation day after None. But, in churches that have no official conventual Mass and in the case of the priest who says Mass for his own devotion, one only of the coinciding Masses is said, the others being (usually) commemorated by saying their collects, secrets, and post-Communions after those of the Mass chosen. To know which Mass to choose one must know their various degrees of dignity. All days or feasts are arranged in this scale: feria, simple, semidouble double, greater double, double of the second class, double of the first class. The greater feast then is the one kept: by transferring feasts to the next free day, it is arranged that two feasts of the same rank do not coincide. Certain important days are privileged, so that a higher feast cannot displace them. Thus, nothing can displace the first Sundays of Advent and Lent, Passion and Palm Sundays. These are the so-called first-class Sundays. In the same way nothing can displace Ash Wednesday or any day of Holy Week. Other days (for instance the so-called second-class Sundays, that is the others in Advent and Lent, and Septuagesima, Sexagesima, and Quinquagesima) can only be replaced by doubles of the first class.

Ordinary Sundays count as semidoubles, but have precedence over other semidoubles. The days of an octave are semidoubles; the octave day is a double. The octaves of Epiphany, Easter, and Pentecost (the original three greatest feasts of all) are closed against any other feast. The displaced feast is commemorated, except in the case of a great inferiority: the rules for this are given among the *"Rubricæ generales"* of the Missal (VII: *de Commemorationibus*). On semidoubles and days below that in rank other collects are always added to that of the day to make up an uneven number. Certain ones are prescribed regularly in the Missal, the celebrant may add others at his discretion. The bishop of the diocese may also order collects for special reasons (the so-called *Orationes imperat*). As a general rule the Mass must correspond to the Office of the day, including its commemorations. But the Missal contains a collection of Votive Masses, that may be said on days not above a semidouble in rank. The bishop or pope may order a Votive Mass for a public cause to be said on any day but the very highest. All these rules are explained in detail by Le Vavasseur (*op. cit.*, I, 216-31) as well as in the rubrics of the Missal (*Rubr. gen.*, IV). There are two other Masses which, inasmuch as they do not correspond to the office, may be considered a kind of Votive Mass: the Nuptial Mass (*missa pro sponso et sponsa*), said at weddings, and the Requiem Mass, said for the faithful departed, which have a number of special characteristics. The calendar (*Ordo*) published yearly in each diocese or province gives the office and Mass for every day.

That the Mass, around which such complicated rules have grown, is the central feature of the Catholic religion hardly needs to be said, During the Reformation and always the Mass has been the test. The word of the Reformers: "It is the Mass that matters," was true. The Cornish insurgents in 1549 rose against the new religion, and expressed their whole cause in their demand to have the Prayer-book Communion Service taken away and the old Mass restored. The long persecution of Catholics in England took the practical form of laws chiefly against saying Mass; for centuries the occupant of the English throne was obliged to manifest his Protestantism, not by a general denial of the whole system of Catholic dogma but by a formal repudiation of the doctrine of Transubstantiation and of the Mass. As union with Rome is the bond between Catholics, so is our common share in this, the most venerable rite in Christendom, the witness and safeguard of that bond. It is by his share in the Mass in Communion that the Catholic proclaims his union with the great Church. As excommunication means the loss of that right in those who are expelled so the Mass and Communion are the visible bond between people, priest, and bishop, who are all one body who share the one Bread.

History of the Christian Altar:
The Orientation of the Altar

Maurice Hassett
The Catholic Encyclopedia of 1913

The custom of praying with faces turned towards the East is probably as old as Christianity. The earliest allusion to it in Christian literature is in the second book of the Apostolic Constitutions (200-250, probably) which prescribes that a church should be oblong "with its head to the East." Tertullian also speaks of churches as erected in "high and open places, and facing the light (Adv. Valent., iii). The reason for this practice, which did not originate with Christianity, was given by St. Gregory of Nyssa (De *Orat. Dominic.*, P. G., XLIV, 1183), is that the Orient is the first home of the human race, the seat of the earthly paradise. In the Middle Ages additional reasons for orientation were given, namely, that Our Lord from the Cross looked towards the West, and from the East He shall come for the Last Judgment (*Durand, Rationale*, V, 2; St. Thomas, *Summa Theologica* II-II:84:3). The existence of the custom among pagans is referred to by Clement of Alexandria, who states that their "most ancient temples looked towards the West, that people might be taught to turn to the East when facing the images" (Stromata, vii. 17, 43). The form of orientation which in the Middle Ages was generally adopted consisted in placing the apse and altar in the Eastern end of the basilica. A system of orientation exactly the opposite of this was adopted in the basilicas of the age of Constantine. The Lateran, St. Peter's, St. Paul's, and San Lorenzo in Rome, as well as the Basilicas of Tyre and Antioch and the Church of the Resurrection at Jerusalem, had their apses facing the West. Thus, in these cases the bishop from his throne in the apse looked towards the East. At Rome the second Basilica of St. Paul, erected in 389, and the Basilica of San Pietro in Vincoli, erected probably in the latter half of the fourth century reversed this order and complied with the rule. The Eastern apse is the rule also in the churches of Ravenna, and generally throughout the East. Whether this form of orientation exercised any influence on the change of the celebrant from the back to the front of the altar cannot well be determined but at all events this custom gradually supplanted the older one, and it became the rule for both priest and people to look in the same direction, namely, towards the East (Mabillon, Museum Italicum, ii, 9). Strict adherence to either form of orientation was, necessarily, in many instances impossible, the direction of streets in cities naturally governed the position of churches. Some of the most ancient churches of Rome were directed towards various points of the compass.

Why in Latin?

Rev. George Bampfield
The Catholic Truth Society, 1922

Part I

"And you, an Englishman of the present century, brought up in a Protestant school and in a Protestant University, you boldly say that it is right and well for the Mass to be said in Latin?"

I do. Righter and better, more reasonable, and more Scriptural—yes, you may open your eyes, more Scriptural—than to say it in English.

"Well! If that is not wonderful! Why, I went the other day into your church. There was bending and bowing, and standing and kneeling, boys going here and boys going there, lighting of candles and swinging of incense, the choir singing and the priest trying to sing, and a thundering big organ drowning everybody in the church with a deluge of sound; but what it was all about I could not for the life of me understand. The choir sang in Latin, and the priest sang in Latin—at least I suppose it was Latin, it certainly was not English—and when he was not singing you could not hear a word he said. Why, he had his back turned to you nearly all the time, and he spoke quite low to himself, he didn't seem to want anybody to hear; so I came out of the church quite puzzled. I had not said a single prayer, and I had not the slightest idea what it all meant."

I fully understand you, and I thoroughly feel for you. You Protestants, when first you come into our churches, must think us the queerest of creatures. I remember how puzzled I was at the first High Mass I ever saw, a day or two after I became a Catholic. I had never been in a Catholic church before, except to look at the architecture, and I sadly disappointed the good priests of the church, who thought I should be delighted, by telling them honestly that the whole thing was to me a Chinese puzzle, and that I did not enjoy it a bit. I can quite feel for you: it must be very, very hard for you. But now, tell me this: Did you look about you at all at the other people in the Church?

"Well, yes; I did: there was nothing much else for me to do."

Well, now; The poor Catholics in the church, the old apple-woman, and the dirty old beggarman, and the hornyhanded labourer, did they seem puzzled like yourself, or did they look as if they were quite at home and knew all about it?

"I must say they looked very attentive, and they seemed really to be saying prayers. There was that funny old Bridget McGrath, I could not help looking at her: she kept lifting her eyes up, and spreading her hands out, and beating her breast, and sometimes groaning a little, and really—though I did feel a trifle inclined to laugh—yet there was that look of awe and devotion about the queer old creature's face that one could not help seeing that she was in earnest. And most of the people, even the children, seemed, I fancy, to understand."

Was there any part of the service at which they all seemed more devout than at another?

"Well, yes, there was; it was when a bell tinkled two or three times, and the music stopped, and the choir did not sing, and the priest knelt just for a moment, and the people bowed down their heads, and there was such a strange hush and silence through the church that I felt half frightened, and bowed my own head, I scarcely knew why. Even poor Bridget was quieter than usual, and just whispered under her breath, 'Ah! dearest Lord,' I think it was; something of the sort."

Were the children quiet?

"Yes; they were quiet too."

Well, you see, their all showing devotion at one time more than another proves that they all knew something about it. It was not all music and show. They were not staring at the organ and the singers, were they, all the time, or looking at the little boys with candles?

"No: only the Protestants did that."

And were there many poor in the church, or was it only poor Bridget, and a few other old things?

"Oh! It was crammed with poor people."

There it is: poor people would not come Sunday—after Sunday to a worship of which they could make neither head nor tail. Somehow or other this Latin, which seems to you so terrible, neither frightens the poor nor puzzles them. Really they seem to like Latin better than

English; for when I go sometimes into Protestant churches, where everything is in English, I see what is called a "highly respectable" congregation, but I see no dirt and rags. Now, as a matter of my own taste I don't like dirt and I don't like rags, but I do like to see the dirty and the ragged not afraid to go into the House of God. I think you will grant that our Latin Mass draws the poor more than your English prayers?

"You do get the poor somehow, spite of the Latin."

We do, and that is what I want you to think about. It does not follow because you are puzzled when you come into our churches, that even poor and ill-taught Catholics are puzzled also. Our poor, though they know not a word of Latin, understand our Latin Mass far better than your poor understand your English prayers. That they love it better is quite clear from our crowded churches and your empty ones. A Latin Mass brings together a reverent crowd of praying poor; English prayers bring together a comfortable assembly of the well-to-do.

"You are hard upon us; yet there is some truth in what you say. For all that, you have not given us yet any reason for the Mass being in Latin!"

No, I have not, that will come by-and-by. I have merely forced upon you the fact that our poor do understand their Mass, so far as outward appearances go. I have shown you that our Catholic poor are not, as a matter of fact, puzzled by the Mass being in Latin, and that, so far as we can judge from their outward conduct, they know what they are about at the Latin Mass. If we are to judge of things by their fruits, the fruit of the Latin Mass is better than the fruit of the English prayers. If this is so, the understanding of the Mass, though it be in Latin, cannot be so terribly hard a thing, and if you are puzzled by it, the fault, I fancy, must be your own. A little trouble would make it as easy to you as to them.

Now, my next step is to show you how this comes about; it is a strange thing that the poor ignorant creatures should not be puzzled by Latin, and proves that there is something underneath, matters into which you have not yet enquired. When you see why the poor are not puzzled you will see also why there would be no earthly use in the Mass being in English. There are two things I have to prove to you; 1. That there is no use in the Mass being in English; 2. That there is much use in its being in Latin. We will take the first point to-day, that there is no earthly reason for the Mass being in English, and that, so far as the devotions of the people go, they would be as earnest and warm and devout if the Mass were said in ancient Arabic or modern Chinese as if it were said in English. There are other good reasons why Latin should be the tongue, but so far as people's prayers go, it matters not what the tongue is which the priest is using.

"No matter? Why, if our clergyman was to pray in French, and read the Bible in Spanish, and preach in Italian, what would be the good of it all to us?"

What indeed? But then, you see, your service is not our service; our Mass is a different thing from your Morning and Evening Prayer. If your clergyman read your prayers in Latin it would be very absurd, but when our clergyman reads our Mass in Latin it is not at all absurd.

"Oh, you are always full of your puzzles. What is this mighty difference?"

Don't lose your temper with me, but tell me quietly; at your service, what is it your clergyman and you do?

"He prays, preaches, and reads the Bible, and there are psalms and hymns sung."

Nothing else?

"Nothing, except on Communion Sundays; but most people don't stop to that."

Then supposing it were all in Latin, or supposing you were a Frenchman and did not know one word of English, there would be nothing whatever in which you could join?

"Nothing whatever; there's that poor girl, the French servant at Lord Strange's, who comes without any bonnet on, I believe she's some sort of Protestant; but she does look so puzzled in church; she yawns and fidgets and makes great eyes at the clergyman, and the children declare she reads a French novel half the time."

I don't wonder; but you see our poor people don't yawn and fidget and make great eyes; and I will tell you why. In the first place—it sounds a queer question to ask—but I suppose you know that the priest preaches not in Latin, but in English?

"Does he? You surprise me! I was always told he preached in Latin."

God forgive those who told you! It is strange indeed that such monstrous falsehoods should be spread, even by religious men. What odd consciences they must have! No: our priest preaches in English, else where would be the good of his preaching? And though for good reasons he reads the Bible in Latin, yet he reads it immediately afterwards to the people in English.

"Read the Bible! The Bible! You!"

Every Sunday in the English tongue. You've been told, of course, that we never read the Bible.

"I have, often."

Great is Diana of the Ephesians; magnificent in its way is that unearthly power of lying which the truth-loving English enjoy on all Catholic matters.

"Then if the priest preaches and reads the Bible in English, why does he pray in Latin? It makes it queerer still."

He is not only praying; he is doing a work which is greater than prayer; and the people join with him not in the words he is saying, but in the work he is doing. He does not want them to join in the words he is saying; he would rather they did not; so little does he want them to join that he say half the prayers not only in Latin, but quite low to himself: let the people use their own words, say their own prayers, point out to God their own wants, for each heart knows its own grief, and no shoulder bears the same cross; let many different prayers therefore arise to heaven, so long as all join in the one great Act, the grand Work, which gives to all the different prayers their value.

"What is that one great Act?"

Sacrifice. Sacrifice is the worship of God. The Jews of old time had their synagogues—their chapels—all over the Holy Land, and in these synagogues they preached and read the Bible, and prayed. That was good, but it was not the worship of God. The worship of God, the true grand worship of God, was in the Temple, where daily, morning and evening, the Lamb was offered to God, and died—a blameless martyr—to the honour of Him who made it. It was to this worship that three times a year the Jews were ordered, at no little cost and weariness, to travel up. It was the loss of this that made David weep when he was in exile. The Synagogue—the Bible, the Sermon, the Prayer—was not enough: it was for sacrifice, for the worship of God, that he yearned. Now your service is the service of the Synagogue, ours is the service of the Temple. The sacrifice of the Temple is greater than the prayers of the Synagogue.

"But were there no public prayers at the time of sacrifice?"

If there were, they were not the great thing. What God ordered was the sacrifice; we nowhere read that He ordered any form of prayers—what the people were to do was to be present at the sacrifice; each man said his own prayers—the Pharisee his prayer of unholy thanksgiving; this Publican his prayer of holier repentance; David his bitter prayer of sorrow for his sin, of anxiety for his dying babe, or for his sinning Absolom; Hannah, her supplication that she might have a child; Simeon, his earnest cries for the coming of his Lord; but all through the same sacrifice, as each man felt his want. It is quite curious to read what careful directions God gives to Moses for altar, and vestment, and incense, and candlestick, and every act and movement of the priest; but of any form of public prayer no mention whatever. For sin even of ignorance, in thanksgiving for mercies, to ask for future blessings, to turn away dangers, or as an act of simple worship of the great God—for all these things is ordered sacrifice, for none of these things a form of prayer. And the duties of the people were two: 1. To be present in the Temple while the priest sacrificed; 2. To feed upon certain parts of the victim. They joined with the priest in his Act, his great work, of sacrificing; they joined with the priest in his feast, in feeding upon the victim; they did not join with the priest in any public prayer or in any words said. Sometimes they could not see what he was doing, much less hear anything he said; yet they knew what he was doing, and joined in it. When the High Priest went once a year on the Day of Atonement into the Holy of Holies, bearing the blood of the sacrifice, he went alone; and the people were without, not even seeing his action, certainly not joining in any words, but knowing what his action was, and knowing that it was being done and joining in it—each offering the victim's blood with the priest, each with his own prayers, each for his own needs. When Zacharias, St. Luke tells us, went into the Temple of the Lord to offer incense, "all the multitude of the people were praying without" at the hour of incense; not seeing his action but joining in it, doing it with him, offering with him the incense to God, each with his own prayers, each for his own wants.

Clearly, therefore, whatever prayers the High Priest might say in the Holy of Holies, or Zachary at the altar of incense, it could not matter to the people in what language he said them. In the synagogue it would matter, because in the synagogue there was no sacrifice, nothing being done but prayer, and, therefore, if the prayers were in a foreign tongue, there would be nothing whatever in which the people could join. But in the Temple it would not matter. The people joined in the Act of the Priest, not in any words of his; and therefore, if he spoke in the ancient Hebrew, as not impossibly he did, at a time when the people only understood Syriac, they would equally be able to join in all that they joined in before. The tongue would not be understood by the people; the Act would be understood by the people. In the Synagogue, the Prayers, Bible, Preaching, in Syriac; in the Temple, at the sacrifice, any tongue under the sun might be used, for anything it would matter to the people.

So is it still with the Mass. Mass is the everlasting offering of the true Lamb of God. It is the highest Action that is done on earth. Our Blessed Lord, when He was going to Heaven to present to His Father His five wounds there, took thought for His Father's worship on earth, and left Himself on earth as the only worship that was worthy of His Father. And the unceasing offering of the Lamb that was slain—not indeed the slaying it, for it died but once, but the one unceasing offering it—is the great work of Mass. Mark you, I am not now proving to you the truth of our doctrine about Mass; that would take me too long; what I am now doing is showing you that with our doctrine and our worship the use of Latin is reasonable and useful, and better than the use of English. We will suppose that it is true that the Catholic priest is not only as much a priest as the son of Aaron, but an infinitely greater priest; we will suppose it true that the Lamb on the Catholic altar is a sacrifice infinitely higher and greater than the Lamb in the Jewish Temple; and then I say the same rule holds good for the Catholic as held good for the Jew: let each man join in the Great Act, offer the same Sacrifice, put up to God the same five wounds, the same crucified Body of God, the same saving Blood; but let each man offer it up in his own prayers and for his own wants, for each man's need is different, and no one carries the same cross.

Think for one moment of the great worship of God that was done on Calvary. The greatest act of worship ever done was done there by the greatest Priest, the only Priest; but it was done in silence. Mary, St. John, and the Magdalen were beneath, and knew what the great Act was, and as Abraham offered Isaac, so Mary, herself martyred, joined in the sacrifice of her Son; but seven times only amidst the thick darkness rang out the voice of the High Priest, nor always then in prayer. Not all three of those who stood beneath prayed the same prayer; one was the prayer of the Magdalen who saw there before her eyes the terrible work of her own sins, who crouched at her Lord's feet that those scarlet sins of hers might, as the blood dropped down, become white as wool; and another was the prayer of him, the innocent one, the virgin friend of the virgin Heart, who had entered by right of his innocence into all its tenderness, and understood the depths of its love; and another still the Mother's prayer, who drew from that slow-dripping blood a higher, grander salvation than we all—who, saved more than we, had a work to do more than we, and a right to stand there offering the Son who saved her, the blood which she had given Him, for us who were not yet saved, who were not yet one with Him. Each his own prayer, each his own thoughts, as they stood beneath the Cross, but all joined in the One Sacrifice, and to all their prayers and thoughts that one great Act gave their value.

So is it still. It matters not what the language be which the priest may use at the Catholic Altar; what the people join in is the great Act of Worship, not any form of prayer: as the Jew in God's Temple at Jerusalem, as Mary and John and the Magdalen at the foot of the Lamb so silently bleeding His life away in that act of awful, hushed, worship.

Part II.

"You still have to show me why, if it matters not much as regards the people what the language is, Latin should be the tongue actually used. You have not answered that question yet."

No, I have not. I have put and answered a question that must go before it: Why need not the Mass be in English?

"Because the Mass is a Sacrifice, you say."

Yes. Prayer is something said to God; Sacrifice is something done to God. In Prayer the words are all; in Sacrifice the thing done is first, the words said are second. Sacrifice is a gift given; in a gift the grand thing is the act of giving, not the speaking of any particular word. When a multitude of people join in bringing a gift to God, each man of the multitude may have a different reason for bringing the gift. One may be in trouble and bring the gift to get out of his trouble; his neighbour may be in joy and bring the gift to thank God for his joy; a third in temptation, a fourth in sin—and all four bring the same gift, though for different reasons. The important point is that they should all join in offering the one gift, which gift is Jesus Christ, not that they should all join in the same words; joyful words could not express the sad man's sorrow, and sad words would not tell to God the happy man's joy; but both joyful and sorrowful tell their joy and their sorrow to God by the same gift, by the offering of the same Jesus

Christ. The one thing required then is that all men should join in the act of sacrifice; but a form of prayer—prayer in the vulgar tongue which would force itself upon the ear—would be in the way at the Sacrifice of the Mass. It is not the idea nor the wish of the Church that her priest should pray aloud, and be heard, and take the people with him; she leaves each man to his own freedom of prayer. Mass is a time of silent prayers, all put up through the one great Sacrifice. Sacrifice, and prayer without sacrifice, are in the Church's eyes different things. When in the Catholic Church we have what you would call public prayers or common prayer, then our prayers are in English. The evening service in most, or very many, Catholic churches is in English.

"You have prayers in English?"

Certainly: both more prayers and more beautiful prayers than any in your Book of Common Prayer. There is no end to the variety of Catholic devotions. All the good parts of your Prayer Book are sparkles of devotion that you have stolen—and, between you and me, spoiled in the stealing—from Catholic sources. You have no devotion to our dearest Lord half so tender as our Litany of Jesus. You have no prayers about the Passion half so touching as our Stations of the Cross. The best even of your hymns are ours. From St. Bernard down to Fr. Faber you take of our treasures and use them, and then turn round upon us and tell us we do not pray. We have plenty of English prayers, plenty of English hymns, and give them to the people at our evening service; but at the Holy Sacrifice we choose to leave the people at liberty. We think, as many Protestants think, that one common form of prayer can never express the devotion of all hearts: Protestants feel this and try to escape the difficulty by extempore prayer: the Catholic Church knew it long before, and while she bids the people ever do the same act, offer the same sacrifice, pray through the same wounded Lord, she leaves them to put up each his own extempore prayer; one day the prayer of sorrow, one day the thanksgiving of joy, and a third day the agonized cry of the tempted and failing. The sacrifice must be the same for all, the prayer may be different for each.

I am dwelling on this and doing little more than repeating over again what I have already said, because it seems to me so hard for you to understand the difference between our Sacrifice and your Common Prayer. English people have quite lost the notion of Sacrifice. Among the peoples of the earth, from the Creation until now, the English stand almost alone in this. They cannot understand, therefore, praying at a Sacrifice, and their notion of our Mass is a set of Latin prayers in which the people are positively idle, doing nothing, saying nothing, because they understand nothing. Whereas in fact the people are hard at work the whole time, joining with the priest in his great act, and praying—not indeed the same prayers as he, but each his own prayer—the whole time, as you can see for yourself if you will but enter a Catholic church and watch them.

There is another difference between our Mass and your public prayers, a difference which makes it not untrue for me to say—though it would startle you, I know that the Latin of the Mass is really a tongue "understanded of the people."

"Latin understood by the people? You do startle me indeed!"

I did not say Latin, but the Latin of the Mass. The difference is this. The larger part of your service is every day different; there are two or three different Psalms and two different chapters of the Bible at each service, and Psalms and Scripture-reading make the largest part of your Common Prayer; people, therefore, rich or poor, can hardly get to know it by heart. But it is not so with our Mass; the largest part of our Mass, like your Communion Service, is every day the same. Day by day the same service—nay! I know what you are going to say, we do not tire of it, there is no shadow of fear that we should weary of it—day by day the same service, a short service too, is gone through. For those who read there are translations of the Mass into English in their sixpenny prayer-books side by side with the Latin; and the dullest and poorest can pray by themselves in English, if they please, the same prayers which the priest is praying by himself in Latin. Nay, with a very little help they understand the Latin of the Mass almost as well as the priest himself. I am sure the boys of my parish school do. Just look at that little fellow kneeling on the altar steps while the priest is saying Mass. He is answering the priest at times, as the clerks answer—if Ritualism has left any clerks—in the Protestant Church; and he is answering him in Latin. He is but ten years old, and the son of a day-labourer, but I will dare to say that he not only knows what he is about, but knows the meaning of the Latin too. He has been saying it off and on these two years, and it would be odd if he did not. Just wait a while: there will be High Mass directly, and the boys will be singing, some twenty of them, and men joining in. They are singing Latin: they have been singing the same words to that grand Catholic music—the boys these five years, and the men, some of them, these twenty years. Not know the meaning of them because they are in Latin! I do not advise you to say that to the hot-tempered

Irishman with the brawny chest and the big fist in the front of the choir. I fancy that he might be indignant. In truth, though it may not seem so to you, it is scarcely possible that, after a short time, the Latin of the Mass should not be as familiar to a Catholic as his own tongue—more so, indeed, than the language of your Prayer Book and your Bible. Between you and me, I question whether much of your Prayer Book is more "understood by the people" than Hebrew: but of that more by-and-by.

"You said just now that the Mass, though always the same, does not weary. I should have thought it would."

No: I believe this to be not only from the awefulness of the Sacrifice, but from that very freedom of prayer of which I have spoken. Some Protestants love a form of prayer, and feel their devotion aroused and guided by that which is old and familiar: others feel that to pray according to a form is to pray in chains and to imprison their devotion. Both feelings are, no doubt, true instincts of our nature, and both are satisfied by God's true worship of the Mass. as true instincts of the nature God has made must be satisfied by God's religion. The same unchanging Sacrifice is the cause and the guide of our devotion; our liberty to pray during the Sacrifice as we will takes all chains from our devotions and makes the same worship ever new.

"Still you have not told me why the Mass should be in Latin."

No: we have only been carting away rubbish, before beginning to build. We have settled that no possible harm can be done to the people by the Mass being in Latin, for they can join the great Act each with his own prayers, they can use the priest's prayers in English, or they can even come to understand that much of Latin by constant use. And having settled that there is no harm done by the Mass being in Latin, if there is any good in its being in Latin let us by all means have that good.

"But is there any good?"

Very decidedly yes. In the first place, it is a proverbial saving of which you will not doubt the truth, because it is in the Gospels, that we must not cast pearls before swine. The things of God are in a world which is careless and irreverent. Even in the College of Apostles there was a Judas, before whom our loving Lord had bountifully thrown the pearls of His teaching, and who turned again and rent his Master. So in every congregation that kneels in a Catholic church, here and there must be a Judas—one or two who will betray, and one or two who will deny. Besides these there is the multitude without, who know not our Lord—the multitude that throngs and jostles, and knows not whom it is so rudely pressing.

Now the Mass is the Church's pearl of great price. You do not understand that? No, you cannot till you become a Catholic. But the Mass is our pearl of great price. It is the life of the Catholic Church, the one thing for which it lives; nay, the one thing by which it lives— its food, its daily bread. Now, we give this food, this manna, to those who know it; from those who know it not we hide and protect it. Who cares to bare the secrets of a loving heart to a scoffing stranger? So we do not care to put our holiest things in plain English before the common scoffer. He who comes to learn will learn easily and surely: he who comes to scoff will turn away baffled; there will be no holy words for him to carry away as a jest for his fellow-laugher. Look how it is with the Scriptures that you have made so common, that hang upon the station walls, and lie side by side in the tap-room with the daily prints. Look how Scripture words and sacred sayings of our dearest Lord are flung from the mouths of infidels to point a jest, and scribbled in newspaper articles that they may spice a sentence. Truly, the every-day mouthing of Scripture and the way in which Scripture is made a jest-book are a proof of what becomes of throwing God's pearls before the graceless.

Therefore, now, see the first use of our Latin. It does not hide our Mass for one instant from the believing; it does not puzzle our own people one whit; but it screens our holiest things from the rude gaze of the infidel and the irreverent. The world cannot get easily into our secrets; cannot make a household jest of our pearl; and because it cannot, the world is wrath, and cries out "English prayers for English people," yes, that English scoffers may make a mock! Here, then, you have one good. Were our Mass in English, the scoffer would scoff easily: it is in Latin, and he is baffled. This is better for him, who would sin, and for us, who would be troubled, and for God, who would be insulted.

Part III.

"Latin better than English for the Mass! You are getting on. You said at first there was no harm done by its being in Latin or any other language not known to the people—now you say 'better.'"

Better, most certainly, mark you, for the Mass firstly, and for all the devotions of the Church, the devotions which she would have used by all nations alike everywhere. Each nation, or part of a nation for that matter, can have and has its own prayer books, its own hymns and the rest, in its own tongue:—English prayer books, Welsh prayer books, prayer books in the native Irish, and so on the world through, prayer books in county dialects if you like—but the Church's devotions are for all nations alike everywhere, and for them the one tongue.

"But Latin is a dead language!"

Exactly; that's just why it is better. Mostly living things are better than the dead. But a dead language is not as other dead things. If it rotted and fell to pieces like other dead things, then indeed would it be worse than living tongues. But when its meaning, which is its life, its soul, is fully known; when it has within it authors who cannot die; when any one who studies it, whatever be his nation, can make it live again, using it for speech and for writing—then it is a dead language indeed in one sense, since no whole nation speaks it, but a living language in another sense, most living of all languages, because the best-taught in every nation, making a sort of nation among themselves, can use it and do use it, a world-wide speech to make their thoughts known to each other. To speak or write in French is to speak and write for France, to write in English is to write for the English-speaking races, to write in Latin is to write for the world.

"And this is why Latin is best?"

Part of my reason only. The Church is Catholic, world-wide, and it is clearly good for a world-wide Church to have a world-wide language. So men gathered as on the Day of Pentecost from all nations under heaven, in one monastery, or in one church, can not only be present at the same Sacrifice because it is an Act in which they all join, but can join in the same psalms and the same prayers, in the very same tongue to which they were used each in his own land. The sailor who has heard Mass in Latin at a village church in Devonshire goes off all round the world, and wherever he puts in he hears the same Mass, takes part in the same Act. in the same tongue which he used himself when he served at Mass before he left home; and he can answer the priest, though he were a native of Japan or China or Central Africa, as readily as he answered Father O'Brien on the coast of Devon. Clearly this is good both for layman and priest. The Jesuit who is ordered off at a moment's notice to Timbuctoo, would say his Mass just as quietly when he got there as he had done at Farm Street: but it would sadly puzzle your Church of England clergyman if he had to read prayers at a moment's notice to a congregation of Laplanders in their native tongue.

Why in Latin?

"Then is this your chief reason?"

No. A dead language can be made, without waking the jealousy of any living nation, a language for all men: but its deadness gives us—in religious matters—a greater good still.

"Greater?"

Far greater: you will grant me, I think, that the first duty of the Society which our Lord founded must be to keep the Truth which our Lord taught: exactly the same Truth. Christianity changed is not Christianity; Christianity added to, or Christianity taken from, is not the Christianity of Christ. The care of the Truth is the great and first duty of the Society of Christ. She would be a false bride to Him if she taught what He did not teach. This is so?

"You put it strongly; but yes, you must be right."

Well, then, the Church must guard against anything which might in any way change that Truth, or bring wrong notions about it into people's minds.

"Granted: but what has that to do with Latin?"

This to do with it:—a dead language is better for this end than a living one.

"Why so?"

Because the meaning of its words is fixed and cannot alter. Latin, as I said, is dead in one way, but not in another. A dead language is somewhat like those dead bodies of some Saints which still do not corrupt and still the limbs can be bent and moved by others. It is death, but a death which lets you see the exact figure and form of the Saint in life, and the look upon her face—a form and a face and an expression in that face which does not change. As her companions saw her three centuries or more ago so we see her still. Limbs will not grow nor change, and we know that our notion of her is what theirs was so long ago.

"How do you apply this to Latin?"

The meaning of the words cannot change. What Cicero meant when first he spoke the words in the parliament of Rome—what SS. Jerome and Augustine meant and the writers who went before, and came after—that same is meant to-day and will be meant when the world ends. And what an Englishman means by the Latin word, that the Frenchman means, and that same the Italian and the Austrian and the

Hindoo student in our colleges and the Japanese who is studying Latin.

"I think I see: but with living languages."

It is not the same. It is hard to find in some tongues even a word that should express aright the Christian thought of God. It is impossible, as we know, to turn some French words into English, so we take the word bodily and make it our own. To translate from one tongue to another is the most difficult of tasks. The Truth then, if it were left to be tossed about by a variety of tongues, would be in danger of taking a variety of meanings; and the One Truth of the Church of Christ would take different colours and shapes. Nor is this the only danger; there would be a like difficulty in each of all the countless tongues in the world, for a living tongue, like a living body, grows and changes. They tell us our living body changes once in seven years: our dead Saint neither changes nor corrupts. As with the body so with the living language—it changes. Have you ever tried to read Chaucer? You will find it hard without notes. There are words which have dropped out of use, and words which have changed their sense, or which are getting new senses besides their old ones. So a word which was a true word for a doctrine two centuries ago might be a very bad one now, and give us a thought almost the opposite of truth.

"Give me an instance or two."

Well, this may do. You object to Catholics worshipping Our Lady?

"Yes, certainly. They must not treat her as God."

Of course they must not, and they don't. The word "worship" never meant in old times to treat as God. It mostly is taken to mean that now, though even now it is used sometimes in the old sense. When a magistrate is addressed as "Your Worship," certainly no divine honour is intended. When a bridegroom says to his bride, "With My Body I thee worship," he is far from saying, unless in the high-falutin language of love, that the lady is more than human flesh and blood. And yet, so much has the meaning of the word changed, that you can accuse us to-day of idolatry because we may still use the word "worship" about the honour shown to Our Lady.

Now this change is going on, not in English only, but in the countless languages of the world. Think what danger there might be of changing that Truth which cannot be changed if the doctrines and devotions of the world's Church were left to be expressed by the changing words of countless tongues! By the use of Latin these doctrines and devotions are embalmed in one unchanging tongue—as unchangeable as the doctrine. And hence no wrong idea can be brought by the growth of the language into the first Christianity: and in this we have another reason why Latin is best.

Part IV.

A dead tongue, then, is better than a living one—vastly better than a variety of living ones—for a worldwide Church, meant equally for all nations:—

Because in all nations equally it helps to guard holy things and holy truths from careless using:

Because it gives a world-language—an universal language—a language such as commerce tried to make for itself in "Volapuk"—for all the teachers in every nation, of the truths most important to man, and for all worshippers in the one grand Act of worship:

Because, if any living tongue were so used to unite men, the Church would seem to favour one race above the rest, and jealousy would spring up:

Because, above all, truths are preserved unchanging in an unchanging tongue—you have seen flies in amber?

"Yes."

You can see them quite clearly, and the most delicate little bit of them is there quite perfect, and quite perfect it will remain—no change, no corruption. In a living stream, a stream that was still flowing on, larger things than flies would be in danger of destruction or of change; but the amber has ceased to flow, and the smallest atom of the fly's wing will be as now till the world's end: and so it is with Truth, and with a worship which is embalmed in an unchanging tongue. Its meaning can in no way alter nor be corrupted. The very same words, with the very same sense, were used in Rome and over all the Roman Empire for the very same truths well nigh two thousand years ago, and will be used until the death of the great world at the last day.

"But Latin is not the only dead tongue?"

There may be many dead tongues for aught I know—tongues of races which themselves are dead or nearly so, of races that never were in any way world-wide: but there are three world-wide dead tongues, three living-dead tongues, three amber tongues preserving truths.

"They are?"

The Hebrew, the Greek, the Latin; the three in which the inscription was written above the thorn-crowned Head—"Jesus of Nazareth the King of the Jews." Those were the languages chosen to tell the great truth to the whole world; if anything could make tongues sacred it would be this: Apostolic languages, witnessing to the Truth, and— you will think me fanciful, but if fancy can make Truth plain, it is well to use it—dying there upon the Cross with a death like the death of the Lord to whom they witnessed: a death that yet was to live on, proclaiming truth for ever.

"Were all three languages living then?"

The Hebrew was already dead, used only in the services of the Jewish Church, just as Latin is now in the Catholic Church; the old Scriptures preserved in it so as not to change were read in the Synagogue and then explained in the living tongue, just as with the Latin now: our Lord Himself and His Mother used a dead language for their worship. So with the Hebrews: but the Greek and Latin were then living— living with a strong life unlikely to die, yet both now by God's Providence dead: the New Testament and the Old "ambered"—to coin a word—in an unchanging dead tongue.

It is God's own hand which has slain those tongues and left His divine truths guarded within them. And now at last I can give full answer to your question, "Why in Latin?" Because Latin is the tongue given to the Church by God Himself. Of all the great empires that conquered nations and joined many in a natural Oneness, Rome, as you know, was by very far the widest: and the tongue of the Roman was Latin. There were no nations then as there are to-day: there was one world, clamped together by the iron arms of force, and one capital city of that world—Rome: and the nations, as we know them now, were split up into tribes—each petty, and each at war with all the rest. And Rome had the great work to do of giving law and knowledge and manners and all that is meant by civilization to these wild tribes, and had to take their rude imperfect tongues and fashion each into a language. And so, when the Roman Empire died, leaving many peoples, its living world-wide language died also, leaving many children; so that to-day every tongue of every European nation is formed largely out of Latin. Of the three dead tongues, therefore, Latin is the easiest and nearest to us—our mother tongue, out of which have sprung hosts of our own living words.

Thus, then, each nation learned to speak its own Latin-born tongue: but the Church, which is for all nations and for all times, kept her dead Latin—as the Jews kept their dead Hebrew—as the safest to preserve unchanged the truth already preached and written in it, and yet the easiest for her many peoples to understand. How could she cast away the one tongue through which she had converted her peoples; the tongue in which their laws were written; the tongue in which their learning was preserved; the tongue above all in which undying Truth had been taught by her saints, and a never-ceasing Worship had for centuries gone up to God?

And this is "Why in Latin." Because Latin was the language of Europe, and because Europe has spread itself the world over; and while, as we have said, a dead language is for many reasons the best tongue to use for world-wide and time-long truths, Latin is the best of the world-wide speeches that have died.

So now you will be content to take the little trouble needed that you may learn Latin enough to join in the Mass, and now and then in Vespers; and you will be content to think that the Church has done wisely to keep her worship in the old undying tongue by which the happy miracle of Whitsunday, undoing the curse of Babel, is in some sense continued.

Go, become a Catholic, and learn, like yonder little lad of ten, to serve Mass in the dear old tongue which was writ for the world to read above the Cross.

**Printed and Published by The Catholic Truth Society,
72 Victoria Street, London, S.W.
March 1922**

Divini Cultus:
On Divine Worship

Pope Pius XI
December 20, 1928

Since the Church has received from Christ her Founder the office of safeguarding the sanctity of divine worship, it is certainly incumbent upon her, while leaving intact the substance of the Sacrifice and the sacraments, to prescribe ceremonies, rites, formulae, prayers, and chant for the proper regulation of that august public ministry, whose special name is "Liturgy," as being the eminently sacred action.

For the Liturgy is indeed a sacred thing, since by it we are raised to God and united to Him, thereby professing our faith and our deep obligation to Him for the benefits we have received and the help of which we stand in constant need. There is thus a close connection between dogma and the sacred Liturgy, and between Christian worship and the sanctification of the faithful. Hence, Pope Celestine I saw the standard of faith expressed in the sacred formulae of the Liturgy. "The rule of our faith," he says, "is indicated by the law of our worship. When those who are set over the Christian people fulfill the function committed to them, they plead the cause of the human race in the sight of God's clemency, and pray and supplicate in conjunction with the whole Church."

These public prayers, called at first "the work of God" and later "the divine office" or the daily "debt" which man owes to God, used to be offered both day and night in the presence of a great concourse of the faithful. From the earliest times the simple chants which graced the sacred prayers and the Liturgy gave a wonderful impulse to the piety of the people. History tells us how in the ancient basilicas, where bishop, clergy, and people alternately sang the divine praises, the liturgical chant played no small part in converting many barbarians to Christianity and civilization. It was in the churches that heretics came to understand more fully the meaning of the communion of saints; thus the Emperor Valens, an Arian, being present at Mass celebrated by Saint Basil, was overcome by an extraordinary seizure and fainted. At Milan, Saint Ambrose was accused by heretics of attracting the crowds by means of liturgical chants. It was due to these that Saint Augustine made up his mind to become a Christian. It was in the churches, finally, where practically the whole city formed a great joint choir, that the workers, builders, artists, sculptors, and writers gained from the Liturgy that deep knowledge of theology which is now so apparent in the monuments of the Middle Ages.

No wonder, then, that the Roman Pontiffs have been so solicitous to safeguard and protect the Liturgy. They have used the same care in making laws for the regulation of the Liturgy, in preserving it from adulteration, as they have in giving accurate expression to the dogmas of the faith. This is the reason why the Fathers made both spoken and written commentary upon the Liturgy or "the law of worship;" for this reason the Council of Trent ordained that the Liturgy should be expounded and explained to the faithful.

In our times too, the chief object of Pope Pius X, in the *Motu Proprio* [*Tra le Sollecitudini*] which he issued twenty-five years ago, making certain prescriptions concerning Gregorian Chant and sacred music, was to arouse and foster a Christian spirit in the faithful, by wisely excluding all that might ill befit the sacredness and majesty of our churches. The faithful come to church in order to derive piety from its chief source, by taking an active part in the venerated mysteries and the public solemn prayers of the Church. It is of the utmost importance, therefore, that anything that is used to adorn the Liturgy should be controlled by the Church, so that the arts may take their proper place as most noble ministers in sacred worship. Far from resulting in a loss to art, such an arrangement will certainly make for the greater splendor and dignity of the arts that are used in the Church. This has been especially true of sacred music. Wherever the regulations on this subject have been carefully observed, a new life has been given to this delightful art, and the spirit of religion has prospered; the faithful have gained a deeper understanding of the sacred Liturgy, and have taken part with greater zest in the ceremonies of the Mass, in the singing of the psalms and the public prayers. Of this We Ourselves had happy experience when, in the first year of Our Pontificate, We celebrated solemn High Mass in the Vatican Basilica to the noble accompaniment of a choir of clerics of all nationalities, singing in Gregorian Chant.

It is, however, to be deplored that these most wise laws in some places have not been fully observed, and therefore their intended results not obtained. We know that some have declared these laws, though so solemnly promulgated, were not binding upon their obedience. Others obeyed them at first, but have since come gradually to give countenance to a type of music which should be altogether banned from our churches. In some cases, especially when the memory of some famous musician was being celebrated, the opportunity has been taken of performing in church certain works which, however excellent, should never have been performed there, since they were entirely out of keeping with the sacredness of the place and of the Liturgy.

In order to urge the clergy and faithful to a more scrupulous observance of these laws and directions which are to be carefully obeyed by the whole Church, We think it opportune to set down here something of the fruits of Our experience during the last twenty-five years. We celebrate not only the memory of the reform of sacred music to which We have referred, but also the centenary of the monk Guido of Arezzo. Nine hundred years ago Guido, at the bidding of the pope, came to Rome and produced his wonderful invention, whereby the ancient and traditional chants might be more easily published, circulated and preserved intact for posterity—to the great benefit and glory of the Church and of art.

It was in the Lateran Palace that Gregory the Great, having made his famous collection of the traditional treasures of plainsong, editing them with additions of his own, had wisely founded his great *Schola* in order to perpetuate the true interpretation of the liturgical chant. It was in the same building that the monk Guido gave a demonstration of his marvelous invention before the Roman clergy and the Roman Pontiff himself. The pope, by his approbation and high praise of it, was responsible for the gradual spread of the new system throughout the whole world, and thus for the great advantages that accrued therefrom to musical art in general.

We wish, then, to make certain recommendations to the bishops and ordinaries, whose duty it is, since they are the custodians of the Liturgy, to promote ecclesiastical art. We are thus acceding to the requests which, as a result of many musical congresses and especially that recently held at Rome, have been made to Us by not a few bishops and learned masters in the musical art. To these We accord due meed of praise; and We ordain that the following directions, as here-under set forth, with the practical methods indicated, be put into effect.

All those who aspire to the priesthood, whether in seminaries or in religious houses, from their earliest years are to be taught Gregorian Chant and sacred music. At that age they are able more easily to learn to sing, and to modify, if not entirely to overcome, any defects in their voices, which in later years would be quite incurable. Instruction in music and singing must be begun in the elementary, and continued in the higher classes. In this way, those who are about to receive sacred orders, having become gradually experienced in chant, will be able during their theological course quite easily to undertake the higher and "aesthetic" study of plainsong and sacred music, of polyphony and the organ, concerning which the clergy certainly ought to have a thorough knowledge.

In seminaries, and in other houses of study for the formation of the clergy both secular and regular there should be a frequent and almost daily lecture or practice—however short—in Gregorian Chant and sacred music. If this is carried out in the spirit of the Liturgy, the students will find it a relief rather than a burden to their minds, after the study of the more exacting subjects. Thus, a more complete education of both branches of the clergy in liturgical music will result in the restoration to its former dignity and splendor of the choral Office, a most important part of divine worship; moreover, the *scholae* and choirs will be invested again with their ancient glory.

Those who are responsible for, and engaged in divine worship in basilicas and cathedrals, in collegiate and conventual churches of religious, should use all their endeavors to see that the choral Office is carried out duly—i.e., in accordance with the prescriptions of the Church. And this, not only as regards the precept of reciting the divine Office "worthily, attentive, and devoutly," but also as regards the chant. In singing the psalms attention should be paid to the right tone, with its appropriate mediation and termination, and a suitable pause at the asterisk; so that every verse of the psalms and every strophe of the hymns may be sung by all in perfect time together. If this were rightly observed, then all who worthily sing the psalms would signify their unity of intention in worshipping God and, as one side of the choir sings in answer to the other, would seem to emulate the everlasting praise of the Seraphim who cried one to the other "Holy, Holy, Holy."

Lest anyone in future should invent easy excuses for exempting himself from obedience to the laws of the Church, let every chapter and religious community deal with these matters at meetings held for the purpose; and just as formerly there used to be a "Cantor" or director of the choir, so in future let one be chosen from each chapter or choir of religious, whose duty it will be to see that the rules of the Liturgy and of choral chant are observed and, both individually and generally, to correct the faults of the choir. In this connection it should be observed that, according to the ancient discipline of the Church and the constitutions of chapters still in force, all those at least who are bound to office in choir, are obliged to be familiar with Gregorian Chant. And the Gregorian Chant which is to be used in every church of whatever order, is the text which, revised according to the ancient manuscripts, has been authentically published by the Church from the Vatican Press.

We wish here to recommend, to those whom it may concern, the formation of choirs. These in the course of time came to replace the ancient *scholae* and were established in the basilicas and greater churches especially for the singing of polyphonic music. Sacred polyphony, We may here remark, is rightly held second only to Gregorian Chant. We are desirous, therefore, that such choirs, as they flourished from the fourteenth to the sixteenth century, should now also be created anew and prosper especially in churches where the scale on which the Liturgy is carried out demands a greater number and a more careful selection of singers.

Choir-schools for boys should be established not only for the greater churches and cathedrals, but also for smaller parish churches. The boys should be taught by the choirmaster to sing properly, so that, in accordance with the ancient custom of the Church, they may sing in the choir with the men, especially as in polyphonic music the highest part, the *cantus*, ought to be sung by boys. Choir-boys, especially in the sixteenth century, have given us masters of polyphony: first and foremost among them, the great Palestrina.

As We have learned that in some places an attempt is being made to reintroduce a type of music which is not entirely in keeping with the performance of the sacred Office, particularly owing to the excessive use made of musical instruments, We hereby declare that singing with orchestra accompaniment is not regarded by the Church as a more perfect form of music or as more suitable for sacred purposes. Voices, rather than instruments, ought to be heard in the church: the voices of the clergy, the choir and the congregation. Nor should it be deemed that the Church, in preferring the human voice to any musical instrument, is obstructing the progress of music; for no instrument, however perfect, however excellent, can surpass the human voice in expressing human thought, especially when it is used by the mind to offer up prayer and praise to Almighty God.

The traditionally appropriate musical instrument of the Church is the organ, which, by reason of its extraordinary grandeur and majesty, has been considered a worthy adjunct to the Liturgy, whether for accompanying the chant or, when the choir is silent, for playing harmonious music at the prescribed times. But here too must be avoided that mixture of the profane with the sacred which, through the fault partly of organ-builders and partly of certain performers who are partial to the singularities of modern music, may result eventually in diverting this magnificent instrument from the purpose for which it is intended. We wish, within the limits prescribed by the Liturgy, to encourage the development of all that concerns the organ; but We cannot but lament the fact that, as in the case of certain types of music which the Church has rightly forbidden in the past, so now attempts are being made to introduce a profane spirit into the Church by modern forms of music; which forms, if they begin to enter in, the Church would likewise be bound to condemn. Let our churches resound with organ-music that gives expression to the majesty of the edifice and breathes the sacredness of the religious rites; in this way will the art both of those who build the organs and of those who play them flourish afresh and render effective service to the sacred liturgy.

In order that the faithful may more actively participate in divine worship, let them be made once more to sing the Gregorian Chant, so far as it belongs to them to take part in it. It is most important that when the faithful assist at the sacred ceremonies, or when pious sodalities take part with the clergy in a procession, they should not be merely detached and silent spectators, but, filled with a deep sense of the beauty of the Liturgy, they should sing alternately with the clergy or the choir, as it is prescribed. If this is done, then it will no longer happen that the people either make no answer at all to the public prayers—whether in the language of the Liturgy or in the vernacular—or at best utter the responses in a low and subdued manner.

Let the clergy, both secular and regular, under the lead of their bishops and ordinaries devote their energies either directly, or through other trained teachers, to instructing the people in the Liturgy and in music, as being matters closely associated with Christian doctrine. This will be best effected by teaching liturgical chant in schools, pious confraternities and similar associations. Religious communities of men and women should devote particular attention to the achievement of this purpose in the various educational institutions committed to their care. Moreover, We are confident that this object will be greatly furthered by those societies which, under the control of ecclesiastical authority, are striving to reform sacred music according to the laws of the Church.

To achieve all that We hope for in this matter numerous trained teachers will be required. And in this connection We accord due praise to all the schools and institutes throughout the Catholic world, which by giving careful instruction in these subjects are forming good and suitable teachers. But We have a special word of commendation for the "Pontifical Higher School of Sacred Music," founded in Rome in the year 1910. This school, which was greatly encouraged by Pope Benedict XV and was by him endowed with new privileges, is most particularly favored by Us; for We regard it as a precious heritage left to Us by two Sovereign Pontiffs, and We therefore wish to recommend it in a special way to all the Bishops.

We are well aware that the fulfillment of these injunctions will entail great trouble and labor. But do we not all know how many artistic works our forefathers, undaunted by difficulties, have handed down to posterity, imbued as they were with pious zeal and with the spirit of the Liturgy? Nor is this to be wondered at; for anything that is the fruit of the interior life of the Church surpasses even the most perfect works of this world. Let the difficulties of this sacred task, far from deterring, rather stimulate and encourage the bishops of the Church, who, by their universal and unfailing obedience to Our behests, will render to the Sovereign Bishop a service most worthy of their episcopal office.

Dated in Rome, 20 December 1928, in the seventh year of our pontificate.

"The Rites Derived from the Roman Mass" from Ninth-Sixteenth Centuries"

The Rt. Rev. Dom Fernand Cabrol
The Mass of the Western Rites, 1934

If a special place has been given in these chapters to the Roman Mass, it is not only because this liturgy is that of the whole Latin church with the few exceptions mentioned; it is also because it is the most ancient of all, or at least that about which exist the most ancient and numerous documents. Again, it appears incontestable that the Roman liturgy excels all others in its dogmatic authority, and even in its literary beauty.

If the Mozarabic, Gallican, and Eastern liturgies show a trace of lyrical inspiration; if they are more dramatic in character, more fervent in piety than that of Rome; if this latter has perhaps less originality and brilliance, it makes up for it by the possession of qualities which are those of the Roman genius; those which strike us in the architectural monuments of Rome: solidity, grandeur, strength, and a simplicity which excludes neither nobility nor elegance.

This remark is especially deserved by the ancient Roman liturgy of the fifth-seventh centuries, for this was its Golden Age. Two hundred years after the time of St. Gregory, in the ninth century, the scepter had passed to other lands: to France, England, Switzerland, Germany, and Spain. It was in those countries that liturgical initiative was found, that new Feasts and fresh rites were created, new formulas composed, a more rational system instituted for the distribution of liturgical books, as well as fresh technical methods of decorating and illuminating them.

In consequence of political circumstances Rome was about to lose all she had gained as to the liturgy; and it was not for two or three hundred years that she would recover her scepter. But by a rather curious stroke of fortune all the new customs originated in the countries just mentioned came back to Rome. They returned there under the covers of the Missal, the Pontifical, Ritual, Breviary, and those other books called Roman, but which are really and more justly Gallicano or Germano-Roman. And, from the eleventh century onwards, Rome got back all her advantages. The reawakening of her liturgical activity was manifested by the efforts of Pope Alexander II (1061-1073), and later by those of St. Gregory VII (1073-1085) to establish the Roman liturgy in Spain instead of the Mozarabic. This episode is instructive; the latter Pope in his letters on this subject to the Kings of Aragon, Castile, and Navarre reminds them energetically of the Papal right to the charge of Divine worship, and also to that of establishing the Roman liturgy in all Catholic countries, especially in Spain.

Another indication of the supremacy of the Roman liturgy is that it was adopted by the new Orders, Carthusians, Praemonstratensians, Dominicans, Franciscans, and even by the Carmelites, who had an ancient liturgy of their own; and very soon all these Orders were to become active agents for its spread through all the countries of the West; not, however, without having occasionally modified it. In this great work the Franciscans played the most important part.

The Roman Curia, which until then had celebrated the same Offices as those of the Roman Basilicas, notably of that of the Lateran, which was the cathedral church of Rome, and considered the mother and mistress of all churches, separated itself from these at the beginning of the twelfth century, and fixed its own Office for the Breviary. The substance of this Breviary was actually that of the Lateran, but it differed on several points, and, above all, it was very much abridged. The same thing happened in the case of the Missal. The subsequent history of these books is rather curious. Innocent III (1198-1206) revised them. In 1223 St. Francis of Assisi ordained that the Franciscans should henceforth adopt the Roman Office; for hitherto they had simply followed the Office of whatever province they had chanced to find themselves in. This was a means of establishing amongst the Friars Minor that liturgical unity which had previously suffered a great deal. But the liturgy they adopted both for Mass and Office was neither that of the Lateran nor of the Roman Basilicas, but actually that of the Roman Curia, established at the beginning of the twelfth century. This fact was big with consequences for the future. The activity of the Franciscans at that time was prodigious; and in all the countries through which they passed as missionaries they established this use of the Missal and Breviary which they themselves followed; though they slightly modified it, especially in the case of the Franciscan Feasts. In 1277 Nicholas III ordered it to be used by the Roman Basilicas; Gregory IX, from the year 1240, had thought of imposing it on the Universal Church; but that important duty devolved on St. Pius V (1566-1572). In the sixteenth century the Council of Trent, having declared that the liturgical books required revision, confided the task to the Pope, who undertook a work at once difficult and complicated. In 1568 the correction of the Breviary was completed; in 1570, that of the Missal. Every church which could not prove a local use of at least two hundred years was obliged to adopt the Breviary and the Roman Missal. But long before this date, since the thirteenth, and even the eleventh century, the Religious Orders, both new and old, had adopted a liturgy directly derived from the Roman, especially for Mass. This point deserves an explanation. We speak sometimes of the Dominican or Franciscan liturgy, or again, that of Lyon, or of the Carmelites, as well as of the English "Uses" of Sarum, Hereford, York, etc. But these terms are rather misleading, for such liturgies are not autonomous, with clearly defined characteristics . . . Not only are they all derived from the Roman liturgy, but some of them are purely and simply that liturgy just as it existed from the eleventh-thirteenth centuries before it underwent certain reforms or suffered the changes imposed upon it subsequently. The Orders and churches in question did not accept these changes, so that the student today finds himself in presence of a liturgy which is that of Rome between the eleventh and thirteenth centuries, with a few insignificant exceptions. And as we are about to see this is specially the case with regard to the Mass.

THE RITE OF LYON. It is unnecessary to say that we reject the hypothesis according to which this rite was brought from Asia by St. Pothinus and St. Irenaeus. In studying the origins of the Gallican liturgy we have stated that this "Johannic" thesis has no solid foundation.

Nor can it be said that this is the old Gallican liturgy, better preserved in this church than in others. Like all the other Gallican churches, Lyon was obliged to accept the reforms of Pepin and Charlemagne, and to adopt the Roman liturgy, with the addition of certain ancient local uses. But today it is generally agreed that the part played by Gallican influence in the rite of Lyon may be increasingly reduced, as indeed is the case with all the other Franco-Gallican rites from the tenth century onwards.

History tells us that towards 789 Charlemagne caused Leidrade, one of his "*Missi Dominici*," to be elected Archbishop of Lyon; and that he charged him to reorganize public worship on the lines of the customs of the Palatine chapel at Aix-la-Chapelle. The cause of the difference which still exists, on a few points, between the rite of Lyon and those of some other churches, is that the ecclesiastics of Lyon jealously preserved the liturgy given them by Leidrade, without accepting the changes and reforms adopted in the course of the centuries by the Roman Curia. It was not till the eighteenth century that De Montazet, Archbishop of Lyon (1758-1788), unfortunately replaced the venerable liturgy of his church by a neo-Gallican one. Therefore in the nineteenth century Lyon, like all the other churches which had adopted these liturgies, had to come back to that of Rome, though she succeeded in saving some of her ancient usages. Thus, she has more numerous Proses: to the fifteen Prefaces of the Roman Mass Lyon adds eight. The prayers at the beginning of Mass, the "*Suscipe Sancta Trinitas*" and some others, present a slightly different text; the "*Libera nos*" after the "*Pater*" is sung at High Mass, as on Good Friday, while after this prayer a blessing is given, as in the old Gallican rite; the beautiful chant of the Fraction "*Venite, populi*" has been preserved; Pontifical Mass is celebrated with especial solemnity, etc.

THE CARTHUSIANS. It is a rather curious fact in liturgical history that the Carthusians have preserved the ancient rite more faithfully than the Lyonnais themselves. The liturgical revolution mentioned as having taken place in the eighteenth century was not felt by the Carthusians. This Order, founded in 1084 by St. Bruno, in the mountains of the Chartreuse, had taken the liturgical uses of Grenoble, Vienne, but specially those of Lyon. Its founder, who at first had followed the Rule of St. Benedict, kept some of its practices. These different usages were codified at various periods in the Constitutions which have been preserved, and of which the most complete are the "*Statuta Antiqua*." The prayer "*Pone, Domine, custodiam ori meo*," and another, "*De latere Domini*," recited at Mass, are derived from the rite of Lyon. On certain Feasts three Lessons at the Pre-Mass have been retained. The wine is poured into the chalice at the beginning of Mass, as in the Dominican rite. The oblations of bread and wine (after they have been offered) are covered with the Corporal, as was the custom before the use of the "*Palla*" had been introduced. "*Domine, Jesu Christe*" is the only one of the three prayers said before the Communion; those present in choir remain standing during both Consecration and Communion; the Mass terminates with "*Ite, Missa est*." Before the fourteenth century the Mass of the Dead had a different text from the "Requiem." Some Benedictine uses have been preserved in the Breviary; while others seem to have been derived from the rite of Lyon. For a long time the Carthusian calendar remained the same as the old Roman one; it was only after a very long period that Feasts instituted after the thirteenth century were admitted, and then not without difficulty. In the sixteenth century some reforms were brought about, either as to the correction of the ancient books, or as to bringing them into line with the new rules.

BENEDICTINE LITURGY On the whole it may be said that the Benedictines have always followed the Roman practice for the Mass. Instituted in the first part of the sixth century, it appears probable that they first followed the Gelasian Sacramentary, adopting the Gregorian in the next generation; this latter being the work of St. Gregory, who was himself a disciple of St. Benedict. But for the daily Office it is quite a different matter. St. Benedict, while doubtless borrowing a certain number of customs from the Roman Office then in use, organized the Psalter and the Day and Night Hours according to a particular plan which has been followed by the Benedictine Order throughout the centuries, till the present day. Liturgiologists are still discussing what has been the respective influence of one use upon another; but this question cannot be entered into here.

CISTERCIANS. As is well known, the Cistercians are a reform of the Benedictine Order. Their founder, St. Robert of Molesmes, wished to return to the primitive observance of the Rule in 1098. To this end he rejected all constitutions or additions made since the sixth century. His principle was the same for the liturgy: to bring back the Office as St. Benedict had instituted it. This principle was a good one, but difficult in application, for it was not exactly known in what the "cursus" of St. Benedict's time consisted. Therefore from the beginning there was a good deal of uncertainty. Then scandal was caused by certain suppressions, and in the twelfth and thirteenth centuries they came back to their first attempts as far as the Office was concerned.

As to the Mass, it has been said that the Benedictine Order followed the use of Rome from the beginning. But the Cluniac monks had accepted modifications made since the ninth century, and had introduced a very great solemnity into both Mass and Office. The Cistercian reform consisted in the suppression of all which seemed superfluous, and as concerned the sacred vases and ornaments, in the return to the greatest simplicity. Thus, it was not till quite late, at the beginning of the eighteenth century, that the different liturgical colors were admitted. A certain number of Feasts was also suppressed in the calendar. In the seventeenth century the General Chapters ordered a general revision of the liturgical books, and more ancient rites were abandoned.

CARMELITES. This rite presents a special case. It is that of the church of the Holy Sepulcher at Jerusalem, which was imposed on the Carmelites about 1210 by St. Albert, Patriarch of Jerusalem, and which they kept for a long time. It is nothing but a Gallicano-Roman use, brought to Jerusalem by the Crusaders. The Office gave a particular place to all which could recall the Holy Land, such as the Mystery of the Resurrection, or devotion to Our Lady, and had besides several other special customs. In the course of ages the Carmelite liturgy underwent various modifications. The Ordinal of Master Sibert de Beka (d. 1332), which has been most carefully published, preserves all the ancient uses onformably to the rite of the Holy Sepulcher. It is in this document that the Carmelite liturgy should be studied.

DOMINICANS. This Order had no special liturgy at its beginning, but adopted that of the provinces through which the Friars first spread. To prevent the inconvenience of this variety the Order sought, from the year 1245, to establish liturgical unity. To this end efforts were made in 1244,1246, and 1251. Finally Humbert de Romans, the Master-General (1254-1263), was charged with this revision. He accomplished an enormous work; and in fourteen volumes published the Lectionary, Antiphonary, Psalter, book of Collects, Martyrology, Processional, Gradual, a Missal for the high altar and one for the other altars in the church, a Breviary for the Choir and a portable Breviary, a book of the Epistles, and another of the Gospels. When in 1568 and 1570 St. Pius V imposed the corrected Missal and Breviary on the whole Church, the Dominicans were allowed to retain their own use, which dated back more than 200 years. This liturgy is not, as has been thought, a Gallican, and more specifically, a Parisian liturgy. It is simply Roman, dating from the thirteenth century, and has not evolved as the actual Roman liturgy has done; thus, retaining all the ancient customs elsewhere fallen into disuse. Thus, a thesis which at first sight appears paradoxical has been advanced, to the effect that the Dominican liturgy is more Roman than that of Rome herself. This, however, is the case with the greater number of these rites, which did not accept the transformations of the Roman liturgy.

FRANCISCANS. It has been already explained how the Franciscans adopted the liturgy which was that of the Roman Curia at the opening of the thirteenth century. To this they added certain special uses, beginning with the Feasts of the Saints of their Order: St. Francis first; then St. Clare; St. Anthony of Padua; St. Louis, King of France; the Stigmata of St. Francis; St. Elizabeth of Hungary; St. Paschal Baylon; St. Bonaventure. Some of the Feasts of Our Lord and of Our Lady owe, if not their actual institution, at least their speedy popularity to the Franciscans. Such are the Holy Name of Jesus, the Immaculate Conception, the Visitation, and the Presentation. Each Religious Order, each diocese has its own Feasts, its own Patrons, which they celebrate with great solemnity; they are the "Proper," as it is called, of the diocese or Order.

What should be particularly noted about the Franciscans is that, having adopted the liturgy of the Roman Curia, they made a "second edition of it," as Msgr. Batiffol remarks; and this was almost the same as that imposed upon the whole Church for Breviary and Missal by St. Pius V.

PRAEMONSTRATENSIANS. The Order of St. Norbert, being an Order of Canons, was bound to give special attention to the liturgy. Its Founder adopted that of Rome, just as it was practiced in France at the beginning of the twelfth century, at Premontre, in the diocese of Laon. Until the eighteenth century they kept it piously; and their books are mentioned as being one of the purest sources of the Roman liturgy of the twelfth century. Thanks to this antiquity they too benefited by the exception made by St. Pius V in 1570 in favor of ancient customs. Unfortunately, in the eighteenth century the French Praemonstratensians succumbed to the general temptation, and modified their books in the neo-Gallican sense. In other countries, however, the ancient books were preserved.

THE ROMAN LITURGY IN ENGLAND. Celtic rites had dominated in England until the arrival of St. Augustine of Canterbury (596). But with the Roman monks the Roman liturgy was established without difficulty wherever Christianity was firmly settled in the land; and the Anglo-Saxons followed it faithfully. Their Bishops and Abbots made frequent journeys to Rome, either to procure the necessary singing-books and those of liturgical interest, or to study the rites more closely. The Norman Conquest of 1066 changed nothing in this regard, for, like all the other French provinces, Normandy had long been conquered by the Roman liturgy. Thus, the various rites called the Use of Sarum (Salisbury), York, Bangor, Hereford, and other places, are, like those of the different Orders we have just been studying, only the Roman liturgy previous to the fourteenth century, with a few rare local customs added to it.

Mediator Dei:
Encyclical on the Sacred Liturgy

Pope Pius XII
November 20, 1947

Venerable Brethren,
Health and Apostolic Benediction.

Mediator between God and men [1] and High Priest who has gone before us into heaven, Jesus the Son of God [2] quite clearly had one aim in view when He undertook the mission of mercy which was to endow mankind with the rich blessings of supernatural grace. Sin had disturbed the right relationship between man and his Creator; the Son of God would restore it. The children of Adam were wretched heirs to the infection of original sin; He would bring them back to their heavenly Father, the primal source and final destiny of all things. For this reason He was not content, while He dwelt with us on earth, merely to give notice that redemption had begun, and to proclaim the long-awaited Kingdom of God, but gave Himself besides in prayer and sacrifice to the task of saving souls, even to the point of offering Himself, as He hung from the Cross, a Victim unspotted unto God, to purify our conscience of dead works, to serve the living God. [3] Thus, happily were all men summoned back from the byways leading them down to ruin and disaster, to be set squarely once again upon the path that leads to God. Thanks to the shedding of the Blood of the Immaculate Lamb, now each might set about the personal task of achieving his own sanctification, so rendering to God the glory due to Him.

2. But what is more, the divine Redeemer has so willed it that the priestly life begun with the supplication and sacrifice of His mortal Body should continue without intermission down the ages in His Mystical Body which is the Church. That is why He established a visible priesthood to offer everywhere the clean oblation [4] which would enable men from East to West, freed from the shackles of sin, to offer God that unconstrained and voluntary homage which their conscience dictates.

3. In obedience, therefore, to her Founder's behest, the Church prolongs the priestly mission of Jesus Christ mainly by means of the sacred liturgy. She does this in the first place at the altar, where constantly the sacrifice of the Cross is represented [5] and with a single difference in the manner of its offering, renewed.[6] She does it next by means of the sacraments, those special channels through which men are made partakers in the supernatural life. She does it, finally, by offering to God, all Good and Great, the daily tribute of her prayer of praise. "What a spectacle for heaven and earth," observes Our predecessor of happy memory, Pius XI, "is not the Church at prayer! For centuries without interruption, from midnight to midnight, the divine psalmody of the inspired canticles is repeated on earth; there is no hour of the day that is not hallowed by its special liturgy; there is no state of human life that has not its part in the thanksgiving, praise, supplication, and reparation of this common prayer of the Mystical Body of Christ which is His Church!"[7]

4. You are of course familiar with the fact, Venerable Brethren, that a remarkably widespread revival of scholarly interest in the sacred liturgy took place towards the end of the last century and has continued through the early years of this one. The movement owed its rise to commendable private initiative and more particularly to the zealous and persistent labor of several monasteries within the distinguished Order of Saint Benedict. Thus, there developed in this field among many European nations, and in lands beyond the seas as well, a rivalry as welcome as it was productive of results. Indeed, the salutary fruits of this rivalry among the scholars were plain for all to see, both in the sphere of the sacred sciences, where the liturgical rites of the Western and Eastern Church were made the object of extensive research and profound study, and in the spiritual life of considerable numbers of individual Christians.

5. The majestic ceremonies of the sacrifice of the altar became better known, understood and appreciated. With more widespread and more frequent reception of the sacraments, with the beauty of the liturgical prayers more fully savored, the worship of the Eucharist came to be regarded for what it really is: the fountain-head of genuine Christian devotion. Bolder relief was given likewise to the fact that all the faithful make up a single and very compact Body with Christ for its Head, and that the Christian community is in duty bound to participate in the liturgical rites according to their station.

6. You are surely well aware that this Apostolic See has always made careful provision for the schooling of the people committed to its charge in the correct spirit and practice of the liturgy; and that it has been no less careful to insist that the sacred rites should be performed with due external dignity. In this connection We ourselves, in the course of our traditional address to the Lenten preachers of this gracious city of Rome in 1943, urged them warmly to exhort their respective hearers to more faithful participation in the eucharistic sacrifice. Only a short while previously, with the design of rendering the prayers of the liturgy more correctly understood and their truth and unction more easy to perceive, We arranged to have the Book of Psalms, which forms such an important part of these prayers in the Catholic Church, translated again into Latin from their original text.[8]

7. But while We derive no little satisfaction from the wholesome results of the movement just described, duty obliges Us to give serious attention to this "revival" as it is advocated in some quarters, and to take proper steps to preserve it at the outset from excess or outright perversion.

8. Indeed, though we are sorely grieved to note, on the one hand, that there are places where the spirit, understanding or practice of the sacred liturgy is defective, or all but inexistent, We observe with considerable anxiety and some misgiving, that elsewhere certain enthusiasts, over-eager in their search for novelty, are straying beyond the path of sound doctrine and prudence. Not seldom, in fact, they interlard their plans and hopes for a revival of the sacred liturgy with principles which compromise this holiest of causes in theory or practice, and sometimes even taint it with errors touching Catholic faith and ascetical doctrine.

9. Yet the integrity of faith and morals ought to be the special criterion of this sacred science, which must conform exactly to what the Church out of the abundance of her wisdom teaches and prescribes. It is, consequently, Our prerogative to commend and approve whatever is done properly, and to check or censure any aberration from the path of truth and rectitude.

10. Let not the apathetic or half-hearted imagine, however, that We agree with them when We reprove the erring and restrain the overbold. No more must the imprudent think that we are commending

them when We correct the faults of those who are negligent and sluggish.

11. If in this encyclical letter We treat chiefly of the Latin liturgy, it is not because We esteem less highly the venerable liturgies of the Eastern Church, whose ancient and honorable ritual traditions are just as dear to Us. The reason lies rather in a special situation prevailing in the Western Church, of sufficient importance, it would seem, to require this exercise of Our authority.

12. With docile hearts, then, let all Christians hearken to the voice of their Common Father, who would have them, each and every one, intimately united with him as they approach the altar of God, professing the same faith, obedient to the same law, sharing in the same Sacrifice with a single intention and one sole desire. This is a duty imposed, of course, by the honor due to God. But the needs of our day and age demand it as well. After a long and cruel war which has rent whole peoples asunder with its rivalry and slaughter, men of good will are spending themselves in the effort to find the best possible way to restore peace to the world. It is, notwithstanding, Our belief that no plan or initiative can offer better prospect of success than that fervent religious spirit and zeal by which Christians must be formed and guided; in this way their common and whole-hearted acceptance of the same truth, along with their united obedience and loyalty to their appointed pastors, while rendering to God the worship due to Him, makes of them one brotherhood: "for we, being many, are one Body: all that partake of one bread."[9]

13. It is unquestionably the fundamental duty of man to orientate his person and his life towards God. "For He it is to whom we must first be bound, as to an unfailing principle; to whom even our free choice must be directed as to an ultimate objective. It is He, too, whom we lose when carelessly we sin. It is He whom we must recover by our faith and trust."[10] But man turns properly to God when he acknowledges His Supreme majesty and supreme authority; when he accepts divinely revealed truths with a submissive mind; when he scrupulously obeys divine law, centering in God his every act and aspiration; when he accords, in short, due worship to the One True God by practicing the virtue of religion.

14. This duty is incumbent, first of all, on men as individuals. But it also binds the whole community of human beings, grouped together

by mutual social ties: mankind, too, depends on the sovereign authority of God.

15. It should be noted, moreover, that men are bound by his obligation in a special way in virtue of the fact that God has raised them to the supernatural order.

16. Thus, we observe that when God institutes the Old Law, He makes provision besides for sacred rites, and determines in exact detail the rules to be observed by His people in rendering Him the worship He ordains. To this end He established various kinds of sacrifice and designated the ceremonies with which they were to be offered to Him. His enactments on all matters relating to the Ark of the Covenant, the Temple and the holy days are minute and clear. He established a sacerdotal tribe with its high priest, selected and described the vestments with which the sacred ministers were to be clothed, and every function in any way pertaining to divine worship. [11] Yet this was nothing more than a faint foreshadowing [12] of the worship which the High Priest of the New Testament was to render to the Father in heaven.

17. No sooner, in fact, "is the Word made flesh" [13] than he shows Himself to the world vested with a priestly office, making to the Eternal Father an act of submission which will continue uninterruptedly as long as He lives: "When He cometh into the world he saith. . . 'behold I come . . . to do Thy Will." [14] This act He was to consummate admirably in the bloody Sacrifice of the Cross: "It is in this will we are sanctified by the oblation of the Body of Jesus Christ once."[15] He plans His active life among men with no other purpose in view. As a child He is presented to the Lord in the Temple. To the Temple He returns as a grown boy, and often afterwards to instruct the people and to pray. He fasts for forty days before beginning His public ministry. His counsel and example summon all to prayer, daily and at night as well. As Teacher of the truth He "enlighteneth every man" [16] to the end that mortals may duly acknowledge the immortal God, "not withdrawing unto perdition, but faithful to the saving of the soul."[17] As Shepherd He watches over His flock, leads it to life-giving pasture, lays down a law that none shall wander from His side, off the straight path He has pointed out, and that all shall lead holy lives imbued with His spirit and moved by His active aid. At the Last Supper He celebrates a new Pasch with solemn rite and ceremonial, and provides for its continuance through the divine institution of the Eucharist. On the morrow, lifted up

between heaven and earth, He offers the saving sacrifice of His life, and pours forth, as it were, from His pierced Heart the sacraments destined to impart the treasures of redemption to the souls of men. All this He does with but a single aim: the glory of His Father and man's ever greater sanctification.

18. But it is His will, besides, that the worship He instituted and practiced during His life on earth shall continue ever afterwards without intermission. For He has not left mankind an orphan. He still offers us the support of His powerful, unfailing intercession, acting as our "advocate with the Father." [18] He aids us likewise through His Church, where He is present indefectibly as the ages run their course: through the Church which He constituted "the pillar of truth" [19] and dispenser of grace, and which by His sacrifice on the Cross, He founded, consecrated and confirmed forever. [20]

19. The Church has, therefore, in common with the Word Incarnate the aim, the obligation, and the function of teaching all men the truth, of governing and directing them aright, of offering to God the pleasing and acceptable sacrifice; in this way the Church re-establishes between the Creator and His creatures that unity and harmony to which the Apostle of the Gentiles alludes in these words: "Now, therefore, you are no more strangers and foreigners; but you are fellow citizens with the saints and domestics of God, built upon the foundation of the apostles and prophets, Jesus Christ Himself being the chief corner-stone; in whom all the building, being framed together, groweth up into a holy temple in the Lord, in whom you also are built together in a habitation of God in the Spirit."[21] Thus, the society founded by the divine Redeemer, whether in her doctrine and government, or in the sacrifice and sacraments instituted by Him, or finally, in the ministry, which He has confided to her charge with the outpouring of His prayer and the shedding of His blood, has no other goal or purpose than to increase ever in strength and unity.

20. This result is, in fact, achieved when Christ lives and thrives, as it were, in the hearts of men, and when men's hearts in turn are fashioned and expanded as though by Christ. This makes it possible for the sacred temple, where the Divine Majesty receives the acceptable worship which His law prescribes, to increase and prosper day by day in this land of exile of earth. Along with the Church, therefore, her Divine Founder is present at every liturgical function: Christ is present at the august sacrifice of the altar both in the person

of His minister and above all under the eucharistic species. He is present in the sacraments, infusing into them the power which makes them ready instruments of sanctification. He is present, finally, in prayer of praise and petition we direct to God, as it is written: "Where there are two or three gathered together in My Name, there am I in the midst of them."[22] The sacred liturgy is, consequently, the public worship which our Redeemer as Head of the Church renders to the Father, as well as the worship which the community of the faithful renders to its Founder, and through Him to the heavenly Father. It is, in short, the worship rendered by the Mystical Body of Christ in the entirety of its Head and members.

21. Liturgical practice begins with the very founding of the Church. The first Christians, in fact, "were persevering in the doctrine of the apostles and in the communication of the breaking of bread and in prayers."[23] Whenever their pastors can summon a little group of the faithful together, they set up an altar on which they proceed to offer the sacrifice, and around which are ranged all the other rites appropriate for the saving of souls and for the honor due to God. Among these latter rites, the first place is reserved for the sacraments, namely, the seven principal founts of salvation. There follows the celebration of the divine praises in which the faithful also join, obeying the behest of the Apostle Paul, "In all wisdom, teaching and admonishing one another in psalms, hymns, and spiritual canticles, singing in grace in your hearts to God."[24] Next comes the reading of the Law, the prophets, the gospel, and the apostolic epistles; and last of all the homily or sermon in which the official head of the congregation recalls and explains the practical bearing of the commandments of the divine Master and the chief events of His life, combining instruction with appropriate exhortation and illustration of the benefit of all his listeners.

22. As circumstances and the needs of Christians warrant, public worship is organized, developed and enriched by new rites, ceremonies and regulations, always with the single end in view, "that we may use these external signs to keep us alert, learn from them what distance we have come along the road, and by them be heartened to go on further with more eager step; for the effect will be more precious the warmer the affection which precedes it."[25] Here then is a better and more suitable way to raise the heart to God. Thenceforth the priesthood of Jesus Christ is a living and continuous reality through all the ages to the end of time, since the liturgy is

nothing more nor less than the exercise of this priestly function. Like her divine Head, the Church is forever present in the midst of her children. She aids and exhorts them to holiness, so that they may one day return to the Father in heaven clothed in that beauteous raiment of the supernatural. To all who are born to life on earth she gives a second, supernatural kind of birth. She arms them with the Holy Spirit for the struggle against the implacable enemy. She gathers all Christians about her altars, inviting and urging them repeatedly to take part in the celebration of the Mass, feeding them with the Bread of angels to make them ever stronger. She purifies and consoles the hearts that sin has wounded and soiled. Solemnly she consecrates those whom God has called to the priestly ministry. She fortifies with new gifts of grace the chaste nuptials of those who are destined to found and bring up a Christian family. When as last she has soothed and refreshed the closing hours of this earthly life by holy Viaticum and extreme unction, with the utmost affection she accompanies the mortal remains of her children to the grave, lays them reverently to rest, and confides them to the protection of the cross, against the day when they will triumph over death and rise again. She has a further solemn blessing and invocation for those of her children who dedicate themselves to the service of God in the life of religious perfection. Finally, she extends to the souls in purgatory, who implore her intercession and her prayers, the helping hand which may lead them happily at last to eternal blessedness in heaven.

23. The worship rendered by the Church to God must be, in its entirety, interior as well as exterior. It is exterior because the nature of man as a composite of body and soul requires it to be so. Likewise, because divine Providence has disposed that "while we recognize God visibly, we may be drawn by Him to love of things unseen."[26] Every impulse of the human heart, besides, expresses itself naturally through the senses; and the worship of God, being the concern not merely of individuals but of the whole community of mankind, must therefore be social as well. This obviously it cannot be unless religious activity is also organized and manifested outwardly. Exterior worship, finally, reveals and emphasizes the unity of the mystical Body, feeds new fuel to its holy zeal, fortifies its energy, intensifies its action day by day: "for although the ceremonies themselves can claim no perfection or sanctity in their own right, they are, nevertheless, the outward acts of religion, designed to rouse the heart, like signals of a sort, to veneration of the sacred realities, and to raise the mind to meditation on the supernatural. They serve to foster piety,

to kindle the flame of charity, to increase our faith and deepen our devotion. They provide instruction for simple folk, decoration for divine worship, continuity of religious practice. They make it possible to tell genuine Christians from their false or heretical counterparts."[27]

24. But the chief element of divine worship must be interior. For we must always live in Christ and give ourselves to Him completely, so that in Him, with Him and through Him the heavenly Father may be duly glorified. The sacred liturgy requires, however, that both of these elements be intimately linked with each another. This recommendation the liturgy itself is careful to repeat, as often as it prescribes an exterior act of worship. Thus, we are urged, when there is question of fasting, for example, "to give interior effect to our outward observance."[28] Otherwise religion clearly amounts to mere formalism, without meaning and without content. You recall, Venerable Brethren, how the divine Master expels from the sacred temple, as unworthily to worship there, people who pretend to honor God with nothing but neat and well-turned phrases, like actors in a theater, and think themselves perfectly capable of working out their eternal salvation without plucking their inveterate vices from their hearts.[29] It is, therefore, the keen desire of the Church that all of the faithful kneel at the feet of the Redeemer to tell Him how much they venerate and love Him. She wants them present in crowds—like the children whose joyous cries accompanied His entry into Jerusalem— to sing their hymns and chant their song of praise and thanksgiving to Him who is King of Kings and Source of every blessing. She would have them move their lips in prayer, sometimes in petition, sometimes in joy and gratitude, and in this way experience His merciful aid and power like the apostles at the lakeside of Tiberias, or abandon themselves totally, like Peter on Mount Tabor, to mystic union with the eternal God in contemplation.

25. It is an error, consequently, and a mistake to think of the sacred liturgy as merely the outward or visible part of divine worship or as an ornamental ceremonial. No less erroneous is the notion that it consists solely in a list of laws and prescriptions according to which the ecclesiastical hierarchy orders the sacred rites to be performed.

26. It should be clear to all, then, that God cannot be honored worthily unless the mind and heart turn to Him in quest of the perfect life, and that the worship rendered to God by the Church in union with her divine Head is the most efficacious means of achieving sanctity.

27. This efficacy, where there is question of the eucharistic sacrifice and the sacraments, derives first of all and principally from the act itself (*ex opere operato*). But if one considers the part which the Immaculate Spouse of Jesus Christ takes in the action, embellishing the sacrifice and sacraments with prayer and sacred ceremonies, or if one refers to the "sacramentals" and the other rites instituted by the hierarchy of the Church, then its effectiveness is due rather to the action of the church (*ex opere operantis Ecclesiae*), inasmuch as she is holy and acts always in closest union with her Head.

28. In this connection, Venerable Brethren, We desire to direct your attention to certain recent theories touching a so-called "objective" piety. While these theories attempt, it is true, to throw light on the mystery of the Mystical Body, on the effective reality of sanctifying grace, on the action of God in the sacraments and in the Mass, it is nonetheless apparent that they tend to belittle, or pass over in silence, what they call "subjective," or "personal," piety.

29. It is an unquestionable fact that the work of our redemption is continued, and that its fruits are imparted to us, during the celebration of the liturgy, notable in the august sacrifice of the altar. Christ acts each day to save us, in the sacraments and in His holy sacrifice. By means of them He is constantly atoning for the sins of mankind, constantly consecrating it to God. Sacraments and sacrifice do, then, possess that "objective" power to make us really and personally sharers in the divine life of Jesus Christ. Not from any ability of our own, but by the power of God, are they endowed with the capacity to unite the piety of members with that of the head, and to make this, in a sense, the action of the whole community. From these profound considerations some are led to conclude that all Christian piety must be centered in the mystery of the Mystical Body of Christ, with no regard for what is "personal," or "subjective, as they would have it. As a result they feel that all other religious exercises not directly connected with the sacred liturgy, and performed outside public worship should be omitted.

30. But though the principles set forth above are excellent, it must be plain to everyone that the conclusions drawn from them respecting two sorts of piety are false, insidious, and quite pernicious.

31. Very truly, the sacraments and the sacrifice of the altar, being Christ's own actions, must be held to be capable in themselves of

conveying and dispensing grace from the divine Head to the members of the Mystical Body. But if they are to produce their proper effect, it is absolutely necessary that our hearts be properly disposed to receive them. Hence, the warning of Paul the Apostle with reference to holy communion, "But let a man first prove himself; and then let him eat of this bread and drink of the chalice."[30] This explains why the Church in a brief and significant phrase calls the various acts of mortification, especially those practiced during the season of Lent, "the Christian army's defenses."[31] They represent, in fact, the personal effort and activity of members who desire, as grace urges and aids them, to join forces with their Captain—"that we may discover . . . in our Captain," to borrow St. Augustine's words, "the fountain of grace itself."[32] But observe that these members are alive, endowed and equipped with an intelligence and will of their own. It follows that they are strictly required to put their own lips to the fountain, imbibe and absorb for themselves the life-giving water, and rid themselves personally of anything that might hinder its nutritive effect in their souls. Emphatically, therefore, the work of redemption, which in itself is independent of our will, requires a serious interior effort on our part if we are to achieve eternal salvation.

32. If the private and interior devotion of individuals were to neglect the august sacrifice of the altar and the sacraments, and to withdraw them from the stream of vital energy that flows from Head to members, it would indeed be sterile, and deserve to be condemned. But when devotional exercises, and pious practices in general, not strictly connected with the sacred liturgy, confine themselves to merely human acts, with the express purpose of directing these latter to the Father in heaven, of rousing people to repentance and holy fear of God, of weaning them from the seductions of the world and its vice, and leading them back to the difficult path of perfection, then certainly such practices are not only highly praiseworthy but absolutely indispensable, because they expose the dangers threatening the spiritual life; because they promote the acquisition of virtue; and because they increase the fervor and generosity with which we are bound to dedicate all that we are and all that we have to the service of Jesus Christ. Genuine and real piety, which the Angelic Doctor calls "devotion," and which is the principal act of the virtue of religion—that act which correctly relates and fitly directs men to God; and by which they freely and spontaneously give themselves to the worship of God in its fullest sense [33]—piety of this authentic sort needs

meditation on the supernatural realities and spiritual exercises, if it is to be nurtured, stimulated and sustained, and if it is to prompt us to lead a more perfect life. For the Christian religion, practiced as it should be, demands that the will especially be consecrated to God and exert its influence on all the other spiritual faculties. But every act of the will presupposes an act of the intelligence, and before one can express the desire and the intention of offering oneself in sacrifice to the eternal Godhead, a knowledge of the facts and truths which make religion a duty is altogether necessary. One must first know, for instance, man's last end and the supremacy of the Divine Majesty; after that, our common duty of submission to our Creator; and, finally, the inexhaustible treasures of love with which God yearns to enrich us, as well as the necessity of supernatural grace for the achievement of our destiny, and that special path marked out for us by divine Providence in virtue of the fact that we have been united, one and all, like members of a body, to Jesus Christ the Head. But further, since our hearts, disturbed as they are at times by the lower appetites, do not always respond to motives of love, it is also extremely helpful to let consideration and contemplation of the justice of God provoke us on occasion to salutary fear, and guide us thence to Christian humility, repentance, and amendment.

33. But it will not do to possess these facts and truths after the fashion of an abstract memory lesson or lifeless commentary. They must lead to practical results. They must impel us to subject our senses and their faculties to reason, as illuminated by the Catholic faith. They must help to cleanse and purify the heart, uniting it to Christ more intimately every day, growing ever more to His likeness, and drawing from Him the divine inspiration and strength of which it stands in need. They must serve as increasingly effective incentives to action: urging men to produce good fruit, to perform their individual duties faithfully, to give themselves eagerly to the regular practice of their religion and the energetic exercise of virtue. "You are Christ's, and Christ is God's."[34] Let everything, therefore, have its proper place and arrangement; let everything be "theocentric," so to speak, if we really wish to direct everything to the glory of God through the life and power which flow from the divine Head into our hearts: "Having, therefore, brethren, a confidence in the entering into the holies by the blood of Christ, a new and living way which He both dedicated for us through the veil, that is to say, His flesh, and a high priest over the house of God; let us draw near with a true heart, in fullness of faith, having our hearts sprinkled from an evil conscience and our bodies

washed with clean water, let us hold fast the confession of our hope without wavering . . . and let us consider one another, to provoke unto charity and to good works."[35]

34. Here is the source of the harmony and equilibrium which prevails among the members of the Mystical Body of Jesus Christ. When the Church teaches us our Catholic faith and exhorts us to obey the commandments of Christ, she is paving a way for her priestly, sanctifying action in its highest sense; she disposes us likewise for more serious meditation on the life of the divine Redeemer and guides us to profounder knowledge of the mysteries of faith where we may draw the supernatural sustenance, strength and vitality that enable us to progress safely, through Christ, towards a more perfect life. Not only through her ministers but with the help of the faithful individually, who have imbibed in this fashion the spirit of Christ, the Church endeavors to permeate with this same spirit the life and labors of men—their private and family life, their social, even economic and political life—that all who are called God's children may reach more readily the end He has proposed for them.

35. Such action on the part of individual Christians, then, along with the ascetic effort promoting them to purify their hearts, actually stimulates in the faithful those energies which enable them to participate in the august sacrifice of the altar with better dispositions. They now can receive the sacraments with more abundant fruit, and come from the celebration of the sacred rites more eager, more firmly resolved to pray and deny themselves like Christians, to answer the inspirations and invitation of divine grace and to imitate daily more closely the virtues of our Redeemer. And all of this not simply for their own advantage, but for that of the whole Church, where whatever good is accomplished proceeds from the power of her Head and redounds to the advancement of all her members.

36. In the spiritual life, consequently, there can be no opposition between the action of God, who pours forth His grace into men's hearts so that the work of the redemption may always abide, and the tireless collaboration of man, who must not render vain the gift of God.[36] No more can the efficacy of the external administration of the sacraments, which comes from the rite itself (*ex opere operato*), be opposed to the meritorious action of their ministers of recipients, which we call the agent's action (*opus operantis*). Similarly, no conflict exists between public prayer and prayers in private, between morality and contemplation, between the ascetical life and devotion to

the liturgy. Finally, there is no opposition between the jurisdiction and teaching office of the ecclesiastical hierarchy, and the specifically priestly power exercised in the sacred ministry.

37. Considering their special designation to perform the liturgical functions of the holy sacrifice and divine office, the Church has serious reason for prescribing that the ministers she assigns to the service of the sanctuary and members of religious institutes betake themselves at stated times to mental prayer, to examination of conscience, and to various other spiritual exercises.[37] Unquestionably, liturgical prayer, being the public supplication of the illustrious Spouse of Jesus Christ, is superior in excellence to private prayers. But this superior worth does not at all imply contrast or incompatibility between these two kinds of prayer. For both merge harmoniously in the single spirit which animates them, "Christ is all and in all."[38] Both tend to the same objective: until Christ be formed in us.[39]

38. For a better and more accurate understanding of the sacred liturgy another of its characteristic features, no less important, needs to be considered.

39. The Church is a society, and as such requires an authority and hierarchy of her own. Though it is true that all the members of the Mystical Body partake of the same blessings and pursue the same objective, they do not all enjoy the same powers, nor are they all qualified to perform the same acts. The divine Redeemer has willed, as a matter of fact, that His Kingdom should be built and solidly supported, as it were, on a holy order, which resembles in some sort the heavenly hierarchy.

40. Only to the apostles, and thenceforth to those on whom their successors have imposed hands, is granted the power of the priesthood, in virtue of which they represent the person of Jesus Christ before their people, acting at the same time as representatives of their people before God. This priesthood is not transmitted by heredity or human descent. It does not emanate from the Christian community. It is not a delegation from the people. Prior to acting as representative of the community before the throne of God, the priest is the ambassador of the divine Redeemer. He is God's vice-regent in the midst of his flock precisely because Jesus Christ is Head of that body of which Christians are the members. The power entrusted to

him, therefore, bears no natural resemblance to anything human. It is entirely supernatural. It comes from God. "As the Father hath sent me, I also send you [40]. . . he that heareth you heareth me [41]. . . go ye into the whole world and preach the gospel to every creature; he that believeth and is baptized shall be saved."[42]

41. That is why the visible, external priesthood of Jesus Christ is not handed down indiscriminately to all members of the Church in general, but is conferred on designated men, through what may be called the spiritual generation of holy orders.

42. This latter, one of the seven sacraments, not only imparts the grace appropriate to the clerical function and state of life, but imparts an indelible "character" besides, indicating the sacred ministers' conformity to Jesus Christ the Priest and qualifying them to perform those official acts of religion by which men are sanctified and God is duly glorified in keeping with the divine laws and regulations.

43. In the same way, actually that baptism is the distinctive mark of all Christians, and serves to differentiate them from those who have not been cleansed in this purifying stream and consequently are not members of Christ, the sacrament of holy orders sets the priest apart from the rest of the faithful who have not received this consecration. For they alone, in answer to an inward supernatural call, have entered the august ministry, where they are assigned to service in the sanctuary and become, as it were, the instruments God uses to communicate supernatural life from on high to the Mystical Body of Jesus Christ. Add to this, as We have noted above, the fact that they alone have been marked with the indelible sign "conforming" them to Christ the Priest, and that their hands alone have been consecrated "in order that whatever they bless may be blessed, whatever they consecrate may become sacred and holy, in the name of our Lord Jesus Christ"[43] Let all, then, who would live in Christ flock to their priests. By them they will be supplied with the comforts and food of the spiritual life. From them they will procure the medicine of salvation assuring their cure and happy recovery from the fatal sickness of their sins. The priest, finally, will bless their homes, consecrate their families and help them, as they breathe their last, across the threshold of eternal happiness.

44. Since, therefore, it is the priest chiefly who performs the sacred liturgy in the name of the Church, its organization, regulation and details cannot but be subject to Church authority. This conclusion,

based on the nature of Christian worship itself, is further confirmed by the testimony of history.

45. Additional proof of this indefeasible right of the ecclesiastical hierarchy lies in the circumstances that the sacred liturgy is intimately bound up with doctrinal propositions which the Church proposes to be perfectly true and certain, and must as a consequence conform to the decrees respecting Catholic faith issued by the supreme teaching authority of the Church with a view to safeguarding the integrity of the religion revealed by God.

46. On this subject We judge it Our duty to rectify an attitude with which you are doubtless familiar, Venerable Brethren. We refer to the error and fallacious reasoning of those who have claimed that the sacred liturgy is a kind of proving ground for the truths to be held of faith, meaning by this that the Church is obliged to declare such a doctrine sound when it is found to have produced fruits of piety and sanctity through the sacred rites of the liturgy, and to reject it otherwise. Hence, the epigram, *"Lex orandi, lex credendi"*—the law for prayer is the law for faith.

47. But this is not what the Church teaches and enjoins. The worship she offers to God, all good and great, is a continuous profession of Catholic faith and a continuous exercise of hope, and charity, as Augustine puts it tersely. "God is to be worshipped," he says, "by faith, hope, and charity."[44] In the sacred liturgy we profess the Catholic faith explicitly and openly, not only by the celebration of the mysteries, and by offering the holy sacrifice and administering the sacraments, but also by saying or singing the credo or Symbol of the faith—it is indeed the sign and badge, as it were, of the Christian— along with other texts, and likewise by the reading of holy scripture, written under the inspiration of the Holy Ghost. The entire liturgy, therefore, has the Catholic faith for its content, inasmuch as it bears public witness to the faith of the Church.

48. For this reason, whenever there was question of defining a truth revealed by God, the Sovereign Pontiff and the Councils in their recourse to the "theological sources," as they are called, have not seldom drawn many an argument from this sacred science of the liturgy. For an example in point, Our predecessor of immortal memory, Pius IX, so argued when he proclaimed the Immaculate Conception of the Virgin Mary. Similarly during the discussion of a

doubtful or controversial truth, the Church and the Holy Fathers have not failed to look to the age-old and age-honored sacred rites for enlightenment. Hence, the well-known and venerable maxim, *"Legem credendi lex statuat supplicandi"*—let the rule for prayer determine the rule of belief.[45] The sacred liturgy, consequently, does not decide or determine independently and of itself what is of Catholic faith. More properly, since the liturgy is also a profession of eternal truths, and subject, as such, to the supreme teaching authority of the Church, it can supply proofs and testimony, quite clearly, of no little value, towards the determination of a particular point of Christian doctrine. But if one desires to differentiate and describe the relationship between faith and the sacred liturgy in absolute and general terms, it is perfectly correct to say, *"Lex credendi legem statuat supplicandi"*—let the rule of belief determine the rule of prayer. The same holds true for the other theological virtues also, *"In . . . fide, spe, caritate continuato desiderio semper oramus"*—we pray always, with constant yearning in faith, hope, and charity.[46]

49. From time immemorial the ecclesiastical hierarchy has exercised this right in matters liturgical. It has organized and regulated divine worship, enriching it constantly with new splendor and beauty, to the glory of God and the spiritual profit of Christians. What is more, it has not been slow—keeping the substance of the Mass and sacraments carefully intact—to modify what it deemed not altogether fitting, and to add what appeared more likely to increase the honor paid to Jesus Christ and the august Trinity, and to instruct and stimulate the Christian people to greater advantage.[47]

50. The sacred liturgy does, in fact, include divine as well as human elements. The former, instituted as they have been by God, cannot be changed in any way by men. But the human components admit of various modifications, as the needs of the age, circumstance and the good of souls may require, and as the ecclesiastical hierarchy, under guidance of the Holy Spirit, may have authorized. This will explain the marvelous variety of Eastern and Western rites. Here is the reason for the gradual addition, through successive development, of particular religious customs and practices of piety only faintly discernible in earlier times. Hence, likewise it happens from time to time that certain devotions long since forgotten are revived and practiced anew. All these developments attest the abiding life of the immaculate Spouse of Jesus Christ through these many centuries. They are the sacred language she uses, as the ages run their course, to

profess to her divine Spouse her own faith along with that of the nations committed to her charge, and her own unfailing love. They furnish proof, besides, of the wisdom of the teaching method she employs to arouse and nourish constantly the "Christian instinct."

51. Several causes, really have been instrumental in the progress and development of the sacred liturgy during the long and glorious life of the Church.

52. Thus, for example, as Catholic doctrine on the Incarnate Word of God, the eucharistic sacrament and sacrifice, and Mary the Virgin Mother of God came to be determined with greater certitude and clarity, new ritual forms were introduced through which the acts of the liturgy proceeded to reproduce this brighter light issuing from the decrees of the teaching authority of the Church, and to reflect it, in a sense so that it might reach the minds and hearts of Christ's people more readily.

53. The subsequent advances in ecclesiastical discipline for the administering of the sacraments, that of penance for example; the institution and later suppression of the catechumenate; and again, the practice of eucharistic communion under a single species, adopted in the Latin Church; these developments were assuredly responsible in no little measure for the modification of the ancient ritual in the course of time, and for the gradual introduction of new rites considered more in accord with prevailing discipline in these matters.

54. Just as notable a contribution to this progressive transformation was made by devotional trends and practices not directly related to the sacred liturgy, which began to appear, by God's wonderful design, in later periods, and grew to be so popular. We may instance the spread and ever mounting ardor of devotion to the Blessed Eucharist, devotion to the most bitter passion of our Redeemer, devotion to the most Sacred Heart of Jesus, to the Virgin Mother of God, and to her most chaste spouse.

55. Other manifestations of piety have also played their circumstantial part in this same liturgical development. Among them may be cited the public pilgrimages to the tombs of the martyrs prompted by motives of devotion, the special periods of fasting instituted for the same reason, and lastly, in this gracious city of Rome, the penitential recitation of the litanies during the "station" processions, in which even the Sovereign Pontiff frequently joined.

56. It is likewise easy to understand that the progress of the fine arts, those of architecture, painting, and music above all, has exerted considerable influence on the choice and disposition of the various external features of the sacred liturgy.

57. The Church has further used her right of control over liturgical observance to protect the purity of divine worship against abuse from dangerous and imprudent innovations introduced by private individuals and particular churches. Thus, it came about—during the 16th century, when usages and customs of this sort had become increasingly prevalent and exaggerated, and when private initiative in matters liturgical threatened to compromise the integrity of faith and devotion, to the great advantage of heretics and further spread of their errors—that in the year 1588, Our predecessor Sixtus V of immortal memory established the Sacred Congregation of Rites, charged with the defense of the legitimate rites of the Church and with the prohibition of any spurious innovation.[48] This body fulfills even today the official function of supervision and legislation with regard to all matters touching the sacred liturgy.[49]

58. It follows from this that the Sovereign Pontiff alone enjoys the right to recognize and establish any practice touching the worship of God, to introduce and approve new rites, as also to modify those he judges to require modification.[50] Bishops, for their part, have the right and duty carefully to watch over the exact observance of the prescriptions of the sacred canons respecting divine worship.[51] Private individuals, therefore, even though they be clerics, may not be left to decide for themselves in these holy and venerable matters, involving as they do the religious life of Christian society along with the exercise of the priesthood of Jesus Christ and worship of God; concerned as they are with the honor due to the Blessed Trinity, the Word Incarnate and His august mother and the other saints, and with the salvation of souls as well. For the same reason no private person has any authority to regulate external practices of this kind, which are intimately bound up with Church discipline and with the order, unity, and concord of the Mystical Body and frequently even with the integrity of Catholic faith itself.

59. The Church is without question a living organism, and as an organism, in respect of the sacred liturgy also, she grows, matures, develops, adapts, and accommodates herself to temporal needs and circumstances, provided only that the integrity of her doctrine be safeguarded. This notwithstanding, the temerity and daring of those

who introduce novel liturgical practices, or call for the revival of obsolete rites out of harmony with prevailing laws and rubrics, deserve severe reproof. It has pained Us grievously to note, Venerable Brethren, that such innovations are actually being introduced, not merely in minor details but in matters of major importance as well. We instance, in point of fact, those who make use of the vernacular in the celebration of the august eucharistic sacrifice; those who transfer certain feast-days—which have been appointed and established after mature deliberation—to other dates; those, finally, who delete from the prayerbooks approved for public use the sacred texts of the Old Testament, deeming them little suited and inopportune for modern times.

60. The use of the Latin language, customary in a considerable portion of the Church, is a manifest and beautiful sign of unity, as well as an effective antidote for any corruption of doctrinal truth. In spite of this, the use of the mother tongue in connection with several of the rites may be of much advantage to the people. But the Apostolic See alone is empowered to grant this permission. It is forbidden, therefore, to take any action whatever of this nature without having requested and obtained such consent, since the sacred liturgy, as We have said, is entirely subject to the discretion and approval of the Holy See.

61. The same reasoning holds in the case of some persons who are bent on the restoration of all the ancient rites and ceremonies indiscriminately. The liturgy of the early ages is most certainly worthy of all veneration. But ancient usage must not be esteemed more suitable and proper, either in its own right or in its significance for later times and new situations, on the simple ground that it carries the savor and aroma of antiquity. The more recent liturgical rites likewise deserve reverence and respect. They, too, owe their inspiration to the Holy Spirit, who assists the Church in every age even to the consummation of the world.[52] They are equally the resources used by the majestic Spouse of Jesus Christ to promote and procure the sanctity of man.

62. Assuredly it is a wise and most laudable thing to return in spirit and affection to the sources of the sacred liturgy. For research in this field of study, by tracing it back to its origins, contributes valuable assistance towards a more thorough and careful investigation of the significance of feast-days, and of the meaning of the texts and sacred

ceremonies employed on their occasion. But it is neither wise nor laudable to reduce everything to antiquity by every possible device. Thus, to cite some instances, one would be straying from the straight path were he to wish the altar restored to its primitive tableform; were he to want black excluded as a color for the liturgical vestments; were he to forbid the use of sacred images and statues in Churches; were he to order the crucifix so designed that the divine Redeemer's body shows no trace of His cruel sufferings; and lastly were he to disdain and reject polyphonic music or singing in parts, even where it conforms to regulations issued by the Holy See.

63. Clearly no sincere Catholic can refuse to accept the formulation of Christian doctrine more recently elaborated and proclaimed as dogmas by the Church, under the inspiration and guidance of the Holy Spirit with abundant fruit for souls, because it pleases him to hark back to the old formulas. No more can any Catholic in his right senses repudiate existing legislation of the Church to revert to prescriptions based on the earliest sources of canon law. Just as obviously unwise and mistaken is the zeal of one who in matters liturgical would go back to the rites and usage of antiquity, discarding the new patterns introduced by disposition of divine Providence to meet the changes of circumstances and situation.

64. This way of acting bids fair to revive the exaggerated and senseless antiquarianism to which the illegal Council of Pistoia gave rise. It likewise attempts to reinstate a series of errors which were responsible for the calling of that meeting as well as for those resulting from it, with grievous harm to souls, and which the Church, the ever watchful guardian of the "deposit of faith" committed to her charge by her divine Founder, had every right and reason to condemn.[53] For perverse designs and ventures of this sort tend to paralyze and weaken that process of sanctification by which the sacred liturgy directs the sons of adoption to their Heavenly Father of their souls' salvation.

65. In every measure taken, then, let proper contact with the ecclesiastical hierarchy be maintained. Let no one arrogate to himself the right to make regulations and impose them on others at will. Only the Sovereign Pontiff, as the successor of Saint Peter, charged by the divine Redeemer with the feeding of His entire flock,[54] and with him, in obedience to the Apostolic See, the bishops "whom the Holy Ghost has placed . . . to rule the Church of God,"[55] have the right and the duty to govern the Christian people. Consequently, Venerable

Brethren, whenever you assert your authority—even on occasion with wholesome severity—you are not merely acquitting yourselves of your duty; you are defending the very will of the Founder of the Church.

66. The mystery of the most Holy Eucharist which Christ, the High Priest instituted, and which He commands to be continually renewed in the Church by His ministers, is the culmination and center, as it were, of the Christian religion. We consider it opportune in speaking about the crowning act of the sacred liturgy, to delay for a little while and call your attention, Venerable Brethren, to this most important subject.

67. Christ the Lord, "Eternal Priest according to the order of Melchisedech,"[56] "loving His own who were of the world,"[57] "at the last supper, on the night He was betrayed, wishing to leave His beloved Spouse, the Church, a visible sacrifice such as the nature of men requires, that would re-present the bloody sacrifice offered once on the cross, and perpetuate its memory to the end of time, and whose salutary virtue might be applied in remitting those sins which we daily commit, . . . offered His Body and Blood under the species of bread and wine to God the Father, and under the same species allowed the apostles, whom he at that time constituted the priests of the New Testament, to partake thereof; commanding them and their successors in the priesthood to make the same offering."[58]

68. The august sacrifice of the altar, then, is no mere empty commemoration of the passion and death of Jesus Christ, but a true and proper act of sacrifice, whereby the High Priest by an unbloody immolation offers Himself a most acceptable victim to the Eternal Father, as He did upon the Cross. "It is one and the same victim; the same person now offers it by the ministry of His priests, who then offered Himself on the cross, the manner of offering alone being different."[59]

69. The priest is the same, Jesus Christ, whose sacred Person His minister represents. Now the minister, by reason of the sacerdotal consecration which he has received, is made like to the High Priest and possesses the power of performing actions in virtue of Christ's very person.[60] Wherefore in his priestly activity he in a certain manner "lends his tongue, and gives his hand" to Christ.[61]

70. Likewise the victim is the same, namely, our divine Redeemer in His human nature with His true Body and Blood. The manner, however, in which Christ is offered is different. On the Cross He completely offered Himself and all His sufferings to God, and the immolation of the victim was brought about by the bloody death, which He underwent of His free will. But on the altar, by reason of the glorified state of His human nature, "death shall have no more dominion over Him,"[62] and so the shedding of His blood is impossible; still, according to the plan of divine wisdom, the sacrifice of our Redeemer is shown forth in an admirable manner by external signs which are the symbols of His death. For by the "transubstantiation" of bread into the body of Christ and of wine into His Blood, His Body and Blood are both really present: now the eucharistic species under which He is present symbolize the actual separation of His Body and Blood. Thus, the commemorative representation of His death, which actually took place on Calvary, is repeated in every sacrifice of the altar, seeing that Jesus Christ is symbolically shown by separate symbols to be in a state of victimhood.

71. Moreover, the appointed ends are the same. The first of these is to give glory to the Heavenly Father. From His birth to His death Jesus Christ burned with zeal for the divine glory; and the offering of His blood upon the cross rose to heaven in an odor of sweetness. To perpetuate this praise, the members of the Mystical Body are united with their divine Head in the eucharistic sacrifice, and with Him, together with the Angels and Archangels, they sing immortal praise to God[63] and give all honor and glory to the Father Almighty.[64]

72. The second end is duly to give thanks to God. Only the divine Redeemer, as the eternal Father's most beloved Son whose immense love He knew, could offer Him a worthy return of gratitude. This was His intention and desire at the Last Supper when He "gave thanks."[65] He did not cease to do so when hanging upon the cross, nor does He fail to do so in the august sacrifice of the altar, which is an act of thanksgiving or a "eucharistic" act; since this "is truly meet and just, right and availing unto salvation."[66]

73. The third end proposed is that of expiation, propitiation, and reconciliation. Certainly, no one was better fitted to make satisfaction to Almighty God for all the sins of men than was Christ. Therefore, He desired to be immolated upon the cross "as a propitiation for our sins, not for ours only but also for those of the whole world"[67] and

likewise He daily offers Himself upon our altars for our redemption, that we may be rescued from eternal damnation and admitted into the company of the elect. This He does, not for us only who are in this mortal life, but also "for all who rest in Christ, who have gone before us with the sign of faith and repose in the sleep of peace;"[68] for whether we live, or whether we die "still we are not separated from the one and only Christ."[69]

74. The fourth end, finally, is that of impetration. Man, being the prodigal son, has made bad use of and dissipated the goods which he received from his heavenly Father. Accordingly, he has been reduced to the utmost poverty and to extreme degradation. However, Christ on the cross "offering prayers and supplications with a loud cry and tears, has been heard for His reverence."[70] Likewise, upon the altar He is our mediator with God in the same efficacious manner, so that we may be filled with every blessing and grace.

75. It is easy, therefore, to understand why the holy Council of Trent lays down that by means of the eucharistic sacrifice the saving virtue of the cross is imparted to us for the remission of the sins we daily commit.[71]

76. Now the Apostle of the Gentiles proclaims the copious plenitude and the perfection of the sacrifice of the Cross, when he says that Christ by one oblation has perfected for ever them that are sanctified.[72] For the merits of this sacrifice, since they are altogether boundless and immeasurable, know no limits; for they are meant for all men of every time and place. This follows from the fact that in this sacrifice the God-Man is the priest and victim; that His immolation was entirely perfect, as was His obedience to the will of His eternal Father; and also that He suffered death as the Head of the human race: "See how we were bought: Christ hangs upon the Cross, see at what a price He makes His purchase . . . He sheds His Blood, He buys with His blood, He buys with the Blood of the Spotless Lamb, He buys with the Blood of God's only Son. He who buys is Christ; the price is His Blood; the possession bought is the world."[73]

77. This purchase, however, does not immediately have its full effect; since Christ, after redeeming the world at the lavish cost of His own blood, still must come into complete possession of the souls of men. Wherefore, that the redemption and salvation of each person and of

future generations unto the end of time may be effectively accomplished, and be acceptable to God, it is necessary that men should individually come into vital contact with the sacrifice of the cross, so that the merits, which flow from it, should be imparted to them. In a certain sense it can be said that on Calvary Christ built a font of purification and salvation which He filled with the Blood He shed; but if men do not bathe in it and there wash away the stains of their iniquities, they can never be purified and saved.

78. The cooperation of the faithful is required so that sinners may be individually purified in the Blood of the Lamb. For though, speaking generally, Christ reconciled by His painful death the whole human race with the Father, He wished that all should approach and be drawn to His Cross, especially by means of the sacraments and the eucharistic sacrifice, to obtain the salutary fruits produced by Him upon it. Through this active and individual participation, the members of the Mystical Body not only become daily more like to their divine Head, but the life flowing from the Head is imparted to the members, so that we can each repeat the words of St. Paul, "With Christ I am nailed to the Cross: I live, now not I, but Christ liveth in me."[74] We have already explained sufficiently and of set purpose on another occasion, that Jesus Christ "when dying on the cross, bestowed upon His Church, as a completely gratuitous gift, the immense treasure of the redemption. But when it is a question of distributing this treasure, He not only commits the work of sanctification to His Immaculate Spouse, but also wishes that, to a certain extent, sanctity should derive from her activity."[75]

79. The august sacrifice of the altar is, as it were, the supreme instrument whereby the merits won by the divine Redeemer upon the Cross are distributed to the faithful: "as often as this commemorative sacrifice is offered, there is wrought the work of our Redemption."[76] This, however, so far from lessening the dignity of the actual sacrifice on Calvary, rather proclaims and renders more manifest its greatness and its necessity, as the Council of Trent declares.[77] Its daily immolation reminds us that there is no salvation except in the Cross of our Lord Jesus Christ[78] and that God Himself wishes that there should be a continuation of this sacrifice "from the rising of the sun till the going down thereof,"[79] so that there may be no cessation of the hymn of praise and thanksgiving which man owes to God, seeing that he required His

help continually and has need of the Blood of the Redeemer to remit sin which challenges God's justice.

80. It is, therefore, desirable, Venerable Brethren, that all the faithful should be aware that to participate in the eucharistic sacrifice is their chief duty and supreme dignity, and that not in an inert and negligent fashion, giving way to distractions and day-dreaming, but with such earnestness and concentration that they may be united as closely as possible with the High Priest, according to the Apostle, "Let this mind be in you which was also in Christ Jesus."[80] And together with Him and through Him let them make their oblation, and in union with Him let them offer up themselves.

81. It is quite true that Christ is a priest; but He is a priest not for Himself but for us, when in the name of the whole human race He offers our prayers and religious homage to the eternal Father; He is also a victim and for us since He substitutes Himself for sinful man. Now the exhortation of the Apostle, "Let this mind be in you which was also in Christ Jesus," requires that all Christians should possess, as far as is humanly possible, the same dispositions as those which the divine Redeemer had when He offered Himself in sacrifice: that is to say, they should in a humble attitude of mind, pay adoration, honor, praise and thanksgiving to the supreme majesty of God. Moreover, it means that they must assume to some extent the character of a victim, that they deny themselves as the Gospel commands, that freely and of their own accord they do penance and that each detests and satisfies for his sins. It means, in a word, that we must all undergo with Christ a mystical death on the Cross so that we can apply to ourselves the words of St. Paul, "With Christ I am nailed to the Cross."[81]

82. The fact, however, that the faithful participate in the eucharistic sacrifice does not mean that they also are endowed with priestly power. It is very necessary that you make this quite clear to your flocks.

83. For there are today, Venerable Brethren, those who, approximating to errors long since condemned[82] teach that in the New Testament by the word "priesthood" is meant only that priesthood which applies to all who have been baptized; and hold that the command by which Christ gave power to His apostles at the Last Supper to do what He Himself had done, applies directly to the entire Christian Church, and that thence, and thence only, arises the hierarchical priesthood.

Hence, they assert that the people are possessed of a true priestly power, while the priest only acts in virtue of an office committed to him by the community. Wherefore, they look on the eucharistic sacrifice as a "concelebration," in the literal meaning of that term, and consider it more fitting that priests should "concelebrate" with the people present than that they should offer the sacrifice privately when the people are absent.

84. It is superfluous to explain how captious errors of this sort completely contradict the truths which we have just stated above, when treating of the place of the priest in the Mystical Body of Jesus Christ. But we deem it necessary to recall that the priest acts for the people only because he represents Jesus Christ, who is Head of all His members and offers Himself in their stead. Hence, he goes to the altar as the minister of Christ, inferior to Christ but superior to the people.[83] The people, on the other hand, since they in no sense represent the divine Redeemer and are not mediator between themselves and God, can in no way possess the sacerdotal power.

85. All this has the certitude of faith. However, it must also be said that the faithful do offer the divine Victim, though in a different sense.

86. This has already been stated in the clearest terms by some of Our predecessors and some Doctors of the Church. "Not only," says Innocent III of immortal memory, "do the priests offer the sacrifice, but also all the faithful: for what the priest does personally by virtue of his ministry, the faithful do collectively by virtue of their intention."[84] We are happy to recall one of St. Robert Bellarmine's many statements on this subject. "The sacrifice," he says "is principally offered in the person of Christ. Thus, the oblation that follows the consecration is a sort of attestation that the whole Church consents in the oblation made by Christ, and offers it along with Him."[85]

87. Moreover, the rites and prayers of the eucharistic sacrifice signify and show no less clearly that the oblation of the Victim is made by the priests in company with the people. For not only does the sacred minister, after the oblation of the bread and wine when he turns to the people, say the significant prayer: "Pray brethren, that my sacrifice and yours may be acceptable to God the Father Almighty;"[86] but also the prayers by which the divine Victim is offered to God are generally expressed in the plural number: and in these it is indicated

more than once that the people also participate in this august sacrifice inasmuch as they offer the same. The following words, for example, are used: "For whom we offer, or who offer up to Thee . . . We therefore beseech thee, O Lord, to be appeased and to receive this offering of our bounded duty, as also of thy whole household. . . We thy servants, as also thy whole people . . . do offer unto thy most excellent majesty, of thine own gifts bestowed upon us, a pure victim, a holy victim, a spotless victim."[87]

88. Nor is it to be wondered at, that the faithful should be raised to this dignity. By the waters of baptism, as by common right, Christians are made members of the Mystical Body of Christ the Priest, and by the "character" which is imprinted on their souls, they are appointed to give worship to God. Thus, they participate, according to their condition, in the priesthood of Christ.

89. In every age of the Church's history, the mind of man, enlightened by faith, has aimed at the greatest possible knowledge of things divine. It is fitting, then, that the Christian people should also desire to know in what sense they are said in the canon of the Mass to offer up the sacrifice. To satisfy such a pious desire, then, We shall here explain the matter briefly and concisely.

90. First of all, the more extrinsic explanations are these: it frequently happens that the faithful assisting at Mass join their prayers alternately with those of the priest, and sometimes—a more frequent occurrence in ancient times—they offer to the ministers at the altar bread and wine to be changed into the Body and Blood of Christ, and, finally, by their alms they get the priest to offer the divine victim for their intentions.

91. But there is also a more profound reason why all Christians, especially those who are present at Mass, are said to offer the sacrifice.

92. In this most important subject it is necessary, in order to avoid giving rise to a dangerous error, that we define the exact meaning of the word "offer." The unbloody immolation at the words of consecration, when Christ is made present upon the altar in the state of a victim, is performed by the priest and by him alone, as the representative of Christ and not as the representative of the faithful. But it is because the priest places the divine victim upon the altar that he offers it to God the Father as an oblation for the glory of the

Blessed Trinity and for the good of the whole Church. Now the faithful participate in the oblation, understood in this limited sense, after their own fashion and in a twofold manner, namely, because they not only offer the sacrifice by the hands of the priest, but also, to a certain extent, in union with him. It is by reason of this participation that the offering made by the people is also included in liturgical worship.

93. Now it is clear that the faithful offer the sacrifice by the hands of the priest from the fact that the minister at the altar, in offering a sacrifice in the name of all His members, represents Christ, the Head of the Mystical Body. Hence, the whole Church can rightly be said to offer up the victim through Christ. But the conclusion that the people offer the sacrifice with the priest himself is not based on the fact that, being members of the Church no less than the priest himself, they perform a visible liturgical rite; for this is the privilege only of the minister who has been divinely appointed to this office: rather it is based on the fact that the people unite their hearts in praise, impetration, expiation, and thanksgiving with prayers or intention of the priest, even of the High Priest himself, so that in the one and same offering of the victim and according to a visible sacerdotal rite, they may be presented to God the Father. It is obviously necessary that the external sacrificial rite should, of its very nature, signify the internal worship of the heart. Now the sacrifice of the New Law signifies that supreme worship by which the principal Offerer himself, who is Christ, and, in union with Him and through Him, all the members of the Mystical Body pay God the honor and reverence that are due to Him.

94. We are very pleased to learn that this teaching, thanks to a more intense study of the liturgy on the part of many, especially in recent years, has been given full recognition. We must, however, deeply deplore certain exaggerations and over-statements which are not in agreement with the true teaching of the Church.

95. Some in fact disapprove altogether of those Masses which are offered privately and without any congregation, on the ground that they are a departure from the ancient way of offering the sacrifice; moreover, there are some who assert that priests cannot offer Mass at different altars at the same time, because, by doing so, they separate the community of the faithful and imperil its unity; while some go so far as to hold that the people must confirm and ratify the sacrifice if it is to have its proper force and value.

96. They are mistaken in appealing in this matter to the social character of the eucharistic sacrifice, for as often as a priest repeats what the divine Redeemer did at the Last Supper, the sacrifice is really completed. Moreover, this sacrifice, necessarily and of its very nature, has always and everywhere the character of a public and social act, inasmuch as he who offers it acts in the name of Christ and of the faithful, whose Head is the divine Redeemer, and he offers it to God for the holy Catholic Church, and for the living and the dead.[88] This is undoubtedly so, whether the faithful are present—as we desire and commend them to be in great numbers and with devotion—or are not present, since it is in no wise required that the people ratify what the sacred minister has done.

97. Still, though it is clear from what We have said that the Mass is offered in the name of Christ and of the Church and that it is not robbed of its social effects though it be celebrated by a priest without a server, nonetheless, on account of the dignity of such an august mystery, it is our earnest desire—as Mother Church has always commanded—that no priest should say Mass unless a server is at hand to answer the prayers, as canon 813 prescribes.

98. In order that the oblation by which the faithful offer the divine Victim in this sacrifice to the heavenly Father may have its full effect, it is necessary that the people add something else, namely, the offering of themselves as a victim.

99. This offering in fact is not confined merely to the liturgical sacrifice. For the Prince of the Apostles wishes us, as living stones built upon Christ, the cornerstone, to be able as "a holy priesthood, to offer up spiritual sacrifices, acceptable to God by Jesus Christ."[89] St. Paul the Apostle addresses the following words of exhortation to Christians, without distinction of time, "I beseech you, therefore, . . . that you present your bodies, a living sacrifice, holy, pleasing unto God, your reasonable service."[90] But at that time especially when the faithful take part in the liturgical service with such piety and recollection that it can truly be said of them: "whose faith and devotion is known to Thee,"[91] it is then, with the High Priest and through Him they offer themselves as a spiritual sacrifice, that each one's faith ought to become more ready to work through charity, his piety more real and fervent, and each one should consecrate himself to the furthering of the divine glory, desiring to become as like as possible to Christ in His most grievous sufferings.

100. This we are also taught by those exhortations which the Bishop, in the Church's name, addresses to priests on the day of their ordination, "Understand what you do, imitate what you handle, and since you celebrate the mystery of the Lord's death, take good care to mortify your members with their vices and concupiscences."[92] In almost the same manner the sacred books of the liturgy advise Christians who come to Mass to participate in the sacrifice: "At this . . . altar let innocence be in honor, let pride be sacrificed, anger slain, impurity and every evil desire laid low, let the sacrifice of chastity be offered in place of doves and instead of the young pigeons the sacrifice of innocence."[93] While we stand before the altar, then, it is our duty so to transform our hearts, that every trace of sin may be completely blotted out, while whatever promotes supernatural life through Christ may be zealously fostered and strengthened even to the extent that, in union with the immaculate Victim, we become a victim acceptable to the eternal Father.

101. The prescriptions in fact of the sacred liturgy aim, by every means at their disposal, at helping the Church to bring about this most holy purpose in the most suitable manner possible. This is the object not only of readings, homilies, and other sermons given by priests, as also the whole cycle of mysteries which are proposed for our commemoration in the course of the year, but it is also the purpose of vestments, of sacred rites, and their external splendor. All these things aim at "enhancing the majesty of this great Sacrifice, and raising the minds of the faithful by means of these visible signs of religion and piety, to the contemplation of the sublime truths contained in this sacrifice."[94]

102. All the elements of the liturgy, then, would have us reproduce in our hearts the likeness of the divine Redeemer through the mystery of the Cross, according to the words of the Apostle of the Gentiles, "With Christ I am nailed to the Cross. I live, now not I, but Christ liveth in me."[95] Thus, we become a victim, as it were, along with Christ to increase the glory of the eternal Father.

103. Let this, then, be the intention and aspiration of the faithful, when they offer up the divine Victim in the Mass. For if, as St. Augustine writes, our mystery is enacted on the Lord's table, that is Christ our Lord Himself,[96] who is the Head and symbol of that union through which we are the body of Christ[97] and members of His Body;[98] if St. Robert Bellarmine teaches, according to the mind of the Doctor of Hippo, that in the sacrifice of the altar there is

signified the general sacrifice by which the whole Mystical Body of Christ, that is, all the city of redeemed, is offered up to God through Christ, the High Priest:[99] nothing can be conceived more just or fitting than that all of us in union with our Head, who suffered for our sake, should also sacrifice ourselves to the eternal Father. For in the sacrament of the altar, as the same St. Augustine has it, the Church is made to see that in what she offers she herself is offered.[100]

104. Let the faithful, therefore, consider to what a high dignity they are raised by the sacrament of Baptism. They should not think it enough to participate in the eucharistic sacrifice with that general intention which befits members of Christ and children of the Church, but let them further, in keeping with the spirit of the sacred liturgy, be most closely united with the High Priest and His earthly minister, at the time the consecration of the divine Victim is enacted, and at that time especially when those solemn words are pronounced, "By Him and with Him and in Him is to Thee, God the Father almighty, in the unity of the Holy Ghost, all honor and glory for ever and ever;"[101] to these words in fact the people answer, "Amen." Nor should Christians forget to offer themselves, their cares, their sorrows, their distress, and their necessities in union with their divine Savior upon the Cross.

105. Therefore, they are to be praised who, with the idea of getting the Christian people to take part more easily and more fruitfully in the Mass, strive to make them familiar with the "Roman Missal," so that the faithful, united with the priest, may pray together in the very words and sentiments of the Church. They also are to be commended who strive to make the liturgy even in an external way a sacred act in which all who are present may share. This can be done in more than one way, when, for instance, the whole congregation, in accordance with the rules of the liturgy, either answer the priest in an orderly and fitting manner, or sing hymns suitable to the different parts of the Mass, or do both, or finally in high Masses when they answer the prayers of the minister of Jesus Christ and also sing the liturgical chant.

100. These methods of participation in the Mass are to be approved and recommended when they are in complete agreement with the precepts of the Church and the rubrics of the liturgy. Their chief aim is to foster and promote the people's piety and intimate union with Christ and His visible minister and to arouse those internal sentiments

and dispositions which should make our hearts become like to that of the High Priest of the New Testament. However, though they show also in an outward manner that the very nature of the sacrifice, as offered by the Mediator between God and men,[102] must be regarded as the act of the whole Mystical Body of Christ, still they are by no means necessary to constitute it a public act or to give it a social character. And besides, a "dialogue" Mass of this kind cannot replace the high Mass, which, as a matter of fact, though it should be offered with only the sacred ministers present, possesses its own special dignity due to the impressive character of its ritual and the magnificence of its ceremonies. The splendor and grandeur of a high Mass, however, are very much increased if, as the Church desires, the people are present in great numbers and with devotion.

107. It is to be observed, also, that they have strayed from the path of truth and right reason who, led away by false opinions, make so much of these accidentals as to presume to assert that without them the Mass cannot fulfill its appointed end.

108. Many of the faithful are unable to use the Roman missal even though it is written in the vernacular; nor are all capable of understanding correctly the liturgical rites and formulas. So varied and diverse are men's talents and characters that it is impossible for all to be moved and attracted to the same extent by community prayers, hymns, and liturgical services. Moreover, the needs and inclinations of all are not the same, nor are they always constant in the same individual. Who, then, would say, on account of such a prejudice, that all these Christians cannot participate in the Mass nor share its fruits? On the contrary, they can adopt some other method which proves easier for certain people; for instance, they can lovingly meditate on the mysteries of Jesus Christ or perform other exercises of piety or recite prayers which, though they differ from the sacred rites, are still essentially in harmony with them.

109. Wherefore We exhort you, Venerable Brethren, that each in his diocese or ecclesiastical jurisdiction supervise and regulate the manner and method in which the people take part in the liturgy, according to the rubrics of the missal and in keeping with the injunctions which the Sacred Congregation of Rites and the Code of canon law have published. Let everything be done with due order and dignity, and let no one, not even a priest, make use of the sacred edifices according to his whim to try out experiments. It is also Our wish that in each diocese an advisory committee to promote the

liturgical apostolate should be established, similar to that which cares for sacred music and art, so that with your watchful guidance everything may be carefully carried out in accordance with the prescriptions of the Apostolic See.

110. In religious communities let all those regulations be accurately observed which are laid down in their respective constitutions, nor let any innovations be made which the superiors of these communities have not previously approved.

111. But however much variety and disparity there may be in the exterior manner and circumstances in which the Christian laity participate in the Mass and other liturgical functions, constant and earnest effort must be made to unite the congregation in spirit as much as possible with the divine Redeemer, so that their lives may be daily enriched with more abundant sanctity, and greater glory be given to the heaven Father.

112. The august sacrifice of the altar is concluded with communion or the partaking of the divine feast. But, as all know, the integrity of the sacrifice only requires that the priest partake of the heavenly food. Although it is most desirable that the people should also approach the holy table, this is not required for the integrity of the sacrifice.

113. We wish in this matter to repeat the remarks which Our predecessor Benedict XIV makes with regard to the definitions of the Council of Trent: "First We must state that none of the faithful can hold that private Masses, in which the priest alone receives holy communion, are therefore unlawful and do not fulfill the idea of the true, perfect, and complete unbloody sacrifice instituted by Christ our Lord. For the faithful know quite well, or at least can easily be taught, that the Council of Trent, supported by the doctrine which the uninterrupted tradition of the Church has preserved, condemned the new and false opinion of Luther as opposed to this tradition."[103] "If anyone shall say that Masses in which the priest only receives communion, are unlawful, and therefore should be abolished, let him be anathema."[104]

114. They, therefore, err from the path of truth who do not want to have Masses celebrated unless the faithful communicate; and those are still more in error who, in holding that it is altogether necessary for the faithful to receive holy communion as well as the priest, put forward the captious argument that here there is question not of a

sacrifice merely, but of a sacrifice and a supper of brotherly union, and consider the general communion of all present as the culminating point of the whole celebration.

115. Now it cannot be over-emphasized that the eucharistic sacrifice of its very nature is the unbloody immolation of the divine Victim, which is made manifest in a mystical manner by the separation of the sacred species and by their oblation to the eternal Father. Holy communion pertains to the integrity of the Mass and to the partaking of the august sacrament; but while it is obligatory for the priest who says the Mass, it is only something earnestly recommended to the faithful.

116. The Church, as the teacher of truth, strives by every means in her power to safeguard the integrity of the Catholic faith, and like a mother solicitous for the welfare of her children, she exhorts them most earnestly to partake fervently and frequently of the richest treasure of our religion.

117. She wishes in the first place that Christians—especially when they cannot easily receive holy communion—should do so at least by desire, so that with renewed faith, reverence, humility, and complete trust in the goodness of the divine Redeemer, they may be united to Him in the spirit of the most ardent charity.

118. But the desire of Mother Church does not stop here. For since by feasting upon the bread of angels we can by a "sacramental" communion, as we have already said, also become partakers of the sacrifice, she repeats the invitation to all her children individually, "Take and eat. . . Do this in memory of Me"[105] so that "we may continually experience within us the fruit of our redemption"[106] in a more efficacious manner. For this reason the Council of Trent, re-echoing, as it were, the invitation of Christ and His immaculate Spouse, has earnestly exhorted "the faithful when they attend Mass to communicate not only by a spiritual communion but also by a sacramental one, so that they may obtain more abundant fruit from this most holy sacrifice."[107] Moreover, our predecessor of immortal memory, Benedict XIV, wishing to emphasize and throw fuller light upon the truth that the faithful by receiving the Holy Eucharist become partakers of the divine sacrifice itself, praises the devotion of those who, when attending Mass, not only elicit a desire to receive holy communion but also want to be nourished by hosts consecrated during the Mass, even though, as he himself states, they

really and truly take part in the sacrifice should they receive a host which has been duly consecrated at a previous Mass. He writes as follows: "And although in addition to those to whom the celebrant gives a portion of the Victim he himself has offered in the Mass, they also participate in the same sacrifice to whom a priest distributes the Blessed Sacrament that has been reserved; however, the Church has not for this reason ever forbidden, nor does she now forbid, a celebrant to satisfy the piety and just request of those who, when present at Mass, want to become partakers of the same sacrifice, because they likewise offer it after their own manner, nay more, she approves of it and desires that it should not be omitted and would reprehend those priests through whose fault and negligence this participation would be denied to the faithful."[108]

119. May God grant that all accept these invitations of the Church freely and with spontaneity. May He grant that they participate even every day, if possible, in the divine sacrifice, not only in a spiritual manner, but also by reception of the august sacrament, receiving the body of Jesus Christ which has been offered for all to the eternal Father. Arouse Venerable Brethren, in the hearts of those committed to your care, a great and insatiable hunger for Jesus Christ. Under your guidance let the children and youth crowd to the altar rails to offer themselves, their innocence and their works of zeal to the divine Redeemer. Let husbands and wives approach the holy table so that nourished on this food they may learn to make the children entrusted to them conformed to the mind and heart of Jesus Christ.

120. Let the workers be invited to partake of this sustaining and never failing nourishment that it may renew their strength and obtain for their labors an everlasting recompense in heaven; in a word, invite all men of whatever class and compel them to come in;[109] since this is the bread of life which all require. The Church of Jesus Christ needs no other bread than this to satisfy fully our souls' wants and desires, and to unite us in the most intimate union with Jesus Christ, to make us "one body,"[110] to get us to live together as brothers who, breaking the same bread, sit down to the same heavenly table, to partake of the elixir of immortality.[111]

121. Now it is very fitting, as the liturgy otherwise lays down, that the people receive holy communion after the priest has partaken of the divine repast upon the altar; and, as we have written above, they should be commended who, when present at Mass, receive hosts

consecrated at the same Mass, so that it is actually verified, "that as many of us, as, at this altar, shall partake of and receive the most holy Body and Blood of thy Son, may be filled with every heavenly blessing and grace."[112]

122. Still sometimes there may be a reason, and that not infrequently, why holy communion should be distributed before or after Mass and even immediately after the priest receives the sacred species—and even though hosts consecrated at a previous Mass should be used. In these circumstances—as we have stated above—the people duly take part in the eucharistic sacrifice and not seldom they can in this way more conveniently receive holy communion. Still, though the Church with the kind heart of a mother strives to meet the spiritual needs of her children, they, for their part, should not readily neglect the directions of the liturgy and, as often as there is no reasonable difficulty, should aim that all their actions at the altar manifest more clearly the living unity of the Mystical Body.

123. When the Mass, which is subject to special rules of the liturgy, is over, the person who has received holy communion is not thereby freed from his duty of thanksgiving; rather, it is most becoming that, when the Mass is finished, the person who has received the Eucharist should recollect himself, and in intimate union with the divine Master hold loving and fruitful converse with Him. Hence, they have departed from the straight way of truth, who, adhering to the letter rather than the sense, assert and teach that, when Mass has ended, no such thanksgiving should be added, not only because the Mass is itself a thanksgiving, but also because this pertains to a private and personal act of piety and not to the good of the community.

124. But, on the contrary, the very nature of the sacrament demands that its reception should produce rich fruits of Christian sanctity. Admittedly, the congregation has been officially dismissed, but each individual, since he is united with Christ, should not interrupt the hymn of praise in his own soul, "always returning thanks for all in the name of our Lord Jesus Christ to God the Father."[113] The sacred liturgy of the Mass also exhorts us to do this when it bids us pray in these words, "Grant, we beseech thee, that we may always continue to offer thanks[114] . . . and may never cease from praising thee."[115] Wherefore, if there is no time when we must not offer God thanks, and if we must never cease from praising Him, who would dare to reprehend or find fault with the Church, because she advises her priests[116] and faithful to converse with the divine Redeemer for at

least a short while after holy communion, and inserts in her liturgical books, fitting prayers, enriched with indulgences, by which the sacred ministers may make suitable preparation before Mass and holy communion or may return thanks afterwards? So far is the sacred liturgy from restricting the interior devotion of individual Christians, that it actually fosters and promotes it so that they may be rendered like to Jesus Christ and through Him be brought to the heavenly Father; wherefore this same discipline of the liturgy demands that whoever has partaken of the sacrifice of the altar should return fitting thanks to God. For it is the good pleasure of the divine Redeemer to hearken to us when we pray, to converse with us intimately and to offer us a refuge in His loving Heart.

125. Moreover, such personal colloquies are very necessary that we may all enjoy more fully the supernatural treasures that are contained in the Eucharist and according to our means, share them with others, so that Christ our Lord may exert the greatest possible influence on the souls of all.

126. Why then, Venerable Brethren, should we not approve of those who, when they receive holy communion, remain on in closest familiarity with their divine Redeemer even after the congregation has been officially dismissed, and that not only for the consolation of conversing with Him, but also to render Him due thanks and praise and especially to ask help to defend their souls against anything that may lessen the efficacy of the sacrament and to do everything in their power to cooperate with the action of Christ who is so intimately present. We exhort them to do so in a special manner by carrying out their resolutions, by exercising the Christian virtues, as also by applying to their own necessities the riches they have received with royal Liberality. The author of that golden book *The Imitation of Christ* certainly speaks in accordance with the letter and the spirit of the liturgy, when he gives the following advice to the person who approaches the altar, "Remain on in secret and take delight in your God; for He is yours whom the whole world cannot take away from you."[117]

127. Therefore, let us all enter into closest union with Christ and strive to lose ourselves, as it were, in His most holy soul and so be united to Him that we may have a share in those acts with which He adores the Blessed Trinity with a homage that is most acceptable, and by which He offers to the eternal Father supreme praise and thanks

which find an harmonious echo throughout the heavens and the earth, according to the words of the prophet, "All ye works of the Lord, bless the Lord."[118] Finally, in union with these sentiments of Christ, let us ask for heavenly aid at that moment in which it is supremely fitting to pray for and obtain help in His name.[119] For it is especially in virtue of these sentiments that we offer and immolate ourselves as a victim, saying, "make of us thy eternal offering."[120]

128. The divine Redeemer is ever repeating His pressing invitation, "Abide in Me."[121] Now by the sacrament of the Eucharist, Christ remains in us and we in Him, and just as Christ, remaining in us, lives and works, so should we remain in Christ and live and work through Him.

129. The Eucharistic Food contains, as all are aware, "truly, really and substantially the Body and Blood together with soul and divinity of our Lord Jesus Christ."[122] It is no wonder, then, that the Church, even from the beginning, adored the Body of Christ under the appearance of bread; this is evident from the very rites of the august sacrifice, which prescribe that the sacred ministers should adore the most holy sacrament by genuflecting or by profoundly bowing their heads.

130. The Sacred Councils teach that it is the Church's tradition right from the beginning, to worship "with the same adoration the Word Incarnate as well as His own Flesh,"[123] and St. Augustine asserts that, "No one eats that Flesh, without first adoring It," while he adds that "not only do we not commit a sin by adoring It, but that we do sin by not adoring It."[124]

131. It is on this doctrinal basis that the cult of adoring the Eucharist was founded and gradually developed as something distinct from the sacrifice of the Mass. The reservation of the sacred species for the sick and those in danger of death introduced the praiseworthy custom of adoring the blessed Sacrament which is reserved in our churches. This practice of adoration, in fact, is based on strong and solid reasons. For the Eucharist is at once a sacrifice and a sacrament; but it differs from the other sacraments in this that it not only produces grace, but contains in a permanent manner the Author of grace Himself. When, therefore, the Church bids us adore Christ hidden behind the eucharistic veils and pray to Him for spiritual and temporal favors, of which we ever stand in need, she manifests living faith in

her divine Spouse who is present beneath these veils, she professes her gratitude to Him and she enjoys the intimacy of His friendship.

132. Now, the Church in the course of centuries has introduced various forms of this worship which are ever increasing in beauty and helpfulness: as, for example, visits of devotion to the tabernacles, even every day; benediction of the Blessed Sacrament; solemn processions, especially at the time of Eucharistic Congress, which pass through cities and villages; and adoration of the Blessed Sacrament publicly exposed. Sometimes these public acts of adoration are of short duration. Sometimes they last for one, several, and even for forty hours. In certain places they continue in turn in different churches throughout the year, while elsewhere adoration is perpetual day and night, under the care of religious communities, and the faithful quite often take part in them.

133. These exercises of piety have brought a wonderful increase in faith and supernatural life to the Church militant upon earth and they are reechoed to a certain extent by the Church triumphant in heaven which sings continually a hymn of praise to God and to the Lamb "who was slain."[125] Wherefore, the Church not merely approves these pious practices, which in the course of centuries have spread everywhere throughout the world, but makes them her own, as it were, and by her authority commends them.[126] They spring from the inspiration of the liturgy and if they are performed with due propriety and with faith and piety, as the liturgical rules of the Church require, they are undoubtedly of the very greatest assistance in living the life of the liturgy.

134. Nor is it to be admitted that by this Eucharistic cult men falsely confound the historical Christ, as they say, who once lived on earth, with the Christ who is present in the august Sacrament of the altar, and who reigns glorious and triumphant in heaven and bestows supernatural favors. On the contrary, it can be claimed that by this devotion the faithful bear witness to and solemnly avow the faith of the Church that the Word of God is identical with the Son of the Virgin Mary, who suffered on the Cross, who is present in a hidden manner in the Eucharist and who reigns upon His heavenly throne. Thus, St. John Chrysostom states: "When you see It [the Body of Christ] exposed, say to yourself: Thanks to this Body, I am no longer dust and ashes, I am no more a captive but a freeman: hence, I hope to obtain heaven and the good things that are there in store for me,

eternal life, the heritage of the angels, companionship with Christ; death has not destroyed this Body which was pierced by nails and scourged, . . . this is that Body which was once covered with Blood, pierced by a lance, from which issued saving fountains upon the world, one of Blood and the other of water. . . This Body He gave to us to keep and eat, as a mark of His intense love."[127]

135. That practice in a special manner is to be highly praised according to which many exercises of piety, customary among the faithful, and with benediction of the blessed Sacrament. For excellent and of great benefit is that custom which makes the priest raise aloft the Bread of Angels before congregations with heads bowed down in adoration, and forming with It the sign of the Cross implores the heavenly Father to deign to look upon His Son who for love of us was nailed to the Cross, and for His sake and through Him who willed to be our Redeemer and our brother, be pleased to shower down heavenly favors upon those whom the immaculate Blood of the Lamb has redeemed.[128]

136. Strive then, Venerable Brethren, with your customary devoted care so the churches, which the faith and piety of Christian peoples have built in the course of centuries for the purpose of singing a perpetual hymn of glory to God almighty and of providing a worthy abode for our Redeemer concealed beneath the eucharistic species, may be entirely at the disposal of greater numbers of the faithful who, called to the feet of their Savior, hearken to His most consoling invitation, "Come to Me all you who labor and are heavily burdened, and I will refresh you."[129] Let your churches be the house of God where all who enter to implore blessings rejoice in obtaining whatever they ask[130] and find there heavenly consolation.

137. Only thus can it be brought about that the whole human family settling their differences may find peace, and united in mind and heart may sing this song of hope and charity, "Good Pastor, truly bread— Jesus have mercy on us—feed us, protect us—bestow on us the vision of all good things in the land of the living."[131]

138. The ideal of Christian life is that each one be united to God in the closest and most intimate manner. For this reason, the worship that the Church renders to God, and which is based especially on the eucharistic sacrifice and the use of the sacraments, is directed and arranged in such a way that it embraces by means of the divine office,

the hours of the day, the weeks and the whole cycle of the year, and reaches all the aspects and phases of human life.

139. Since the divine Master commanded "that we ought always to pray and not to faint,"[132] the Church faithfully fulfills this injunction and never ceases to pray: she urges us in the words of the Apostle of the Gentiles, "by him Jesus let us offer the sacrifice of praise always to God."[133]

140. Public and common prayer offered to God by all at the same time was customary in antiquity only on certain days and at certain times. Indeed, people prayed to God not only in groups but in private houses and occasionally with neighbors and friends. But soon in different parts of the Christian world the practice arose of setting aside special times for praying, as for example, the last hour of the day when evening set in and the lamps were lighted; or the first, heralded, when the night was coming to an end, by the crowing of the cock, and the rising of the morning star. Other times of the day, as being more suitable for prayer are indicated in Sacred Scripture, in Hebrew customs, or in keeping with the practice of every-day life. According to the acts of the Apostles, the disciples of Jesus Christ all came together to pray at the third hour, when they were all filled with the Holy Ghost;[134] and before eating, the Prince of the Apostles went up to the higher parts of the house to pray, about the sixth hour;[135] Peter and John "went up into the Temple at the ninth hour of prayer"[136] and at "midnight Paul and Silas praying . . . praised God."[137]

141. Thanks to the work of the monks and those who practice asceticism, these various prayers in the course of time become ever more perfected and by the authority of the Church are gradually incorporated into the sacred liturgy.

142. The divine office is the prayer of the Mystical Body of Jesus Christ, offered to God in the name and on behalf of all Christians, when recited by priests and other ministers of the Church and by religious who are deputed by the Church for this.

143. The character and value of the divine office may be gathered from the words recommended by the Church to be said before starting the prayers of the office, namely, that they be said "worthily, with attention and devotion."

144. By assuming human nature, the Divine Word introduced into this earthly exile a hymn which is sung in heaven for all eternity. He unites to Himself the whole human race and with it sings this hymn to the praise of God. As we must humbly recognize that "we know not what we should pray for, as we ought, the Spirit Himself asketh for us with unspeakable groanings."[138] Moreover, through His Spirit in us, Christ entreats the Father, "God could not give a greater gift to men . . . [Jesus] prays for us, as our Priest; He prays in us as our Head; we pray to Him as our God . . . we recognize in Him our voice and His voice in us . . . He is prayed to as God, He prays under the appearance of a servant; in heaven He is Creator; here, created though not changed, He assumes a created nature which is to be changed and makes us with Him one complete man, head and body."[139]

145. To this lofty dignity of the Church's prayer, there should correspond earnest devotion in our souls. For when in prayer the voice repeats those hymns written under the inspiration of the Holy Ghost and extols God's infinite perfections, it is necessary that the interior sentiment of our souls should accompany the voice so as to make those sentiments our own in which we are elevated to heaven, adoring and giving due praise and thanks to the Blessed Trinity; "so let us chant in choir that mind and voice may accord together."[140] It is not merely a question of recitation or of singing which, however perfect according to norms of music and the sacred rites, only reaches the ear, but it is especially a question of the ascent of the mind and heart to God so that, united with Christ, we may completely dedicate ourselves and all our actions to Him.

146. On this depends in no small way the efficacy of our prayers. These prayers in fact, when they are not addressed directly to the Word made man, conclude with the phrase "though Jesus Christ our Lord." As our Mediator with God, He shows to the heavenly Father His glorified wounds, "always living to make intercessions for us."[141]

147. The Psalms, as all know, form the chief part of the divine office. They encompass the full round of the day and sanctify it. Cassiodorus speaks beautifully about the Psalms as distributed in his day throughout the divine office: "With the celebration of matins they bring a blessing on the coming day, they set aside for us the first hour and consecrate the third hour of the day, they gladden the sixth hour with the breaking of bread, at the ninth they terminate our fast, they

bring the evening to a close and at nightfall they shield our minds from darkness."[142]

148. The Psalms recall to mind the truths revealed by God to the chosen people, which were at one time frightening and at another filled with wonderful tenderness; they keep repeating and fostering the hope of the promised Liberator which in ancient times was kept alive with song, either around the hearth or in the stately temple; they show forth in splendid light the prophesied glory of Jesus Christ: first, His supreme and eternal power, then His lowly coming to this terrestrial exile, His kingly dignity and priestly power and, finally, His beneficent labors, and the shedding of His blood for our redemption. In a similar way they express the joy, the bitterness, the hope and fear of our hearts and our desire of loving God and hoping in Him alone, and our mystic ascent to divine tabernacles.

149. "The psalm is . . . a blessing for the people, it is the praise of God, the tribute of the nation, the common language and acclamation of all, it is the voice of the Church, the harmonious confession of faith, signifying deep attachment to authority; it is the joy of freedom, the expression of happiness, an echo of bliss."[143]

150. In an earlier age, these canonical prayers were attended by many of the faithful. But this gradually ceased, and, as We have already said, their recitation at present is the duty only of the clergy and of religious. The laity have no obligation in this matter. Still, it is greatly to be desired that they participate in reciting or chanting vespers sung in their own parish on feast days. We earnestly exhort you, Venerable Brethren, to see that this pious practice is kept up, and that wherever it has ceased you restore it if possible. This, without doubt, will produce salutary results when vespers are conducted in a worthy and fitting manner and with such helps as foster the piety of the faithful. Let the public and private observance of the feasts of the Church, which are in a special way dedicated and consecrated to God, be kept inviolable; and especially the Lord's day which the Apostles, under the guidance of the Holy Ghost, substituted for the sabbath. Now, if the order was given to the Jews: "Six days shall you do work; in the seventh day is the sabbath, the rest holy to the Lord. Every one that shall do any work on this day, shall die;"[144] how will these Christians not fear spiritual death who perform servile work on feast-days, and whose rest on these days is not devoted to religion and piety but given over to the allurements of the world? Sundays and

holydays, then, must be made holy by divine worship, which gives homage to God and heavenly food to the soul. Although the Church only commands the faithful to abstain from servile work and attend Mass and does not make it obligatory to attend evening devotions, still she desires this and recommends it repeatedly. Moreover, the needs of each one demand it, seeing that all are bound to win the favor of God if they are to obtain His benefits. Our soul is filled with the greatest grief when We see how the Christian people of today profane the afternoon of feast days; public places of amusement and public games are frequented in great numbers while the churches are not as full as they should be. All should come to our churches and there be taught the truth of the Catholic faith, sing the praises of God, be enriched with benediction of the blessed Sacrament given by the priest and be strengthened with help from heaven against the adversities of this life. Let all try to learn those prayers which are recited at vespers and fill their souls with their meaning. When deeply penetrated by these prayers, they will experience what St. Augustine said about himself: "How much did I weep during hymns and verses, greatly moved at the sweet singing of thy Church. Their sound would penetrate my ears and their truth melt my heart, sentiments of piety would well up, tears would flow and that was good for me."[145]

151. Throughout the entire year, the Mass and the divine office center especially around the person of Jesus Christ. This arrangement is so suitably disposed that our Savior dominates the scene in the mysteries of His humiliation, of His redemption and triumph.

152. While the sacred liturgy calls to mind the mysteries of Jesus Christ, it strives to make all believers take their part in them so that the divine Head of the mystical Body may live in all the members with the fullness of His holiness. Let the souls of Christians be like altars on each one of which a different phase of the sacrifice, offered by the High priest, comes to life again, as it were: pains and tears which wipe away and expiate sin; supplication to God which pierces heaven; dedication and even immolation of oneself made promptly, generously and earnestly; and, finally, that intimate union by which we commit ourselves and all we have to God, in whom we find our rest. "The perfection of religion is to imitate whom you adore."[146]

153. By these suitable ways and methods in which the liturgy at stated times proposes the life of Jesus Christ for our meditation, the Church gives us examples to imitate, points out treasures of sanctity for us to make our own, since it is fitting that the mind believes what the lips

sing, and that what the mind believes should be practiced in public and private life.

154. In the period of Advent, for instance, the Church arouses in us the consciousness of the sins we have had the misfortune to commit, and urges us, by restraining our desires and practicing voluntary mortification of the body, to recollect ourselves in meditation, and experience a longing desire to return to God who alone can free us by His grace from the stain of sin and from its evil consequences.

155. With the coming of the birthday of the Redeemer, she would bring us to the cave of Bethlehem and there teach that we must be born again and undergo a complete reformation; that will only happen when we are intimately and vitally united to the Word of God made man and participate in His divine nature, to which we have been elevated.

156. At the solemnity of the Epiphany, in putting before us the call of the Gentiles to the Christian faith, she wishes us daily to give thanks to the Lord for such a blessing; she wishes us to seek with lively faith the living and true God, to penetrate deeply and religiously the things of heaven, to love silence and meditation in order to perceive and grasp more easily heavenly gifts.

157. During the days of Septuagesima and Lent, our Holy Mother the Church over and over again strives to make each of us seriously consider our misery, so that we may be urged to a practical emendation of our lives, detest our sins heartily, and expiate them by prayer and penance. For constant prayer and penance done for past sins obtain for us divine help, without which every work of ours is useless and unavailing.

158. In Holy Week, when the most bitter sufferings of Jesus Christ are put before us by the liturgy, the Church invites us to come to Calvary and follow in the blood-stained footsteps of the divine Redeemer, to carry the cross willingly with Him, to reproduce in our own hearts His spirit of expiation and atonement, and to die together with Him.

159. At the Paschal season, which commemorates the triumph of Christ, our souls are filled with deep interior joy: we, accordingly, should also consider that we must rise, in union with the Redeemer, from our cold and slothful life to one of greater fervor and holiness by

giving ourselves completely and generously to God, and by forgetting this wretched world in order to aspire only to the things of heaven: "If you be risen with Christ, seek the things that are above . . . mind the things that are above."[147]

160. Finally, during the time of Pentecost, the Church by her precept and practice urges us to be more docile to the action of the Holy Spirit who wishes us to be on fire with divine love so that we may daily strive to advance more in virtue and thus become holy as Christ our Lord and His Father are holy.

161. Thus, the liturgical year should be considered as a splendid hymn of praise offered to the heavenly Father by the Christian family through Jesus, their perpetual Mediator. Nevertheless, it requires a diligent and well ordered study on our part to be able to know and praise our Redeemer ever more and more. It requires a serious effort and constant practice to imitate His mysteries, to enter willingly upon His path of sorrow and thus finally share His glory and eternal happiness.

162. From what We have already explained, Venerable Brethren, it is perfectly clear how much modern writers are wanting in the genuine and true liturgical spirit who, deceived by the illusion of a higher mysticism, dare to assert that attention should be paid not to the historic Christ but to a "pneumatic" or glorified Christ. They do not hesitate to assert that a change has taken place in the piety of the faithful by dethroning, as it were, Christ from His position; since they say that the glorified Christ, who liveth and reigneth forever and sitteth at the right hand of the Father, has been overshadowed and in His place has been substituted that Christ who lived on earth. For this reason, some have gone so far as to want to remove from the churches images of the divine Redeemer suffering on the cross.

163. But these false statements are completely opposed to the solid doctrine handed down by tradition. "You believe in Christ born in the flesh," says St. Augustine, "and you will come to Christ begotten of God."[148] In the sacred liturgy, the whole Christ is proposed to us in all the circumstances of His life, as the Word of the eternal Father, as born of the Virgin Mother of God, as He who teaches us truth, heals the sick, consoles the afflicted, who endures suffering and who dies; finally, as He who rose triumphantly from the dead and who, reigning in the glory of heaven, sends us the Holy Paraclete and who abides in His Church forever; "Jesus Christ, yesterday and today, and the same

forever."[149] Besides, the liturgy shows us Christ not only as a model to be imitated but as a master to whom we should listen readily, a Shepherd whom we should follow, Author of our salvation, the Source of our holiness and the Head of the Mystical Body whose members we are, living by His very life.

164. Since His bitter sufferings constitute the principal mystery of our redemption, it is only fitting that the Catholic faith should give it the greatest prominence. This mystery is the very center of divine worship since the Mass represents and renews it every day and since all the sacraments are most closely united with the cross.[150]

165. Hence, the liturgical year, devotedly fostered and accompanied by the Church, is not a cold and lifeless representation of the events of the past, or a simple and bare record of a former age. It is rather Christ Himself who is ever living in His Church. Here, He continues that journey of immense mercy which He lovingly began in His mortal life, going about doing good,[151] with the design of bringing men to know His mysteries and in a way live by them. These mysteries are ever present and active not in a vague and uncertain way as some modern writers hold, but in the way that Catholic doctrine teaches us. According to the Doctors of the Church, they are shining examples of Christian perfection, as well as sources of divine grace, due to the merit and prayers of Christ; they still influence us because each mystery brings its own special grace for our salvation. Moreover, our holy Mother the Church, while proposing for our contemplation the mysteries of our Redeemer, asks in her prayers for those gifts which would give her children the greatest possible share in the spirit of these mysteries through the merits of Christ. By means of His inspiration and help and through the cooperation of our wills we can receive from Him living vitality as branches do from the tree and members from the head; thus slowly and laboriously we can transform ourselves "unto the measure of the age of the fullness of Christ."[152]

166. In the course of the liturgical year, besides the mysteries of Jesus Christ, the feasts of the saints are celebrated. Even though these feasts are of a lower and subordinate order, the Church always strives to put before the faithful examples of sanctity in order to move them to cultivate in themselves the virtues of the divine Redeemer.

167. We should imitate the virtues of the saints just as they imitated Christ, for in their virtues there shines forth under different aspects the splendor of Jesus Christ. Among some of these saints the zeal of the apostolate stood out, in others courage prevailed even to the shedding of blood, constant vigilance marked others out as they kept watch for the divine Redeemer, while in others the virginal purity of soul was resplendent and their modesty revealed the beauty of Christian humility; there burned in all of them the fire of charity towards God and their neighbor. The sacred liturgy puts all these gems of sanctity before us so that we may consider them for our salvation, and "rejoicing at their merits, we may be inflamed by their example."[153] It is necessary, then, to practice "in simplicity innocence, in charity concord, in humility modesty, diligence in government, readiness in helping those who labor, mercy in serving the poor, in defending truth, constancy, in the strict maintenance of discipline justice, so that nothing may be wanting in us of the virtues which have been proposed for our imitation. These are the footprints left by the saints in their journey homeward, that guided by them we might follow them into glory."[154] In order that we may be helped by our senses, also, the Church wishes that images of the saints be displayed in our churches, always, however, with the same intention "that we imitate the virtues of those whose images we venerate."[155]

168. But there is another reason why the Christian people should honor the saints in heaven, namely, to implore their help and "that we be aided by the pleadings of those whose praise is our delight."[156] Hence, it is easy to understand why the sacred liturgy provides us with many different prayers to invoke the intercession of the saints.

169. Among the saints in heaven the Virgin Mary Mother of God is venerated in a special way. Because of the mission she received from God, her life is most closely linked with the mysteries of Jesus Christ, and there is no one who has followed in the footsteps of the Incarnate Word more closely and with more merit than she: and no one has more grace and power over the most Sacred Heart of the Son of God and through Him with the Heavenly Father. Holier than the Cherubim and Seraphim, she enjoys unquestionably greater glory than all the other saints, for she is "full of grace,"[157] she is the Mother of God, who happily gave birth to the Redeemer for us. Since she is, therefore, "Mother of mercy, our life, our sweetness and our hope," let us all cry to her "mourning and weeping in this vale of tears,"[158] and confidently place ourselves and all we have under her patronage.

She became our Mother also when the divine Redeemer offered the sacrifice of Himself; and hence by this title also, we are her children. She teaches us all the virtues; she gives us her Son and with Him all the help we need, for God "wished us to have everything through Mary."[159]

170. Throughout this liturgical journey which begins anew for us each year under the sanctifying action of the Church, and strengthened by the help and example of the saints, especially of the Immaculate Virgin Mary, "let us draw near with a true heart, in fullness of faith having our hearts sprinkled from an evil conscience, and our bodies washed with clean water,"[160] let us draw near to the "High Priest"[161] that with Him we may share His life and sentiments and by Him penetrate "even within the veil,"[162] and there honor the heavenly Father for ever and ever.

171. Such is the nature and the object of the sacred liturgy: it treats of the Mass, the sacraments, the divine office; it aims at uniting our souls with Christ and sanctifying them through the divine Redeemer in order that Christ be honored and, through Him and in Him, the most Holy Trinity, *Glory be to the Father and to the Son and to the Holy Ghost.*

172. In order that the errors and inaccuracies, mentioned above, may be more easily removed from the Church, and that the faithful following safer norms may be able to use more fruitfully the liturgical apostolate, We have deemed it opportune, Venerable Brethren, to add some practical applications of the doctrine which We have explained.

173. When dealing with genuine and solid piety We stated that there could be no real opposition between the sacred liturgy and other religious practices, provided they be kept within legitimate bounds and performed for a legitimate purpose. In fact, there are certain exercises of piety which the Church recommends very much to clergy and religious.

174. It is Our wish also that the faithful, as well, should take part in these practices. The chief of these are: meditation on spiritual things, diligent examination of conscience, enclosed retreats, visits to the blessed sacrament, and those special prayers in honor of the Blessed Virgin Mary among which the rosary, as all know, has pride of place.[163]

175. From these multiple forms of piety, the inspiration and action of the Holy Spirit cannot be absent. Their purpose is, in various ways, to attract and direct our souls to God, purifying them from their sins, encouraging them to practice virtue and, finally, stimulating them to advance along the path of sincere piety by accustoming them to meditate on the eternal truths and disposing them better to contemplate the mysteries of the human and divine natures of Christ. Besides, since they develop a deeper spiritual life of the faithful, they prepare them to take part in sacred public functions with greater fruit, and they lessen the danger of liturgical prayers becoming an empty ritualism.

176. In keeping with your pastoral solicitude, Venerable Brethren, do not cease to recommend and encourage these exercises of piety from which the faithful, entrusted to your care, cannot but derive salutary fruit. Above all, do not allow—as some do, who are deceived under the pretext of restoring the liturgy or who idly claim that only liturgical rites are of any real value and dignity—that churches be closed during the hours not appointed for public functions, as has already happened in some places: where the adoration of the august Sacrament and visits to our Lord in the tabernacles are neglected; where confession of devotion is discouraged; and devotion to the Virgin Mother of God, a sign of "predestination" according to the opinion of holy men, is so neglected, especially among the young, as to fade away and gradually vanish. Such conduct most harmful to Christian piety is like poisonous fruit, growing on the infected branches of a healthy tree, which must be cut off so that the life-giving sap of the tree may bring forth only the best fruit.

177. Since the opinions expressed by some about frequent confession are completely foreign to the spirit of Christ and His Immaculate Spouse and are also most dangerous to the spiritual life, let Us call to mind what with sorrow We wrote about this point in the encyclical on the Mystical Body. We urgently insist once more that what We expounded in very serious words be proposed by you for the serious consideration and dutiful obedience of your flock, especially to students for the priesthood and young clergy.

178. Take special care that as many as possible, not only of the clergy but of the laity and especially those in religious organizations and in the ranks of Catholic Action, take part in monthly days of recollection and in retreats of longer duration made with a view to growing in virtue. As We have previously stated, such spiritual exercises are

most useful and even necessary to instill into souls solid virtue, and to strengthen them in sanctity so as to be able to derive from the sacred liturgy more efficacious and abundant benefits.

179. As regards the different methods employed in these exercises, it is perfectly clear to all that in the Church on earth, no less in the Church in heaven, there are many mansions,[164] and that asceticism cannot be the monopoly of anyone. It is the same spirit who breatheth where He will,[165] and who with differing gifts and in different ways enlightens and guides souls to sanctity. Let their freedom and the supernatural action of the Holy Spirit be so sacrosanct that no one presume to disturb or stifle them for any reason whatsoever.

180. However, it is well known that the spiritual exercise according to the method and norms of St. Ignatius have been fully approved and earnestly recommended by Our predecessors on account of their admirable efficacy. We, too, for the same reason have approved and commended them and willingly do We repeat this now.

181. Any inspiration to follow and practice extraordinary exercises of piety must most certainly come from the Father of Lights, from whom every good and perfect gift descends;[166] and, of course, the criterion of this will be the effectiveness of these exercises in making the divine cult loved and spread daily ever more widely, and in making the faithful approach the sacraments with more longing desire, and in obtaining for all things holy due respect and honor. If, on the contrary, they are an obstacle to principles and norms of divine worship, or if they oppose or hinder them, one must surely conclude that they are not in keeping with prudence and enlightened zeal.

182. There are, besides, other exercises of piety which, although not strictly belonging to the sacred liturgy, are, nevertheless, of special import and dignity, and may be considered in a certain way to be an addition to the liturgical cult; they have been approved and praised over and over again by the Apostolic See and by the bishops. Among these are the prayers usually said during the month of May in honor of the Blessed Virgin Mother of God, or during the month of June to the most Sacred Heart of Jesus: also novenas and triduums, stations of the cross, and other similar practices.

183. These devotions make us partakers in a salutary manner of the liturgical cult, because they urge the faithful to go frequently to the sacrament of penance, to attend Mass and receive communion with

devotion, and, as well, encourage them to meditate on the mysteries of our redemption and imitate the example of the saints.

184. Hence, he would do something very wrong and dangerous who would dare to take on himself to reform all these exercises of piety and reduce them completely to the methods and norms of liturgical rites. However, it is necessary that the spirit of the sacred liturgy and its directives should exercise such a salutary influence on them that nothing improper be introduced nor anything unworthy of the dignity of the house of God or detrimental to the sacred functions or opposed to solid piety.

185. Take care then, Venerable Brethren, that this true and solid piety increases daily and more under your guidance and bears more abundant fruit. Above all, do not cease to inculcate into the minds of all that progress in the Christian life does not consist in the multiplicity and variety of prayers and exercises of piety, but rather in their helpfulness towards spiritual progress of the faithful and constant growth of the Church universal. For the eternal Father "chose us in Him [Christ] before the foundation of the world that we should be holy and unspotted in His sight."[167] All our prayers, then, and all our religious practices should aim at directing our spiritual energies towards attaining this most noble and lofty end.

186. We earnestly exhort you, Venerable Brethren, that after errors and falsehoods have been removed, and anything that is contrary to truth or moderation has been condemned, you promote a deeper knowledge among the people of the sacred liturgy so that they more readily and easily follow the sacred rites and take part in them with true Christian dispositions.

187. First of all, you must strive that with due reverence and faith all obey the decrees of the Council of Trent, of the Roman Pontiffs, and the Sacred Congregation of Rites, and what the liturgical books ordain concerning external public worship.

188. Three characteristics of which Our predecessor Pius X spoke should adorn all liturgical services: sacredness, which abhors any profane influence; nobility, which true and genuine arts should serve and foster; and universality, which, while safeguarding local and legitimate custom, reveals the catholic unity of the Church.[168]

189. We desire to commend and urge the adornment of churches and altars. Let each one feel moved by the inspired word, "the zeal of thy house hath eaten me up;"[169] and strive as much as in him lies that everything in the church, including vestments and liturgical furnishings, even though not rich nor lavish, be perfectly clean and appropriate, since all is consecrated to the Divine Majesty. If we have previously disapproved of the error of those who would wish to outlaw images from churches on the plea of reviving an ancient tradition, We now deem it Our duty to censure the inconsiderate zeal of those who propose for veneration in the Churches and on the altars, without any just reason, a multitude of sacred images and statues, and also those who display unauthorized relics, those who emphasize special and insignificant practices, neglecting essential and necessary things. They thus bring religion into derision and lessen the dignity of worship.

190. Let us recall, as well, the decree about "not introducing new forms of worship and devotion."[170] We commend the exact observance of this decree to your vigilance.

191. As regards music, let the clear and guiding norms of the Apostolic See be scrupulously observed. Gregorian chant, which the Roman Church considers her own as handed down from antiquity and kept under her close tutelage, is proposed to the faithful as belonging to them also. In certain parts of the liturgy the Church definitely prescribes it;[171] it makes the celebration of the sacred mysteries not only more dignified and solemn but helps very much to increase the faith and devotion of the congregation. For this reason, Our predecessors of immortal memory, Pius X and Pius XI, decree—and We are happy to confirm with Our authority the norms laid down by them—that in seminaries and religious institutes, Gregorian chant be diligently and zealously promoted, and moreover that the old *Scholae Cantorum* be restored, at least in the principal churches. This has already been done with happy results in not a few places.[172]

192. Besides, "so that the faithful take a more active part in divine worship, let Gregorian chant be restored to popular use in the parts proper to the people. Indeed it is very necessary that the faithful attend the sacred ceremonies not as if they were outsiders or mute onlookers, but let them fully appreciate the beauty of the liturgy and take part in the sacred ceremonies, alternating their voices with the priest and the choir, according to the prescribed norms. If, please

God, this is done, it will not happen that the congregation hardly ever or only in a low murmur answer the prayers in Latin or in the vernacular."[173] A congregation that is devoutly present at the sacrifice, in which our Savior together with His children redeemed with His sacred Blood sings the nuptial hymn of His immense love, cannot keep silent, for "song befits the lover"[174] and, as the ancient saying has it, "he who sings well prays twice." Thus, the Church militant, faithful as well as clergy, joins in the hymns of the Church triumphant and with the choirs of angels, and, all together, sing a wondrous and eternal hymn of praise to the most Holy Trinity in keeping with words of the preface, "with whom our voices, too, thou wouldst bid to be admitted."[175]

193. It cannot be said that modern music and singing should be entirely excluded from Catholic worship. For, if they are not profane nor unbecoming to the sacredness of the place and function, and do not spring from a desire of achieving extraordinary and unusual effects, then our churches must admit them since they can contribute in no small way to the splendor of the sacred ceremonies, can lift the mind to higher things and foster true devotion of soul.

194. We also exhort you, Venerable Brethren, to promote with care congregational singing, and to see to its accurate execution with all due dignity, since it easily stirs up and arouses the faith and piety of large gatherings of the faithful. Let the full harmonious singing of our people rise to heaven like the bursting of a thunderous sea[176] and let them testify by the melody of their song to the unity of their hearts and minds[177], as becomes brothers and the children of the same Father.

195. What We have said about music, applies to the other fine arts, especially to architecture, sculpture, and painting. Recent works of art which lend themselves to the materials of modern composition, should not be universally despised and rejected through prejudice. Modern art should be given free scope in the due and reverent service of the church and the sacred rites, provided that they preserve a correct balance between styles tending neither to extreme realism nor to excessive "symbolism," and that the needs of the Christian community are taken into consideration rather than the particular taste or talent of the individual artist. Thus, modern art will be able to join its voice to that wonderful choir of praise to which have contributed, in honor of the Catholic faith, the greatest artists throughout the centuries. Nevertheless, in keeping with the duty of Our office, We

cannot help deploring and condemning those works of art, recently introduced by some, which seem to be a distortion and perversion of true art and which at times openly shock Christian taste, modesty, and devotion, and shamefully offend the true religious sense. These must be entirely excluded and banished from our churches, like "anything else that is not in keeping with the sanctity of the place."[178]

196. Keeping in mind, Venerable Brethren, pontifical norms and decrees, take great care to enlighten and direct the minds and hearts of the artists to whom is given the task today of restoring or rebuilding the many churches which have been ruined or completely destroyed by war. Let them be capable and willing to draw their inspiration from religion to express what is suitable and more in keeping with the requirements of worship. Thus, the human arts will shine forth with a wondrous heavenly splendor, and contribute greatly to human civilization, to the salvation of souls and the glory of God. The fine arts are really in conformity with religion when "as noblest handmaids they are at the service of divine worship."[179]

197. But there is something else of even greater importance, Venerable Brethren, which We commend to your apostolic zeal, in a very special manner. Whatever pertains to the external worship has assuredly its importance; however, the most pressing duty of Christians is to live the liturgical life, and increase and cherish its supernatural spirit.

198. Readily provide the young clerical student with facilities to understand the sacred ceremonies, to appreciate their majesty, and beauty and to learn the rubrics with care, just as you do when he is trained in ascetics, in dogma, and in a canon law and pastoral theology. This should not be done merely for cultural reasons and to fit the student to perform religious rites in the future, correctly and with due dignity, but especially to lead him into closest union with Christ, the Priest, so that he may become a holy minister of sanctity.

199. Try in every way, with the means and helps that your prudence deems best, that the clergy and people become one in mind and heart, and that the Christian people take such an active part in the liturgy that it becomes a truly sacred action of due worship to the eternal Lord in which the priest, chiefly responsible for the souls of his parish, and the ordinary faithful are united together.

200. To attain this purpose, it will greatly help to select carefully good and upright young boys from all classes of citizens who will come generously and spontaneously to serve at the altar with careful zeal and exactness. Parents of higher social standing and culture should greatly esteem this office for their children. If these youths, under the watchful guidance of the priests, are properly trained and encouraged to fulfill the task committed to them punctually, reverently and constantly, then from their number will readily come fresh candidates for the priesthood. The clergy will not then complain—as, alas, sometimes happens even in Catholic places—that in the celebration of the august sacrifice they find no one to answer or serve them.

201. Above all, try with your constant zeal to have all the faithful attend the eucharistic sacrifice from which they may obtain abundant and salutary fruit; and carefully instruct them in all the legitimate ways we have described above so that they may devoutly participate in it. The Mass is the chief act of divine worship; it should also be the source and center of Christian piety. Never think that you have satisfied your apostolic zeal until you see your faithful approach in great numbers the celestial banquet which is a sacrament of devotion, a sign of unity, and a bond of love.[180]

202. By means of suitable sermons and particularly by periodic conferences and lectures, by special study weeks and the like, teach the Christian people carefully about the treasures of piety contained in the sacred liturgy so that they may be able to profit more abundantly by these supernatural gifts. In this matter, those who are active in the ranks of Catholic Action will certainly be a help to you, since they are ever at the service of the hierarchy in the work of promoting the kingdom of Jesus Christ.

203. But in all these matters, it is essential that you watch vigilantly lest the enemy come into the field of the Lord and sow cockle among the wheat;[181] in other words, do not let your flocks be deceived by the subtle and dangerous errors of false mysticism or quietism—as you know We have already condemned these errors;[182] also do not let a certain dangerous "humanism" lead them astray, nor let there be introduced a false doctrine destroying the notion of Catholic faith, nor finally an exaggerated zeal for antiquity in matters liturgical. Watch with like diligence lest the false teaching of those be propagated who wrongly think and teach that the glorified human nature of Christ really and continually dwells in the "just" by His presence and that

one and numerically the same grace, as they say, unites Christ with the members of His Mystical Body.

204. Never be discouraged by the difficulties that arise, and never let your pastoral zeal grow cold. "Blow the trumpet in Sion . . . call an assembly, gather together the people, sanctify the Church, assemble the ancients, gather together the little ones, and them that suck at the breasts,"[183] and use every help to get the faithful everywhere to fill the churches and crowd around the altars so that they may be restored by the graces of the sacraments and joined as living members to their divine Head, and with Him and through Him celebrate together the august sacrifice that gives due tribute of praise to the Eternal Father.

205. These, Venerable Brethren, are the subjects We desired to write to you about. We are moved to write that your children, who are also Ours, may more fully understand and appreciate the most precious treasures which are contained in the sacred liturgy: namely, the eucharistic sacrifice, representing and renewing the sacrifice of the cross, the sacraments which are the streams of divine grace and of divine life, and the hymn of praise, which heaven and earth daily offer to God.

206. We cherish the hope that these Our exhortations will not only arouse the sluggish and recalcitrant to a deeper and more correct study of the liturgy, but also instill into their daily lives its supernatural spirit according to the words of the Apostle, "extinguish not the spirit."[184]

207. To those whom an excessive zeal occasionally led to say and do certain things which saddened Us and which We could not approve, we repeat the warning of St. Paul, "But prove all things, hold fast that which is good."[185] Let Us paternally warn them to imitate in their thoughts and actions the Christian doctrine which is in harmony with the precepts of the immaculate Spouse of Jesus Christ, the mother of saints.

208. Let Us remind all that they must generously and faithfully obey their holy pastors who possess the right and duty of regulating the whole life, especially the spiritual life, of the Church. "Obey your prelates and be subject to them. For they watch as being to render an account of your souls; that they may do this with joy and not with grief."[186]

209. May God, whom we worship, and who is "not the God of dissension but of peace,"[187] graciously grant to us all that during our earthly exile we may with one mind and one heart participate in the sacred liturgy which is, as it were, a preparation and a token of that heavenly liturgy in which we hope one day to sing together with the most glorious Mother of God and our most loving Mother, "To Him that sitteth on the throne, and to the Lamb, benediction and honor, and glory and power for ever and ever."[188]

210. In this joyous hope, We most lovingly impart to each and every one of you, Venerable Brethren, and to the flocks confided to your care, as a pledge of divine gifts and as a witness of Our special love, the apostolic benediction.

Given at Castel Gandolfo, near Rome, on the 20th day of November in the year 1947, the 9th of Our Pontificate.

PIUS XII

---

1. 1 Tim. 2:5.
2. Cf. Heb. 4:14.
3. Cf. Heb. 9:14.
4. Cf. Mal.1:11.
5. Cf. Council of Trent Sess. 22, c. 1.
6. Cf. *ibid.*, c. 2.
7. Encyclical Letter *Caritate Christi*, May 3, 1932.
8. Cf. Apostolic Letter (Motu Proprio) *In cotidianis precibus*, March 24, 1945.
9. 1 Cor. 10:17.
10. Saint Thomas, *Summa Theologica*, II^a II^{a3} q. 81, art. 1.
11. Cf. Book of Leviticus.
12. Cf. Heb.10:1.
13. John, 1:14.
14. Heb.10:5-7.
15. *Ibid.* 10:10.
16. John, 1:9.
17. Heb.10:39.
18. Cf. 1 John, 2:1.
19. Cf. 1 Tim. 3:15.
20. Cf. Boniface IX, *Ab origine mundi*, October 7, 1391; Callistus III, *Summus Pontifex*, January 1, 1456; Pius II, *Triumphans Pastor*, April 22, 1459; Innocent XI, *Triumphans Pastor*, October 3, 1678.

21. Eph. 2:19-22.
22. Matt. 18:20.
23. Acts, 2:42.
24. Col. 3:16.
25. Saint Augustine, *Epist. 130, ad Probam*, 18.
26. Roman Missal, Preface for Christmas.
27. Giovanni Cardinal Bona, *De divina psalmodia*, c. 19, par. 3, 1.
28. Roman Missal, Secret for Thursday after the Second Sunday of Lent.
29. Cf. Mark, 7:6 and Isaias, 29:13.
30. 1 Cor.11:28.
31. Roman Missal, Ash Wednesday; Prayer after the imposition of ashes.
32. *De praedestinatione sanctorum*, 31.
33. Cf. Saint Thomas, *Summa Theologica*, II^a II^{a3}, q. 82, art. 1.
34. Cf. 1 Cor. 3:23.
35. Heb. 10:19-24.
36. Cf. 2 Cor. 6:1.
37. Cf. Code of Canon Law, can. 125, 126, 565, 571, 595, 1367.
38. Col. 3:11.
39. Cf. Gal. 4:19.
40. John, 20:21.
41. Luke, 10:16.
42. Mark, 16:15-16.
43. Roman Pontifical, Ordination of a priest: anointing of hands.
44. *Enchiridion*, c. 3.
45. *De gratia Dei* "Indiculus."
46. Saint Augustine, *Epist. 130, ad Probam,* 18.
47. Cf. Constitution *Divini cultus*, December 20, 1928.
48. Constitution *Immensa*, January 22, 1588.
49. Code of Canon Law, can. 253.
50. Cf. Code of Canon Law, can. 1257.
51. Cf. Code of Canon Law, can. 1261.
52. Cf. Matt. 28:20.
53. Cf. Pius VI, Constitution *Auctorem fidei*, August 28, 1794, nn. 31-34, 39, 62, 66, 69-74.
54. Cf. John, 21:15-17.
55. Acts, 20:28.
56. Ps.109:4.
57. John, 13:1.
58. Council of Trent, Sess. 22, c. 1.
59. *Ibid.*, c. 2.

60. Cf. Saint Thomas, *Summa Theologica*, III^a, q. 22, art. 4.
61. Saint John Chrysostom, *In Joann. Hom.,* 86:4.
62. Rom. 6:9.
63. Cf. Roman Missal, Preface.
64. Cf. *Ibid.*, Canon.
65. Mark, 14:23.
66. Roman Missal, Preface.
67. 1 John, 2:2.
68. Roman Missal, Canon of the Mass.
69. Saint Augustine, *De Trinit.*, Book XIII, c. 19.
70. Heb. 5:7.
71. Cf. Sess. 22, c. 1.
72. Cf. Heb. 10:14.
73. Saint Augustine, *Enarr. in Ps.* 147, n. 16.
74. Gal. 2:19-20.
75. Encyclical Letter, *Mystici Corporis*, June 29, 1943.
76. Roman Missal, Secret of the Ninth Sunday after Pentecost.
77. Cf. Sess. 22, c. 2. and can. 4.
78. Cf. Gal. 6:14.
79. Mal. 1:11.
80. Phil. 2:5.
81. Gal. 2:19.
82. Cf. Council of Trent, Sess. 23. c. 4.
83. Cf. Saint Robert Bellarmine, *De Missa, 2, c.4.*
84. *De Sacro Altaris Mysterio*, 3:6.
85. *De Missa,* 1, c. 27.
86. Roman Missal, Ordinary of the Mass.
87. *Ibid.*, Canon of the Mass.
88. Roman Missal, Canon of the Mass.
89. 1 Peter, 2:5.
90. Rom. 12:1.
91. Roman Missal, Canon of the Mass.
92. Roman Pontifical, Ordination of a priest.
93. *Ibid.*, Consecration of an altar, Preface.
94. Cf. Council of Trent, Sess. 22, c. 5.
95. Gal. 2:19-20.
96. Cf. *Serm.* 272.
97. Cf. 1 Cor. 12:27.
98. Cf. Eph. 5:30.
99. Cf. Saint Robert Bellarmine, *De Missa*, 2, c. 8.
100. Cf. *De Civitate Dei,* Book 10, c. 6.
101. Roman Missal, Canon of the Mass.

102. Cf. 1 Tim. 2:5.
103. Encyclical Letter *Certiores effecti*, November 13, 1742, par. 1.
104. Council of Trent, Sess. 22, can. 8.
105. 1 Cor. 11:24.
106. Roman Missal, Collect for Feast of Corpus Christi.
107. Sess. 22, c. 6.
108. Encyclical Letter *Certiores effecti*, par. 3.
109. Cf. Luke, 14:23.
110. 1 Cor. 10:17.
111. Cf. Saint Ignatius Martyr, *Ad Eph.* 20.
112. Roman Missal, Canon of the Mass.
113. Eph. 5:20.
114. Roman Missal, Postcommunion for Sunday within the Octave of Ascension.
115. *Ibid.*, Postcommunion for First Sunday after Pentecost.
116. Code of Canon Law, can. 810.
117. Book IV, c. 12.
118. Dan. 3:57.
119. Cf. John 16: 3.
120. Roman Missal, Secret for Mass of the Most Blessed Trinity.
121. John, 15:4.
122. Council of Trent, Sess. 13, can. 1.
123. Second Council of Constantinople, *Anath, de trib. Capit.*, can. 9; compare Council of Ephesus, *Anath. Cyrill*, can 8. Cf. Council of Trent, Sess. 13, can. 6; Pius VI Constitution *Auctorem fidei*, n. 61.
124. Cf. *Enarr in Ps.* 98:9.
125. Apoc. 5:12, cp. 7:10.
126. Cf. Council of Trent, Sess. 13, c. 5 and can. 6.
127. *In I ad Cor.*, 24:4.
128. Cf. 1 Peter, 1:19.
129. Matt. 11:28.
130. Cf. Roman Missal, Collect for Mass for the Dedication of a Church.
131. Roman Missal, Sequence *Lauda Sion* in Mass for Feast of Corpus Christi.
132. Luke, 18:1.
133. Heb. 13:15.
134. Cf. Acts, 2:1-15.
135. *Ibid.*, 10:9.
136. *Ibid.*, 3:1.
137. *Ibid.*, 16:25.
138. Rom. 8:26.

---

139. Saint Augustine, *Enarr. in Ps.* 85, n. 1.
140. Saint Benedict, *Regula Monachorum*, c. 19.
141. Heb. 7:25.
142. *Explicatio in Psalterium*, Preface. Text as found in Migne, Parres Larini, 70:10. But some are of the opinion that part of this passage should not be attributed to Cassiodorus.
143. Saint Ambrose, *Enarr in Ps.* 1, n. 9.
144. Exod. 31:15.
145. *Confessions*, Book 9, c. 6.
146. Saint Augustine, *De Civitate Dei*, Book 8, c. 17.
147. Col.3:1-2.
148. Saint Augustine, *Enarr. in Ps.* 123, n. 2.
149. Heb. 13:8.
150. Saint Thomas, *Summa Theologica* III^a, q. 49 and q. 62, art. 5.
151. Cf. Acts, 10:38.
152. Eph. 4:13.
153. Roman Missal, Collect for Third Mass of Several Martyrs outside Paschaltide.
154. Saint Bede the Venerable, *Hom. subd. 70* for Feast of All Saints.
155. Roman Missal, Collect for Mass of Saint John Damascene.
156. Saint Bernard, *Sermon 2 for Feast of All Saints.*
157. Luke, 1:28.
158. "Salve Regina."
159. Saint Bernard, *In Nativ. B.M.V., 7.*
160. Heb. 10:22.
161. *Ibid.*, 10:21.
162. *Ibid.*, 6:19.
163. Cf. Code of Canon Law, Can. 125.
164. Cf. John, 14:2.
165. John, 3:8.
166. Cf. James, 1:17.
167. Eph. 1:4.
168. Cf. Apostolic Letter (Motu Proprio) *Tra le sollecitudini,* November 22, 1903.
169. Ps. 68:9; John, 2:17.
170. Supreme Sacred Congregation of the Holy Office, Decree of May 26, 1937.
171. Cf. Pius X, Apostolic Letter (Motu Proprio) *Tra le sollectitudini.*
172. Cf. Pius X, *loc. cit.*; Pius XI, Constitution *Divini cultus,* 2, 5.
173. Pius XI, Constitution *Divini cultus,* 9.
174. Saint Augustine, *Serm. 336*, n. 1.
175. Roman Missal, Preface.

176. Saint Ambrose, *Hexameron*, 3:5, 23.
177. Cf. Acts, 4:32.
178. Code of Canon Law, can. 1178.
179. Pius XI, Constitution *Divini cultus.*
180. Cf. Saint Augustine, *Tract. 26 in John 13.*
181. Cf. Matt. 13:24-25.
182. Encyclical letter *Mystici Corporis.*
183. Joel, 2:15-16.
184. I Thess. 5:19.
185. *Ibid.*, 5:21.
186. Heb. 13:17
187. 1 Cor.14:33.
188. Apoc. 5:13.

Christus Dominus:
Concerning the Discipline to be Observed
With Respect to the Eucharistic Fast

The Apostolic Constitution of
His Holiness Pope Pius XII
January 6, 1953

P ius, Bishop, Servant of the Servants of God for an everlasting remembrance.

Christ the Lord "on the night in which He was betrayed"[1] when for the last time He kept the Pasch of the old law, after He had supped[2] took bread, and giving thanks broke, and gave to His disciples, saying: "This is My Body which shall be given up for you"[3]; and He likewise presented the chalice to them saying: "This is my Blood of the new covenant, which is being shed for many,"[4] "Do this in remembrance of Me."[5] From these passages out of Holy Scripture it is completely obvious that our Divine Redeemer wished to substitute, in place of this final Passover ceremony in which a lamb was eaten according to the rite of the Hebrews, a new Pasch which would endure until the end of the world, that is, the eating of the Immaculate Lamb who was to be immolated for the life of the world. Thus the new Pasch of the new law put an end to the old Passover and the truth emerged from the shadow.[6]

But since the conjoining of the two suppers was so arranged as to signify the transfer from the old Pasch to the new, it is easy to see why the Church, in renewing the Eucharistic Sacrifice at the command of the Divine Redeemer and in commemoration of Him, could depart from the custom of the ancient love-feast and introduce the Eucharistic fast.

From the very earliest time the custom was observed of administering the Eucharist to the faithful who were fasting.[7] Towards the end of the fourth century fasting was prescribed by many Councils for those who were going to celebrate the Eucharistic Sacrifice. So it was that the Council of Hippo in the year 393 issued this decree: "The Sacrament of the altar shall be offered only by those who are fasting."[8] Shortly afterwards, in the year 397, the Third Council of Carthage issued this same command, using the very same words.[9] At the beginning of the fifth century this custom can be called quite common and immemorial. Hence, St. Augustine affirms that the Holy Eucharist is always received by people who are fasting and likewise that this custom is observed throughout the entire world.[10]

Doubtless this way of doing things was based upon very serious reasons, among which there can be mentioned first of all the one the Apostle of the Gentiles deplores when he is dealing with the brotherly love-feast of the Christians.[11] Abstinence from food and drink is in accord with that supreme reverence we owe to the supreme majesty of Jesus Christ when we are going to receive Him hidden under the veils of the Eucharist. And moreover, when we receive His precious Body and Blood before we take any food, we show clearly that this is the first and loftiest nourishment by which our soul is fed and its holiness increased. Hence, the same St. Augustine gives this warning: "It has pleased the Holy Ghost that, to honor so great a Sacrament, the Lord's Body should enter the mouth of the Christian before other food."[12]

Not only does the Eucharistic fast pay due honor to our Divine Redeemer, it fosters piety also; and hence it can help to increase in us those most salutary fruits of holiness which Christ, the Source and Author of all good, wishes us who are enriched by His Grace to bring forth.

Moreover, everyone with experience will recognize that, by the very laws of human nature, when the body is not weighted down by food the mind more easily is lifted up and is by a more ardent virtue moved to meditate upon that hidden and transcendent Mystery that works in the soul, as in a temple, to the increase of divine charity.

The solicitude of the Church for the preservation of the Eucharistic fast may be perceived also from the fact that the Church, in decreeing this fast, imposed serious penalties for its violation. Thus the Seventh Council of Toledo in the year 646 threatened with excommunication anyone who should say Mass after having broken his fast.[13] In the year 672 the Third Council of Braga,[14] and in the year 685 the Second Council of Macon[15] had already pronounced that anyone who incurred this guilt should be deposed from his office and deprived of his honors.

As time went by, however, on careful consideration it was sometimes judged opportune because of particular circumstances to relax in some measure this law of fasting as it affected the faithful. So it is that the Council of Constance, in the year 1416, while confirming the venerable law of fasting, somewhat moderated it: ". . . the authority of the sacred canons and the praiseworthy and approved custom of the Church have observed and do observe the following: that Mass should not be said after the celebrant has taken food, nor should Holy Communion be received by the faithful without fasting, unless in case of illness or of some other necessity conceded or admitted by right or by the Church."[16]

It has pleased Us to recall these things so that all may understand that We, despite the fact that new conditions of the times and of affairs have moved Us to grant not a few faculties and favors on this subject, still wish through this Apostolic Letter to confirm the supreme force of the law and custom dealing with the Eucharistic fast; and that We wish also to admonish those who are able to observe that same law that they should continued diligently to observe it, so that only those who need these concessions can enjoy them according to the nature of their need.

We are most effectively consoled—and it is right to speak of this here, even though briefly—when We see that devotion to the Blessed Sacrament of the Altar is increasing day by day, not only in the souls of the faithful, but also in what has to do with the splendor of the divine worship, which has often been made evident in public popular demonstrations. The careful directions of Sovereign Pontiffs have doubtless contributed a great deal to this effect, and especially that of the Blessed Pius X who, summoning all to renew the primitive custom of the Church, urged them to receive the Bread of Angels very frequently, even daily if possible.[17] Inviting the little ones to this heavenly food, he wisely decreed that the precept of holy Confession and Holy Communion has reference to every one of those who have reached the use of reason.[18] This same rule is prescribed in the Code of Canon Law.[19] The faithful responding generously and willingly to these directions of the Sovereign Pontiffs, have approached ever more frequently to the sacred Table. May this hunger for the heavenly Bread and the thirst for the Sacred Blood burn in all men of every age and of every walk of life!

It should, nevertheless, be noted that the times in which we live and their peculiar conditions have brought many modifications in the habits of society and in the activities of common life. Out of these there may arise serious difficulties which could keep men from partaking of the divine mysteries if the law of the Eucharistic fast is to be observed in the way in which it had to be observed up to the present time.

In the first place, it is evident to all that today the clergy are not sufficiently numerous to cope with the increasingly serious needs of the faithful. Especially on feast days they are subject to overwork, when they have to offer the Eucharistic Sacrifice at a late hour and frequently twice or three times the same day, and when at times they are forced to travel a great distance so as not to leave considerable portions of their flocks without Holy Mass. Such tiring apostolic work undoubtedly weakens the health of priests. This is all the more true because, over and above the offering of the Holy Mass and the explanation of the Gospel, they must likewise hear confession, give catechetical instruction, devote ever-increasing care and take ever more pains in completing the duties of the other parts of their ministry. They must also diligently look after those matters that are demanded by the warfare against God and His Church, a warfare that has grown so widespread and bitter at the present time.

Now our mind and heart go out to those especially who, working far from their own native country in far distant lands, have generously answered the invitation and the command of the Lord: "Go, therefore, and make disciples of all nations."[20] We are speaking of the heralds of the Gospel who, overcoming the most difficult and multitudinous labors and all manner of difficulty in traveling, strive with all their might to have the light of the Christian religion illumine all, and to nourish their flocks, who but very recently received the Catholic faith, with the Bread of Angels which nourishes virtue and fosters piety.

Almost in the same situation are those Catholics who, living in many localities cared for by Catholic missionaries, or who, living in other places and not having among them their own priests, must wait until a late hour for the coming of another priest that they may partake of the Eucharist and nourish themselves with the divine Food.

Furthermore, since the introduction of machines for every sort of use, it very often happens that many workers—in factories, or in the land and water transportation fields, or in other public utility services—are employed not only during the day, but even during the night, in alternate shifts. As a result, their weakened condition compels them at times to take some nourishment. But, in this way, they are prevented from approaching the Eucharist fasting.

Mothers also are often unable to approach the Eucharist before they take care of their household duties, duties that demand of them many hours of work.

In the same way, it happens that there are many boys and girls in school who desire to respond to the divine invitation: 'Let the little children come to me."[21] They are entirely confident that "He who dwells among the lilies" will protect their innocence of soul and purity of life against the enticements to which youth is subjected, the snares of the world. But at times it is most difficult for them, before going to school, to go to church and be nourished with the Bread of Angels and then return home to partake of the food they need.

Furthermore, it should be noted that it often happens, at the present time, that great crowds of people travel from one place to another in the afternoon hours to take part in religious celebrations or to hold meetings on social questions. Now, if on these occasions it were allowed to offer the Eucharistic Sacrifice, which is the living Fruit of divine grace and which commands our will to burn with the desire of acquiring virtue, there is no doubt that strength could be drawn from this by which all would be stirred profoundly to think and act in a Christian manner and to obey legitimate laws.

To these special considerations it seems opportune to add some which have reference to all. Although in our days medical science and that study which is called hygiene have made great progress and have helped greatly to cut down the number of deaths, especially among the young, nevertheless conditions of life at the present time and the hardships which flow from the cruel wars of this century are of such nature that they have greatly weakened bodily constitution and health.

For these reasons, and especially so that renewed piety towards the Eucharist may be all the more readily increased, many Bishops from various countries have asked, in official letters, that this law of fast be somewhat mitigated. Actually, the Apostolic See has kindly granted special faculties and permissions, in this regard, to both priests and faithful. As regards these concessions, We can cite the Decree, entitled, "*Post Editum*," given for the sick by the Sacred Congregation of the Council, December 7, 1906;[22] and the Letter of the 22nd of May, 1923, from the Sacred Congregation of the Holy Office to the local Ordinaries in favor of priests.[23]

In these latter days, the petitions of the Bishops have become more frequent and urgent, and the faculties granted were more ample, especially those that were bestowed in view of the war. This, without doubt, clearly indicates that there are new and grave reasons, reasons that are not occasional but rather general, because of which it is very difficult, in these diversified circumstances, both for the priest to celebrate the Eucharistic Sacrifice, and for the faithful to receive the Bread of Angels fasting.

Wherefore, that we may meet these grave inconveniences and difficulties, that the different indults may not lead to inconsistent practice, We have deemed it necessary to lay down the discipline of the Eucharistic fast, by mitigating it in such a way that, in the greatest manner possible, all, in view of the peculiar circumstances of time, place, and the faithful, may be able to fulfill this law more easily. We, by this decree, trust that We may be able to add not a little to the increase of Eucharistic piety, and in this way to move and stir up all to partake at the Table of the Angels. This, without doubt, will increase the glory of God and the holiness of the Mystical Body of Christ.

By Our Apostolic authority We decree and command all the following:

I. The law of the Eucharistic fast from midnight continues in force for all of those who do not come under the special conditions which We are going to set forth in this Apostolic Letter. In the future it shall be a general and common principle for all, both priests and faithful, that natural water does not break the Eucharistic fast.

II. The sick, even when they are not confined to bed, can, on the prudent advice of a confessor, take something in the form of beverage or of true medicine. This does not hold for alcoholic beverages. The same faculty is given to sick priests who are going to say Mass.

III. Priests who are going to say Mass at late hours, or after onerous work of the sacred ministry, or after a long journey, can take something by way of beverage. They cannot take alcoholic beverages. They should abstain, however, for the space of one hour before they say Mass.

IV. Those who say Mass twice or three times can consume the ablutions. In such cases, however, the ablution must be made with water alone, not with wine.

V. Likewise the faithful, even those not sick, who by reason of some serious inconvenience—that is, by reason of tiring work, by reason of the late hours at which alone it is possible for them to attend Mass, or by reason of a long journey which they must take—could not approach the Eucharistic table completely fasting, can, on the advice of a prudent confessor, while the need lasts, take something to drink, to the exclusion of alcoholic beverages, but they must abstain at least for the space of one hour before they are nourished by the Bread of Angels.

VI. If the circumstance calls for it as necessary, We grant to the local Ordinaries the right to permit the celebration of Mass in the evening, as we said, but in such wise that the Mass shall not begin before four o'clock in the afternoon, on holy days of obligation still observed, on those which formerly were observed, on the first Friday of every month, and also on those days on which solemn celebrations are held with a large attendance, and also, in addition to these days, on one day a week; with the requirement that the priest observe a fast of three hours from solid food and alcoholic beverages, and of one hour from non-alcoholic beverages. At these Masses the faithful may approach the Holy Table, observing the same rule as regards the Eucharistic fast, the presumption of Canon 857 remaining in force.

In mission territories, in consideration of the very unusual conditions there prevailing, on account of which it often happens that there are only a few priests to visit the distant missions, the local Ordinaries can grant to the preachers of the Gospel faculties to celebrate evening Masses on other days of the week also.

Local Ordinaries shall carefully see that every interpretation is avoided that would stretch these faculties and that all abuse and irreverence in this matter is prevented. For in granting these faculties which the conditions of persons, places and times demand today, We ardently desire to emphasize the force and the value of the Eucharistic fast for those who are to receive our Divine Redeemer hidden under the Eucharistic veils. Besides, as often as the inconvenience of the body is diminished, the soul must supply as far as it can, either by internal penance or by other means, in accordance with the traditional custom of the Church which is wont to command other works to be done when it mitigates the fast. Hence, those who may enjoy the faculties granted in this matter should raise fervent prayers to heaven to adore God, to thank Him, and especially to expiate for sins and beg Him for new heavenly aid. Since all must recognize that the Eucharist "has been instituted as the permanent memorial of the Passion,[24] let them from their hearts elicit those sentiments of Christian humility and Christian patience which meditation on the sufferings and death of our Divine Redeemer must arouse. Also, to our Divine Redeemer who, ever immolating Himself on our altars is repeating the greatest proof of His love, let all offer increased fruits of charity toward their neighbors. For this reason all shall cooperate toward daily fulfilling the words of the Apostle of the Gentiles: "Because the bread is one, we though many, are one body, all of us who partake of the one bread."[25]

Whatever decrees are contained in this letter we wish to be stable, ratified and valid, notwithstanding anything to the contrary, even what may be worthy of most special mention. All other privileges and faculties, in whatever way they may have been granted by the Holy See, are abolished, so that all may everywhere properly and equally observe this legislation.

All that has been decreed above shall be in force from the day of promulgation through the [*Acta Apostolicae Sedis*].

Given at St. Pete's in Rome, January 6, 1953, the Feast of the Epiphany, in the fourteenth year of our Pontificate.

POPE PIUS XII.

AN INSTRUCTION ON THE DISCIPLINE TO BE OBSERVED WITH REFERENCE TO THE EUCHARISTIC FAST

Issued by the Sacred Congregation of the Holy Office on January 6, 1953.

The Apostolic Constitution "Christus Dominus," issued today by the Sovereign Pontiff Pius XII happily reigning, grants several faculties and dispensations with respect to the observance of the law of the Eucharistic fast. It also confirms, in great measure and substantially, the rules of the Code of Canon Law[26] for the priests and the faithful able to observe that law of the Eucharistic fast. Nevertheless, the favorable first order of this Constitution, according to which natural water (that is, without the addition of any element) no longer breaks the Eucharistic fast (Const., Rule I), is extended to these also. But, with regard to the other concessions, these can be used only by priests and by the faithful who find themselves in the conditions described in the Constitution, or by those who say evening Masses or receive Holy Communion at such Masses authorized by the Ordinaries within the limits of the new faculties granted to them.

And so, in order that the rules with regard to such concessions may be observed uniformly everywhere, in order to avoid any interpretation which would make these faculties appear more extensive than they really are, and in order to prevent every abuse in this matter, this Supreme Sacred Congregation of the Holy Office, at the direction and by the command of the Sovereign Pontiff himself, has issued the following:

With Regard to the Sick, Either the Priests or the Faithful (Rule II of the Constitution)

1. The faithful who are sick, even though not confined to bed, may take something in the form of beverage, though not an alcoholic beverage, if, by reason of their sickness they cannot, without real inconvenience, observe a complete fast up to the time they receive Holy Communion. They can also take something in the line of medicine, either liquid (but not alcoholic), or solid, as long as what they take is real medicine, prescribed by a physician or commonly esteemed as such. It must be noted that any solid taken as nourishment cannot be considered as medicine.

2. The conditions under which a person may be able to take advantage of this dispensation from the law of fasting for which no time limit preceding Holy Communion is prescribed must be judged very prudently by the confessor. Without his advice no one can use this dispensation. The confessor, however, can give his advice either when he is hearing confessions or privately apart from the confessional. He may also give this advice once so that the person to whom he gives it may always act upon it as long as the conditions of this same sickness last.

3. Sick priests, even though they are not confined to their beds, may use a like dispensation if they are going to say Mass or receive the Holy Eucharist.

With Regard to Priests Placed in Special Circumstances (Constitution, Rules III and IV)

4. Priests who are not sick, but who are going to say Mass

> a. at a late hour (that is, after nine o'clock),

> b. after onerous work of the sacred ministry (for example, from early in the morning or for a long time), or

> c. after a long journey (that is, at least about two kilometers walking or a proportionally longer trip in terms of the classes of vehicles used, the difficulties of the journey, and the condition of the person), may take something in the form of drink, but not any alcoholic beverage.

5. The three cases indicated above are such as to take in all the circumstances in which the legislator intends to grant the above-mentioned faculty. Consequently every interpretation which would make these faculties seem more extensive must be avoided.

6. Priests who are in such circumstances can take something in the line of drink one or many times, but they must keep the fast for one hour before they say Mass.

7. Moreover, all priests who are going to say Mass twice or three times the same day can, in the earlier Masses, consume the two ablutions prescribed by the rubrics of the Missal, but using only the water which, according to the new principle, does not break the fast.

The priest who says three Masses, one after the other, on Christmas or on All Souls Day is bound to follow the rubrics with regard to the ablutions.

8. If it should happen that a priest who is obliged to say Mass two or three times the same day should inadvertently consume wine in the ablution, he is not prevented from saying the second and the third Mass.

With Regard to the Faithful Placed in Special Circumstances (Constitution, Rule V)

9. Likewise the faithful who are unable to keep the Eucharistic fast, not by reason of sickness, but because of some serious difficulty, can take something in the line of drink. They cannot, however, take any alcoholic beverage, and they must fast for an hour before the reception of Holy Communion.

10. The cases of serious difficulty (*gravis incommodi*) are these three. It is wrong to add any others.

> a. Work that weakens, started before Holy Communion. Such as the function of laborers in factories, transport and dock workers, or workers in other public utilities employed in day and night shifts; or those who, by reason of duty or of charity, must stay awake during the night (for example, nurses, night watchmen, etc.); and of pregnant women and mothers of families who must spend a long time on their household duties before they can go to Church, etc.

> b. The late hour at which Holy Communion is received. There are many of the faithful who can have a priest to say Mass among them only at a late hour. There are likewise

many children for whom it would be too difficult, before going to school, to go to the Church, receive Holy Communion, and then to go back home to eat breakfast, etc.

c. A long journey which must be made in order to reach the Church. As has been explained above (n. 4), a trip is to be considered long for this purpose if it covers a walk of about a mile and a quarter, or a journey that is longer in proportion to the vehicles used, the difficulty of the journey itself, or the condition of the person making the journey.

11. The nature of such serious difficulty must be judged prudently by a confessor either while he is hearing confessions or in a private conversation with the one seeking advice. The faithful cannot receive the Holy Eucharist not fasting without the confessor's advice. The confessor can give his advice once and for all, to be effective as long as the cause of the serious difficulty remains.

With Reference to Evening Masses
(Constitution, Rule VI)

By the force of the Constitution the Ordinaries of places[27] have the faculty of permitting the saying of evening Masses in their own territory, should circumstances render this necessary. This holds true despite the command of canon 821, #1. The common good sometimes demands the saying of Mass after midday: For example, for the workers in some industries who work their shifts even on feast days, for those categories of workers who must be on the job during the morning hours of feast days, like dock workers, and likewise for those who have come in great numbers and from considerable distances for some religious or social celebration, etc.

12. Such Masses, however, may not be said before four o'clock in the afternoon, and may be celebrated only on the following definitely stated days. These are:

a. Holy days of obligation according to the rule of Canon 1247, #1;

b. Feasts which were formerly holy days of obligation but which now are not. These are listed in the index published by the Sacred Congregation of the Council on December 28, 1919.[28]

c. First Fridays of the month.

d. Other solemn occasions which are celebrated with great gatherings of the people.

e. On one day of the week other than those enumerated above, if the good of special classes of persons should demand it.

13. Priests who say afternoon Masses, as well as the faithful who receive Holy Communion at these Masses, may, at the meal which is permitted up to three hours before the beginning of Mass or Communion, take with due moderation the alcoholic beverages which are ordinarily taken at meals, (for example, wine, beer, and the like). They may not take strong liquors. With regard to beverages, which can be taken before or after the above-mentioned meal, up to one hour before Mass or Communion, everything alcoholic is excluded.

14. Priests may not say a morning and an evening Mass on the same day unless they have the explicit permission to say Mass twice or three times the same day, according to the rule of canon 806.

Likewise the faithful cannot receive Holy Communion in the morning and the evening of the same day, according to the norm of canon 857.

15. The faithful, even though they may not be of the number of those for whom the offering of an evening Mass was decreed, may freely receive Holy Communion, at this Mass or immediately before it (cf. Can. 846, # 1), or immediately after it, if they obey the directions given above with reference to the Eucharistic fast.

16. In places where the law for the missions rather than the general law is in force, the Ordinaries may permit evening Masses on all the days of the week under the same conditions.

Admonitions on the Observance of the Rules

17. Ordinaries must carefully see to it that every abuse and irreverence towards the Blessed Sacrament is entirely avoided.

18. They must also take care that the new discipline be observed uniformly by all their subjects, and they must teach these subjects that all faculties and dispensations, both territorial and personal, which have hitherto been granted by the Holy See, have been revoked.

19. The interpretation of the Constitution and of this Instruction must faithfully keep to the text, and must not in any way enlarge the highly favorable faculties which have been granted. With regard to customs which may differ from the new discipline, let the abrogating clause be

kept in mind: "Notwithstanding any disposition whatever to the contrary, even those worthy of most special mention."

20. The Ordinaries and the priests, who ought to take advantage of these faculties granted by the Holy See, should zealously stir up the faithful to assist at Mass and receive Holy Communion frequently. They should take advantage of every opportunity, especially by preaching, to promote the spiritual good for the sake of which the Sovereign Pontiff Pius XII has published the Constitution.

The Sovereign Pontiff, approving this Instruction, decreed that it should be promulgated by publication in the [*Acta Apostolicae Sedis*], together with the Apostolic Constitution [*Christus Dominus*].

From the Palace of the Holy Office, on the 6th day of January, in the year 1953.

S./S/ JOSEPH CARDINAL PIZZARDO, Secretary. L./S/ ALFREDO ottaviani, Assessor.

ENDNOTES

1. Cor., 11-23.

2. Cf. Luke, 22:20.

3. I Cor., 11:24.

4. Matt., 26:28.

5. Cf. I Cor., 11:24 f.

6. Cf. the Hymn "*Lauda Sion*" in the Roman Missal.

7. Cf. Pope Benedict XIV, [*De synodo diocesano*], 6, cap. 8, n. 10.

8. Conc. Hipp., can. 28: [*Mansi*], III, 923.

9. Conc. Carth. III, cap. 29: [*Mansi*], III, 885.

10 Cf. St. Augustine, Ep. 54, [*Ad Jan.*], cap. 6: [*Migne*], PL, 33, 203.

11. Cf. I Cor., 11-21 ff.

12. St. Augustine, [*loc. cit.*]

13. Conc. Tolet. VII, cap. 2: [*Mansi*], X, 768.

14. Con. Bracar. III, can. 10; [*Mansi*], IX, 841.

15. Conc. Matiscon. II, can 6: [*Mansi*], IX, 952.

16. Conc. Constant. sess. XIII: [*Mansi*], XXVII, 727.

17. *S. Congr. Concilii, Decretum "Sacra Tridentina Synodus,"* Dec. 20, 1905: [Acta S. Sedis] XVIII, 400 ff.

18. *S. Congr. de Sac., Decretum "Quam singulari,"* Aug. 8, 1910: AAS, II 577 ff.

19. CIC, can. 863; cf. can. 854, # 5.

20. Matth. 28, 19.

21. Mark 10. 14.

22. [*Acta S. Sedis*], XXXIX, p. 603 ff.

23. *S. S. Congregationis S. Officii Litterae Locorum Ordinariis datae super ieiunio eucharistico ante Missam*: AAS, XV, p. 151 ff.

24. S. Thom., [*Opusc*]. LVII, Office for the Feast of Corpus Christi, 4th lesson: [*Opera Omnia,*] Rome, 1570, vol. XVII.

25. I Cor., 10:17.

26 Can. 808 and 858. # 1.

27. Cf. can. 198

28. AAS, XII, 1920, 42 f.

Musicae Sacrae:
Encyclical on Sacred Music

Pope Pius XII
December 25, 1955

To Our Venerable Brethren, the Patriarchs, Primates, Archbishops, Bishops, and other Local Ordinaries in Peace and Communion with the Apostolic See: Health and Apostolic Benediction.

The subject of sacred music has always been very close to Our heart. Hence, it has seemed appropriate to us in this encyclical letter to give an orderly explanation of the topic and also to answer somewhat more completely several questions which have been raised and discussed during the past decades. We are doing so in order that this noble and distinguished art may contribute more every day to greater splendor in the celebration of divine worship and to the more effective nourishment of spiritual life among the faithful.

2. At the same time We have desired to grant what many of you, venerable brethren, have requested in our wisdom and also what has been asked by outstanding masters of this liberal art and distinguished students of sacred music at meetings devoted to the subject. The experience of pastoral life and the advances being made in the study of this art have persuaded Us that this step is timely.

3. We hope, therefore, that what St. Pius X rightly decreed in the document which he accurately called the "legal code of sacred music"[1] may be confirmed and inculcated anew, shown in a new light and strengthened by new proofs. We hope that the noble art of sacred music—adapted to contemporary conditions and in some way enriched—may ever more perfectly accomplish its mission.

4. Music is among the many and great gifts of nature with which God, in Whom is the harmony of the most perfect concord and the most perfect order, has enriched men, whom He has created in His image and likeness.[2] Together with the other liberal arts, music contributes to spiritual joy and the delight of the soul.

5. On this subject St. Augustine has accurately written: "Music, that is the science or the sense of proper modulation, is likewise given by God's generosity to mortals having rational souls in order to lead them to higher things."[3]

6. No one, therefore, will be astonished that always and everywhere, even among pagan peoples, sacred song and the art of music have been used to ornament and decorate religious ceremonies. This is proved by many documents, both ancient and new. No one will be astonished that these arts have been used especially for the worship of the true and sovereign God from the earliest times. Miraculously preserved unharmed from the Red Sea by God's power, the people of God sang a song of victory to the Lord, and Miriam, the sister of Moses, their leader, endowed with prophetic inspiration, sang with the people while playing a tambourine.[4]

7. Later, when the ark of God was taken from the house of Abinadab to the city of David, the king himself and "all Israel played before the Lord on all manner of instruments made of wood, on harps and lutes and timbrels and cornets and cymbals."[5] King David himself established the order of the music and singing used for sacred worship.[6] This order was restored after the people's return from exile and was observed faithfully until the Divine Redeemer's coming.

8. St. Paul showed us clearly that sacred chant was used and held in honor from the very beginning in the Church founded by the Divine Redeemer when he wrote to the Ephesians: "Be filled with the Spirit, speaking to one another in psalms and hymns and spiritual songs."[7] He indicates that this custom of singing hymns was in force in the assemblies of Christians when he says: "When you come together each of you has a hymn."[8]

9. Pliny testifies that the same thing held true after apostolic times. He writes that apostates from the Faith said that "this was their greatest fault or error, that they were accustomed to gather before dawn on a certain day and sing a hymn to Christ as if He were God."[9] These words of the Roman proconsul in Bithynia show very clearly that the sound of church singing was not completely silenced even in times of persecution.

10. Tertullian confirms this when he says that in the assemblies of the Christians "the Scriptures are read, the psalms are sung, sermons are preached."[10]

11. There are many statements of the fathers and ecclesiastical writers testifying that after freedom and peace had been restored to the Church the psalms and hymns of liturgical worship were in almost daily use. Moreover, new forms of sacred chant were gradually created and new types of songs were invented. These were developed more and more by the choir schools attached to cathedrals and other important churches, especially by the School of Singers in Rome.

12. According to tradition, Our predecessor of happy memory, St. Gregory the Great, carefully collected and wisely arranged all that had been handed down by the elders and protected the purity and integrity of sacred chant with fitting laws and regulations.

13. From Rome, the Roman mode of singing gradually spread to other parts of the West. Not only was it enriched by new forms and modes, but a new kind of sacred singing, the religious song, frequently sung in the vernacular, was also brought into use.

14. The choral chant began to be called "Gregorian" after St. Gregory, the man who revived it. It attained new beauty in almost all parts of Christian Europe after the 8th or 9th century because of its accompaniment by a new musical instrument called the "organ." Little by little, beginning in the 9th century, polyphonic singing was added to this choral chant. The study and use of polyphonic singing were developed more and more during the centuries that followed and were raised to a marvelous perfection under the guidance of magnificent composers during the 15th and 16th centuries.

15. Since the Church always held this polyphonic chant in the highest esteem, it willingly admitted this type of music even in the Roman basilicas and in pontifical ceremonies in order to increase the glory of the sacred rites. Its power and splendor were increased when the sounds of the organ and other musical instruments were joined with the voices of the singers.

16. Thus, with the favor and under the auspices of the Church the study of sacred music has gone a long way over the course of the centuries. In this journey, although sometimes slowly and laboriously, it has gradually progressed from the simple and ingenuous Gregorian

modes to great and magnificent works of art. To these works not only the human voice, but also the organ and other musical instruments, add dignity, majesty and a prodigious richness.

17. The progress of this musical art clearly shows how sincerely the Church has desired to render divine worship ever more splendid and more pleasing to the Christian people. It likewise shows why the Church must insist that this art remain within its proper limits and must prevent anything profane and foreign to divine worship from entering into sacred music along with genuine progress, and perverting it.

18. The Sovereign Pontiffs have always diligently fulfilled their obligation to be vigilant in this matter. The Council of Trent also forbids "those musical works in which something lascivious or impure is mixed with organ music or singing."[11] In addition, not to mention numerous other Sovereign Pontiffs, Our predecessor Benedict XIV of happy memory in an encyclical letter dated February 19, 1749, which prepared for a Holy Year and was outstanding for its great learning and abundance of proofs, particularly urged Bishops to firmly forbid the illicit and immoderate elements which had arrogantly been inserted into sacred music.[12]

19. Our predecessors Leo XII, Pius VII, Gregory XVI, Pius IX, and Leo XIII[13] followed the same line.

20. Nevertheless it can rightly be said that Our predecessor of immortal memory, St. Pius X, made as it were the highest contribution to the reform and renewal of sacred music when he restated the principles and standards handed down from the elders and wisely brought them together as the conditions of modern times demanded.[14] Finally, like Our immediate predecessor of happy memory, Pius XI, in his Apostolic Constitution *Divini cultus sanctitatem* (The Holiness of Divine Worship), issued December 20, 1929,[15] We ourself in the encyclical *Mediator Dei* (On the Sacred Liturgy), issued November 20, 1947,[16] have enriched and confirmed the orders of the older Pontiffs.

21. Certainly no one will be astonished that the Church is so vigilant and careful about sacred music. It is not a case of drawing up laws of aesthetics or technical rules that apply to the subject of music. It is the intention of the Church, however, to protect sacred music against

anything that might lessen its dignity, since it is called upon to take part in something as important as divine worship.

22. On this score sacred music obeys laws and rules which are no different from those prescribed for all religious art and, indeed, for art in general. Now we are aware of the fact that during recent years some artists, gravely offending against Christian piety, have dared to bring into churches works devoid of any religious inspiration and completely at variance with the right rules of art. They try to justify this deplorable conduct by plausible-looking arguments which they claim are based on the nature and character of art itself. They go on to say that artistic inspiration is free and that it is wrong to impose upon it laws and standards extraneous to art, whether they are religious or moral, since such rules seriously hurt the dignity of art and place bonds and shackles on the activity of an inspired artist.

23. Arguments of this kind raise a question which is certainly difficult and serious, and which affects all art and every artist. It is a question which is not to be answered by an appeal to the principles of art or of aesthetics, but which must be decided in terms of the supreme principle of the final end, which is the inviolate and sacred rule for every man and every human act.

24. The ordination and direction of man to his ultimate end—which is God—by absolute and necessary law based on the nature and the infinite perfection of God Himself is so solid that not even God could exempt anyone from it. This eternal and unchangeable law commands that man himself and all his actions should manifest and imitate, so far as possible, God's infinite perfection for the praise and glory of the Creator. Since man is born to attain this supreme end, he ought to conform himself and through his actions direct all powers of his body and his soul, rightly ordered among themselves and duly subjected to the end they are meant to attain, to the divine Model. Therefore even art and works of art must be judged in the light of their conformity and concord with man's last end.

25. Art certainly must be listed among the noblest manifestations of human genius. Its purpose is to express in human works the infinite divine beauty of which it is, as it were, the reflection. Hence, that outworn dictum "art for art's sake" entirely neglects the end for which every creature is made. Some people wrongly assert that art should be exempted entirely from every rule which does not spring from art

itself. Thus, this dictum either has no worth at all or is gravely offensive to God Himself, the Creator and Ultimate End.

26. Since the freedom of the artist is not a blind instinct to act in accordance with his own whim or some desire for novelty, it is in no way restricted or destroyed, but actually ennobled and perfected, when it is made subject to the divine law.

27. Since this is true of works of art in general, it obviously applies also to religious and sacred art. Actually religious art is even more closely bound to God and the promotion of His praise and glory, because its only purpose is to give the faithful the greatest aid in turning their minds piously to God through the works it directs to their senses of sight and hearing. Consequently the artist who does not profess the truths of the faith or who strays far from God in his attitude or conduct should never turn his hand to religious art. He lacks, as it were, that inward eye with which he might see what God's majesty and His worship demand. Nor can he hope that his works, devoid of religion as they are, will ever really breathe the piety and faith that befit God's temple and His holiness, even though they may show him to be an expert artist who is endowed with visible talent. Thus, he cannot hope that his works will be worthy of admission into the sacred buildings of the Church, the guardian and arbiter of religious life.

28. But the artist who is firm in his faith and leads a life worthy of a Christian, who is motivated by the love of God and reverently uses the powers the Creator has given him, expresses and manifests the truths he holds and the piety he possesses so skillfully, beautifully and pleasingly in colors and lines or sounds and harmonies that this sacred labor of art is an act of worship and religion for him. It also effectively arouses and inspires people to profess the faith and cultivate piety.

29. The Church has always honored and always will honor this kind of artist. It opens wide the doors of its temples to them because what these people contribute through their art and industry is a welcome and important help to the Church in carrying out its apostolic ministry more effectively.

30. These laws and standards for religious art apply in a stricter and holier way to sacred music because sacred music enters more intimately into divine worship than many other liberal arts, such as

architecture, painting, and sculpture. These last serve to prepare a worthy setting for the sacred ceremonies. Sacred music, however, has an important place in the actual performance of the sacred ceremonies and rites themselves. Hence, the Church must take the greatest care to prevent whatever might be unbecoming to sacred worship or anything that might distract the faithful in attendance from lifting their minds up to God from entering into sacred music, which is the servant, as it were, of the sacred liturgy.

31. The dignity and lofty purpose of sacred music consist in the fact that its lovely melodies and splendor beautify and embellish the voices of the priest who offers Mass and of the Christian people who praise the Sovereign God. Its special power and excellence should lift up to God the minds of the faithful who are present. It should make the liturgical prayers of the Christian community more alive and fervent so that everyone can praise and beseech the Triune God more powerfully, more intently and more effectively.

32. The power of sacred music increases the honor given to God by the Church in union with Christ, its Head. Sacred music likewise helps to increase the fruits which the faithful, moved by the sacred harmonies, derive from the holy liturgy. These fruits, as daily experience and many ancient and modern literary sources show, manifest themselves in a life and conduct worthy of a Christian.

33. St. Augustine, speaking of chants characterized by "beautiful voice and most apt melody," says: "I feel that our souls are moved to the ardor of piety by the sacred words more piously and powerfully when these words are sung than when they are not sung, and that all the affections of our soul in their variety have modes of their own in song and chant by which they are stirred up by an indescribable and secret sympathy."[17]

34. It is easy to infer from what has just been said that the dignity and force of sacred music are greater the closer sacred music itself approaches to the supreme act of Christian worship, the Eucharistic sacrifice of the altar. There can be nothing more exalted or sublime than its function of accompanying with beautiful sound the voice of the priest offering up the Divine Victim, answering him joyfully with the people who are present and enhancing the whole liturgical ceremony with its noble art.

35. To this highest function of sacred music We must add another which closely resembles it, that is its function of accompanying and beautifying other liturgical ceremonies, particularly the recitation of the Divine Office in choir. Thus, the highest honor and praise must be given to liturgical music.

36. We must also hold in honor that music which is not primarily a part of the sacred liturgy, but which by its power and purpose greatly aids religion. This music is therefore rightly called religious music. The Church has possessed such music from the beginning and it has developed happily under the Church's auspices. As experience shows, it can exercise great and salutary force and power on the souls of the faithful, both when it is used in churches during non-liturgical services and ceremonies, or when it is used outside churches at various solemnities and celebrations.

37. The tunes of these hymns, which are often sung in the language of the people, are memorized with almost no effort or labor. The mind grasps the words and the music. They are frequently repeated and completely understood. Hence, even boys and girls, learning these sacred hymns at a tender age, are greatly helped by them to know, appreciate, and memorize the truths of the faith. Therefore they also serve as a sort of catechism. These religious hymns bring pure and chaste joy to young people and adults during times of recreation. They give a kind of religious grandeur to their more solemn assemblies and gatherings. They bring pious joy, sweet consolation, and spiritual progress to Christian families themselves. Hence, these popular religious hymns are of great help to the Catholic apostolate and should be carefully cultivated and promoted.

38. Therefore when We praised the manifold power and the apostolic effectiveness of sacred music, We spoke of something that can be a source of great joy and solace to all who have in any way dedicated themselves to its study and practice. All who use the art they possess to compose such musical compositions, to teach them or to perform them by singing or using musical instruments, undoubtedly exercise in many ways a true and genuine apostolate. They will receive from Christ the Lord the generous rewards and honors of apostles for the work they have done so faithfully.

39. Consequently they should hold their work in high esteem, not only as artists and teachers of art, but also as ministers of Christ the Lord and as His helpers in the work of the apostolate. They should

likewise show in their conduct and their lives the dignity of their calling.

40. Since, as We have just shown, the dignity and effectiveness of sacred music and religious chant are so great, it is very necessary that all of their parts should be diligently and carefully arranged to produce their salutary results in a fitting manner.

41. First of all the chants and sacred music which are immediately joined with the Church's liturgical worship should be conducive to the lofty end for which they are intended. This music—as our predecessor Pius X has already wisely warned us—"must possess proper liturgical qualities, primarily holiness and goodness of form; from which its other note, universality, is derived."[18]

42. It must be holy. It must not allow within itself anything that savors of the profane nor allow any such thing to slip into the melodies in which it is expressed. The Gregorian chant which has been used in the Church over the course of so many centuries, and which may be called, as it were, its patrimony, is gloriously outstanding for this holiness.

43. This chant, because of the close adaptation of the melody to the sacred text, is not only most intimately conformed to the words, but also in a way interprets their force and efficacy and brings delight to the minds of the hearers. It does this by the use of musical modes that are simple and plain, but which are still composed with such sublime and holy art that they move everyone to sincere admiration and constitute an almost inexhaustible source from which musicians and composers draw new melodies.

44. It is the duty of all those to whom Christ the Lord has entrusted the task of guarding and dispensing the Church's riches to preserve this precious treasure of Gregorian chant diligently and to impart it generously to the Christian people. Hence, what Our predecessors, St. Pius X, who is rightly called the renewer of Gregorian chant,[19] and Pius XI[20] have wisely ordained and taught, We also, in view of the outstanding qualities which genuine Gregorian chant possesses, will and prescribe that this be done. In the performance of the sacred liturgical rites this same Gregorian chant should be most widely used and great care should be taken that it should be performed properly, worthily, and reverently. And if, because of recently instituted feast days, new Gregorian melodies must be composed, this should be done

by true masters of the art. It should be done in such a way that these new compositions obey the laws proper to genuine Gregorian chant and are in worthy harmony with the older melodies in their virtue and purity.

45. If these prescriptions are really observed in their entirety, the requirements of the other property of sacred music—that property by virtue of which it should be an example of true art—will be duly satisfied. And if in Catholic churches throughout the entire world Gregorian chant sounds forth without corruption or diminution, the chant itself, like the sacred Roman liturgy, will have a characteristic of universality, so that the faithful, wherever they may be, will hear music that is familiar to them and a part of their own home. In this way they may experience, with much spiritual consolation, the wonderful unity of the Church. This is one of the most important reasons why the Church so greatly desires that the Gregorian chant traditionally associated with the Latin words of the sacred liturgy be used.

46. We are not unaware that, for serious reasons, some quite definite exceptions have been conceded by the Apostolic See. We do not want these exceptions extended or propagated more widely, nor do We wish to have them transferred to other places without due permission of the Holy See. Furthermore, even where it is licit to use these exemptions, local Ordinaries and the other pastors should take great care that the faithful from their earliest years should learn at least the easier and more frequently used Gregorian melodies, and should know how to employ them in the sacred liturgical rites, so that in this way also the unity and the universality of the Church may shine forth more powerfully every day.

47. Where, according to old or immemorial custom, some popular hymns are sung in the language of the people after the sacred words of the liturgy have been sung in Latin during the solemn Eucharistic sacrifice, local Ordinaries can allow this to be done "if, in the light of the circumstances of the locality and the people, they believe that (custom) cannot prudently be removed."[21] The law by which it is forbidden to sing the liturgical words themselves in the language of the people remains in force, according to what has been said.

48. In order that singers and the Christian people may rightly understand the meaning of the liturgical words joined to the musical melodies, it has pleased Us to make Our own the exhortation made by

the Fathers of the Council of Trent. "Pastors and all those who have care of souls," were especially urged that "often, during the celebration of Mass, they or others whom they delegate explain something about what is read in the Mass and, among other things, tell something about the mystery of this most holy sacrifice. This is to be done particularly on Sundays and holy days."[22]

49. This should be done especially at the time when catechetical instruction is being given to the Christian people. This may be done more easily and readily in this age of ours than was possible in times past, because translations of the liturgical texts into the vernacular tongues and explanations of these texts in books and pamphlets are available. These works, produced in almost every country by learned writers, can effectively help and enlighten the faithful to understand and share in what is said by the sacred ministers in the Latin language.

50. It is quite obvious that what We have said briefly here about Gregorian chant applies mainly to the Latin Roman Rite of the Church. It can also, however, be applied to a certain extent to the liturgical chants of other rites—either to those of the West, such as the Ambrosian, Gallican, or Mozarabic, or to the various eastern rites.

51. For as all of these display in their liturgical ceremonies and formulas of prayer the marvelous abundance of the Church, they also, in their various liturgical chants, preserve treasures which must be guarded and defended to prevent not only their complete disappearance, but also any partial loss or distortion.

52. Among the oldest and most outstanding monuments of sacred music the liturgical chants of the different eastern rites hold a highly important place. Some of the melodies of these chants, modified in accordance with the character of the Latin liturgy, had a great influence on the composition of the musical works of the Western Church itself. It is Our hope that the selection of sacred eastern rite hymns—which the Pontifical Institute of Oriental Studies, with the help of the Pontifical Institute of Sacred Music, is busily working to complete—will achieve good doctrinal and practical results. Thus, eastern rite seminarians, well trained in sacred chant, can make a significant contribution to enhancing the beauty of God's house after they have been ordained priests.

53. It is not Our intention in what We have just said in praise and commendation of the Gregorian chant to exclude sacred polyphonic music from the rites of the Church. If this polyphonic music is endowed with the proper qualities, it can be of great help in increasing the magnificence of divine worship and of moving the faithful to religious dispositions. Everyone certainly knows that many polyphonic compositions, especially those that date from the 16th century, have an artistic purity and richness of melody which render them completely worthy of accompanying and beautifying the Church's sacred rites.

54. Although over the course of the centuries genuine polyphonic art gradually declined and profane melodies often crept into it, during recent decades the indefatigable labors of experts have brought about a restoration. The works of the old composers have been carefully studied and proposed as models to be imitated and rivaled by modern composers.

55. So it is that in the basilicas, cathedrals, and churches of religious communities these magnificent works of the old masters and the polyphonic compositions of more recent musicians can be performed, contributing greatly to the beauty of the sacred rite. Likewise We know that simpler but genuinely artistic polyphonic compositions are often sung even in smaller churches.

56. The Church favors all these enterprises. As Our predecessor of immortal memory, St. Pius X, says, the Church "unceasingly encourages and favors the progress of the arts, admitting for religious use all the good and the beautiful that the mind of man has discovered over the course of the centuries, but always respecting the liturgical laws."[23]

57. These laws warn that great prudence and care should be used in this serious matter in order to keep out of churches polyphonic music which, because of its heavy and bombastic style, might obscure the sacred words of the liturgy by a kind of exaggeration, interfere with the conduct of the liturgical service or, finally, lower the skill and competence of the singers to the disadvantage of sacred worship.

58. These norms must be applied to the use of the organ or other musical instruments. Among the musical instruments that have a place in church the organ rightly holds the principal position, since it is especially fitted for the sacred chants and sacred rites. It adds a

wonderful splendor and a special magnificence to the ceremonies of the Church. It moves the souls of the faithful by the grandeur and sweetness of its tones. It gives minds an almost heavenly joy and it lifts them up powerfully to God and to higher things.

59. Besides the organ, other instruments can be called upon to give great help in attaining the lofty purpose of sacred music, so long as they play nothing profane nothing clamorous or strident and nothing at variance with the sacred services or the dignity of the place. Among these the violin and other musical instruments that use the bow are outstanding because, when they are played by themselves or with other stringed instruments or with the organ, they express the joyous and sad sentiments of the soul with an indescribable power. Moreover, in the encyclical *Mediator Dei*, We Ourselves gave detailed and clear regulations concerning the musical modes that are to be admitted into the worship of the Catholic religion.

60. "For, if they are not profane or unbecoming to the sacredness of the place and function and do not spring from a desire to achieve extraordinary and unusual effects, then our churches must admit them, since they can contribute in no small way to the splendor of the sacred ceremonies, can lift the mind to higher things, and can foster true devotion of the soul."[24]

61. It should hardly be necessary to add the warning that, when the means and talent available are unequal to the task, it is better to forego such attempts than to do something which would be unworthy of divine worship and sacred gatherings.

62. As We have said before, besides those things that are intimately associated with the Church's sacred liturgy, there are also popular religious hymns which derive their origin from the liturgical chant itself. Most of these are written in the language of the people. Since these are closely related to the mentality and temperament of individual national groups, they differ considerably among themselves according to the character of different races and localities.

63. If hymns of this sort are to bring spiritual fruit and advantage to the Christian people, they must be in full conformity with the doctrine of the Catholic faith. They must also express and explain that doctrine accurately. Likewise they must use plain language and simple melody and must be free from violent and vain excess of words. Despite the fact that they are short and easy, they should manifest a religious

dignity and seriousness. When they are fashioned in this way these sacred canticles, born as they are from the most profound depths of the people's soul, deeply move the emotions and spirit and stir up pious sentiments. When they are sung at religious rites by a great crowd of people singing as with one voice, they are powerful in raising the minds of the faithful to higher things.

64. As we have written above, such hymns cannot be used in Solemn High Masses without the express permission of the Holy See. Nevertheless at Masses that are not sung solemnly these hymns can be a powerful aid in keeping the faithful from attending the Holy Sacrifice like dumb and idle spectators. They can help to make the faithful accompany the sacred services both mentally and vocally and to join their own piety to the prayers of the priest. This happens when these hymns are properly adapted to the individual parts of the Mass, as We rejoice to know is being done in many parts of the Catholic world.

65. In rites that are not completely liturgical religious hymns of this kind—when, as We have said, they are endowed with the right qualities—can be of great help in the salutary work of attracting the Christian people and enlightening them, in imbuing them with sincere piety and filling them with holy joy. They can produce these effects not only within churches, but outside of them also, especially on the occasion of pious processions and pilgrimages to shrines and at the time of national or international congresses. They can be especially useful, as experience has shown, in the work of instructing boys and girls in Catholic truth, in societies for youth and in meetings of pious associations.

66. Hence, We can do no less than urge you, venerable brethren, to foster and promote diligently popular religious singing of this kind in the dioceses entrusted to you. There is among you no lack of experts in this field to gather hymns of this sort into one collection, where this has not already been done, so that all of the faithful can learn them more easily, memorize them and sing them correctly.

67. Those in charge of the religious instruction of boys and girls should not neglect the proper use of these effective aids. Those in charge of Catholic youth should make prudent use of them in the highly important work entrusted to them. Thus, there will be hope of happily attaining what everyone desires, namely the disappearance of worldly songs which because of the quality of their melodies or the

frequently voluptuous and lascivious words that go with them are a danger to Christians, especially the young, and their replacement by songs that give chaste and pure pleasure, that foster and increase faith and piety.

68. May it thus come about that the Christian people begin even on this earth to sing that song of praise it will sing forever in heaven: "To Him who sits upon the throne, and to the Lamb, blessing and honor and glory and dominion forever and ever."[25]

69. What we have written thus far applies primarily to those nations where the Catholic religion is already firmly established. In mission lands it will not be possible to accomplish all these things until the number of Christians has grown sufficiently, larger church buildings have been erected, the children of Christians properly attend schools established by the Church and, finally, until there is an adequate number of sacred ministers. Still We urgently exhort apostolic workers who are laboring strenuously in these extensive parts of the Lord's vineyard to pay careful attention to this matter as one of the serious problems of their ministry.

70. Many of the peoples entrusted to the ministry of the missionaries take great delight in music and beautify the ceremonies dedicated to the worship of idols with religious singing. It is not prudent, then, for the heralds of Christ, the true God, to minimize or neglect entirely this effective help in their apostolate. Hence, the preachers of the Gospel in pagan lands should sedulously and willingly promote in the course of their apostolic ministry the love for religious song which is cherished by the men entrusted to their care. In this way these people can have, in contrast to their own religious music which is frequently admired even in cultivated countries, sacred Christian hymns in which the truths of the faith, the life of Christ the Lord, and the praises of the Blessed Virgin Mary and the Saints can be sung in a language and in melodies familiar to them.

71. Missionaries should likewise be mindful of the fact that, from the beginning, when the Catholic Church sent preachers of the Gospel into lands not yet illumined by the light of faith, it took care to bring into those countries, along with the sacred liturgical rites, musical compositions, among which were the Gregorian melodies. It did this so that the people who were to be converted might be more easily led to accept the truths of the Christian religion by the attractiveness of these melodies.

72. So that the desired effect may be produced by what We have recommended and ordered in this encyclical, following in the footsteps of Our predecessors, you, venerable brethren, must carefully use all the aids offered by the lofty function entrusted to you by Christ the Lord and committed to you by the Church. As experience teaches, these aids are employed to great advantage in many churches throughout the Christian world.

73. First of all see to it that there is a good school of singers in the cathedral itself and, as far as possible, in other major churches of your diocese. This school should serve as an example to others and influence them to carefully develop and perfect sacred chant.

74. Where it is impossible to have schools of singers or where there are not enough choir boys, it is allowed that "a group of men and women or girls, located in a place outside the sanctuary set apart for the exclusive use of this group, can sing the liturgical texts at Solemn Mass, as long as the men are completely separated from the women and girls and everything unbecoming is avoided. The Ordinary is bound in conscience in this matter."[26]

75. Great care must be taken that those who are preparing for the reception of sacred orders in your seminaries and in missionary or religious houses of study are properly instructed in the doctrine and use of sacred music and Gregorian chant according to the mind of the Church by teachers who are experts in this field, who esteem the traditional customs and teachings and who are entirely obedient to the precepts and norms of the Holy See.

76. If, among the students in the seminary or religious house of study, anyone shows remarkable facility in or liking for this art, the authorities of the seminary or house of study should not neglect to inform you about it. Then you may avail yourself of the opportunity to cultivate these gifts further and send him either to the Pontifical Institute of Sacred Music in Rome or to some other institution of learning in which this subject is taught, provided that the student manifests the qualities and virtues upon which one can base a hope that he will become an excellent priest.

77. In this matter care must also be taken that local Ordinaries and heads of religious communities have someone whose help they can use in this important area which, weighed down as they are by so many occupations, they cannot easily take care of themselves.

78. It would certainly be best if in diocesan Councils of Christian Art there were someone especially expert in the fields of religious music and chant who could carefully watch over what is being done in the diocese, inform the Ordinary about what has been done and what is going to be done, receive the Ordinary's commands and see that they are obeyed. If in any diocese there is one of these associations, which have been wisely instituted to foster sacred music and have been greatly praised and commended by the Sovereign Pontiffs, the Ordinary in his prudence may employ this association in the task of fulfilling responsibility.

79. Pious associations of this kind, which have been founded to instruct the people in sacred music or for advanced study in this subject, can contribute greatly by words and example to the advance of sacred music.

80. Help and promote such associations, venerable brethren, so that they may lead an active life, may employ the best and the most effective teachers, and so that, throughout the entire diocese, they may diligently promote the knowledge, love and use of sacred music and religious harmonies, with due observance of the Church's laws and due obedience to Ourselves.

81. Moved by paternal solicitude, We have dealt with this matter at some length. We are entirely confident that you, venerable brethren, will diligently apply all of your pastoral solicitude to this sacred subject which contributes so much to the more worthy and magnificent conduct of divine worship.

82. It is Our hope that whoever in the Church supervises and directs the work of sacred music under your leadership may be influenced by Our encyclical letter to carry on this glorious apostolate with new ardor and new effort, generously, enthusiastically and strenuously.

83. Hence, We hope that this most noble art, which has been so greatly esteemed throughout the Church's history and which today has been brought to real heights of holiness and beauty, will be developed and continually perfected and that on its own account it will happily work to bring the children of the Church to give due praise, expressed in worthy melodies and sweet harmonies, to the Triune God with stronger faith, more flourishing hope and more ardent charity.

84. May it produce even outside the walls of churches—in Christian families and gatherings of Christians—what St. Cyprian beautifully spoke of to Donatus, "Let the sober banquet resound with Psalms. And if your memory by good and your voice pleasant, approach this work according to custom. You give more nourishment to those dearest to you if we hear spiritual things and if religious sweetness delights the ears."[27]

85. In the meantime, buoyed up by the hope of richer and more joyous fruits which We are confident will come from this exhortation of Ours, as a testimony of Our good will and as an omen of heavenly gifts to each one of you, venerable brethren, to the flock entrusted to your care and to those who observe Our wishes and work to promote sacred music, with abundant charity, We impart the Apostolic Benediction.

86. Given at St. Peter's in Rome, December 25, on the feast of the Nativity of Our Lord Jesus Christ, in the year 1955, the 17th of Our Pontificate.

REFERENCES:

1. Motu proprio, *Fra le sollecitudini*, Acta Pii X, 1, 77.
2. Cf. Gen. 1.26.
3. Epis. 161. *De origine animae hominis*, 1,2;PL XXXIII, 725.
4. Cf. Ex. 15. 1-20.
5. II Sam. 6. 5.
6. Cf. I Para. 23. 5; 25. 2-31.
7. Eph. 5. 18ff; cf. Col. 3. 16.
8. I Cor. 14. 26.
9. Pliny, Epis. X, 96-97.
10. *Tertullian, De anima*, ch. 9; PL 11, 701; and Apol. 39; PL 1, 540.
11. Council of Trent, Session XXII: *Decretum de observandis et evitandis in celebratione Missae.*
12. Cf. encyclical letter of Benedict XIV *Annus qui, Opera omnia* (Prati edition, vol. 17, 1, page 16).
13. Cf. apostolic letter *Bonum est confiteri Domino*, August 2, 1828; Cf. Bulla *Tium Romanum*, Prati edition, ex Typ. Aldina, IX, 139ff.
14. Cf. Acta Pii X, 1 75-87; *Acta Sanctae Sedis*, XXXVI (1903-1904) 329-39, 387-95.
15. Cf. AAS., XXI, 33ff.
16. Cf. AAS., XXXIX, 521-95.

---

17. St. Augustine, Confessions, Book X, chap. 33, MPL, XXXII, 799ff.

18. Acta Pii X, *loc. cit.*, 78.

19. Letter to Card. Respighi, Acta PII X, loc. cit. 68-74, see 73ff.; *Acta Sanctae Sedis*, XXXVI (1903-04), 325-29, 395-98, see 398.

20. Pius Xl, apostolic constitution. *Divini cultus*, AAS, XXI (1929), 33ff

21. Code of Canon Law, Can. 5.

22. Council of Trent, Session XXII, *De Sacrificio Missae*, C. Vlll.

23. Acta Pii X, *loc. cit.*, 80.

24. AAS, XXXIX (1947), 590.

25. Apoc. 5. 13.

26. Decrees of the Sacred Congregation of Rites, No's. 3964, 4201, 4231.

27. St. Cyprian, Letter to Donatus (Letter 1, n. 16) PL, IV, 227.

Sacram Communionem:
On Laws of Fasting and The Evening Mass

Motu Proprio of His Holiness Pope Pius XII in which permissions granted by the Apostolic Constitution "Christus Dominus" are extended. Issued March 19, 1957

In the early part of 1953 [January 6] We issued the Apostolic Constitution [*Christus Dominus*], by which We eased the rigor of the law on the Eucharistic fast so that the faithful could receive Holy Communion more frequently and more easily fulfill the precept of hearing Holy Mass on holy days. For this purpose We granted to local Ordinaries the power to allow the celebration of Mass and distribution of Holy Communion in early evening hours, provided certain conditions be fulfilled.

We lessened the time of fasting to be observed before the celebration of Mass and the reception of Holy Communion in the afternoon to three hours for solid food and to one hour for non-alcoholic liquids.

The Bishops expressed to Us their profound gratitude for these concessions, which had brought abundant fruits, and many of them have insistently asked Us to authorize them to allow daily celebration of Mass in the afternoon hours, in view of the great benefit which the faithful would derive from it.

They have also asked Us to decree that an equal period of fasting be observed prior to the celebration of Mass or the reception of Holy Communion, in the morning hours.

Having taken into consideration the considerable changes which have occurred in working and office hours and in all social life, We deemed it advisable to comply with the insistent requests of the Bishops and have therefore decreed:

1. Ordinaries of places, excluding vicars general who are not in possession of a special mandate, may permit Holy Mass to be celebrated every day after midday, should this be necessary for the spiritual welfare of a considerable number of the faithful.

2. Priests and faithful, before Holy Mass or Holy Communion respectively, must abstain for three hours from solid foods and alcoholic liquids, for one hour from non-alcoholic liquids. Water does not break the fast.

3. From now on, the fast must be observed for the period of time indicated in Number Two, even by those who celebrate or receive Holy Communion at midnight or in the first hours of the day.

4. The infirm, even if not bedridden, may take nonalcoholic liquids and that which is really and properly medicine, either in liquid or solid form, before Mass or Holy Communion without any time limit.

We strongly exhort priests and faithful who are able to do so to observe the old and venerable form of the Eucharistic fast before Mass and Holy Communion. All those who will make use of these concessions must compensate for the good received by becoming shining examples of a Christian life and principally with works of penance and charity.

The dispositions of this Motu Proprio will go into effect on March 25, 1957, the Feast of the Annunciation of the Blessed Virgin Mary. Every disposition whatsoever to the contrary is abrogated, even if it is worthy of special mention.

Given at Rome at St. Peter's, March 19, the Feast of St. Joseph, Patron of the Universal Church, 1957, the 19th year of Our pontificate.

Veterum Sapientia:
Apostolic Constitution on the Promotion of the Study of Latin

Pope John XXIII
February 22, 1962

The wisdom of the ancient world, enshrined in Greek and Roman literature, and the truly memorable teaching of ancient peoples, served, surely, to herald the dawn of the Gospel which God's Son, "the judge and teacher of grace and truth, the light and guide of the human race,"[1] proclaimed on earth.

Such was the view of the Church Fathers and Doctors. In these outstanding literary monuments of antiquity, they recognized man's spiritual preparation for the supernatural riches which Jesus Christ communicated to mankind "to give history its fulfilment."[2]

Thus, the inauguration of Christianity did not mean the obliteration of man's past achievements. Nothing was lost that was in any way true, just, noble, and beautiful.

Venerable languages

The Church has ever held the literary evidences of this wisdom in the highest esteem. She values especially the Greek and Latin languages in which wisdom itself is cloaked, as it were, in a vesture of gold. She has likewise welcomed the use of other venerable languages, which flourished in the East. For these too have had no little influence on the progress of humanity and civilization. By their use in sacred liturgies and in versions of Holy Scripture, they have remained in force in certain regions even to the present day, bearing constant witness to the living voice of antiquity.

A primary place

But amid this variety of languages a primary place must surely be given to that language which had its origins in *Latium*, and later proved so admirable a means for the spreading of Christianity throughout the West.

And since in God's special Providence this language united so many nations together under the authority of the Roman Empire—and that for so many centuries—it also became the rightful language of the Apostolic See.[3] Preserved for posterity, it proved to be a bond of unity for the Christian peoples of Europe.

The nature of Latin

Of its very nature Latin is most suitable for promoting every form of culture among peoples. It gives rise to no jealousies. It does not favor any one nation, but presents itself with equal impartiality to all and is equally acceptable to all.

Nor must we overlook the characteristic nobility of Latin formal structure. Its "concise, varied and harmonious style, full of majesty and dignity"[4] makes for singular clarity and impressiveness of expression.

Preservation of Latin by the Holy See

For these reasons the Apostolic See has always been at pains to preserve Latin, deeming it worthy of being used in the exercise of her teaching authority "as the splendid vesture of her heavenly doctrine and sacred laws."[5] She further requires her sacred ministers to use it, for by so doing they are the better able, wherever they may be, to acquaint themselves with the mind of the Holy See on any matter, and communicate the more easily with Rome and with one another.

Thus, the "knowledge and use of this language," so intimately bound up with the Church's life, "is important not so much on cultural or literary grounds, as for religious reasons."[6] These are the words of Our Predecessor Pius XI, who conducted a scientific inquiry into this whole subject, and indicated three qualities of the Latin language which harmonize to a remarkable degree with the Church's nature. "For the Church, precisely because it embraces all nations and is destined to endure to the end of time . . . of its very nature requires a language which is universal, immutable, and non-vernacular."[7]

Universal

Since "every Church must assemble round the Roman Church,"[8] and since the Supreme Pontiffs have "true episcopal power, ordinary and immediate, over each and every Church and each and every Pastor, as well as over the faithful"[9] of every rite and language, it seems particularly desirable that the instrument of mutual communication be uniform and universal, especially between the Apostolic See and the Churches which use the same Latin rite.

When, therefore, the Roman Pontiffs wish to instruct the Catholic world, or when the Congregations of the Roman Curia handle matters or draw up decrees which concern the whole body of the faithful, they invariably make use of Latin, for this is a maternal voice acceptable to countless nations.

Immutable

Furthermore, the Church's language must be not only universal but also immutable. Modern languages are liable to change, and no single one of them is superior to the others in authority. Thus, if the truths of the Catholic Church were entrusted to an unspecified number of them, the meaning of these truths, varied as they are, would not be manifested to everyone with sufficient clarity and precision. There would, moreover, be no language which could serve as a common and constant norm by which to gauge the exact meaning of other renderings.

But Latin is indeed such a language. It is set and unchanging. It has long since ceased to be affected by those alterations in the meaning of words which are the normal result of daily, popular use. Certain Latin words, it is true, acquired new meanings as Christian teaching developed and needed to be explained and defended, but these new meanings have long since become accepted and firmly established.

Non-vernacular

Finally, the Catholic Church has a dignity far surpassing that of every merely human society, for it was founded by Christ the Lord. It is altogether fitting, therefore, that the language it uses should be noble, majestic, and non-vernacular.

In addition, the Latin language "can be called truly catholic."[10] It has been consecrated through constant use by the Apostolic See, the mother and teacher of all Churches, and must be esteemed "a treasure . . . of incomparable worth."[11] It is a general passport to the proper understanding of the Christian writers of antiquity and the documents of the Church's teaching.[12] It is also a most effective bond, binding the Church of today with that of the past and of the future in wonderful continuity.

Educational value of Latin

There can be no doubt as to the formative and educational value either of the language of the Romans or of great literature generally. It is a most effective training for the pliant minds of youth. It exercises, matures and perfects the principal faculties of mind and spirit. It sharpens the wits and gives keenness of judgment. It helps the young mind to grasp things accurately and develop a true sense of values. It is also a means for teaching highly intelligent thought and speech.

A natural result

It will be quite clear from these considerations why the Roman Pontiffs have so often extolled the excellence and importance of Latin, and why they have prescribed its study and use by the secular and regular clergy, forecasting the dangers that would result from its neglect.

A resolve to uphold Latin

And We also, impelled by the weightiest of reasons—the same as those which prompted Our Predecessors and provincial synods [13]— are fully determined to restore this language to its position of honor, and to do all We can to promote its study and use. The employment of Latin has recently been contested in many quarters, and many are asking what the mind of the Apostolic See is in this matter. We have therefore decided to issue the timely directives contained in this document, so as to ensure that the ancient and uninterrupted use of Latin be maintained and, where necessary, restored.

We believe that We made Our own views on this subject sufficiently clear when We said to a number of eminent Latin scholars:

> "It is a matter of regret that so many people, unaccountably dazzled by the marvelous progress of science, are taking it upon themselves to oust or restrict the study of Latin and other kindred subjects. . . . Yet, in spite of the urgent need for science, Our own view is that the very contrary policy should be followed. The greatest impression is made on the mind by those things which correspond more closely to man's nature and dignity. And therefore the greatest zeal should be shown

in the acquisition of whatever educates and ennobles the mind. Otherwise poor mortal creatures may well become like the machines they build—cold, hard, and devoid of love."[14]

Provisions for the Promotion of Latin Studies

With the foregoing considerations in mind, to which We have given careful thought, We now, in the full consciousness of Our Office and in virtue of Our authority, decree and command the following:

Responsibility for enforcement

1. Bishops and superiors-general of religious orders shall take pains to ensure that in their seminaries and in their schools where adolescents are trained for the priesthood, all shall studiously observe the Apostolic See's decision in this matter and obey these Our prescriptions most carefully.

2. In the exercise of their paternal care they shall be on their guard lest anyone under their jurisdiction, eager for revolutionary changes, writes against the use of Latin in the teaching of the higher sacred studies or in the Liturgy, or through prejudice makes light of the Holy See's will in this regard or interprets it falsely.

Study of Latin as a prerequisite

3. As is laid down in Canon Law (can. 1364) or commanded by Our Predecessors, before Church students begin their ecclesiastical studies proper they shall be given a sufficiently lengthy course of instruction in Latin by highly competent masters, following a method designed to teach them the language with the utmost accuracy. "And that too for this reason: lest later on, when they begin their major studies . . . they are unable by reason of their ignorance of the language to gain a full understanding of the doctrines or take part in those scholastic disputations which constitute so excellent an intellectual training for young men in the defense of the faith."[15]

We wish the same rule to apply to those whom God calls to the priesthood at a more advanced age, and whose classical studies have either been neglected or conducted too superficially. No one is to be admitted to the study of philosophy or theology except he be thoroughly grounded in this language and capable of using it.

Traditional curriculum to be restored

4. Wherever the study of Latin has suffered partial eclipse through the assimilation of the academic program to that which obtains in State public schools, with the result that the instruction given is no longer so thorough and well-grounded as formerly, there the traditional method of teaching this language shall be completely restored. Such is Our will, and there should be no doubt in anyone's mind about the necessity of keeping a strict watch over the course of studies followed by Church students; and that not only as regards the number and kinds of subjects they study, but also as regards the length of time devoted to the teaching of these subjects.

Should circumstances of time and place demand the addition of other subjects to the curriculum besides the usual ones, then either the course of studies must be lengthened, or these additional subjects must be condensed or their study relegated to another time.

Sacred sciences to be taught in Latin

5. In accordance with numerous previous instructions, the major sacred sciences shall be taught in Latin, which, as we know from many centuries of use, "must be considered most suitable for explaining with the utmost facility and clarity the most difficult and profound ideas and concepts."[16] For apart from the fact that it has long since been enriched with a vocabulary of appropriate and unequivocal terms, best calculated to safeguard the integrity of the Catholic faith, it also serves in no slight measure to prune away useless verbiage.

Hence, professors of these sciences in universities or seminaries are required to speak Latin and to make use of textbooks written in Latin. If ignorance of Latin makes it difficult for some to obey these instructions, they shall gradually be replaced by professors who are suited to this task. Any difficulties that may be advanced by students or professors must be overcome by the patient insistence of the bishops or religious superiors, and the good will of the professors.

A Latin Academy

6. Since Latin is the Church's living language, it must be adequate to daily increasing linguistic requirements. It must be furnished with new words that are apt and suitable for expressing modern things,

words that will be uniform and universal in their application and constructed in conformity with the genius of the ancient Latin tongue. Such was the method followed by the sacred Fathers and the best writers among the scholastics.

To this end, therefore, We commission the Sacred Congregation of Seminaries and Universities to set up a Latin Academy staffed by an international body of Latin and Greek professors. The principal aim of this Academy—like the national academies founded to promote their respective languages—will be to superintend the proper development of Latin, augmenting the Latin lexicon where necessary with words which conform to the particular character and color of the language.

It will also conduct schools for the study of Latin of every era, particularly the Christian one. The aim of these schools will be to impart a fuller understanding of Latin and the ability to use it and to write it with proper elegance. They will exist for those who are destined to teach Latin in seminaries and ecclesiastical colleges, or to write decrees and judgments or conduct correspondence in the ministries of the Holy See, diocesan curias, and the offices of religious orders.

The teaching of Greek

7. Latin is closely allied to Greek both in formal structure and in the importance of its extant writings. Hence—as Our Predecessors have frequently ordained—future ministers of the altar must be instructed in Greek in the lower and middle schools. Thus, when they come to study the higher sciences—and especially if they are aiming for a degree in Sacred Scripture or theology—they will be enabled to follow the Greek sources of scholastic philosophy and understand them correctly; and not only these, but also the original texts of Sacred Scripture, the Liturgy, and the sacred Fathers.[17]

A syllabus for the teaching of Latin

8. We further commission the Sacred Congregation of Seminaries and Universities to prepare a syllabus for the teaching of Latin which all shall faithfully observe. The syllabus will be designed to give those who follow it an adequate understanding of the language and its use. Episcopal boards may indeed rearrange this syllabus if circumstances warrant, but they must never curtail it or alter its nature. Ordinaries

may not take it upon themselves to put their own proposals into effect until these have been examined and approved by the Sacred Congregation.

Finally, in virtue of Our apostolic authority, We will and command that all the decisions, decrees, proclamations and recommendations of this Our Constitution remain firmly established and ratified, notwithstanding anything to the contrary, however worthy of special note.

Given at Rome, at Saint Peter's, on the feast of Saint Peter's Throne on the 22ⁿᵈ day of February in the year 1962, the fourth of Our pontificate.

END NOTES:

1. Tertullian, Apol. 21: *Migne*, FL 1, 294.
2. Ephesians 1, 10.
3. Epist. S. Cong. Stud. *Vehementer sane, ad Ep. universos*, July 1, 1908: Ench. Cler., N. 820. Cf. also *Epist. Ap. Pius XI, Unigenitus Dei Filius,* Mar. 19, 1924: AAS 16 (1924), 141.
4. Pius XI, *Epist. Ap. Officiorum omnium,* Aug. 1, 1922: AAS 14 (1922), 452-453.
5. Pius XI, *Motu proprio Litterarum latinarum,* Oct. 20, 1924: AAS 16 (1924), 417.
6. Pius XI, *Epist. Ap. Officiorum omnium,* Aug. 1, 1922: AAS 14 (1922), 452.
7. Ibid.
8. Saint Iren., *Adv. Haer.* 3, 3, 2: *Migne* PG 7, 848.
9. Cf. CIC, can. 218, pars. 2.
10. Cf. Pius XI, *Epist. Ap. Officiorum omnium,* Aug. 1, 1922: AAS 14 (1922), 453.
11. Pius XII, *Al. Magis quam,* Nov. 23, 1951: AAS 43 (1951), 737.
12. Leo XIII, *Epist. Encycl. Depuis le jour,* Sept. 8, 1899: *Acta Leonis XIII,* 19 (1899), 166.
13. Cf. *Collectio Lacensis,* espec. vol. III, 1018s. (*Conc. Prov. Westmonasteriense,* a (1859); Vol. IV, 29 (*Conc. Prov. Parisiense,* a 1849); Vol. IV, 149, 153 (*Conc. Prov. Rhemense,* a 1849); Vol. IV, 359, 861 (*Conc. Prov. Avenionense,* a 1849); Vol. IV, 394, 396 (*Conc. Prov. Burdigalense,* a 1850); Vol. V, 61 (*Conc. Strigoniense,* a 1858); Vol. V. 664 (*Conc. Prov. Colocense,* a 1863); Vol. VI, 619 (*Synod. Vicariatus Suchnensis,* a 1803).

14. International Convention for the Promotion of Ciceronian Studies, Sept. 7, 1959, in *Discorsi Messaggi Colloqui del Santo Padre Giovanni XXIII*, I, pp. 234-235. [English translation in TPS, V, 421.] Cf. also Address to Roman Pilgrims of the Diocese of Piacenza, April 15, 1959, in *L'Osservatore Romano* April 16, 1959; *Epist. Pater misericordiarum,* Aug. 22, 1961, in A.4S 53 (1961), 677; Address given on the occasion of the solemn inauguration of the College of the Philippine Islands at Rome, Oct. 7, 1961, in *L'Osservatore Romano,* Oct. 9-10, 1961; *Epist. Iucunda laudatio,* Dec. 8, 1961: AAS 53 (1961), 812 [English summary in TPS, VII, 367-8.]

15. Pius XII, *Epist. Ap. Officiorum omnium,* Aug. 1, 1922: AAS 14 (1922), 453.

16. *Epist. S. C. Stud., Vehementer sane,* July 1, 1908: Ench. Cler., N. 821.

17. Leo XIII. *Lit. Encyci. Providentissimus Deus*, Nov. 18, 1893: Acta Leonis XIII 13 (1893), 342; Epist. *Plane quidem intelligis,* May 20, 1885, *Acta*, 5, 63-64; Pius XII, *Alloc. Magis quam,* Sept. 23, 1951: AAS 43 (1951), 737.

Constitution on The Sacred Liturgy
Sacrosanctum Concilium

Pope Paul VI
December 4, 1963

INTRODUCTION

1. This sacred Council has several aims in view: it desires to impart an ever increasing vigor to the Christian life of the faithful; to adapt more suitably to the needs of our own times those institutions which are subject to change; to foster whatever can promote union among all who believe in Christ; to strengthen whatever can help to call the whole of mankind into the household of the Church. The Council therefore sees particularly cogent reasons for undertaking the reform and promotion of the liturgy.

2. For the liturgy, "through which the work of our redemption is accomplished,"[1] most of all in the divine sacrifice of the Eucharist, is the outstanding means whereby the faithful may express in their lives, and manifest to others, the mystery of Christ and the real nature of the true Church. It is of the essence of the Church that she be both human and divine, visible and yet invisibly equipped, eager to act and yet intent on contemplation, present in this world and yet not at home in it; and she is all these things in such wise that in her the human is directed and subordinated to the divine, the visible likewise to the invisible, action to contemplation, and this present world to that city yet to come, which we seek.[2] While the liturgy daily builds up those who are within into a holy temple of the Lord, into a dwelling place for God in the Spirit,[3] to the mature measure of the fullness of Christ,[4] at the same time it marvelously strengthens their power to preach Christ, and thus shows forth the Church to those who are outside as a sign lifted up among the nations [5] under which the scattered children of God may be gathered together,[6] until there is one sheepfold and one shepherd.[7]

3. Wherefore the sacred Council judges that the following principles concerning the promotion and reform of the liturgy should be called to mind, and that practical norms should be established.

Among these principles and norms there are some which can and should be applied both to the Roman rite and also to all the other rites. The practical norms which follow, however, should be taken as applying only to the Roman rite, except for those which, in the very nature of things, affect other rites as well.

4. Lastly, in faithful obedience to tradition, the sacred Council declares that holy Mother Church holds all lawfully acknowledged rites to be of equal right and dignity; that she wishes to preserve them in the future and to foster them in every way. The Council also desires that, where necessary, the rites be revised carefully in the light of sound tradition, and that they be given new vigor to meet the circumstances and needs of modern times.

CHAPTER I

GENERAL PRINCIPLES FOR THE: RESTORATION AND PROMOTION OF THE SACRED LITURGY

1. The Nature of the Sacred Liturgy and Its Importance in the Church's Life

5. God who "wills that all men be saved and come to the knowledge of the truth" (1 Tim. 2:4), "who in many and various ways spoke in times past to the fathers by the prophets" (Heb. 1:1), when the fullness of time had come sent His Son, the Word made flesh, anointed by the Holy Spirit, to preach the the gospel to the poor, to heal the contrite of heart,[8] to be a "bodily and spiritual medicine,"[9] the Mediator between God and man.[10] For His humanity, united with the person of the Word, was the instrument of our salvation. Therefore in Christ "the perfect achievement of our reconciliation came forth, and the fullness of divine worship was given to us."[11]

The wonderful works of God among the people of the Old Testament were but a prelude to the work of Christ the Lord in redeeming mankind and giving perfect glory to God. He achieved His task principally by the paschal mystery of His blessed passions resurrection from the dead, and the glorious ascension, whereby "dying, he destroyed our death and, rising, he restored our life."[12] For it was from the side of Christ as He slept the sleep of death upon the Cross that there came forth "the wondrous sacrament of the whole Church."[13]

6. Just as Christ was sent by the Father, so also He sent the apostles, filled with the Holy Spirit. This He did that, by preaching the gospel to every creature,[14] they might proclaim that the Son of God, by His death and resurrection, had freed us from the power of Satan [15] and from death, and brought us into the kingdom of His Father. His purpose also was that they might accomplish the work of salvation which they had proclaimed, by means of sacrifice and sacraments, around which the entire liturgical life revolves. Thus, by baptism men are plunged into the paschal mystery of Christ: they die with Him, are buried with Him, and rise with Him;[16] they receive the spirit of adoption as sons "in which we cry: Abba, Father" (Rom. 8 :15), and thus become true adorers whom the Father seeks.[17] In like manner, as often as they eat the supper of the Lord they proclaim the death of the Lord until He comes.[18] For that reason, on the very day of Pentecost, when the Church appeared before the world, "those who received the word" of Peter "were baptized." And "they continued steadfastly in the teaching of the apostles and in the communion of the breaking of bread and in prayers . . . praising God and being in favor with all the people" (Acts 2:41-47). From that time onwards the Church has never failed to come together to celebrate the paschal mystery: reading those things "which were in all the scriptures concerning him" (Luke 24:27), celebrating the eucharist in which "the victory and triumph of his death are again made present;"[19] and at the same time giving thanks "to God for his unspeakable gift" (2 Cor. 9:15) in Christ Jesus, "in praise of his glory" (Eph. 1:12), through the power of the Holy Spirit.

7. To accomplish so great a work, Christ is always present in His Church, especially in her liturgical celebrations. He is present in the sacrifice of the Mass, not only in the person of His minister, "the same now offering, through the ministry of priests, who formerly offered Himself on the Cross,"[20] but especially under the Eucharistic species. By His power He is present in the sacraments, so that when a man baptizes it is really Christ Himself who baptizes.[21] He is present in His word, since it is He Himself who speaks when the holy scriptures are read in the Church. He is present, lastly, when the Church prays and sings, for He promised: "Where two or three are gathered together in my name, there am I in the midst of them" (Matt. 18:20).

Christ indeed always associates the Church with Himself in this great work wherein God is perfectly glorified and men are sanctified. The

Church is His beloved Bride who calls to her Lord, and through Him offers worship to the Eternal Father.

Rightly, then, the liturgy is considered as an exercise of the priestly office of Jesus Christ. In the liturgy the sanctification of the man is signified by signs perceptible to the senses, and is effected in a way which corresponds with each of these signs; in the liturgy the whole public worship is performed by the Mystical Body of Jesus Christ, that is, by the Head and His members.

From this it follows that every liturgical celebration, because it is an action of Christ the priest and of His Body which is the Church, is a sacred action surpassing all others; no other action of the Church can equal its efficacy by the same title and to the same degree.

8. In the earthly liturgy we take part in a foretaste of that heavenly liturgy which is celebrated in the holy city of Jerusalem toward which we journey as pilgrims, where Christ is sitting at the right hand of God, a minister of the holies and of the true tabernacle;[22] we sing a hymn to the Lord's glory with all the warriors of the heavenly army; venerating the memory of the saints, we hope for some part and fellowship with them; we eagerly await the Saviour, Our Lord Jesus Christ, until He, our life, shall appear and we too will appear with Him in glory.[23]

9. The sacred liturgy does not exhaust the entire activity of the Church. Before men can come to the liturgy they must be called to faith and to conversion: "How then are they to call upon him in whom they have not yet believed? But how are they to believe him whom they have not heard? And how are they to hear if no one preaches? And how are men to preach unless they be sent?" (Rom. 10:14-15).

Therefore, the Church announces the good tidings of salvation to those who do not believe, so that all men may know the true God and Jesus Christ whom He has sent, and may be converted from their ways, doing penance.[24] To believers also the Church must ever preach faith and penance, she must prepare them for the sacraments, teach them to observe all that Christ has commanded,[25] and invite them to all the works of charity, piety, and the apostolate. For all these works make it clear that Christ's faithful, though not of this world, are to be the light of the world and to glorify the Father before men.

10. Nevertheless, the liturgy is the summit toward which the activity of the Church is directed; at the same time it is the font from which all her power flows. For the aim and object of apostolic works is that all

who are made sons of God by faith and baptism should come together to praise God in the midst of His Church, to take part in the sacrifice, and to eat the Lord's supper.

The liturgy in its turn moves the faithful, filled with "the paschal sacraments," to be "one in holiness;"[26] it prays that "they may hold fast in their lives to what they have grasped by their faith;"[27] the renewal in the Eucharist of the covenant between the Lord and man draws the faithful into the compelling love of Christ and sets them on fire. From the liturgy, therefore, and especially from the Eucharist, as from a font, grace is poured forth upon us; and the sanctification of men in Christ and the glorification of God, to which all other activities of the Church are directed as toward their end, is achieved in the most efficacious possible way.

11. But in order that the liturgy may be able to produce its full effects, it is necessary that the faithful come to it with proper dispositions, that their minds should be attuned to their voices, and that they should cooperate with divine grace lest they receive it in vain.[28]. Pastors of souls must therefore realize that, when the liturgy is celebrated, something more is required than the mere observation of the laws governing valid and licit celebration; it is their duty also to ensure that the faithful take part fully aware of what they are doing, actively engaged in the rite, and enriched by its effects.

12. The spiritual life, however, is not limited solely to participation in the liturgy. The Christian is indeed called to pray with his brethren, but he must also enter into his chamber to pray to the Father, in secret;[29] yet more, according to the teaching of the Apostle, he should pray without ceasing.[30] We learn from the same Apostle that we must always bear about in our body the dying of Jesus, so that the life also of Jesus may be made manifest in our bodily frame.[31] This is why we ask the Lord in the sacrifice of the Mass that, "receiving the offering of the spiritual victim," he may fashion us for Himself "as an eternal gift."[32]

13. Popular devotions of the Christian people are to be highly commended, provided they accord with the laws and norms of the Church, above all when they are ordered by the Apostolic See.

Devotions proper to individual Churches also have a special dignity if they are undertaken by mandate of the bishops according to customs or books lawfully approved.

But these devotions should be so drawn up that they harmonize with the liturgical seasons, accord with the sacred liturgy, are in some fashion derived from it, and lead the people to it, since, in fact, the liturgy by its very nature far surpasses any of them.

II. The Promotion of Liturgical Instruction and Active Participation

14. Mother Church earnestly desires that all the faithful should be led to that fully conscious, and active participation in liturgical celebrations which is demanded by the very nature of the liturgy. Such participation by the Christian people as "a chosen race, a royal priesthood, a holy nation, a redeemed people" (1 Pet. 2:9; cf. 2:4-5), is their right and duty by reason of their baptism.

In the restoration and promotion of the sacred liturgy, this full and active participation by all the people is the aim to be considered before all else; for it is the primary and indispensable source from which the faithful are to derive the true Christian spirit; and, therefore, pastors of souls must zealously strive to achieve it, by means of the necessary instruction, in all their pastoral work.

Yet it would be futile to entertain any hopes of realizing this unless the pastors themselves, in the first place, become thoroughly imbued with the spirit and power of the liturgy, and undertake to give instruction about it. A prime need, therefore, is that attention be directed, first of all, to the liturgical instruction of the clergy. Wherefore the sacred Council has decided to enact as follows:

15. Professors who are appointed to teach liturgy in seminaries, religious houses of study, and theological faculties must be properly trained for their work in institutes which specialize in this subject.

16. The study of sacred liturgy is to be ranked among the compulsory and major courses in seminaries and religions houses of studies; in theological faculties it is to rank among the principal courses. It is to be taught under its theological, historical, spiritual, pastoral, and juridical aspects. Moreover, other professors, while striving to expound the mystery of Christ and the history of salvation from the angle proper to each of their own subjects, must, nevertheless, do so in a way which will clearly bring out the connection between their subjects and the liturgy, as also the unity which underlies all priestly training. This consideration is especially important for professors of dogmatic, spiritual, and pastoral theology and for those of holy scripture.

17. In seminaries and houses of religious, clerics shall be given a liturgical formation in their spiritual life. For this they will need proper direction, so that they may be able to understand the sacred

rites and take part in them wholeheartedly; and they will also need personally to celebrate the sacred mysteries, as well as popular devotions which are imbued with the spirit of the liturgy. In addition they must learn how to observe the liturgical laws, so that life in seminaries and houses of religious may be thoroughly influenced by the spirit of the liturgy.

18. Priests, both secular and religious, who are already working in the Lord's vineyard are to be helped by every suitable means to understand ever more fully what it is that they are doing when they perform sacred rites; they are to be aided to live the liturgical life and to share it with the faithful entrusted to their care.

19. With zeal and patience, pastors of souls must promote the liturgical instruction of the faithful, and also their active participation in the liturgy both internally and externally, taking into account their age and condition, their way of life, and standard of religious culture. By so doing, pastors will be fulfilling one of the chief duties of a faithful dispenser of the mysteries of God; and in this matter they must lead their flock not only in word but also by example.

20. Transmissions of the sacred rites by radio and television shall be done with discretion and dignity, under the leadership and direction of a suitable person appointed for this office by the bishops. This is especially important when the service to be broadcast is the Mass.

III. The Reform of the Sacred Liturgy

21. In order that the Christian people may more certainly derive an abundance of graces from the sacred liturgy, holy Mother Church desires to undertake with great care a general restoration of the liturgy itself. For the liturgy is made up of immutable elements divinely instituted, and of elements subject to change. These not only may but ought to be changed with the passage of time if they have suffered from the intrusion of anything out of harmony with the inner nature of the liturgy or have become unsuited to it.

In this restoration, both texts and rites should be drawn up so that they express more clearly the holy things which they signify; the Christian people, so far as possible, should be enabled to understand them with ease and to take part in them fully, actively, and as befits a community.

Wherefore the sacred Council establishes the following general norms:

Sacrosanctum Concilium: Constitution on The Sacred Liturgy

A) General norms

22. 1. Regulation of the sacred liturgy depends solely on the authority of the Church, that is, on the Apostolic See and, as laws may determine, on the bishop.

2. In virtue of power conceded by the law, the regulation of the liturgy within certain defined limits belongs also to various kinds of competent territorial bodies of bishops legitimately established.

3. Therefore no other person, even if he be a priest, may add, remove, or change anything in the liturgy on his own authority.

23. That sound tradition may be retained, and yet the way remain open to legitimate progress careful investigation is always to be made into each part of the liturgy which is to be revised. This investigation should be theological, historical, and pastoral. Also the general laws governing the structure and meaning of the liturgy must be studied in conjunction with the experience derived from recent liturgical reforms and from the indults conceded to various places. Finally, there must be no innovations unless the good of the Church genuinely and certainly requires them; and care must be taken that any new forms adopted should in some way grow organically from forms already existing.

As far as possible, notable differences between the rites used in adjacent regions must be carefully avoided.

24. Sacred scripture is of the greatest importance in the celebration of the liturgy. For it is from scripture that lessons are read and explained in the homily, and psalms are sung; the prayers, collects, and liturgical songs are scriptural in their inspiration and their force, and it is from the scriptures that actions and signs derive their meaning. Thus, to achieve the restoration, progress, and adaptation of the sacred liturgy, it is essential to promote that warm and living love for scripture to which the venerable tradition of both eastern and western rites gives testimony.

25. The liturgical books are to be revised as soon as possible; experts are to be employed on the task, and bishops are to be consulted, from various parts of the world.

B) Norms drawn from the hierarchic and communal nature of the Liturgy

26. Liturgical services are not private functions, but are celebrations of the Church, which is the "sacrament of unity," namely, the holy people united and ordered under their bishops.[33]

Therefore liturgical services pertain to the whole body of the Church; they manifest it and have effects upon it; but they concern the individual members of the Church in different ways, according to their differing rank, office, and actual participation.

27. It is to be stressed that whenever rites, according to their specific nature, make provision for communal celebration involving the presence and active participation of the faithful, this way of celebrating them is to be preferred, so far as possible, to a celebration that is individual and quasi-private.

This applies with especial force to the celebration of Mass and the administration of the sacraments, even though every Mass has of itself a public and social nature.

28. In liturgical celebrations each person, minister or layman, who has an office to perform, should do all of, but only, those parts which pertain to his office by the nature of the rite and the principles of liturgy.

29. Servers, lectors, commentators, and members of the choir also exercise a genuine liturgical function. They ought, therefore, to discharge their office with the sincere piety and decorum demanded by so exalted a ministry and rightly expected of them by God's people.

Consequently they must all be deeply imbued with the spirit of the liturgy, each in his own measure, and they must be trained to perform their functions in a correct and orderly manner.

30. To promote active participation, the people should be encouraged to take part by means of acclamations, responses, psalmody, antiphons, and songs, as well as by actions, gestures, and bodily attitudes. And at the proper times all should observe a reverent silence.

31. The revision of the liturgical books must carefully attend to the provision of rubrics also for the people's parts.

32. The liturgy makes distinctions between persons according to their liturgical function and sacred Orders, and there are liturgical laws

providing for due honors to be given to civil authorities. Apart from these instances, no special honors are to be paid in the liturgy to any private persons or classes of persons, whether in the ceremonies or by external display.

C) Norms based upon the didactic and pastoral nature of the Liturgy

33. Although the sacred liturgy is above all things the worship of the divine Majesty, it likewise contains much instruction for the faithful.[34] For in the liturgy God speaks to His people and Christ is still proclaiming His gospel. And the people reply to God both by song and prayer.

Moreover, the prayers addressed to God by the priest who presides over the assembly in the person of Christ are said in the name of the entire holy people and of all present. And the visible signs used by the liturgy to signify invisible divine things have been chosen by Christ or the Church. Thus, not only when things are read "which were written for our instruction" (Rom. 15:4), but also when the Church prays or sings or acts, the faith of those taking part is nourished and their minds are raised to God, so that they may offer Him their rational service and more abundantly receive His grace.

Wherefore, in the revision of the liturgy, the following general norms should be observed:

34. The rites should be distinguished by a noble simplicity; they should be short, clear, and unencumbered by useless repetitions; they should be within the people's powers of comprehension, and normally should not require much explanation.

35. That the intimate connection between words and rites may be apparent in the liturgy:

1) In sacred celebrations there is to be more reading from holy scripture, and it is to be more varied and suitable.

2) Because the sermon is part of the liturgical service, the best place for it is to be indicated even in the rubrics, as far as the nature of the rite will allow; the ministry of preaching is to be fulfilled with exactitude and fidelity. The sermon, moreover, should draw its content mainly from scriptural and liturgical sources, and its character should be that of a proclamation of God's wonderful works in the history of salvation, the mystery of Christ, ever made present and active within us, especially in the celebration of the liturgy.

3) Instruction which is more explicitly liturgical should also be given in a variety of ways; if necessary, short directives to be spoken by the priest or proper minister should be provided within the rites themselves. But they should occur only at the more suitable moments, and be in prescribed or similar words.

4) Bible services should be encouraged, especially on the vigils of the more solemn feasts, on some weekdays in Advent and Lent, and on Sundays and feast days. They are particularly to be commended in places where no priest is available; when this is so, a deacon or some other person authorized by the bishop should preside over the celebration.

36. 1. Particular law remaining in force, the use of the Latin language is to be preserved in the Latin rites.

2. But since the use of the mother tongue, whether in the Mass, the administration of the sacraments, or other parts of the liturgy, frequently may be of great advantage to the people, the limits of its employment may be extended. This will apply in the first place to the readings and directives, and to some of the prayers and chants, according to the regulations on this matter to be laid down separately in subsequent chapters.

3. These norms being observed, it is for the competent territorial ecclesiastical authority mentioned in Art. 22, 2, to decide whether, and to what extent, the vernacular language is to be used; their decrees are to be approved, that is, confirmed, by the Apostolic See. And, whenever it seems to be called for, this authority is to consult with bishops of neighboring regions which have the same language.

4. Translations from the Latin text into the mother tongue intended for use in the liturgy must be approved by the competent territorial ecclesiastical authority mentioned above.

D) Norms for adapting the Liturgy to the culture and traditions of peoples

37. Even in the liturgy, the Church has no wish to impose a rigid uniformity in matters which do not implicate the faith or the good of the whole community; rather does she respect and foster the genius and talents of the various races and peoples. Anything in these peoples' way of life which is not indissolubly bound up with superstition and error she studies with sympathy and, if possible, preserves intact. Sometimes in fact she admits such things into the

liturgy itself, so long as they harmonize with its true and authentic spirit.

38. Provisions shall also be made, when revising the liturgical books, for legitimate variations and adaptations to different groups, regions, and peoples, especially in mission lands, provided that the substantial unity of the Roman rite is preserved; and this should be borne in mind when drawing up the rites and devising rubrics.

39. Within the limits set by the typical editions of the liturgical books, it shall be for the competent territorial ecclesiastical authority mentioned in Art. 22, 2, to specify adaptations, especially in the case of the administration of the sacraments, the sacramentals, processions, liturgical language, sacred music, and the arts, but according to the fundamental norms laid down in this Constitution.

40. In some places and circumstances, however, an even more radical adaptation of the liturgy is needed, and this entails greater difficulties. Wherefore:

1) The competent territorial ecclesiastical authority mentioned in Art. 22, 2, must, in this matter, carefully and prudently consider which elements from the traditions and culture of individual peoples might appropriately be admitted into divine worship. Adaptations which are judged to be useful or necessary should when be submitted to the Apostolic See, by whose consent they may be introduced.

2) To ensure that adaptations may be made with all the circumspection which they demand, the Apostolic See will grant power to this same territorial ecclesiastical authority to permit and to direct, as the case requires, the necessary preliminary experiments over a determined period of time among certain groups suited for the purpose.

3) Because liturgical laws often involve special difficulties with respect to adaptation, particularly in mission lands, men who are experts in these matters must be employed to formulate them.

E) Promotion of Liturgical Life in Diocese and Parish

41. The bishop is to be considered as the high priest of his flock, from whom the life in Christ of his faithful is in some way derived and dependent.

Therefore, all should hold in great esteem the liturgical life of the diocese centered around the bishop, especially in his cathedral church; they must be convinced that the pre-eminent manifestation of the Church consists in the full active participation of all God's holy people in these liturgical celebrations, especially in the same eucharist, in a single prayer, at one altar, at which there presides the bishop surrounded by his college of priests and by his ministers.[35]

42. But because it is impossible for the bishop always and everywhere to preside over the whole flock in his Church, he cannot do other than establish lesser groupings of the faithful. Among these the parishes, set up locally under a pastor who takes the place of the bishop, are the most important: for in some manner they represent the visible Church constituted throughout the world.

And therefore the liturgical life of the parish and its relationship to the bishop must be fostered theoretically and practically among the faithful and clergy; efforts also must be made to encourage a sense of community within the parish, above all in the common celebration of the Sunday Mass.

F) The Promotion of Pastoral-Liturgical Action

43. Zeal for the promotion and restoration of the liturgy is rightly held to be a sign of the providential dispositions of God in our time, as a movement of the Holy Spirit in His Church. It is today a distinguishing mark of the Church's life, indeed of the whole tenor of contemporary religious thought and action.

So that this pastoral-liturgical action may become even more vigorous in the Church, the sacred Council decrees:

44. It is desirable that the competent territorial ecclesiastical authority mentioned in Art. 22, 2, set up a liturgical commission, to be assisted by experts in liturgical science, sacred music, art, and pastoral practice. So far as possible the commission should be aided by some kind of Institute for Pastoral Liturgy, consisting of persons who are eminent in these matters, and including laymen as circumstances suggest. Under the direction of the above-mentioned territorial ecclesiastical authority the commission is to regulate pastoral-liturgical action throughout the territory, and to promote studies and necessary experiments whenever there is question of adaptations to be proposed to the Apostolic See.

45. For the same reason every diocese is to have a commission on the sacred liturgy under the direction of the bishop, for promoting the liturgical apostolate.

Sometimes it may be expedient that several dioceses should form between them one single commission which will be able to promote the liturgy by common consultation.

46. Besides the commission on the sacred liturgy, every diocese, as far as possible, should have commissions for sacred music and sacred art.

These three commissions must work in closest collaboration; indeed it will often be best to fuse the three of them into one single commission.

CHAPTER II

THE MOST SACRED MYSTERY OF THE EUCHARIST

47. At the Last Supper, on the night when He was betrayed, our Saviour instituted the eucharistic sacrifice of His Body and Blood. He did this in order to perpetuate the sacrifice of the Cross throughout the centuries until He should come again, and so to entrust to His beloved spouse, the Church, a memorial of His death and resurrection: a sacrament of love, a sign of unity, a bond of charity,[36] a paschal banquet in which Christ is eaten, the mind is filled with grace, and a pledge of future glory is given to us.[37].

48. The Church, therefore, earnestly desires that Christ's faithful, when present at this mystery of faith, should not be there as strangers or silent spectators; on the contrary, through a good understanding of the rites and prayers they should take part in the sacred action conscious of what they are doing, with devotion and full collaboration. They should be instructed by God's word and be nourished at the table of the Lord's Body; they should give thanks to God; by offering the Immaculate Victim, not only through the hands of the priest, but also with him, they should learn also to offer themselves; through Christ the Mediator,[38] they should be drawn day by day into ever more perfect union with God and with each other, so that finally God may be all in all.

49. For this reason the sacred Council, having in mind those Masses which are celebrated with the assistance of the faithful, especially on Sundays and feasts of obligation, has made the following decrees in order that the sacrifice of the Mass, even in the ritual forms of its celebration, may become pastorally efficacious to the fullest degree.

50. The rite of the Mass is to be revised in such a way that the intrinsic nature and purpose of its several parts, as also the connection

between them, may be more clearly manifested, and that devout and active participation by the faithful may be more easily achieved.

For this purpose the rites are to be simplified, due care being taken to preserve their substance; elements which, with the passage of time, came to be duplicated, or were added with but little advantage, are now to be discarded; other elements which have suffered injury through accidents of history are now to be restored to the vigor which they had in the days of the holy Fathers, as may seem useful or necessary.

51. The treasures of the bible are to be opened up more lavishly, so that richer fare may be provided for the faithful at the table of God's word. In this way a more representative portion of the holy scriptures will be read to the people in the course of a prescribed number of years.

52. By means of the homily the mysteries of the faith and the guiding principles of the Christian life are expounded from the sacred text, during the course of the liturgical year; the homily, therefore, is to be highly esteemed as part of the liturgy itself; in fact, at those Masses which are celebrated with the assistance of the people on Sundays and feasts of obligation, it should not be omitted except for a serious reason.

53. Especially on Sundays and feasts of obligation there is to be restored, after the Gospel and the homily, "the common prayer" or "the prayer of the faithful." By this prayer, in which the people are to take part, intercession will be made for holy Church, for the civil authorities, for those oppressed by various needs, for all mankind, and for the salvation of the entire world.[39]

54. In Masses which are celebrated with the people, a suitable place may be allotted to their mother tongue. This is to apply in the first place to the readings and "the common prayer," but also, as local conditions may warrant, to those parts which pertain to the people, according to the norm laid down in Art. 36 of this Constitution.

Nevertheless steps should be taken so that the faithful may also be able to say or to sing together in Latin those parts of the Ordinary of the Mass which pertain to them.

And wherever a more extended use of the mother tongue within the Mass appears desirable, the regulation laid down in Art. 40 of this Constitution is to be observed.

55. That more perfect form of participation in the Mass whereby the faithful, after the priest's communion, receive the Lord's Body from the same sacrifice, is strongly commended.

The dogmatic principles which were laid down by the Council of Trent remaining intact[40], communion under both kinds may be granted when the bishops think fit, not only to clerics and religious, but also to the laity, in cases to be determined by the Apostolic See, as, for instance, to the newly ordained in the Mass of their sacred ordination, to the newly professed in the Mass of their religious profession, and to the newly baptized in the Mass which follows their baptism.

56. The two parts which, in a certain sense, go to make up the Mass, namely, the liturgy of the word and the eucharistic liturgy, are so closely connected with each other that they form but one single act of worship. Accordingly this sacred Synod strongly urges pastors of souls that, when instructing the faithful, they insistently teach them to take their part in the entire Mass, especially on Sundays and feasts of obligation.

57. 1. Concelebration, whereby the unity of the priesthood is appropriately manifested, has remained in use to this day in the Church both in the east and in the west. For this reason it has seemed good to the Council to extend permission for concelebration to the following cases:

1.

    a) on the Thursday of the Lord's Supper, not only at the Mass of the Chrism, but also at the evening Mass.

    b) at Masses during councils, bishops' conferences, and synods;

    c) at the Mass for the blessing of an abbot.

2. Also, with permission of the ordinary, to whom it belongs to decide whether concelebration is opportune:

    a) at conventual Mass, and at the principle Mass in churches when the needs of the faithful do not require that all priests available should celebrate individually;

    b) at Masses celebrated at any kind of priests' meetings, whether the priests be secular clergy or religious.

2.

1. The regulation, however, of the discipline of con-celebration in the diocese pertains to the bishop.

2. Nevertheless, each priest shall always retain his right to celebrate Mass individually, though not at the same time in the same church as a concelebrated Mass, nor on Thursday of the Lord's Supper.

58. A new rite for concelebration is to be drawn up and inserted into the Pontifical and into the Roman Missal.

CHAPTER III

THE OTHER SACRAMENTS AND THE SACRAMENTALS

59. The purpose of the sacraments is to sanctify men, to build up the Body of Christ, and, finally, to give worship to God; because they are signs they also instruct. They not only presuppose faith, but by words and objects they also nourish, strengthen, and express it; that is why they are called "sacraments of faith." They do indeed impart grace, but, in addition, the very act of celebrating them most effectively disposes the faithful to receive this grace in a fruitful manner, to worship God duly, and to practice charity.

It is therefore of the highest importance that the faithful should easily understand the sacramental signs, and should frequent with great eagerness those sacraments which were instituted to nourish the Christian life.

60. Holy Mother Church has, moreover, instituted sacramentals. These are sacred signs which bear a resemblance to the sacraments: they signify effects, particularly of a spiritual kind, which are obtained through the Church's intercession. By them men are disposed to receive the chief effect of the sacraments, and various occasions in life are rendered holy.

61. Thus, for well-disposed members of the faithful, the liturgy of the sacraments and sacramentals sanctifies almost every event in their lives; they are given access to the stream of divine grace which flows from the paschal mystery of the passion, death, the resurrection of Christ, the font from which all sacraments and sacramentals draw their power. There is hardly any proper use of material things which cannot thus be directed toward the sanctification of men and the praise of God.

62. With the passage of time, however, there have crept into the rites of the sacraments and sacramentals certain features which have rendered their nature and purpose far from clear to the people of today; hence, some changes have become necessary to adapt them to the needs of our own times. For this reason the sacred Council decrees as follows concerning their revision.

63. Because of the use of the mother tongue in the administration of the sacraments and sacramentals can often be of considerable help to the people, this use is to be extended according to the following norms:

a) The vernacular language may be used in administering the sacraments and sacramentals, according to the norm of Art. 36.

b) In harmony with the new edition of the Roman Ritual, particular rituals shall be prepared without delay by the competent territorial ecclesiastical authority mentioned in Art. 22, 2, of this Constitution. These rituals, which are to be adapted, also as regards the language employed, to the needs of the different regions, are to be reviewed by the Apostolic See and then introduced into the regions for which they have been prepared. But in drawing up these rituals or particular collections of rites, the instructions prefixed to the individual rites the Roman Ritual, whether they be pastoral and rubrical or whether they have special social import, shall not be omitted.

64. The catechumenate for adults, comprising several distinct steps, is to be restored and to be taken into use at the discretion of the local ordinary. By this, means the time of the catechumenate, which is intended as a period of suitable instruction, may be sanctified by sacred rites to be celebrated at successive intervals of time.

65. In mission lands it is found that some of the peoples already make use of initiation rites. Elements from these, when capable of being adapted to Christian ritual, may be admitted along with those already found in Christian tradition, according to the norm laid down in Art. 37-40, of this Constitution.

66. Both the rites for the baptism of adults are to be revised: not only the simpler rite, but also the more solemn one, which must take into account the restored catechumenate. A special Mass "for the conferring of baptism" is to be inserted into the Roman Missal.

67. The rite for the baptism of infants is to be revised, and it should be adapted to the circumstance that those to be baptized are, in fact,

infants. The roles of parents and godparents, and also their duties, should be brought out more clearly in the rite itself.

68. The baptismal rite should contain variants, to be used at the discretion of the local ordinary, for occasions when a very large number are to be baptized together. Moreover, a shorter rite is to be drawn up, especially for mission lands, to be used by catechists, but also by the faithful in general when there is danger of death, and neither priest nor deacon is available.

69. In place of the rite called the "Order of supplying what was omitted in the baptism of an infant," a new rite is to be drawn up. This should manifest more fittingly and clearly that the infant, baptized by the short rite, has already been received into the Church.

And a new rite is to be drawn up for converts who have already been validly baptized; it should indicate that they are now admitted to communion with the Church.

70. Except during Eastertide, baptismal water may be blessed within the rite of baptism itself by an approved shorter formula.

71. The rite of confirmation is to be revised and the intimate connection which this sacrament has with the whole of Christian initiation is to be more clearly set forth; for this reason it is fitting for candidates to renew their baptismal promises just before they are confirmed.

Confirmation may be given within the Mass when convenient; when it is given outside the Mass, the rite that is used should be introduced by a formula to be drawn up for this purpose.

72. The rite and formulas for the sacrament of penance are to be revised so that they more clearly express both the nature and effect of the sacrament.

73. "Extreme unction," which may also and more fittingly be called "anointing of the sick," is not a sacrament for those only who are at the point of death. Hence, as soon as any one of the faithful begins to be in danger of death from sickness or old age, the fitting time for him to receive this sacrament has certainly already arrived.

74. In addition to the separate rites for anointing of the sick and for viaticum, a continuous rite shall be prepared according to which the sick man is anointed after he has made his confession and before he receives viaticum.

75. The number of the anointings is to be adapted to the occasion, and the prayers which belong to the rite of anointing are to be revised so as to correspond with the varying conditions of the sick who receive the sacrament.

76. Both the ceremonies and texts of the ordination rites are to be revised. The address given by the bishop at the beginning of each ordination or consecration may be in the mother tongue.

When a bishop is consecrated, the laying of hands may be done by all the bishops present.

77. The marriage rite now found in the Roman Ritual is to be revised and enriched in such a way that the grace of the sacrament is more clearly signified and the duties of the spouses are taught.

"If any regions are wont to use other praiseworthy customs and ceremonies when celebrating the sacrament of matrimony, the sacred Synod earnestly desires that these by all means be retained."[41]

Moreover the competent territorial ecclesiastical authority mentioned in Art. 22, 52, of this Constitution is free to draw up its own rite suited to the usages of place and people, according to the provision of Art. 63. But the rite must always conform to the law that the priest assisting at the marriage must ask for and obtain the consent of the contracting parties.

78. Matrimony is normally to be celebrated within the Mass, after the reading of the gospel and the homily, and before "the prayer of the faithful." The prayer for the bride, duly amended to remind both spouses of their equal obligation to remain faithful to each other, may be said in the mother tongue.

But if the sacrament of matrimony is celebrated apart from Mass, the epistle and gospel from the nuptial Mass are to be read at the beginning of the rite, and the blessing should always be given to the spouses.

79. The sacramentals are to undergo a revision which takes into account the primary principle of enabling the faithful to participate intelligently, actively, and easily; the circumstances of our own days must also be considered. When rituals are revised, as laid down in Art. 63, new sacramentals may also be added as the need for these becomes apparent.

Reserved blessings shall be very few; reservations shall be in favor of bishops or ordinaries.

Let provision be made that some sacramentals, at least in special circumstances and at the discretion of the ordinary, may be administered by qualified lay persons.

80. The rite for the consecration of virgins at present found in the Roman Pontifical is to be revised.

Moreover, a rite of religious profession and renewal of vows shall be drawn up in order to achieve greater unity, sobriety, and dignity. Apart from exceptions in particular law, this rite should be adopted by those who make their profession or renewal of vows within the Mass.

Religious profession should preferably be made within the Mass.

81. The rite for the burial of the dead should express more clearly the paschal character of Christian death, and should correspond more closely to the circumstances and traditions found in various regions. This holds good also for the liturgical color to be used.

82. The rite for the burial of infants is to be revised, and a special Mass for the occasion should be provided.

CHAPTER IV

THE DIVINE OFFICE

83. Christ Jesus, high priest of the new and eternal covenant, taking human nature, introduced into this earthly exile that hymn which is sung throughout all ages in the halls of heaven. He joins the entire community of mankind to Himself, associating it with His own singing of this canticle of divine praise.

For He continues His priestly work through the agency of His Church, which is ceaselessly engaged in praising the Lord and interceding for the salvation of the whole world. She does this, not only by celebrating the eucharist, but also in other ways, especially by praying the divine office.

84. By tradition going back to early Christian times, the divine office is devised so that the whole course of the day and night is made holy by the praises of God. Therefore, when this wonderful song of praise is rightly performed by priests and others who are deputed for this purpose by the Church's ordinance, or by the faithful praying together with the priest in the approved form, then it is truly the voice of the bride addressed to her bridegroom; It is the very prayer which Christ Himself, together with His Body, addresses to the Father.

85. Hence, all who render this service are not only fulfilling a duty of the Church, but also are sharing in the greatest honor of Christ's spouse, for by offering these praises to God they are standing before God's throne in the name of the Church their Mother.

86. Priests who are engaged in the sacred pastoral ministry will offer the praises of the hours with greater fervor the more vividly they realize that they must heed St. Paul's exhortation: "Pray without ceasing" (1 Thess. 5:11). For the work in which they labor will effect nothing and bring forth no fruit except by the power of the Lord who said: "Without me you can do nothing" (John 15: 5). That is why the apostles, instituting deacons, said: "We will devote ourselves to prayer and to the ministry of the word" (Acts 6:4).

81. In order that the divine office may be better and more perfectly prayed in existing circumstances, whether by priests or by other members of the Church, the sacred Council, carrying further the restoration already so happily begun by the Apostolic See, has seen fit to decree as follows concerning the office of the Roman rite.

88. Because the purpose of the office is to sanctify the day, the traditional sequence of the hours is to be restored so that once again they may be genuinely related to the time of the day when they are prayed, as far as this may be possible. Moreover, it will be necessary to take into account the modern conditions in which daily life has to be lived, especially by those who are called to labor in apostolic works.

89. Therefore, when the office is revised, these norms are to be observed:

a) By the venerable tradition of the universal Church, Lauds as morning prayer and Vespers as evening prayer are the two hinges on which the daily office turns; hence, they are to be considered as the chief hours and are to be celebrated as such.

b) Compline is to be drawn up so that it will be a suitable prayer for the end of the day.

c) The hour known as Matins, although it should retain the character of nocturnal praise when celebrated in choir, shall be adapted so that it may be recited at any hour of the day; it shall be made up of fewer psalms and longer readings.

d) The hour of Prime is to be suppressed.

e) In choir the hours of Terce, Sext, and None are to be observed. But outside choir it will be lawful to select any one of these three, according to the respective time of the day.

90. The divine office, because it is the public prayer of the Church, is a source of piety, and nourishment for personal prayer. And therefore priests and all others who take part in the divine office are earnestly exhorted in the Lord to attune their minds to their voices when praying it. The better to achieve this, let them take steps to improve their understanding of the liturgy and of the bible, especially of the psalms.

In revising the Roman office, its ancient and venerable treasures are to be so adapted that all those to whom they are handed on may more extensively and easily draw profit from them.

91. So that it may really be possible in practice to observe the course of the hours proposed in Art. 89, the psalms are no longer to be distributed throughout one week, but through some longer period of time.

The work of revising the psalter, already happily begun, is to be finished as soon as possible, and is to take into account the style of Christian Latin, the liturgical use of psalms, also when sung, and the entire tradition of the Latin Church.

92. As regards the readings, the following shall be observed: a) Readings from sacred scripture shall be arranged so that the riches of God's word may be easily accessible in more abundant measure.

b) Readings excerpted from the works of the fathers, doctors, and ecclesiastical writers shall be better selected.

c) The accounts of martyrdom or the lives of the saints are to accord with the facts of history.

93. To whatever extent may seem desirable, the hymns are to be restored to their original form, and whatever smacks of mythology or ill accords with Christian piety is to be removed or changed. Also, as occasion may arise, let other selections from the treasury of hymns be incorporated.

94. That the day may be truly sanctified, and that the hours themselves may be recited with spiritual advantage, it is best that each of them be prayed at a time which most closely corresponds with its true canonical time.

95. Communities obliged to choral office are bound to celebrate the office in choir every day in addition to the conventual Mass. In particular:

a) Orders of canons, of monks, and of nuns, and of other regulars bound by law or constitutions to choral office must celebrate the entire office.

b) Cathedral or collegiate chapters are bound to recite those parts of the office imposed on them by general or particular law.

c) All members of the above communities who are in major orders or who are solemnly professed, except for lay brothers, are bound to recite individually those canonical hours which they do not pray in choir.

96. Clerics not bound to office in choir, if they are in major orders, are bound to pray the entire office every day, either in common or individually, as laid down in Art. 89.

97. Appropriate instances are to be defined by the rubrics in which a liturgical service may be substituted for the divine office.

In particular cases, and for a just reason, ordinaries can dispense their subjects wholly or in part from the obligation of reciting the divine office, or may commute the obligation.

98. Members of any institute dedicated to acquiring perfection who, according to their constitutions, are to recite any parts of the divine office are thereby performing the public prayer of the Church.

They too perform the public prayer of the Church who, in virtue of their constitutions, recite any short office, provided this is drawn up after the pattern of the divine office and is duly approved.

99. Since the divine office is the voice of the Church, that is of the whole mystical body publicly praising God, those clerics who are not obliged to office in choir, especially priests who live together or who assemble for any purpose, are urged to pray at least some part of the divine office in common.

All who pray the divine office, whether in choir or in common, should fulfill the task entrusted to them as perfectly as possible: this refers not only to the internal devotion of their minds but also to their external manner of celebration.

It is, moreover, fitting that the office, both in choir and in common, be sung when possible.

100. Pastors of souls should see to it that the chief hours, especially Vespers, are celebrated in common in church on Sundays and the more solemn feasts. And the laity, too, are encouraged to recite the divine office, either with the priests, or among themselves, or even individually.

101. 1. In accordance with the centuries-old tradition of the Latin rite, the Latin language is to be retained by clerics in the divine office. But in individual cases the ordinary has the power of granting the use of a vernacular translation to those clerics for whom the use of Latin constitutes a grave obstacle to their praying the office properly. The vernacular version, however, must be one that is drawn up according to the provision of Art. 36.

2. The competent superior has the power to grant the use of the vernacular in the celebration of the divine office, even in choir, to nuns and to members of institutes dedicated to acquiring perfection, both men who are not clerics and women. The version, however, must be one that is approved.

3. Any cleric bound to the divine office fulfills his obligation if he prays the office in the vernacular together with a group of the faithful or with those mentioned in 52 above provided that the text of the translation is approved.

CHAPTER V

THE LITURGICAL YEAR

102. Holy Mother Church is conscious that she must celebrate the saving work of her divine Spouse by devoutly recalling it on certain days throughout the course of the year. Every week, on the day which she has called the Lord's day, she keeps the memory of the Lord's resurrection, which she also celebrates once in the year, together with His blessed passion, in the most solemn festival of Easter.

Within the cycle of a year, moreover, she unfolds the whole mystery of Christ, from the incarnation and birth until the ascension, the day of Pentecost, and the expectation of blessed hope and of the coming of the Lord.

Recalling thus the mysteries of redemption, the Church opens to the faithful the riches of her Lord's powers and merits, so that these are in some way made present for all time, and the faithful are enabled to lay hold upon them and become filled with saving grace.

103. In celebrating this annual cycle of Christ's mysteries, holy Church honors with especial love the Blessed Mary, Mother of God, who is joined by an inseparable bond to the saving work of her Son. In her the Church holds up and admires the most excellent fruit of the redemption, and joyfully contemplates, as in a faultless image, that which she herself desires and hopes wholly to be.

104. The Church has also included in the annual cycle days devoted to the memory of the martyrs and the other saints. Raised up to perfection by the manifold grace of God, and already in possession of eternal salvation, they sing God's perfect praise in heaven and offer prayers for us. By celebrating the passage of these saints from earth to heaven the Church proclaims the paschal mystery achieved in the saints who have suffered and been glorified with Christ; she proposes them to the faithful as examples drawing all to the Father through Christ, and through their merits she pleads for God's favors.

105. Finally, in the various seasons of the year and according to her traditional discipline, the Church completes the formation of the faithful by means of pious practices for soul and body, by instruction, prayer, and works of penance and of mercy.

Accordingly the sacred Council has seen fit to decree as follows.

106. By a tradition handed down from the apostles which took its origin from the very day of Christ's resurrection, the Church celebrates the paschal mystery every eighth day; with good reason this, then, bears the name of the Lord's day or Sunday. For on this day Christ's faithful are bound to come together into one place so that; by hearing the word of God and taking part in the eucharist, they may call to mind the passion, the resurrection and the glorification of the Lord Jesus, and may thank God who "has begotten them again, through the resurrection of Jesus Christ from the dead, unto a living hope" (1 Pet. 1:3). Hence, the Lord's day is the original feast day, and it should be proposed to the piety of the faithful and taught to them so that it may become in fact a day of joy and of freedom from work. Other celebrations, unless they be truly of greatest importance, shall not have precedence over the Sunday which is the foundation and kernel of the whole liturgical year.

107. The liturgical year is to be revised so that the traditional customs and discipline of the sacred seasons shall be preserved or restored to suit the conditions of modern times; their specific character is to be retained, so that they duly nourish the piety of the faithful who celebrate the mysteries of Christian redemption, and above all the

paschal mystery. If certain adaptations are considered necessary on account of local conditions, they are to be made in accordance with the provisions of Art. 39 and 40.

108. The minds of the faithful must be directed primarily toward the feasts of the Lord whereby the mysteries of salvation are celebrated in the course of the year. Therefore, the proper of the time shall be given the preference which is its due over the feasts of the saints, so that the entire cycle of the mysteries of salvation may be suitably recalled.

109. The season of Lent has a twofold character: primarily by recalling or preparing for baptism and by penance, it disposes the faithful, who more diligently hear the word of God and devote themselves to prayer, to celebrate the paschal mystery. This twofold character is to be brought into greater prominence both in the liturgy and by liturgical catechesis. Hence:

a) More use is to be made of the baptismal features proper to the Lenten liturgy; some of them, which used to flourish in bygone days, are to be restored as may seem good.

b) The same is to apply to the penitential elements. As regards instruction it is important to impress on the minds of the faithful not only a social consequences of sin but also that essence of the virtue of penance which leads to the detestation of sin as an offence against God; the role of the Church in penitential practices is not to be passed over, and the people must be exhorted to pray for sinners.

110. During Lent penance should not be only internal and individual, but also external and social. The practice of penance should be fostered in ways that are possible in our own times and in different regions, and according to the circumstances of the faithful; it should be encouraged by the authorities mentioned in Art. 22.

Nevertheless, let the paschal fast be kept sacred. Let it be celebrated everywhere on Good Friday and, where possible, prolonged throughout Holy Saturday, so that the joys of the Sunday of the resurrection may be attained with uplifted and clear mind.

111. The saints have been traditionally honored in the Church and their authentic relics and images held in veneration. For the feasts of the saints proclaim the wonderful works of Christ in His servants, and display to the faithful fitting examples for their imitation.

Lest the feasts of the saints should take precedence over the feasts which commemorate the very mysteries of salvation, many of them should be left to be celebrated by a particular Church or nation or family of religious; only those should be extended to the universal Church which commemorate saints who are truly of universal importance.

CHAPTER VI
SACRED MUSIC

112. The musical tradition of the universal Church is a treasure of inestimable value, greater even than that of any other art. The main reason for this pre-eminence is that, as sacred song united to the words, it forms a necessary or integral part of the solemn liturgy.

Holy Scripture, indeed, has bestowed praise upon sacred song,[42] and the same may be said of the fathers of the Church and of the Roman pontiffs who in recent times, led by St. Pius X, have explained more precisely the ministerial function supplied by sacred music in the service of the Lord.

Therefore sacred music is to be considered the more holy in proportion as it is more closely connected with the liturgical action, whether it adds delight to prayer, fosters unity of minds, or confers greater solemnity upon the sacred rites. But the Church approves of all forms of true art having the needed qualities, and admits them into divine worship.

Accordingly, the sacred Council, keeping to the norms and precepts of ecclesiastical tradition and discipline, and having regard to the purpose of sacred music, which is the glory of God and the sanctification of the faithful, decrees as follows.

113. Liturgical worship is given a more noble form when the divine offices are celebrated solemnly in song, with the assistance of sacred ministers and the active participation of the people.

As regards the language to be used, the provisions of Art. 36 are to be observed; for the Mass, Art. 54; for the sacraments, Art. 63; for the divine office. Art. 101.

114. The treasure of sacred music is to be preserved and fostered with great care. Choirs must be diligently promoted, especially in cathedral churches; but bishops and other pastors of souls must be at pains to ensure that, whenever the sacred action is to be celebrated with song, the whole body of the faithful may be able to contribute that active participation which is rightly theirs, as laid down in Art. 28 and 30.

115. Great importance is to be attached to the teaching and practice of music in seminaries, in the novitiates and houses of study of religious of both sexes, and also in other Catholic institutions and schools. To impart this instruction, teachers are to be carefully trained and put in charge of the teaching of sacred music.

It is desirable also to found higher institutes of sacred music whenever this can be done.

Composers and singers, especially boys, must also be given a genuine liturgical training.

116. The Church acknowledges Gregorian chant as specially suited to the Roman liturgy: therefore, other things being equal, it should be given pride of place in liturgical services.

But other kinds of sacred music, especially polyphony, are by no means excluded from liturgical celebrations, so long as they accord with the spirit of the liturgical action, as laid down in Art. 30.

117. The typical edition of the books of Gregorian chant is to be completed; and a more critical edition is to be prepared of those books already published since the restoration by St. Pius X.

It is desirable also that an edition be prepared containing simpler melodies, for use in small churches.

118. Religious singing by the people is to be intelligently fostered so that in devotions and sacred exercises, as also during liturgical services, the voices of the faithful may ring out according to the norms and requirements of the rubrics.

119. In certain parts of the world, especially mission lands, there are peoples who have their own musical traditions, and these play a great part in their religious and social life. For this reason due importance is to be attached to their music, and a suitable place is to be given to it, not only in forming their attitude toward religion, but also in adapting worship to their native genius, as indicated in Art. 39 and 40.

Therefore, when missionaries are being given training in music, every effort should be made to see that they become competent in promoting the traditional music of these peoples, both in schools and in sacred services, as far as may be practicable.

120. In the Latin Church the pipe organ is to be held in high esteem, for it is the traditional musical instrument which adds a wonderful splendor to the Church's ceremonies and powerfully lifts up man's mind to God and to higher things.

But other instruments also may be admitted for use in divine worship, with the knowledge and consent of the competent territorial authority, as laid down in Art. 22, 52, 37, and 40. This may be done, however, only on condition that the instruments are suitable, or can be made suitable, for sacred use, accord with the dignity of the temple, and truly contribute to the edification of the faithful.

121. Composers, filled with the Christian spirit, should feel that their vocation is to cultivate sacred music and increase its store of treasures.

Let them produce compositions which have the qualities proper to genuine sacred music, not confining themselves to works which can be sung only by large choirs, but providing also for the needs of small choirs and for the active participation of the entire assembly of the faithful.

The texts intended to be sung must always be in conformity with Catholic doctrine; indeed they should be drawn chiefly from holy scripture and from liturgical sources.

CHAPTER VII

SACRED ART AND SACRED FURNISHINGS

122. Very rightly the fine arts are considered to rank among the noblest activities of man's genius, and this applies especially to religious art and to its highest achievement, which is sacred art. These arts, by their very nature, are oriented toward the infinite beauty of God which they attempt in some way to portray by the work of human hands; they achieve their purpose of redounding to God's praise and glory in proportion as they are directed the more exclusively to the single aim of turning men's minds devoutly toward God.

Holy Mother Church has therefore always been the friend of the fine arts and has ever sought their noble help, with the special aim that all things set apart for use in divine worship should be truly worthy, becoming, and beautiful, signs and symbols of the supernatural world, and for this purpose she has trained artists. In fact, the Church has, with good reason, always reserved to herself the right to pass judgment upon the arts, deciding which of the works of artists are in accordance with faith, piety, and cherished traditional laws, and thereby fitted for sacred use.

The Church has been particularly careful to see that sacred furnishings should worthily and beautifully serve the dignity of worship, and has admitted changes in materials, style, or ornamentation prompted by the progress of the technical arts with he passage of time.

Wherefore it has pleased the Fathers to issue the following decrees on these matters.

123. The Church has not adopted any particular style of art as her very own; she has admitted styles from every period according to the natural talents and circumstances of peoples, and the needs of the various rites. Thus, in the course of the centuries, she has brought into being a treasury of art which must be very carefully preserved. The art of our own days, coming from every race and region, shall also be given free scope in the Church, provided that it adorns the sacred buildings and holy rites with due reverence and honor; thereby it is enabled to contribute its own voice to that wonderful chorus of praise in honor of the Catholic faith sung by great men in times gone by.

124. Ordinaries, by the encouragement and favor they show to art which is truly sacred, should strive after noble beauty rather than mere sumptuous display. This principle is to apply also in the matter of sacred vestments and ornaments.

Let bishops carefully remove from the house of God and from other sacred places those works of artists which are repugnant to faith, morals, and Christian piety, and which offend true religious sense either by depraved forms or by lack of artistic worth, mediocrity, and pretense.

And when churches are to be built, let great care be taken that they be suitable for the celebration of liturgical services and for the active participation of the faithful.

125. The practice of placing sacred images in churches so that they may be venerated by the faithful is to be maintained. Nevertheless their number should be moderate and their relative positions should reflect right order. For otherwise they may create confusion among the Christian people and foster devotion of doubtful orthodoxy.

126. When passing judgment on works of art, local ordinaries shall give a hearing to the diocesan commission on sacred art and, if needed, also to others who are especially expert, and to the commissions referred to in Art. 44, 45, and 46.

Ordinaries must be very careful to see that sacred furnishings and works of value are not disposed of or dispersed; for they are the ornaments of the house of God.

127. Bishops should have a special concern for artists, so as to imbue them with the spirit of sacred art and of the sacred liturgy. This they may do in person or through suitable priests who are gifted with a knowledge and love of art.

It is also desirable that schools or academies of sacred art should be founded in those parts of the world where they would be useful, so that artists may be trained.

All artists who, prompted by their talents, desire to serve God's glory in holy Church, should ever bear in mind that they are engaged in a kind of sacred imitation of God the Creator, and are concerned with works destined to be used in Catholic worship, to edify the faithful, and to foster their piety and their religious formation.

128. Along with the revision of the liturgical books, as laid down in Art. 25, there is to be an early revision of the canons and ecclesiastical statutes which govern the provision of material things involved in sacred worship. These laws refer especially to the worthy and well planned construction of sacred buildings, the shape and construction of altars, the nobility, placing, and safety of the eucharistic tabernacle, the dignity and suitability of the baptistery, the proper ordering of sacred images, embellishments, and vestments. Laws which seem less suited to the reformed liturgy are to be brought into harmony with it, or else abolished; and any which are helpful are to be retained if already in use, or introduced where they are lacking.

According to the norm of Art. 22 of this Constitution, the territorial bodies of bishops are empowered to adapt such things to the needs and customs of their different regions; this applies especially to the materials and form of sacred furnishings and vestments.

129. During their philosophical and theological studies, clerics are to be taught about the history and development of sacred art, and about the sound principles governing the production of its works. In consequence they will be able to appreciate and preserve the Church's venerable monuments, and be in a position to aid, by good advice, artists who are engaged in producing works of art.

130. It is fitting that the use of pontificals be reserved to those ecclesiastical persons who have episcopal rank or some particular jurisdiction.

APPENDIX

A DECLARATION OF THE SECOND ECUMENICAL COUNCIL OF THE VATICAN ON REVISION OF THE CALENDAR

The Second Ecumenical Sacred Council of the Vatican, recognizing the importance of the wishes expressed by many concerning the assignment of the feast of Easter to a fixed Sunday and concerning an unchanging calendar, having carefully considered the effects which could result from the introduction of a new calendar, declares as follows:

1. The Sacred Council would not object if the feast of Easter were assigned to a particular Sunday of the Gregorian Calendar, provided that those whom it may concern, especially the brethren who are not in communion with the Apostolic See, give their assent.

2. The sacred Council likewise declares that it does not oppose efforts designed to introduce a perpetual calendar into civil society.

But among the various systems which are being suggested to stabilize a perpetual calendar and to introduce it into civil life, the Church has no objection only in the case of those systems which retain and safeguard a seven-day week with Sunday, without the introduction of any days outside the week, so that the succession of weeks may be left intact, unless there is question of the most serious reasons. Concerning these the Apostolic See shall judge.

NOTES

[1] Secret of the ninth Sunday after Pentecost.
[2] Cf. *Heb.* 13:14.
[3] Cf. *Eph.* 2:21-22.
[4] Cf. *Eph.* 4:13.
[5] Cf. *Is.* 11:12.

[6] Cf. *John* 11:52.
[7] Cf. *John* 10:16.
[8] Cf. Is. 61:1; *Luke* 4:18.
[9] St. Ignatius of Antioch, *To the Ephesians*, 7, 2.
[10] Cf. 1 *Tim.* 2:5.
[11] *Sacramentarium Veronese* (ed. Mohlberg), n. 1265; cf. also n. 1241, 1248.
[12] Easter Preface of the Roman Missal.

[13] Prayer before the second lesson for Holy Saturday, as it was in the Roman Missal before the restoration of Holy Week.

[14] Cf. *Mark* 16:15.

[15] Cf. *Acts* 26:18.

[16] Cf. *Rom.* 6:4; *Eph.* 2:6; *Col.* 3:1; 2 Tim. 2:11.

[17] Cf. *John* 4:23.

[18] Cf. 1 *Cor.* 11:26.

[19] Council of Trent, Session XIII, *Decree on the Holy Eucharist*, c.5.

[20] Council of Trent, Session XXII, *Doctrine on the Holy Sacrifice of the Mass*, c. 2.

[21] Cf. St. Augustine, *Tractatus in Ioannem*, VI, n. 7.

[22] Cf. *Apoc.* 21:2; *Col.* 3:1; *Heb.* 8:2.

[23] Cf. *Phil.* 3:20; *Col.* 3:4.

[24] Cf. *John* 17:3; *Luke* 24:27; *Acts* 2:38.

[25] Cf. *Matt.* 28:20.

[26] Postcommunion for both Masses of Easter Sunday.

[27] Collect of the Mass for Tuesday of Easter Week.

[28] Cf. 2 *Cor.* 6:1.

[29] Cf. *Matt.* 6:6.

[30] Cf. 1 *Thess.* 5:17.

[31] Cf. 2 *Cor.* 4:10-11.

[32] Secret for Monday of Pentecost Week.

[33] St. Cyprian, *On the Unity of the Catholic Church*, 7; cf. *Letter 66*, n. 8, 3.

[34] Cf. Council of Trent, Session XXII, *Doctrine on the Holy Sacrifice of the Mass*, c. 8.

[35] Cf. St. Ignatius of Antioch, *To the Smyrnians*, 8; *To the Magnesians*, 7; *To the Philadelphians*, 4.

[36] Cf. St. Augustine, *Tractatus in Ioannem*, VI, n. 13.

[37] Roman Breviary, feast of Corpus Christi, Second Vespers, antiphon to the *Magnificat*.

[38] Cf. St. Cyril of Alexandria, *Commentary on the Gospel of John*, book XI, chap. XI-XII: Migne, Patrologia Graeca, 74, 557-64.

[39] Cf. 1 *Tim.* 2:1-2.

[40] Session XXI, July 16, 1562. *Doctrine on Communion under Both Species*, chap. 1-3: *Condlium Tridentinum. Diariorum, Actorum, Epistolarum, Tractatuum nova collectio* ed. Soc. Goerresiana, tome VIII (Freiburg in Br., 1919), 698-99.

[41] Council of Trent, Session XXIV, November 11, 1563, *On Reform*, chap. I. Cf. Roman Ritual, title VIII, chap. II, n. 6.

[42] Cf. *Eph.* 5:19; Col. 3:16.

Inter Oecumenici: Excerpt from First Instruction on the Orderly Carrying Out of the Constitution on the Liturgy

Sacred Congregation of Rites, September 26, 1964

V. Part Allowed The Vernacular In Mass (Sc Art. 54)

57. For Masses, whether sung or recited, celebrated with a congregation, the competent, territorial ecclesiastical authority on approval, that is, confirmation, of its decisions by the Holy See, may introduce the vernacular into:

    a. the proclaiming of the lessons, epistle, and gospel; the universal prayer or prayer of the faithful;

    b. as befits the circumstances of the place, the chants of the Ordinary of the Mass, namely, the *Kyrie, Gloria, Credo, Sanctus-Benedictus, Agnus Dei*, as well as the introit, offertory, and communion antiphons and the chants between the readings;

    c. acclamations, greeting, and dialogue formularies, the *Ecce Agnus Dei, Domine, non sum dignus, Corpus Christi* at the communion of the faithful, and the Lord's Prayer with its introduction and embolism.

Missals to be used in the liturgy, however, shall contain besides the vernacular version the Latin text as well.

58. The Holy See alone can grant permission for use of the vernacular in those parts of the Mass that the celebrant sings or recites alone.

59. Pastors shall carefully see to it that the Christian faithful, especially members of lay religious institutes, also know how to recite or sing together in Latin, mainly with simple melodies, the parts of the Ordinary of the Mass proper to them.

Optatam Totius:
An Excerpt From A Decree on Priestly Training

His Holiness Pope Paul VI
Rome, October 28, 1965

Before beginning specifically ecclesiastical subjects, seminarians should be equipped with that humanistic and scientific training which young men in their own countries are wont to have as a foundation for higher studies. Moreover they are to acquire a knowledge of Latin which will enable them to understand and make use of the sources of so many sciences and of the documents of the Church. The study of the liturgical language proper to each rite should be considered necessary; a suitable knowledge of the languages of the Bible and of Tradition should be greatly encouraged.

Excerpts from Remarks at an Audience

His Holiness Pope Paul VI
Rome, April 26, 1968

Latinists cannot but feel at home in the house of the Pope, because as expert, intelligent, versatile collaborators in the composition of the noble, important documents of the Apostolic See, they are, so to speak, in their own house. We lack time for what would be an "excursus" of historical erudition. It would be most interesting to see how our Predecessors favoured Latin in every way, enhanced its splendour and promoted its advancement. Moreover, they encouraged its experts and established the foundations of its literary and artistic development which reached heights of splendour in history and art. It is sufficient to recall Saint Jerome's place beside Pope Damasus, and the admirable flowering of illustrious ecclesiastical personalities during the humanistic period and the Renaissance.

Our intention here is not to dwell on the resplendent hours of a past which was characteristically bound to a particular historical and literary pattern. Today, as We welcome you, We only wish to stress that, you as Latinists, are not strangers nor foreigners to the Holy See, but are, by right, its citizens.

The name of Rome has rendered and still renders to the Church a service of incomparable value. First, the organization of the Roman Empire was providentially preordained to lend the highroads of the world subjugated by it to the messengers of the meek, liberating, humble, triumphant, hidden, priceless Good News. Afterwards, it offered the infant Church, as it emerged from the terrible bloody ordeal of persecution, the bond of the Latin tongue for the new liturgy, for ecclesiastical law and as a means of communication between peoples of different origin and culture, making them all one by the use of the same language, in the profound reality of a mysterious unity.

The Latin language contributed largely to the achievement of this marvel of unity. It is an indisputable, historical fact that the language of Rome became that of the Church of the Latin rite, as Our Predecessor, Pius XI, affirmed: "Embracing all nations and destined to subsist till the end of the world, the Church needs a universal language, immutable and not a vernacular" (Pius XI, Epist. Ap. *Officiorum omnium*, 1 aug. 1922: A.A.S. 14, 1922, p. 452). Our immediate Predecessor, John XXIII, while recalling and summarizing the merits of Latin in the magnificent document *Veterum Sapientia*, commented at length and lovingly on the three above mentioned effective attributes (cfr. A.A.S. 54, 1962, pp. 129-135).

We, Ourself, have not only openly confirmed these noble documents of Our Predecessors, but We have instituted, with a Motu Proprio, *Studia Latinitatis* (cfr. A.A.S. 56, 1964, pp. 225-231) the *Pontificium Institutum altioris latinitatis*, for the correct and complete formation of professors of Latin in our Seminaries and Religious houses, and We have again confirmed these directives for these same Seminaries in Our Apostolic Letter *Summi Dei Verbum* (cfr. A. A. S. 55, 1963, pp. 979-995), given upon the occasion of the fourth centenary of the institution of Seminaries by the Council of Trent: "that the study of various languages be placed in the curriculum of the Seminaries and above all Latin, especially for priests of the Latin rite."

For all these reasons, We wish to repeat here and now before this distinguished assembly, that Latin must continue to be fostered, above all, in our Seminaries and in the houses of formation of the Regular Clergy, because it is essential to the mental formation of their students, as well as to the study of the classics and of the Fathers of the Church and, particularly, it will enable them to appreciate the treasures of the Sacred Liturgy. Without Latin, their higher and complete intellectual, theological and liturgical formation—which the modern world demands of priests—would be minimized. The Ecumenical Council Vatican II, in the Decree, *Optatam totius* on the formation of priests, in the Constitution *Sacrosanctum Concilium* on the Liturgy and in other documents, has repeatedly advised and inculcated the necessity of this study and use of Latin. It is precisely for its educative and formative value that We desire that Latin should continue to hold a place of honour in our midst.

Excerpts from Remarks at a General Audience

Pope Paul VI
Rome, November 26, 1969

It is here that the greatest newness is going to be noticed, the newness of language. No longer Latin, but the spoken language will be the principal language of the Mass. The introduction of the vernacular will certainly be a great sacrifice for those who know the beauty, the power and the expressive sacrality of Latin. We are parting with the speech of the Christian centuries; we are becoming like profane intruders in the literary preserve of sacred utterance. We will lose a great part of that stupendous and incomparable artistic and spiritual thing, the Gregorian chant.

We have reason indeed for regret, reason almost for bewilderment. What can we put in the place of that language of the angels? We are giving up something of priceless worth. But why? What is more precious than these loftiest of our Church's values?

Statement by
Scholars, Intellectuals, and Artists
Living in England
Published in the July 6, 1971 edition
of the *Times of London*

If some senseless decree were to order the total or partial destruction of basilicas or cathedrals, then obviously it would be the educated—whatever their personal beliefs—who would rise up in horror to oppose such a possibility.

Now the fact is that basilicas and cathedrals were built so as to celebrate a rite which, until a few months ago, constituted a living tradition. We are referring to the Roman Catholic Mass. Yet, according to the latest information in Rome, there is a plan to obliterate that Mass by the end of the current year.

One of the axioms of contemporary publicity, religious as well as secular, is that modern man in general, and intellectuals in particular, have become intolerant of all forms of tradition and are anxious to suppress them and put something else in their place.

But, like many other affirmations of our publicity machines, this axiom is false. Today, as in times gone by, educated people are in the vanguard where recognition of the value of tradition is concerned, and are the first to raise the alarm when it is threatened.

We are not at this moment considering the religious or spiritual experience of millions of individuals. The rite in question, in its magnificent Latin text, has also inspired a host of priceless achievements in the arts—not only mystical works, but works by poets, philosophers, musicians, architects, painters and sculptors in all countries and epochs. Thus, it belongs to universal culture as well as to churchmen and formal Christians.

In the materialistic and technocratic civilisation that is increasingly threatening the life of mind and spirit in its original creative expression—the word—it seems particularly inhuman to deprive man of word-forms in one of their most grandiose manifestations.

The signatories of this appeal, which is entirely ecumenical and nonpolitical, have been drawn from every branch of modern culture in Europe and elsewhere. They wish to call to the attention of the Holy See, the appalling responsibility it would incur in the history of the human spirit were it to refuse to allow the Traditional Mass to survive, even though this survival took place side by side with other liturgical forms.

Signed,

Harold Acton
Vladimir Ashkenazy
John Bayler
Lennox Berkeley
Maurice Bowra
Agatha Christie
Kenneth Clark
Nevill Coghill
Cyril Connolly
Colin Davis
Hugh Delargy
Robert Exeter
Miles Fitzalen-Howard
Constantine Fitzgibbon
William Glock
Magdalen Gofflin
Robert Graves
Graham Greene
Ian Greenless
Joseph Grimond
Harman Grisewood
Colin Hardie
Rupert Hart-Davis
Barbara Hepworth
Auberon Herbert
John Jolliffe
David Jones
Osbert Lancaster

Cecil Day Lewis
Compton Mackenzie
George Malcolm
Max Mallowan
Alfred Marnau
Yehudi Menuhin
Nancy Mitford
Raymond Mortimer
Malcolm Muggeridge
Iris Murdoch
John Murray
Sean O'Faolain
E.J. Oliver
Oxford and Asquith
F.R. Leavis
William Plomer
Kathleen Raine
William Rees-Mogg
Ralph Richardson
John Ripon
Charles Russell
Rivers Scott
Joan Sutherland
Philip Toynbee
Martin Turnell
Bernard Wall
Patrick Wall
E.I. Watkin

The "English" Indult

The Congregation for Divine Worship
November 5, 1971

Prot. N. 1897/71

Your Eminence,

His Holiness Pope Paul VI, by letter of 30 October 1971, has given special faculties to the undersigned Secretary of this Sacred Congregation to convey to Your Eminence, as Chairman of the Episcopal Conference of England and Wales, the following points regarding the Order of the Mass:

1. Considering the pastoral needs referred to by Your Eminence, it is permitted to the local Ordinaries of England and Wales to grant that certain groups of the faithful may on special occasions be allowed to participate in the Mass celebrated according to the Rites and texts of the former Roman Missal. The edition of the Missal to be used on these occasions should be that published again by the Decree of the Sacred Congregation of Rites (27 January 1965), and with the modifications indicated in the *Instructio altera* (4 May 1967).

This faculty may be granted provided that groups make the request for reasons of genuine devotion, and provided that the permission does not disturb or damage the general communion of the faithful. For this reason the permission is limited to certain groups on special occasions; at all regular parish and other community Masses, the Order of the Mass given in the new Roman Missal should be used. Since the Eucharist is the sacrament of unity, it is necessary that the use of the Order of Mass given in the former Missal should not become a sign or cause of disunity in the Catholic community. For this reason agreement among the Bishops of the Episcopal Conference as to how this faculty is to be exercised will be a further guarantee of unity of praxis in this area.

2. Priests who on occasion wish to celebrate Mass according to the above-mentioned edition of the Roman Missal may do so by consent of their Ordinary and in accordance with the norms given by the

same. When these priests celebrate Mass with the people and wish to use the rites and texts of the former Missal, the conditions and limits mentioned above for celebration by certain groups on special occasions are to be applied.

With my highest respects, I am
Yours sincerely in Christ,
(Signed:) A[nnibale] Bugnini
Secretary
Sacra Congregatio
pro Cultu Divino

Quattuor Abhinc Annos:
Indult for the Use of the Roman Missal of 1962

Congregation for Divine Worship
October 3, 1984

Most Rev. Excellency:

Four years ago, by order of the Supreme Pontiff John Paul II, the bishops of the whole Church were invited to present a report:

> —concerning the way in. which the priests and faithful of their dioceses had received the Missal promulgated in 1970 by authority of Pope Paul VI in accordance with the decisions of the Second Vatican Council

> —concerning the difficulties arising in the implementation of the liturgical reform;

> —concerning possible resistance that may have arisen.

The result of the consultation was sent to all the bishops (cf. *Notitiae,* n. 185 December 1981). On the basis of their replies it appeared that the problem of priests and faithful holding to the so-called "Tridentine" rite was almost completely solved.

Since, however, the same problem continues, the Supreme Pontiff, in a desire to meet the wishes of these groups grants to diocesan bishops the possibility of using an indult whereby priests and faithful, who shall be expressly indicated in the letter of request to be presented to their own bishop, may be able to celebrate Mass by using the Roman Missal according to the 1962 edition, but under the following conditions:

> a) That it be made publicly clear beyond all ambiguity that such priests and their respective faithful in no way share the positions of those who call in question the legitimacy and doctrinal exactitude of the Roman Missal promulgated by Pope Paul VI in 1970.

b) Such celebration must be made only for the benefit of those groups that request it; in churches and oratories indicated by the bishop (not, however, in parish churches, unless the bishop permits it in extraordinary cases); and on the days and under the conditions fixed by the bishop either habitually or in individual cases.

c) These celebrations must be according to the 1962 Missal and in Latin.

d) There must be no interchanging of texts and rites of the two Missals.

e) Each bishop must inform this Congregation of the concessions granted by him, and at the end of a year from the granting of this indult, he must report on the result of its application.

This concession, indicative of the common Father's solicitude for all his children, must be used in such a way as not to prejudice the faithful observance of the liturgical reform in the life of the respective ecclesial communities.

I am pleased to avail myself of this occasion to express to Your Excellency my sentiments of deep esteem.

Yours devotedly in the Lord

Augustin Mayer, Pro-Prefect
Virgilio Noe Secretary

Ecclesia Dei

Pope John Paul II
Apostolic letter given on July 2, 1988

---

1. With great affliction the church has learned of the unlawful episcopal ordination conferred on June 30 by Archbishop Marcel Lefebvre, which has frustrated all the efforts made during the previous years to ensure the full communion with the church of the Priestly Society of St. Pius X founded by the same Archbishop Lefebvre. These efforts, especially intense during recent months, in which the Apostolic See has shown comprehension to the limits of the possible, were all to no avail.[1]

2. This affliction was particularly felt by the successor of Peter, to whom in the first place pertains the guardianship of the unity of the church,[2] even though the number of persons directly involved in these events might be few, since every person is loved by God on his own account and has been redeemed by the blood of Christ shed on the cross for the salvation of all.

The particular circumstances, both objective and subjective, in which Archbishop Lefebvre acted provide everyone with an occasion for profound reflection and for a renewed pledge of fidelity to Christ and to his church.

3. In itself this act was one of disobedience to the Roman pontiff in a very grave matter and of supreme importance for the unity of the church, such as is the ordination of bishops whereby the apostolic succession is sacramentally perpetuated. Hence, such disobedience—which implies in practice the rejection of the Roman primacy—constitutes a schismatic act.[3] In performing such an act, notwithstanding the formal canonical warning sent to them by the cardinal prefect of the Congregation for Bishops last June 17, Archbishop Lefebvre and the priests Bernard Fellay, Bernard Tissier de Mallerais, Richard Williamson, and Alfonso de Galarreta have incurred the grave penalty of excommunication envisaged by ecclesiastical law.[4]

4. The root of this schismatic act can be discerned in an incomplete and contradictory notion of tradition. Incomplete, because it does not take sufficiently into account the living character of tradition, which, as the Second Vatican Council clearly taught, "comes from the apostles and progresses in the church with the help of the Holy Spirit.

There is a growth in insight into the realities and words that are being passed on. This comes about in various ways. It comes through the contemplation and study of believers, who ponder these things in their hearts. It comes from the intimate sense of spiritual realities which they experience. And it comes from the preaching of those who have received, along with their right of succession in the episcopate, the sure charism of truth."[5]

But especially contradictory is a notion of tradition which opposes the universal magisterium of the church possessed by the bishop of Rome and the body of bishops. It is impossible to remain faithful to the tradition while breaking the ecclesial bond with him to whom, in the person of the apostle Peter, Christ himself entrusted the ministry of unity in his church.[6]

5. Faced with the situation that has arisen, I deem it my duty to inform all the Catholic faithful of some aspects which this sad event has highlighted.

a) The outcome of the movement promoted by Archbishop Lefebvre can and must be, for all the Catholic faithful, a motive for sincere reflection concerning their own fidelity to the church's tradition, authentically interpreted by the ecclesiastical magisterium, ordinary and extraordinary, especially in the ecumenical councils from Nicaea to Vatican II. From this reflection all should draw a renewed and efficacious conviction of the necessity of strengthening still more their fidelity by rejecting erroneous interpretations and arbitrary and unauthorized applications in matters of doctrine, liturgy, and discipline.

To the bishops especially it pertains, by reason of their pastoral mission, to exercise the important duty of a clear-sighted vigilance full of charity and firmness, so that this fidelity may be everywhere safeguarded.[7]

However, it is necessary that all the pastors and other faithful have a new awareness, not only of the lawfulness but also of the richness for the church of a diversity of charisms, traditions of spirituality and apostolate, which also constitutes the beauty unity in variety: of that blended "harmony" which the earthly church raises up to heaven under the impulse of the Holy Spirit.

b) Moreover, I should like to remind theologians and other experts in the ecclesiastical sciences that they should feel called upon to answer in the present circumstances.

Indeed, the extent and depth of the teaching of the Second Vatican Council call for a renewed commitment to deeper study in order to reveal clearly the council's continuity with tradition, especially in points of doctrine which, perhaps because they are new, have not yet been well understood by some sections of the church.

c) In the present circumstances I wish especially to make an appeal both solemn and heartfelt, paternal and fraternal, to all those who until now have been linked in various ways to the movement of Archbishop Lefebvre, that they may fulfill the grave duty of remaining united to the vicar of Christ in the unity of the Catholic Church and of ceasing their support in any way for that movement. Everyone should be aware that formal adherence to the schism is a grave offense against God and carries the penalty of excommunication decreed by the church's law.[8]

To all those Catholic faithful who feel attached to some previous liturgical and disciplinary forms of the Latin tradition, I wish to manifest my will to facilitate their ecclesial communion by means of the necessary measures to guarantee respect for their rightful aspirations. In this matter I ask for the support of the bishops and of all those engaged in the pastoral ministry in the church.

6. Taking account of the importance and complexity of the problems referred to in this document, by virtue of my apostolic authority I decree the following:

a) A commission is instituted whose task it will be to collaborate with the bishops, with the departments of the Roman Curia and with the circles concerned, for the purpose of facilitating full ecclesial communion of priests, seminarians, religious communities, or individuals until now linked in various ways to the society founded by Archbishop Lefebvre who may wish to remain united to the successor of Peter in the Catholic Church while preserving their spiritual and liturgical traditions in the light of the protocol signed on last May 5 by [Joseph] Cardinal Ratzinger and Archbishop Lefebvre.

b) This commission is composed of a cardinal-president and other members of the Roman Curia, in a number that will be deemed opportune according to circumstances.

c) Moreover, respect must everywhere by shown for the feelings of all those who are attached to the Latin liturgical tradition by a wide and generous application of the directives already issued some time ago by the Apostolic See for the use of the Roman Missal according to the typical edition of 1962.[9]

7. As this year specially dedicated to the Blessed Virgin is now drawing to a close, I wish to exhort all to join in unceasing prayer, which the vicar of Christ, through the intercession of the mother of the church, addresses to the Father in the very words of the Son: "That they all may be one!"

Given at Rome, at St. Peter's, July 2, 1988, the 10th year of the pontificate.

ENDNOTES

1. Cf. Informatory note of June 16, 1988; *L'Osservatore Romano*, English ed., June 27, 1988, pp. 1-2.
2. Cf. Vatican Council I, "*Pastor Aeternus*," Ch. 3; Denzinger-Schonmetzer 3060.
3. Cf. Code of Canon Law, Canon 751.
4. Cf. *ibid.*, Canon 1382.
5. Vatican Council II, "*Dei Verbum*," 8; cf. Vatican Council I, "*Dei Filius*," Ch. 4; DS 3020.
6. Cf. Mt. 16:18; Lk, 10:16; "*Pastor Aeternus*," Ch. 3; DS 3060.
7. Cf. Canon 386; Paul VI, "*Quique Iam Anni*," Dec. 8, 1970; "*Acta Apostolicae Sedis*" 63 (1971) pp. 97-106.
8. Cf. Canon 1364.
9. Cf. Congregation for Divine Worship, "*Quattuor Abhinc Annos*," Oct. 3, 1984; AAS 76 (1984) pp. 1088-89.

Excerpt from
An Address to the Bishops of Chile
Santiago, Chile

Joseph Cardinal Ratzinger
July 13, 1988

While there are many motives that might have led a great number of people to seek a refuge in the traditional liturgy, the chief one is that they find the dignity of the sacred preserved there. After the Council there were many priests who deliberately raised "desacralization" to the level of a program, on the plea that the New Testament abolished the cult of the Temple: the veil of the Temple which was torn from top to bottom at the moment of Christ's death on the cross is, according to certain people, the sign of the end of the sacred. The death of Jesus, outside the City walls, that is to say, in the public world, is now the true religion. Religion, if it has any being at all, must have it in the nonsacredness of daily life, in love that is lived. Inspired by such reasoning, they put aside the sacred vestments; they have despoiled the churches as much as they could of that splendor which brings to mind the sacred; and they have reduced the liturgy to the language and the gestures of ordinary life, by means of greetings, common signs of friendship, and such things.

There is no doubt that, with these theories and practices, they have entirely disregarded the true connection between the Old and the New Testaments: It is forgotten that this world is not the Kingdom of God, and that the "Holy One of God" (John 6:69) continues to exist in contradiction to this world; that we have need of purification before we draw near to Him; that the profane, even after the death and the Resurrection of Jesus, has not succeeded in becoming "the holy." The Risen One has appeared, but to those whose heart has been opened to Him, to the Holy; He did not manifest Himself to everyone. It is in this way a new space has been opened for the religion to which all of us would now submit; this religion which consists in drawing near to the community of the Risen One, at whose feet the women prostrated themselves and adored Him. I do not want to develop this point any further now; I confine myself to coming straight to this conclusion: we ought to get back the dimension of the sacred in the liturgy. The liturgy is not a festivity; it is not a meeting for the purpose of having a good time. It is of no importance that the parish priest has cudgeled his brains to come up with suggestive ideas or imaginative novelties. The liturgy is what makes the Thrice-Holy God present amongst us; it is the burning bush; it is the Alliance of God with man in Jesus Christ, who has died and risen again. The grandeur of the liturgy does not rest upon the fact that it offers an interesting entertainment, but in rendering tangible the Totally Other, whom we are not capable of summoning. He comes because He wills. In other words, the essential in the liturgy is the mystery, which is realized in the common ritual of the Church; all the rest diminishes it. Men experiment with it in lively fashion, and find themselves deceived, when the mystery is transformed into distraction, when the chief actor in the liturgy is not the Living God but the priest or the liturgical director.

Guidelines for the Celebration of the Tridentine Mass

Pontifical Commission "Ecclesia Dei"
January 1, 1991

I write to you as a brother in the episcopal college charged by the Holy Father to carry out the provisions of his apostolic letter *Ecclesia Dei* of July 2, 1988. My objective is addressing myself to you now is precisely to encourage you in the exercise of your pastoral mission to those who legitimately request the celebration of Holy Mass according to the 1962 typical edition of the Roman Missal.

Perhaps a review of developments which led to the issuance of *Ecclesia Dei* would be helpful in this regard.

1. On Oct. 3, 1984, the Sacred Congregation for Divine Worship issued *Quattuor Abhinc Annos*, in which the Holy Father granted to diocesan bishops "the possibility of using an indult whereby priests and faithful . . . may be able to celebrate Mass by using the Roman Missal according to the 1962 edition."

The following conditions were stipulated: a) that those requesting the permission do not "call into question the legitimacy and doctrinal exactitude of the Roman Missal promulgated by Pope Paul VI in 1970;" b) that such celebrations take place only for groups requesting them, not in parish churches (except with the bishop's permission in extraordinary cases) and under conditions laid down by the bishop; c) that "these celebrations must be according to the 1962 missal and in Latin;" d) that there "be no interchanging of texts and rites of the two missals" and e) that each bishop had to inform the congregation "of the concessions granted by him and at the end of a year from the granting of this indult, he must report on the result of its application.

2. A special *commissio cardinalitia ad hoc ipsum instituta* charged with reviewing the use made of the indult met in December of 1986. At that time the cardinals unanimously agreed that the conditions laid down in *Quattuor Abhinc Annos* were too restrictive and should be relaxed.

3. As you well know, responses to the illicit ordination of bishops at Econe on June 30, 1988, and wishing to uphold the principles which had been established in the previous and unfortunately unfruitful dialogue with Archbishop Marcel Lefebvre, the Holy Father issued *Ecclesia Dei* motu proprio on July 2, 1988.

While insisting that the root of the schismatic act of Archbishop Lefebvre lies in an "incomplete and contradictory notion of tradition" which fails to "take sufficiently into account the living character of tradition," he also maintained with equal firmness that it is necessary that all the pastors and other faithful have a new awareness not only of the lawfulness, but also of the richness for the Church of a diversity of charisms, traditions of spirituality and apostolate."

Consequently, addressing himself "to all those Catholic faithful who feel attached to some previous liturgical and disciplinary forms of the Latin tradition" and not just to former adherents of Archbishop Lefebvre, he expressed his will "to guarantee respect for their rightful aspirations." In order to provide for these legitimate desires of the faithful he established this pontifical commission and indicated his mind with regard to its primary task by stating:

> "Respect must everywhere be shown for the feelings of all those who are attached to the Latin liturgical tradition, by a wide and generous application of the directives already issued some time ago by the Apostolic See for the use of the Roman Missal according to the typical edition."

Consequently, Your Excellency, we wish to encourage you to facilitate the proper and reverent celebration of the liturgical rites according to the Roman Missal of 1962 wherever there is genuine desire for this on the part of priests and faithful. This should not be construed as a promotion of that missal in prejudice to the one promulgated eight years later, but simply a pastoral provision to meet the "rightful aspirations" of those who wish to worship according to the Latin tradition as celebrated for centuries.

In the light of our Holy Father's motu proprio, then, we offer the following guidelines and suggestions:

1. There is no reason now why the so-called "Tridentine" Mass cannot be celebrated in a parish church where this would be a genuine pastoral service to the faithful asking for it. Care should be taken, of

course, for a harmonious integration into the already existing parish liturgical schedule.

2. The regularity and frequency of the celebration of this liturgy, whether to be celebrated on Sundays, holy days and/or weekdays, will depend on the needs of the faithful. Our recommendation is that in places where the faithful have made a request for the regular celebration for the Mass according to the 1962 Roman Missal a weekly Sunday and holy day Mass be scheduled in a central location and at a convenient time on a trial basis for a period of several months. Afterwards further evaluation and adjustment could be made.

3. Of course the celebrant of the "Tridentine" Mass should not fail in their preaching and contacts with the faithful attending such Masses to emphasize their own adherence to the legislation of the universal church and their acknowledgment of the doctrinal and juridical value of the liturgy as revisited after the Second Vatican Council. Under such conditions, it would seem unnecessary, even unduly painful, to impose further restrictions upon those who wish to attend such celebrations.

The very fact that, avoiding the possibilities offered by schismatic groups, they wish to come to celebrations authorized by the bishop of the diocese may be considered a sign of good will and desire of full ecclesial communion.

4. Although the Holy Father has given this pontifical commission the faculty to grant the use of the 1962 typical edition of the Roman Missal to all those who request it while the commission informs the appropriate ordinary thereof, we would much prefer that such faculties be granted by the ordinary himself for the sake of strengthening the bond of ecclesial communion between those priests and faithful and their local pastors.

5. Following upon the "wide and generous application" of the principles laid down in *Quattuor Abhinc Annos* and the directives of the fathers of the Second Vatican Council (cf. *Sacrosanctum Concilium,* nos. 51 and 54), the new lectionary in the vernacular could be used as a way of "providing a richer fare for the faithful at the table of God's Word" in Masses celebrated according to the 1962 missal. However, we believe that this usage should not be imposed on congregations who decidedly wish to maintain the former liturgical tradition in its integrity according to the provision of the motu proprio

Ecclesia Dei. Such an imposition might also be less likely to invite back to full communion with the Church at this time those who have lapsed into schismatic worship.

6. Since a number of older and retired priests who have a deep appreciation of the previous Latin liturgical tradition have approached their individual ordinaries as well as this pontifical commission to obtain the *celebret* for the use of the 1962 missal, it would seem particularly suitable to utilize the services of such priests where possible for the celebration of this Mass. It may well be discovered that even retired priests who have not requested this faculty would nonetheless be willing to provide this special form of pastoral care for those who request it.

Finally, Your Excellency, it is my sincere desire that this fraternal letter will be for us who are members of the episcopal college an incentive to exercise that *munus episcopale* described so beautifully in *Lumen Gentium*, 23:

> "Individual bishops, insofar as they are set over particular churches, exercise their pastoral office over the portion of the people of God assigned to them, not over other churches nor the church universal. But insofar as they are members of the episcopal college and legitimate successors of the apostles by Christ's arrangement and decree, each is bound to have such care and solicitude for the whole church which, though it be not exercised by an act of jurisdiction, does for all that redound in an eminent degree to the advantage of the universal Church. For all the bishops have the obligation of fostering and safeguarding the unity of the faith and of upholding the discipline which is common to the whole Church."

I am pleased to avail myself of this opportunity to extend my best wishes to you in your shepherding of the flock entrusted to your care and to assure you of my willing collaboration that in all circumstances God may be glorified in the worship of his Holy Church.

Cardinal Paul Augustine Mayer, President

Address at the
Annual General Meeting of the
Latin Mass Society of England and Wales

Alfons Cardinal Stickler, SDB
June 20, 1992

Your Movement has Legitimacy in the Church

I have accepted, with great pleasure, the invitation of your Chairman and Secretary to come to your Meeting. Now after reaching my 80's I am free from my ordinary work in the Curia so I can more easily accept such invitations and I do it with great pleasure when I can be helpful to so many of the faithful who today have many difficulties. I will communicate with you some ideas which I have found in many countries. I have been to Italy, France, Austria, Switzerland. I have been last February also in the United States for the opening of the Institute of Dietrich von Hildebrand, with a great High Mass in St. Agnes Church. I was told that the church was never so full since Fulton Sheen preached his Lenten sermons there. From everywhere people were coming so I could realize that in the United States also, the movement and the consideration for the old Mass are very effective.

The first idea I will communicate with you is that you can be sure that your movement has full legitimacy in the Church. Some have said that we are not legitimate. This is not true because, if you remember article 4 of the Liturgical Constitution, the Council Fathers explicitly said all the venerable rites have to be preserved. Some people say this is valid for all the other rites, with the exception of the Roman Latin rite. This is not so. Because article 4 says: all the rites legitimately recognized. This was not only established for the rites existing at that time, during the Council, but also for the rites that should be approved afterwards. Now the Old Latin rite was really recognized after the changing of the former Latin Roman rite because, as you know, exception was given immediately for old priests and, in England, you had fortunately your great Cardinal Heenan, who obtained the Indult for England and Wales in 1971. Then, we had the *Motu Proprio*, the Indult of the Pope, and later on *Ecclesia Dei* which was clearly confirmed by the Pope; for example, when he spoke to the Abbot of

Le Barroux in 1990, who had asked explicitly for this rite. Consequently, a new authority was given to the old Rite on the base of the liturgical Constitution of the Council itself. This recognition is coming from the Holy See, from the Pope, under the conditions given at the moment of the new approbation, which institutes a real legitimation of the Old Rite (and is available now). So, if you fulfill the conditions for the continuation of the Old Rite, it is legitimate for you. This is the external legitimacy of your movement.

Legitimacy from Tradition

Now we have another legitimacy which is coming from the internal sensibility for this rite. You know that worship and worshipping in every region is attached closely to tradition. No worship is easily changed in any religion. All are attached closely to tradition. This is true in a special manner also for our Rite, our Roman Latin Rite. Its changing after the Council was said to be a question of natural development; but, for every Rite, thinking should be only organical, adopted slowly in order to give no impression of changing, of cutting tradition. Unfortunately many people had this impression after the so-called "reform" established by the Commission, which was instituted by Pope Paul VI after the Council. Many things were changed which really cut the hearts of many of the Faithful—I would say sometimes the best of the Faithful. This is also a reason to continue the tradition in the external forms of the Rite we professed before. This is the proof of the old saying *"Lex orandi—Lex credendi."* Unfortunately too many things have confused the common faithful in our Church. This is one of the reasons why they no longer have the security of an unchanging rite. *"Lex orandi—Lex credendi."* If the Law of worshipping is changed so profoundly, our faith has lost the help we had in our worship.

No Polemics

Now the next idea I want to express is that we have to avoid, always in our life and in our discussions, in our general behavior in our association, every kind of polemics, because there is always a danger of hurting others. If there are polemics, they will say "Ah, you are a sect with no more reasoning." So we have to profess our attachment to the Old Rite calmly, reasoning with them but without polemics.

We have to explain also to ourselves the reasons for following the Old Latin Rite and we have many reasons for it. The first I have mentioned already; it is the absolute tradition of Liturgy in every religion to have no change with the past because we have to preserve that rite as the expression of our Faith. You know that the Oriental Church saved the common truth, that is the Catholic Truth, by preserving the rite. They preserved all the Sacraments because they were attached so strongly to the rite which they would never changed. The other heretics—Protestants and so on—have changed the Faith because they have changed the Rite.

The Catholic Church a Communio

The Vatican Council says explicitly that we have "*a communion*" in the Catholic Church, the Pope with the Bishops and with the priests in all parts of the world. We are particular churches but we are all in one Catholic Church. If we have the same faith, even with the different rites, but not in all our fundamental teaching, then we have not the complete Communion. For example, the Oriental Church is a Church not in complete communion because there is not preserved the dogma and truth in the Primacy of the Pope. They have not the whole truth, but most of it they have preserved. All the other churches are not called "churches" in the full sense but religious communities. This means that they have not the complete substance of our Faith. So the Catholic Church in the case of the Rites, who did not absolutely preserve the truths of the Catholic and Latin Rites has not with them this unity. This is very important in order to confirm our sensibilities for the Old Rite which is really that of the "*Lex Credendi*" expressed by the "*Lex Orandi.*"

The Modernity of the Church

We have to consider still another idea. Modern Catholics say, "Now we have to cut away all the old things. We must be modern." But this modernity is not the modernity of the Church because we have to preserve the whole substance which is our heritage from past generations. So if many of the Bishops ask us "Why do you follow the Old Rite?" We can answer very easily: "The new rite was introduced after the Council as a matter of pastoral care. This means that the Faithful should be animated more and more by the new form of rites to be better in Catholic truth and life. But many good people in the world who still believe in the truths of the Catholic Church are not satisfied about the innovations introduced into the Mass. Can you say then that the pastoral purpose has been fulfilled?" I think, through my experience, that there is more and more dissatisfaction becoming stronger always in all the categories of age, social positions, even in many young people.

Further we are told that the truth about the Mass, about the centre of the liturgy has not really changed. But we can ask; have we the same sense, the same reverence we had before—and perhaps still have—when we assist at the Old Roman Rite? Or have we a loss of reverence, of awe of our biggest mystery, our faith in the Holy Mass? In the sacrifice? It was admitted officially when, two years ago, on the Silver Jubilee of the changing of the Rite, authorities in Rome admitted that there was a great loss of awe in the Mass—the most important rite of our worship.

This is the experience of all who travel around everywhere. We have lost what really is at the heart of our worshipping in the Holy Sacrifice. Many times we get the impression that it is man being worshipped but not God. We have a Communion meal, but not a Sacrifice. I think that this has proved one of the most important changes in the general attitude to the Holy Sacrifice of the Mass. When I studied Theology I was told that the centre of the Mass is the Consecration, the Communion is quite necessary for the priest but supposes the sacrificial act already done. Today, at the centre is the meal. What we have to do when confronted with the situation as members of the Association, you represent here. Firstly we have to tell our Bishops and our parish priests that we are not satisfied with the new rite; that we have good reasons for being attached to the Old Mass. We should explain all the reasons why it should be available for those who ask for it. We must also explain that the Holy Father has granted the privilege contained in the *Motu Proprio*; *Ecclesia Dei* and that he wanted to take care of the sensibilities of those attached to the Old Latin Mass.

Loyalty Always to the Holy See

Our fidelity to the Old Rite must always conform to the decisions of the Holy See, with all the conditions satisfied which the Holy See has laid down for this purpose. We should persist in our fidelity to this heritage, which is a heritage of truth and because we can be sure that also today, the old Latin Mass is completely valid and *"Lex Orandi"* reflects the *"Lex Credendi."* If we are faithful in *"Oratione,"* we can be certain to remain also attached to the truth in *"Credendo,"* in full devotion to our heritage of Faith.

Praying *Ad Orientem Versus*

An editorial in *Notitiae*
332, Vol. 29, No. 5, May 1993, pp. 245-249
Reprinted in *Sacred Music,* Winter 1993

1) The Eucharistic celebration is, by definition, connected to the eschatological dimension of the Christian faith. This is true in its most profound identity. Is this not perhaps the sense of the wondrous change (*mirabilis conversio*) of the bread and wine into the Body and Blood of the Lord of glory, who lives always with the Father, perpetuating His paschal mystery?

2) The sober description of the Acts of the Apostles in the first summary concerning the life of the community speaks of the "joy" (*agalliasis*) with which those joined in the assembly (*epi to auto*), broke bread in the homes. This term (*agalliasis*) is the same that Luke used to indicate eschatological joy.

3) There is a logic of Ascension in the Eucharist: "This Jesus that you have seen ascend into heaven, will return. . ." In the Eucharist the Lord returns; He anticipates sacramentally His glorious return, transforming the profound reality of the elements, and He leaves them in the condition of signs of His presence and mediation of communion with His own person. It is for this that the various liturgical families underscored a common point in different ways: with the Eucharistic prayer the Church penetrates the celestial sphere. This is the meaning of the conclusion of the Roman prefaces, of the chant of the *Sanctus* and of the eastern *herubicon*.

4) In analyzing the origins of the Eucharistic prayer one is struck by the typically Christian variant introduced in the initial dialogue. The greeting, *Dominus vobiscum*, and the invitation, *Gratias agamus*, are common to the Jewish *berakha*. Only the Christian one, beginning with the first complete redaction that we possess—the Apostolic Tradition—inserts the *Sursum corda. Habemus ad Dominum.* For the Church, in fact, celebrating the Eucharist is never to put into action something earthly, but rather something heavenly, because it has the awareness that the principal celebrant of the same action is the Lord of glory. The Church necessarily celebrates the Eucharist oriented toward the Lord, in communion with Him and, through His

mediation, toward the Father in unity with the Holy Spirit. The priest, ordained in the Catholic and apostolic communion, is the witness of the authenticity of the celebration and at the same time the sign of the glorious Lord who presides at it. Just as the bread and wine are the elements that Christ assumes in order to "give Himself," the priest is the person that Christ consecrated and invited to "give."

5) The placement of the priest and the faithful in relation to the "mystical table" found different forms in history, some of which can be considered typical to certain places and periods. As is logical when treating liturgical questions, symbolism took on a noteworthy role in these different forms, but it would be difficult to prove that the architectural interpretation of such symbolism could, in any of the forms chosen, have been considered as an integral and basic part of the Christian faith or of the profound attitudes of the celebrating Church.

6) The arrangement of the altar in such a manner that the celebrant and the faithful were looking toward the east—which is a great tradition even if it is not unanimous—is a splendid application of the "parousial" character of the Eucharist. One celebrates the mystery of Christ until He comes again from the heavens (*donec veniat de caelis*). The sun which illuminates the altar during the Eucharist is a pale reference to the "sun that comes from on high" (*exsultans ut gigas ad currendam viam*) (Ps. 18:6) in order to celebrate the paschal victory with His Church. The influence of the symbol of light, and concretely the sun, is frequently found in Christian liturgy. The baptismal ritual of the East still preserves this symbolism. Perhaps the Christian West has not adequately appreciated this, given the consequence of having come to be known as a "gloomy place." But also in the West, at the popular level, we know that there remains a certain fascination for the rising sun. Did not Saint Leo the Great, in the fifth century, remind the faithful in one of his Christmas homilies that "when the sun rises in the first dawning of the day some people are so foolish as to worship it in high places?" He adds: "There are also Christians that still retain that it is part of religious practice to continue this convention and that before entering the Basilica of the Apostle Peter, dedicated to the only and true God, after having climbed the stairs that bear one up to the upper level, turn themselves around toward the rising sun, bow their heads and kneel in order to honor the shining disk" (Homily 27, 4). In fact, the faithful entering the basilica for the Eucharist, in order to be intent on the altar, had to turn their backs to the sun. In order to pray while "turned toward the

east," as it was said, they would have had to turn their backs to the altar, which does not seem probable.

7) The fact that the application of this symbolism in the West, beginning from very early on, progressively diminished, demonstrates that it did not constitute an inviolable element. Therefore, it cannot be considered a traditional fundamental principle in Christian liturgy. From this it also arises that, subsequently, other types of symbolism influenced the construction of altars and their arrangement in churches.

8) In the encyclical *Mediator Dei*, Pius XII regarded as "archeologists" those who presumed to speak of the altar as a simple table. Would it not be equally an archeologizing tendency to consider that the arrangement of the altar toward the East is the decisive key to a correct Eucharistic celebration? In effect, the validity of the liturgical reform is not based only and exclusively on the return to original forms. There can also be completely new elements in it, and in fact there are some, that have been perfectly integrated.

9) The liturgical reform of the II Vatican Council did not invent the arrangement of the altar turned toward the people. One thinks concerning this of the witness of the Roman basilicas, at least as a pre-existing fact. But it was not an historical fact that directed the clear option for an arrangement of the altar that permits a celebration turned toward the people. The authorized interpretors of the reform—Cardinal Lercaro as the president of the Consilium-repeated from the very beginning (see the letters from 1965) that one was not dealing with a question of a liturgy that is continuing or passing away (*quaestio stantis vel cadentis liturgiae*). The fact that the suggestions of Cardinal Lercaro in this matter were, in that moment of euphoria, little taken into consideration, is unfortunately not an isolated case. Changing the orientation of the altar and utilizing the vernacular turned out to be much easier ways for entering into the theological and spiritual meaning of the liturgy, for absorbing its spirit, for studying the history and the meaning of the rites and analyzing the reasons behind the changes that were brought about and their pastoral consequences.

10) The option for celebrations is coherent with the foundational theological idea discovered and proven by the liturgical movement: "Liturgical actions are celebrations of the Church . . . which is the holy people of God gathered and ordered under the bishops" (SC 26). The theology of the common priesthood and the ministerial

priesthood, "distinct in essence, and not in degree" (*essentia, non gradu*) and nevertheless ordered to each other (LG 10) is certainly better expressed with the arrangement of the *altar versus populum*. Did not monks, from ancient times, pray turned toward each other in order to search for the presence of the Lord in their midst? Moreover, a figurative motive is worth underscoring. The symbolic form of the Eucharist is that of a meal, a repetition of the supper of the Lord. One does not doubt that this meal is sacrificial, a memorial of the death and resurrection of Christ, but from the figurative point of view its reference point is the supper.

11) Furthermore, how does one forget that one of the strongest arguments that sustain the continuance of the uninterrupted tradition of the exclusive ordination of men, lies in the fact that the priest, president in virtue of ordination, stands at the altar as a member of the assembly, but also by his sacramental character, before the assembly as Christ is the head of the Church and that for this reason stands there in front of (*gegenuber*) the Church?

12) If from the supports we pass to the applications, we find much material for reflection. The Congregation of Divine Worship, taking into consideration that a series of questions has been rising up in this regard, proposes now the following guiding points:

> 1. The celebration of the Eucharist *versus populum* requires of the priest a greater and more sincere expression of his ministerial conscience: his gestures, his prayer, his facial expression must reveal to the assembly in a more direct way the principal actor, the Lord Jesus. One does not improvise this; one acquires it with some technique. Only a profound sense of the proper priestly identity in *spiritu et veritate* is able to attain this.

> 2. The orientation of the altar *versus populum* requires with great care a correct use of the different areas of the sanctuary: the chair, the ambo and altar, as well as a correct positioning of the people that preside and serve in it. If the altar is turned into a pedestal for everything necessary for celebrating the Eucharist, or into a substitute for the chair in the first part of the Mass, or into a place from which the priest directs the whole celebration (in almost a technical sense), the altar will lose symbolically its identity as the central place of the

Eucharist, the table of mystery, the meeting place between God and men for the sacrifice of the new and eternal covenant.

3. The placement of the altar *versus populum* is certainly something in the present liturgical legislation that is desirable. It is not, nevertheless, an absolute value over and beyond all others. It is necessary to take into account cases in which the sanctuary does not admit of an arrangement of the altar facing the people, or it is not possible to preserve the preceding altar with its ornamentation in such a way that another altar facing the people can be understood to be the principal altar. In these cases, it is more faithful to liturgical sense to celebrate at the existing altar with the back turned to the people rather than maintain two altars in the same sanctuary. The principle of the unicity of the altar is theologically more important than the practice of celebrating facing the people.

4. It is proper to explain clearly that the expression "celebrate facing the people" does not have a theological sense, but only a topographical-positional sense. Every celebration of the Eucharist is praise and glory of God, for our good and the good of all the Church (*ad laudem et gloriam nominis Dei, ad utilitatem quoque nostram, totiusque Ecclesiae suae sanctae*). Theologically, therefore, the Mass is always facing towards God and facing the people. In the form of celebration it is necessary to take care not to switch theology and topography around, above all when the priest is at the altar. The priest speaks to the people only in the dialogue from the altar. All the rest is prayer to the Father, through the mediation of Christ in the Holy Spirit. This theology must be visible.

5. At last, a conjectural consideration that is not to be left in silence. Thirty years have passed since the constitution *Sacrosanctum Concilium*. "Provisional arrangements" cannot be justified any longer. In the re-organization of the sanctuary if a provisional character is maintained which is either pedagogically or artistically badly resolved, then an element of distortion results for catechesis and for the very theology of the celebration. Some criticisms of certain celebrations that are raised are well-founded and can only be taken with seriousness. The effort to improve celebrations is one of the basic elements to assure, in so far as it depends on us, an active and fruitful participation.

Facing the Lord:
On the Building of Churches and Facing East in Prayer
A Commentary on an Editorial in 'Notitiae,' May 1993

Rev. John T. Zuhlsdorf
Sacred Music, Winter 1993

In his book, *The Reform of the Roman Liturgy*, recently published in both French and English translations, Monsignor Klaus Gamber said:

> During the past twenty years, we have experienced a change in the accepted meaning of the Sacrifice. Personally, I believe that the introduction of the "altar of the people," with the celebrant of the Mass facing the people, is of much greater significance and poses greater problems for the future than the introduction of the new missal.

In the May 1993 issue of *Notitiae*, the publication of the Vatican's Congregation of Divine Worship and Discipline of the Sacraments, there is an editorial concerning the orientation of altars and celebrations of the Mass facing the people (See *Sacred Music*, Vol. 120, No. 4, pp. 14-17). In light of the increasing discussion over these very matters, it is opportune to comment on this editorial.

It must be noted that *Notitiae* is the official publication of the Congregation. It relates various speeches of the Holy Father, minutes of plenary sessions of the congregations, various continuing scholarly studies accepted in manuscript or undertaken by the Congregation concerning the liturgy; provides the ordinary prayers for newly beatified or canonized saints to be used in the Mass or the Liturgy of the Hours; publishes decrees of the same congregation; from time to time responds formally and publicly to questions raised about the liturgy with official clarifications or interpretations; and also provides editorials or opinions. While some of the things in *Notitiae* have an official character, such as a decree or clarification, an editorial has no authority other than that derived from the strength of its arguments and ability to persuade. People often mistake opinion for authority, especially in the liturgy. This leads to terrible problems for the use of music, observance of rubrics, construction/destruction of churches, and the like. In this number of *Notitiae*, one notes in the index the title of the editorial in question, but there is no indication that it is in fact an editorial until one glances at the top of the next page. While this may have been an oversight, it could lead to confusion and is best clarified.

After several introductory paragraphs (14), which establish the obvious point that all liturgy is oriented toward God, the editorial begins to address its topic. A clear attempt is made to argue that, at least in part, the arrangement of the altar, people, and celebrant is historically and culturally conditioned. The motive here seems to be this: to prepare the reader later in the editorial to accept as preferable the theological/cultural criteria provided for a positioning of the altar in contrast to any historical/cultural criteria that would acrue for a different arrangement. In otherwords, if it can be shown that altars *ad orientem* are the result of historical or cultural conditions, rather than an organic outgrowth of Christian spirituality and theology, then the arrangement of the altar *versus populum* can be claimed as superior once a theological basis for it can be established.

However, the editorial's argument reveals the first of a series of weaknesses. We read that "symbolism" as expressed in architecture is only proved with difficulty to be "an integral and basic part of Christian faith." While this is the first salvo designed to undermine support for an *ad orientem* altar, it likewise weakens support for a *versus populum* altar if convincing theological and spiritual arguments cannot be provided. Moreover, this is founded on a premise that is hard to admit, namely, that the historical or cultural influences on the development of the altar are to be set in *contrast* with the theological. Basically, the editorial has begun its bid to finesse the reader into being persuaded by what will, at its end, be admitted to be a matter of symbolic emphasis and even taste. It is furthermore ironic that later in the editorial numerous appeals will be made to "symbolism" to support a *versus populum* altar.

There follows a secondary section that continues to associate the *ad orientem* altar with historical and cultural conditions, even pagan influences. The editorial makes a particularly strange use of one of the fathers of the Church, St. Leo the Great. However, at the end of the paragraph, we find probably the real *causa movens* behind *Notitiae*'s apologia:

> In fact, the faithful entering the basilica for the Eucharist in order to be intent on the altar, had to turn their backs to the sun. In order to pray while "turned toward the east," as it was said, they would have had to turn their backs to the altar, which doesn't seem probable.

This is an unmistakable reference to the thesis of Klaus Gamber in his recently and posthumously re-published works that have all but dismantled the archeological arguments favoring the *versus populum* altars that have been the rage of liturgists and the bane of architectural integrity for decades. *In Zum Hernn hin!*[1] Gamber argues very effectively that, regardless of the physical orientation of the building, the priest and people faced the same direction at Mass, symbolically facing the east. The fact that in Roman basilicas the altars were set between the priest celebrating and the people is not sufficient evidence for an ancient practice of *versus populum* celebrations in the modern sense. Put briefly, it is Gamber's thesis, founded on historical evidence and well-documented, that at a certain point in the Basilica of St. Peter, the people literally turned around and faced the east with the result that the priest and people face the same direction, this time with the priest behind the assembly. As time went on and the practice of turning around faded, there were still no *versus populum* Masses (in the modern sense) in the Roman basilicas because of the presence of barriers between the congregations and the altar, screens, curtains, etc.[2]

Though revolutionary, Gamber's well-researched argument is far more convincing than what has been provided in past decades. It is clear that he has frightened not a few people, even in the Congregation for Divine Worship. If Gamber is right, the destruction of countless altars, the violation of sanctuaries, the pain and "disorientation" as it were of the Catholic faithful, will have proved to be a sham founded on a false argument. Some of the people who pushed the reforms after Vatican II are still around, of course, and their spiritual offspring can be found still in the Congregation that provided the editorial . . . But the full impact of the editorial remains to be seen. Nonetheless, it is patent that this editorial is a response to Gamber and his growing posthumous influence.

After having attempted to associate the *ad orientem* altar with a culturally conditioned practice that eventually faded away, the next paragraph goes on to state that, since the practice deriving from that outdated and even pagan symbolism diminished, the celebration of Mass *ad orientem* cannot be considered an "inviolable element" or a "traditional fundamental principle of the liturgy." Following this, the editorial uses Pius XII to show that a desire to perpetuate an *ad orientem* altar is merely archeologizing, and therefore unsound, even bad. This is a further attack on the thesis of Gamber. While appealing to Pius XII seems to be a rather blatant citation of a pope much revered by traditional Catholics, there is a yet more curious point to this. Gamber himself also cites the 1947 encyclical, *Mediator Dei*, which says that "one who wants to change the altar into the old form of the *mensa* is going down the wrong road."[3]

Changing tacks, the editorial goes on to give us this:

> In effect, the validity of the liturgical reform is not based only and exclusively on the return to original forms. There can also be completely new elements in it, and in fact there are some, that have been perfectly integrated.

To this assertion several responses must be made. First, we can see how nervous the defenders of the *versus populum* Mass (clearly the position taken by the editorial writer!) have become if they are now beginning to back-peddle on the very argument by which they justified their altar "revolution" in the first place. "Go back to the original forms!" they once cried, thereby casting aspersions on anything that organically and legitimately developed during more than a dozen intervening centuries. Now they say that a return to the original forms is not the point? Gamber has shown that they are probably wrong in the first place about what they thought original forms were. No wonder they say that the original forms are not the point . . . now. It remains for them to make that assertion on a scholarly level, however. Until then, *gratis asseritur, gratis negatur.*

Second, it seems that they (in the Congregation) are afraid that Gamber was right and that they have no evidence to the contrary. Why else would they now attack the "previous forms" argument when before they lionized it? The whole editorial shows that the proponents of the *versus populum* altar are now being forced to go fishing for a theology to support their projects. But isn't that what they say happened in the intervening centuries of organic liturgical development? Liturgical reformers were ever ready to say that all those developments in the Mass were merely historical encrustations that were later justified with subsequent theological explanations. To this writer's mind, the *Notitiae* editorial is doing precisely the same thing, but with a difference. Whereas the developments in the liturgy unconsciously acquired theological explanations over the years, the Congregation seems to be consciously stitching one together, *ex nihilo*.

Third, this editorial has surely and openly admitted that completely new elements were added to the reform of the liturgy and has implicitly placed the *versus populum* altar among them. Is this anything other than a tacit admission that, while they don't like Gamber's argument, they have to accept it? Whether these new elements in the liturgy have been "perfectly integrated" or not must be balanced against the concrete fruits that they have produced for the two or more generations of Catholics since they were introduced.

It is important to note the phrase, "The option for celebrations *versus populum* is coherent with the foundational theological idea discovered and proven by the liturgical movement . . . " The Italian implies the notion of "option" in the sense of "choose." One could say "the choice in favor of celebrations" or even "the choice to celebrate *versus populum*." The editorial is again tackling Gamber, who comments on these points.[4] At least Gamber went back somewhat farther than the last few decades (a century at best) of the liturgical movement. Why the author of the editorial would want to favor the recent liturgical movement, a clear example of the intertwining of cultural influence on the form of liturgy, over the practice of the ancient Church is puzzling at best, especially since he has gone to such lengths to undermine the historical and cultural criterion arguing for the altar's orientation. Once again the specter of prejudice seems to be raising its head. Why do certain lines of argumentation concerning liturgical questions inevitably prefer the modern over the ancient, oppose the old to the new, create conflict between different periods of Christian expression? It is as if the authentic liturgy began only recently after centuries of benighted wandering and aberrations.

The last few paragraphs of the editorial have the flavor of a very self-conscious *apologia*. This section begins with the dramatic statement that "the liturgical reforms of the Second Vatican Council did not invent the arrangement of the altar turned toward the people." This is odd in light of the next paragraph's discussion of the "liturgical movement." It also seems to be protesting innocence when there had been no accusation.

Moreover, while this paragraph seems in one moment to defend the post-conciliar entity, *Consilium* and its Cardinal Lercaro, the interpolation of their names in this context has the side effect of drawing our attention to just exactly what they did after the Council. The editorial justly uses the argument *abusus non tollit usum*. Still, is this any better than the finger-pointing cry of "its their fault?"

Besides this, what can one make of the statement, "Changing the orientation of the altar and utilizing the vernacular turned out to be much easier ways for entering into the theological and spiritual meaning of the liturgy . . . " This is greatly to be disputed. One could conversely charge that changing the altar and eliminating Latin created confusion and ignorance. While running the risk of extremism, one could argue effectively both ways.

All of this begs the question, however, of why it is necessarily preferable to make everything "easier." Why reduce the sacred and the mysterious always and everywhere to the common denominator? At the beginning of the editorial it was correctly stated that "celebrating the Eucharist is never to put into action something earthly, but rather something heavenly." How does a *versus populum* altar and the vernacular facilitate that fundamental concept better than the previous forms? If once it was not "easy" to "enter into" the liturgy's meaning at all its levels, it can hardly be stated that centuries of saints and martyrs, billions of unknown lay people, clergy, and religious throughout the world were unable to imbibe of the spirit of the liturgy which reflects the eschatological presence of the Lord of glory simply because Latin was used or the altar was *ad orientem*! The editorial's statement is specious. In fact, the older form of liturgy proved itself by its fruits, and the newer form has yet to prove anything by the fact that we haven't as yet seen it authentically implemented.

It has been said that the Church has bequeathed two things to humanity as its rightful heritage: art and saints. The centuries long use of the older form of liturgy certainly inculturated the Christian faith and gave thousands of generations a foretaste of our heavenly promise. This cannot be disputed. We have yet to see what the new-easier-form of the liturgy will give us. Despite the editorial's disclaimer of abuses, if we have seen "something" since the introduction of the reforms, including the "new elements" cited, we have hardly seen a flowering of Catholic art and saints. Time will tell. We must give an authentic reform the chance to bear its own fruits.

The argument that a *versus populum* altar is verified because monks pray facing each other is ridiculous. Going on, the editorial reveals a clear theological bias even though a nod is given in the direction of the sacrificial nature of the Mass (which seems adequately expressed by an *ad orientem* altar) the notion of the supper and the meal is put in high evidence (favoring the *versus populum*). More absurd, and hardly to be understood, is the contention that the *versus populum* altar is "one of the strongest arguments sustaining the uninterrupted tradition of the exclusive ordination of men." One is almost embarrassed by this last point. After several blatant appeals to things revered by traditionally minded Catholics, Fathers of the Church, Pius XII, etc., now the need is felt to tack on a reference to male priesthood as something favoring a *versus populum* altar.

Moving from "theory" to "pastoral application," the final paragraph introduces what the Congregation proposes as "guiding points." First, the use of the title "Congregation" does not change the fact that Gamber's argument has not been systematically addressed.

Nevertheless, as faithful Roman Catholics, it is still praiseworthy to consider and draw upon that which Roman Congregations publish, even if only at the level of an editorial. It is useful then to look at these five "guiding points" in order, and then consider their implications for our pastoral use. These "guiding points," reduced to their core and commented on here are as follows:

1. Priests need to acquire a better liturgical technique, based on a sound faith and theology, since celebrating facing the people is harder to do.

This is hardly to be disputed. Would that the Congregation had insisted on this point over the last thirty years since *Sacrosanctum Concilium*. If, on the other hand, it is true that one does not easily acquire a liturgical "presidential" style for Masses *coram populo*, the same is to be said for those *ad orientem*. It is not to be assumed that celebrating Mass with one's back to the people is automatically easier. Still, this remains a very good point, even if it is partly a response to what Gamber says about the liturgical style prone to the turned-around altar.[5] In addition, one can use this point to draw many implications for other related issues of training for clergy.

2. The altar itself is not a mere table, and its placement makes a difference in how the sanctuary is used.

Certainly this is directed at the abuse or disregard of the altar's special character. The very fact that a guiding point is given on this, shows how vulnerable to abuse the *versus populum* altar is. Also, if the position of the altar *versus populum* requires a rigorous and careful use of sanctuary space, this is no less the case when the altar is fixed to the wall and the sanctuary is more open. The other part of this problem is that the comment arrives at a time when, more often than not, people are asking "what's a sanctuary?" so many have been eliminated. Also, the carefully worked out rubrics of previous missals are certainly more in line with this "guiding point" than the usual chaos seen in most sanctuaries today. This is partly because of the ambiguity of the rubrics remaining in the new books. If the Congregation wants a better liturgical presider and a better use of the altar and sanctuary, then it could start by giving us a clear and detailed ceremonial, even though one shudders at the idea of what we might get.

3. The principle of the unicity of the altar is theologically more important than the practice of celebrating facing the people.

Although this should be an obvious point, in its own way it is the single most important point of the whole editorial. Here the entire argumentation of the editorial falls away only to reveal what everybody already knows, and has known all along. Despite all the talk of historical conditions and previous forms, aside from the theological dance done to persuade the reader that a turned-around altar is to be preferred, in the final analysis the *versus populum* celebration, and therefore all of the editorial's argumentation, is not of absolute value. There are legitimate and obvious reasons why one should have an *ad orientem* altar. This is a most singular statement to find in *Notitiae* after the years and years of polemics throughout the world over this issue!

Reviewed briefly, the reason for this "point" is as follows. If the architectural layout or the artistic value of the *versus ad orientem* altar doesn't allow space for a turned-around altar, keep the old one. The main idea is to defend the focus of attention on one altar. What implications does this have for the table altars that have been set up in churches both large and small where the clear architectural intention was to create lines of sight such that the worshippers' eyes were directed to the high altar and the tabernacle? What conclusions are to be drawn from this "point" for cathedrals and basilicas, richly and beautifully decorated, that have placed a table altar in front of an artistic treasure that dominated the whole sanctuary? What does this mean for overly crowded sanctuaries that have *coram populo* altars squeezed in so that the space is cramped and the main altar, if still extant, turns into the shelf for plants? When in a church one sees nothing else but the high altar, beautifully decorated and by its location at the center of every attention, what implications can be drawn for the little table set up so that the priest can face the people? More sadly, what does this mean for all the altars, artistic treasures, architectural "wholes" that have been destroyed for the sake of *versus populum*?

In addition to momentous practical implications, this "point" has a legitimate and convincing theological aspect too: the one people of God should focus on one altar in their church. This does not mean destroy side altars, which also have significance. The artistic values and architectural space and integrity of altars and churches must be respected. Thus, common sense, theology and good taste converge at last.

4. Do not confuse topography with theology.

In a way, this "guiding point" extends point No. 3, above. Here we read that, theologically, every Mass is facing God. This is an attempt to say that an altar *coram populo* and one *ad orientem* accomplish virtually the same thing, provided, of course, that the celebrant knows what he is doing (point No. 1), the space is used well (point No. 2) and the practical and artistic aspects have been properly handled so that the people are focused on one altar (point No. 3). While this point tries to participate in the clear advantages of an *ad orientem* altar for all situations, it is a good principle and hardly to be disputed, even though the Congregation's editorial keeps saying that *versus populum* is better.

5. "Provisional arrangements" cannot be justified any longer.

Thirty years after *Sacrosanctum Concilium* it is time to settle down. There are at least two ways to read this "guiding point," one superficial and one more reflective. First reading: movable tables should be quickly fixed to the floor as permanent altars, lest something happen and the table altar *versus populum* goes out of style. In this way it will be harder to get rid of and just might weather the storm. Second, a comprehensive reading that takes into consideration some other principles provided by the editorial itself is possible. Take stock of how the liturgy is being celebrated: improve your celebrant's style, get your ceremonies worked out, study your church's design and the artistic value of the main altar and/or the table altar. If, when there are two altars present, the *versus populum* altar is clearly overshadowed and doesn't work harmoniously with the space, get rid of it; use the high altar, and celebrate together facing God, priest's back to the people. This would be the case with most older churches where the sanctuaries have not been "reformed." If on the other hand the *versus populum* altar is clearly harmonious with the space and there is no altar *ad orientem*, then keep things the way they are. This would be the case with most newer churches, designed to have a *coram populo* altar. Here priest and people could celebrate facing God, while facing each other. It is obvious that in churches where there is only one altar *ad orientem* and it works well, and that a *versus populum* altar would disturb the space's organic whole, it should be shunned. Alas, too late for many . . .

This leaves unclarified the case of the older church in which the sanctuary has been reformed or the internal floor plan has been rearranged. In this case the high *ad orientem* altar may have been removed and a *versus populum* altar been introduced, but the result is a confusion of architectural lines and artistic styles that try to force the building to do something it was not designed to do.

Using the editorial's guidelines, the Congregation seems to be saying that the church should be put back the way it was so that the space's artistic and architectural harmony can favor the unicity of the altar and the people's focus on it for the purpose of celebrating facing God. On the other hand, as Cardinal Ratzinger says, after all the upheaval endured in the last years and throughout all the various "renovations" that have been done, maybe it is prudent to give things a rest before putting them back the way they were. Many people already have the idea that the Church is no longer stable because of the last thirty years. Let us not contribute to that by rushing into "denovation" projects too quickly.

After looking at the strengths and weaknesses of this editorial in *Notitiae*, and reviewing with comments the "guiding points" it provides, a final word is in order.

The Congregation, startled into action by the thesis of Klaus Gamber to which it reacts in this editorial, has clearly been forced into a massive retreat. If the Congregation is seen as perpetuating the innovations of the *Consilium*, then the article in *Notitiae* is doubly astonishing, like a trusted rifle backfiring, exploding. If the Holy See's *Notitiae* can be argued to be the balanced and genuine "central line," neither too conservative, nor too radical, then the liturgists of the world will still have a great deal of thinking to do. In fact, it probably lies somewhere in between. Nevertheless, the "experts" of the Congregation have gone back on the principle of returning to original forms, because it is clear now that the forms don't bear out what has been done in their name. While trying to state that historical conditioning is not a central criterion for the arrangement of an altar, they have referred to the liturgical movement of the past few decades. This is a great contradiction. Abandoning historical criteria, they set out to create a theology in order to justify a celebration facing the people, the same organic process which was the bugbear of reformers concerning the older form of liturgy. Having lost every other support, they are reduced to defence of the "unicity" of the altar, in whatever form, in order to salvage the *versus populum*. "Point," set, and match.

Notwithstanding all of the above, the "guiding points," though they have no authority themselves, can provide food for thought to all those who for so long have thought themselves to be secure in their exclusive use of a *versus populum* liturgy. It seems to be a gentle way of breaking the news and giving some guidance.

This editorial of *Notitiae* was in a way an immense concession to those who for decades have been saying that the Church's artistic treasures must be respected and used wisely. Although it deals mainly with the position of the altar and the celebrant, the editorial opened itself up to wider considerations when it brought up the vernacular and various "new elements" in the liturgy. Therefore, we can conclude that if the "guiding points" given can be applied to altars, we can also apply them to liturgical language as well. If the liturgy reflects heaven and not earth, mystery and not commonplace, then the position of the altar, the language used, and the music and other arts employed must foster this. If they do not, they should be changed. This is a solid argument for the use of Latin and the treasury of sacred music at our disposal, so intimately joined to Latin and the liturgical space itself.

The great works of sacred music that we have inherited over the centuries were conceived and born into a certain kind of liturgical space, namely, one that was open, acoustically favorable, and adequate for a solemn liturgical function proportioned to the lofty values and the greatness of the music's own artistic expression. Therefore, the discussion of the altar and Latin are themselves central to the music, for they impact on the space and the language in which the music is performed.

Even the notion given in "guiding point" No. 2 is vital and applicable to a discussion of Latin and music. If a good liturgical style is important to celebrations, and if it must be worked on, practiced, studied, acquired by training, it is even more important to have the Church direct the training of priests particularly in Latin, music, and the other arts. Without Latin, how can a Latin rite priest function authentically? How can he know what music is suitable for the liturgy? Similarly, if the Church does not assure that there are justly paid church musicians with the proper training in their special field, as well as some work in Latin, architecture, theology and liturgy, how can any of our "liturgical spaces" realize what the Congregation says in the fourth paragraph of the editorial:

> celebrating the Eucharist is never to put into action something earthly, but rather something heavenly, because (the Church) has the awareness that the principle celebrant of the same action is the Lord of Glory.

The Second Vatican Council could provide the background for a new renaissance in the third millennium of the Church's pilgrimage toward the Lord of Glory in the heavenly Jerusalem to come. Editorials such as the one in *Notitiae*, though conditioned as they are by many factors, reveal Rome's unchanging desire to guide us, get us to admit mistakes and use common sense, roll up our sleeves and then . . . just do what the Council asked.

ENDNOTES

1. This is published in English as *Facing the Lord: On the Building of Churches and Facing East in Prayer* in a single volume together with another work (which gives the title to the volume) *The Reform of the Roman Liturgy: its problems and background*, Una Voce Press, 1993.

2. op. cit., pp. 159-61.

3. ibid., pp. 142-3.

4. ibid., pp. 142 sq.

5. ibid., pp. 171 sq.

The Attractiveness of the Tridentine Mass

Alfons Cardinal Stickler, SDB
Fort Lee, New Jersey, May 20, 1995

The Tridentine Mass means the rite of the Mass which was fixed by Pope Pius V at the request of the Council of Trent and promulgated on December 5, 1570. This Missal contains the old Roman rite, from which various additions and alterations were removed. When it was promulgated, other rites were retained that had existed for at least 200 years. Therefore, it is more correct to call this Missal the liturgy of Pope Pius V.

Faith and Liturgy

From the very beginning of the Church, faith and liturgy have been intimately connected. A clear proof of this can be found in the Council of Trent itself. It solemnly declared that the sacrifice of the Mass is at the center of the Catholic liturgy, contrary to the heresy of Martin Luther, who denied that the Mass was a sacrifice.

We know from the history of the development of the Faith that this doctrine has been fixed authoritatively by the Magisterium in the teach of popes and councils. We also know that in the whole Church, and especially in the Eastern churches, the Faith was the most important factor in the development and formation of the liturgy, particularly in the case of the Mass.

There are convincing arguments for this from the early centuries of the Church. Pope Celestine I wrote to the bishops of Gaul in 422: *Legem Credendi, lex statuit supplicandi*—the law of praying determines the law of believing. This has subsequently been commonly expressed by the phrase, *lex orandi, lex credendi* [the law of prayer is the law of belief].

The Orthodox churches preserved the Faith through liturgy. This is very important because in the last letter the Pope wrote, seven days ago, he said the Latin Church must learn from the Eastern churches, especially about the liturgy . . .

Conciliar Statements

A matter often neglected is the two types of conciliar statements and decisions: doctrinal (theological) and disciplinary.

In most of the councils we have both doctrinal *and* disciplinary. In some councils we have no disciplinary statements or decisions; we have some councils without doctrinal statements, with only disciplinary statements. Many of the Eastern councils after Nicaea treated only questions of faith. The Second Council of Toulon in 691 was strictly an Oriental council for only disciplinary statements and decisions, because the Eastern churches had been neglected in the preceding councils. It brought discipline up to date for the Eastern churches, especially the Church in Constantinople.

This is important because in the Council of Trent we have explicitly *both:* we have chapters and canons which belong exclusively to faith; and then, in nearly all the sessions, after the theological chapters and canons, we have exclusively disciplinary matters. The distinction is important. In all the theological canons we have the statement that anyone who opposes the decisions of the Council is excluded from the community—*anathema sit*. But the Council never states an anathema for purely disciplinary matters—the Conciliar sanctions are only for doctrinal statements.

Trent on the Mass

This is important for our reflections now. I've already pointed out the connection between faith and prayer—liturgy—and especially between faith and the highest form of liturgy, the common worship.

This connection has its classic expression in the Council of Trent, which dealt with the topic in three sessions: the thirteenth in October 1551, the twentieth session in July 1562, which dealt with the Sacrament of the Eucharist, an especially the twenty-second in September 1562, which produced the dogmatic chapters and canons on the Holy Sacrifice of the Mass. There is also a particular decree that concerns those things that have to be observed and avoided in the celebration of Mass. This is a classical and central statement, authoritative and official, of the Church's mind on the subject.

The decree first considers the nature of the Mass. Martin Luther had clearly and openly denied its very nature by stating that the Mass was not a sacrifice. It is true that, in order not to disturb the simple faithful, the Reformers did not immediately eliminate all those parts of the Mass which reflected the true Faith and ran contrary to their new doctrines. For example, they retained the elevation of the Host between the *Sanctus* and the *Benedictus*.

For Luther and his followers, worship consisted mainly in preaching as a means of instruction and edification, interwoven with prayers and hymns. The reception of Holy Communion was only a secondary event. Luther still maintained the presence of Christ in the bread at the moment of its reception, but he strongly denied the Sacrifice of the Mass. For him the altar could never be a place of sacrifice.

From this denial we can understand the consequent flaws in the Protestant liturgy, which is completely different from that of the Catholic Church. We can also understand why the Council of Trent defined the part of the Catholic Faith which concerns the nature of the Eucharistic sacrifice: it is a real saving, force. In the sacrifice of Jesus Christ the priest is a substitute of Christ Himself. As a result of his ordination he is a true *alter Christus.* By means of the Consecration the bread is changed into the Body of Christ and the wine into His Blood. This implementation of His sacrifice is the adoration of God.

The Council specifies that this sacrifice is not a new one, independent of the unique sacrifice of the Cross; rather it is dependent upon that unique sacrifice of Christ, making it present in a bloodless way such that the Body and Blood of Christ are substantially present, while still remaining under the appearance of bread and wine. Consequently there is no new sacrificial merit; rather, the infinite fruit of the bloody sacrifice of the Cross is effected or realized by Jesus Christ constantly in the Mass.

It follows that the action of the sacrifice consists in the Consecration; the Offertory (by which bread and wine are prepared for the Consecration) and the Communion are integral parts of the Mass, but are not essential ones. The essential part is the Consecration, by which the priest, in the person of Christ, and in the same way, pronounces the consecrating words of Christ.

Thus, the Mass is not and cannot be simply a celebration of Communion, or a mere remembrance or memorial of the sacrifice of the Cross, but rather a true, unbloody making present of this self-same sacrifice of the Cross.

For the same reason we can now understand that the Mass is an effective renewal of the sacrifice of the Cross. It is essentially an adoration of God, offered only to Him. This adoration rightly involves other elements: praise, thanksgiving for all the graces received, sorrow for sins committed, petitions for necessary graces. Naturally the Mass can be offered for one or all of these various intentions. All these doctrines were established and promulgated in the chapters and canons of Session 22 in the Council of Trent.

Trent's Anathemas

Various consequences derive from this fundamental theological nature of the Mass. First, the *Canon Missae.*

In the Roman liturgy there has always been only one Canon, which was introduced by the Church many centuries ago. The Council of Trent expressly stated, in Chapter 4, that this Canon is free from error; in fact it contains nothing that is not full of sanctity and piety and that does not raise the faithful to God. In composition it is based on the words of Our Lord Himself, the tradition of the apostles and the regulation of saintly popes. Canon 6 of Chapter 4 threatens with excommunication those who maintain that the *Canon Missae* contains errors and should therefore be abolished.

In Chapter 5 the Council stated that human nature requires external signs in order to raise the spirit to divine things. For that reason the Church has introduced certain rites and signs: silent or vocal prayer, blessings, candles, incense, vestments, *et cetera*. Many of these signs have their origins in apostolic prescriptions or tradition.

Through these visible signs of faith and piety, the nature of the sacrifice is underscored. The signs strengthen and encourage the faithful in their meditation on the divine elements contained in the sacrifice of the Mass. To safeguard this doctrine, Canon 7 threatens with excommunication all those who consider these external signs as inducing impiety instead of piety. This is an example of what I discussed before: this kind of statement, with the canon of sanctions, has largely a theological meaning, not only a disciplinary meaning.

In Chapter 6 the Council emphasizes the desire of the Church that all the faithful present at Mass should receive Holy Communion, but states that if only the priest who celebrates the Mass receives Holy Communion, this Mass should not then be called private and so be criticized or forbidden. In this case the faithful receive Communion spiritually, and, further, all sacrifices offered by the priest as a public minister of the Church are offered for all the members of the Mystical Body of Christ. Thus, Canon 8 threatens with excommunication all those who say that such Masses are illicit and should therefore be forbidden—another theological statement.

Chapter 8 is dedicated to the peculiar language of worship in the Mass. It is known that in the cult of all religions a sacred language is used. In the Roman Catholic Church during the first three centuries the language was Greek, being the common language employed in the Latin world. From the fourth century on, the Latin language developed into the common idiom in the Roman Empire. Latin remained for centuries in the Roman Catholic Church as the only language for worship. Quite naturally, Latin was also the language of the Roman rite in its central act of worship, the Mass. This remained the case even after Latin was replaced as the living language by the various Romance languages.

Trent on Latin, Silence

Now we come to the question: why not chance again? We answer: divine Providence establishes even secondary things. For example, Palestine—Jerusalem—is the place of the Redemption by Jesus Christ. Rome is the center of the Church. Peter was not born in Rome. He came to Rome. Why? It was the center then of the Roman Empire—that means, of the world. That is the practical background of the diffusion of the Faith by the Roman Empire, only a human thing, a historical thing. But it enters certainly in divine Providence.

A similar process can be seen even in other religions. For the Moslems, the old Arab language is dead and yet it remains the language of their liturgy, of their cult. For the Hindus, the Sanskrit. Due to its necessary connection with the supernatural, worship naturally requires its own particular religious language, which should not be "vulgar" one.

The fathers of the Council knew very well that most of the faithful assisting at the Mass neither understood Latin nor were able to read translations. They were generally illiterate. The fathers also knew that the Mass contains a great deal of instruction for the faithful.

Nevertheless they did not agree with the view held by Protestants that it was necessary to celebrate the Mass only in the vernacular. In order to provide instruction for the faithful, the Council ordered that the old custom approved by the Holy Roman Church—the mother and teacher of all churches—be maintained everywhere, and that care should be had for souls in explaining the central mystery of the Mass.

Canon 9 threatens with excommunication those who affirm that the language of the Mass must only be the vernacular. It is noteworthy that in both chapter and canon the Council of Trent only rejected the *exclusivity* of the "vulgar" language in the sacred rites. On the other hand, we need once again to take into account that these various Conciliar regulations do not only have a disciplinary character. They are based on a doctrinal, theological foundation that involves the Faith itself.

The reasons for this concern can be seen, firstly, in the reverence that is due to the mystery of the Mass. The decree which immediately followed concerning what has to be observed and avoided in the celebration of the Mass states, "Irreverence cannot be separated from impiety." Irreverence always involves impiety. In addition, the Council wished to safeguard the ideas expressed in the Mass, and the precision of the Latin tongue safeguards the content against misunderstanding and potential errors based on linguistic imprecision.

For these reasons the Church has always defended the sacred tongue and even recently Pius XI expressly stated that this language should be *non vulgaris*. For these self-same reasons Canon 9 established excommunication against those who affirm that the rite of the Roman Church, in which a part of the Canon and the words of consecration are pronounced silently, must be condemned. Even silence has a theological background.

Finally, in the first canon of the reform decree, in the twenty-second session of the Council of Trent, we find other regulations which have a somewhat disciplinary character but also complete the doctrinal part—for nothing is more fit to guide worshipers to a deepened understanding of the mystery than the life and example of the ministers of cult. These ministers should mold their lives and behavior to this end, and that is reflected in their dress, their bearing, their speech. In all this they should be dignified, modest, and religious. They also are to avoid even slight faults since in their case they would be considered grave. Thus, superiors were to demand of the sacred ministers the living out of the whole tradition of proper clerical behavior.

The Mass of Pius V and the Mass of Paul VI

Now we can better appreciate and understand the theological background and foundation of the discussions and regulations of the Council of Trent concerning the Mass as the summit of the sacred liturgy. In response to the serious challenge of Protestantism we can now understand the theological attractiveness of the Tridentine Mass, not only for that particular historical period but also as a pattern for the Church and liturgical reform of Vatican II.

In the first place, we have to determine here the correct meaning of this reform. As in the case of the Tridentine Mass, we emphasize the importance of a correct understanding of what was understood by the Mass of Pope Pius V which fulfilled the wishes of the Council fathers at Trent.

Now, we must underline what should be considered the correct name of the Mass of the Second Vatican Council: the Mass of the post-Conciliar liturgical commission. A simple glance at the liturgical constitution of the Second Vatican Council immediately illustrates that the will of the Council and the will of the liturgical commission often do not coincide, and are even evidently contrary.

We'll briefly examine the main differences between the two liturgical reforms as well as what we might term their theological attractiveness.

Firstly, in the light of the Protestant heresy, the Mass of Pius V emphasized the central truth of the Mass as a sacrifice, based on the theological discussions and specific regulations of the Council. The Mass of Paul VI (so-called because the liturgical commission for the reform after Vatican II worked under the ultimate responsibility of the Pope) emphasizes rather the integral part of the Mass, Communion, with the result that the sacrifice is transformed into what could be termed a meal. The great importance given to the readings and to preaching in the new Mass, and even the faculty given to the priest to add private speeches and explications, is another reflection of what can be called an adaptation to the Protestant idea of worship. . . .

French philosopher Jean Guitton says that Pope Paul VI revealed to him that it was his [the Pope's] intention to assimilate as much as possible of the new Catholic liturgy to Protestant worship. Clearly, it is necessary to verify the true meaning of this remark, since all the official statements of Paul VI—especially his excellent eucharistic encyclical *Mysterium Fidei* of 1965, issued before the end of the Council, as well as the *Credo of the People of God* demonstrate his absolute orthodoxy. Now, how can we explain this opposite statement?

Along these same lines we can try to understand the new position of the altar and the priest. According to the well-founded studies of Msgr. Klaus Gamber concerning the position of the altar in the old basilicas of Rome and elsewhere, the criterion for the old position was not that it should face the worshiping assembly, but rather that it should be turned towards the East, which was the symbol of the rising sun of Christ who was to be worshiped. The completely new position of the altar and priest in facing the assembly, previously forbidden, today becomes an expression of the Mass as a meeting of the community.

Secondly, in the old liturgy the Canon is the center of the Mass as sacrifice. According to the testimony of the Council of Trent, the Canon traces itself back to the tradition of the apostles and was substantially complete at the time of Gregory the Great, 600. The Roman Church never had other canons. Even for the *mysterium fidei* in the Consecration form, we have evidence from Innocent III, explicitly, at the inauguration of the Archbishop of Lyons. I don't know if the majority of liturgy reformers know about this fact. St. Thomas Aquinas in a special article justifies this *mysterium fidei*. And the Council of Florence explicitly confirmed the *mysterium fidei* in the Consecration form.

Now, this *mysterium fidei* was eliminated in the Consecration words brought about in the new liturgy. Why? We also find permission given for new canons. The second one—which does not mention the sacrificial character of the Mass—with its merit of being the shortest, has virtually supplanted the old Roman Canon everywhere. Thereby, the profound theological insight given by the Council of Trent has been lost.

The mystery of the divine Sacrifice is actualized in every rite, though in different ways. In the case of the Latin Mass it was emphasized by the Tridentine Council with the silent reading of the Canon in Latin. This has been discarded by the proclamation of the Canon in the new Mass out loud.

Third: the Vatican II reform destroyed or changed the meaning of in much of the rich symbolism in the liturgy (though it remains in the Oriental rites). The importance of this symbolism was emphasized by the Council of Trent. . . .

This fact was deplored even by a well-known atheistic psychoanalyst, who called the Second Vatican Council the "Council of Bookkeepers."

Vulgarizing the Mass

There is one theological principle completely overthrown by the liturgical reform but confirmed both by the Council of Trent *and* by the Second Vatican Council, after a long and sober discussion. (I assisted, and can confirm that the clear resolutions of the final text of the Council constitution substantially reaffirmed it). That principle: the Latin language is to be preserved in the Latin rite. As in the Council of Trent, so in Vatican II the Council fathers admitted the vernacular only as an exception.

But for the reform of Paul VI, the exception has become exclusive. Theological reasons which were stated in both councils for the retention of Latin in the Mass can now be seen to have been justified in the light of the exclusive use of the vernacular introduced by the liturgical reform. The vernacular has often vulgarized the Mass itself, and the translation of the original Latin has resulted in very serious doctrinal misunderstanding and errors.

Furthermore, the vernacular was not formerly permitted for people who were not only illiterate but also completely different from one another. Now that different languages and dialects can be used in worship, by Catholic people of varying tribes and nations, all living closely in a world that becomes smaller every day, this Babel of common worship results in a loss of external unity in the world-wide Catholic Church which was once unified in a common voice. Further, it has become on a number of occasions the cause of internal disunity even in the Mass itself, which should be the spirit and center of external and internal concord among Catholics throughout the world. We have many, many examples of this fact of disunion caused by the vulgar tongue.

And another consideration. . . . Before, every priest in the whole world could say the Mass in Latin for all the communities, and all the priests could understand Latin. Unfortunately, today no priest can say the Mass for all the people in the world. We must admit that, only a few decades after the reform of the liturgical language, we have lost that possibility of praying and singing together even in the great international gatherings, such as Eucharistic conferences, or even during meetings with the Pope, the center of the unity of the Church. No longer can we sing and pray together.

Finally, we have to consider seriously the behavior of the sacred ministers in the light of the Council of Trent—the behavior of the sacred ministers whose deep relationship with their sacred ministry the Council of Trent emphasized. Correct clerical behavior, dress, bearing, comportment, encourage people to follow what they say and teach. Unfortunately, the wretched behavior of many clerics often obliterates the difference between sacred minister and laity, and emphasizes the difference between the sacred minister and the *alter Christus*.

Summarizing our reflections, we can say the theological attractiveness of the Tridentine Mass corresponds with the theological incorrectness of the Vatican [II] Mass. For this reason the Christi Fidelis of the theological tradition should continue to manifest, in the spirit of obedience to legitimate superiors, the legitimate desire and pastoral preference for the Tridentine Mass.

"The Oxford Declaration on the Liturgy"

The Centre for Faith and Culture, Westminster College Oxford, England, June 29, 1996

1. Reflecting on the history of liturgical renewal and reform since the Second Vatican Council, the Liturgy Forum agreed that there have been many positive results. Among these might be mentioned the introduction of the vernacular, the opening up of the treasury of the Sacred Scriptures, increased participation in the liturgy, and the enrichment of the process of Christian initiation. However, the Forum concluded that the preconciliar liturgical movement as well as the manifest intentions of *Sacrosanctum Concilium* have in large part been frustrated by powerful contrary forces, which could be described as bureaucratic, philistine, and secularist.

2. The effect has been to deprive the Catholic people of much of their liturgical heritage. Certainly, many ancient traditions of sacred music, art, and architecture have been all but destroyed, *Sacrosanctum Concilium* gave pride of place to Gregorian chant, yet in many places this "sung theology" of the Roman liturgy has disappeared without trace. Our liturgical heritage is not a superficial embellishment of worship but should properly be regarded as intrinsic to it, as it is also to the process of transmitting the Catholic faith in education and evangelization. Liturgy cannot be separated from culture; it is the living font of a Christian civilization and hence has profound ecumenical significance.

3. The impoverishment of our liturgy after the Council is a fact not yet sufficiently admitted or understood, to which the necessary response must be a revival of the liturgical movement and the initiation of a new cycle of reflection and reform. The liturgical movement which we represent is concerned with the enrichment, correction and resacralization of Catholic liturgical practice. It is concerned with a renewal of liturgical eschatology, cosmology and aesthetics, and with a recovery of the sense of the sacred—mindful that the law of worship is the law of belief. This renewal will be aided by a closer and deeper acquaintance with the liturgical, theological, and iconographic traditions of the Christian East.

4. The revived liturgical movement calls for the promotion of the Liturgy of the Hours, celebrated in song as an action of the Church in cathedrals, parishes, monasteries, and families, and of Eucharistic Adoration, already spreading in many parishes. In this way, the Divine Word and the Presence of Christ's reality in the Mass may resonate throughout the day, making human culture into a dwelling place for God. At the heart of the Church in the world we must be able to find that loving contemplation, that adoring silence, which is the essential complement to the spoken word of Revelation, and the key to active participation in the holy mysteries of faith.

5. We call for a greater pluralism of Catholic rites and uses, so that all these elements of our tradition may flourish and be more widely known during the period of reflection and "essourcement" (going back to the sources) that lies ahead. If the liturgical movement is to prosper, it must seek to rise above differences of opinion and taste to that unity, which is the Holy Spirit's gift to the Body of Christ. Those who love the Catholic tradition in its fullness should strive to work together in charity, bearing each other's burdens in the light of the Holy Spirit, and persevering in prayer with Mary the Mother of Jesus.

6. We hope that any future liturgical reform would not be imposed on the faithful but would proceed, with the utmost caution and sensitivity to the *sensus fidelium*, from a thorough understanding of the organic nature of the liturgical traditions of the Church. Our work should be sustained by prayer, education, and study. This cannot be undertaken in haste, or in anything other than a serene spirit. No matter what difficulties lie ahead, the glory of the Paschal Mystery—Christ's love, his cosmic sacrifice and his childlike trust in the Father—shines through every Catholic liturgy for those who have eyes to see, and in this undeserved grace we await the return of spring.

"The Antiquity and Beauty of the Roman Missal"

Michael Davies
A Short History of the Roman Mass
TAN Books and Publishers, 1997

The antiquity of the Roman Mass is a point which needs to be stressed. There is what Father Fortescue describes as a "prejudice that imagines that everything Eastern must be old." This is a mistake, and there is no existing Eastern liturgy with a history of continual use stretching back as far as that of the Roman Mass. This is particularly true with regard to the traditional Roman Canon. Dom Cabrol, O.S.B., "Father" of the Modern Liturgical Movement, stresses that: 'The Canon of our Roman Rite, which in its main lines was drawn up in the fourth century, is the oldest and most venerable example of all the Eucharistic prayers in use today."[1]

Fr. Louis Bouyer, one of the leaders of the pre-Vatican II Liturgical Movement, also emphasized the fact that the Roman Canon is older than any other ancient Eucharistic prayer:

> The Roman Canon, such as it is today, goes back to St. Gregory the Great. Neither in East nor West is there any Eucharistic prayer remaining in use today that can boast such antiquity. For the Roman Church to throw it overboard would be tantamount, in the eyes not only of the Orthodox, but also of the Anglicans and even Protestants having still to some extent a sense of tradition, to a denial of all claim any more to be the true Catholic Church.[2]

It is scarcely possible to exaggerate the importance of the traditional Roman Missal from any standpoint. Dr. Anton Baumstark (1872-1948), perhaps (he greatest liturgical scholar of this century, expressed this well when he wrote that every worshipper taking part in this liturgy "feels Himself to be at the point which links those who before him, since the very earliest days of Christianity, have offered prayer and sacrifice with those who in time to come will be offering the same prayer and the same sacrifice, long after the last fragment of his mortal remains have crumbled into dust."[3]

Those who reflect upon the nature of the mystery of the Mass will wonder how men dare to celebrate it, how a priest dares to utter the words of Consecration which renew the sacrifice of Calvary, how even the most saintly layman dares to set foot in the building where it is being offered. *Terrihilis est locus isle: hie damns Dei est, et porta coeli; et vocahitur aulu Dei.* ("Awesome is this place: it is the house of God. and the gate of heaven; and it shall be called the court of God.")[4]

It is natural that the Church, the steward of these holy mysteries, should clothe them with the most solemn and beautiful rites and ceremonies possible. It is equally natural that the book containing these rites should appropriate to itself some of the wonder and veneration evoked by the sacred mysteries themselves. This veneration for the traditional Missal is well expressed by Dom Cabrol:

> The Missal, being concerned directly with the Mass and the Holy Eucharist, which is the chief of the Sacraments, has the most right to our veneration, and with it the Pontifical and the Ritual, because those three in the early Church formed one volume, as we have seen when speaking of the Sacramentary. The Church herself seems to teach us by her actions the reverence in which the Missal should be held. At High Mass it is carried by the deacon in solemn procession to read from it the Gospel of the day. He incenses it as a sign. The historical value of the Missal as a living link with the earliest and formative roots of Christian civilization in Europe is another point to which Dom Cabrol draws attention.

If these evidences of antiquity were merely a question of archaeology, we could not enlarge upon them here, but they have another immense importance. They prove the perpetuity of the Church and the continuity of her teaching. We have life by our tradition, but the Western Church has never confused fidelity to tradition with antiquarianism: she lives and grows with the time, ever advancing towards her goal: the liturgy of the Missal with its changes and developments throughout the centuries is a proof of this, but it proves also that the Church does not deny her past: she possesses a treasure from which she can draw the new and the old; and this is the secret of her adaptability, which is recognized even by her enemies. Though she adopts certain reforms, she never forgets her past history and guards preciously her relics of antiquity.

Here we have the explanation of the growing respect for the liturgy and of the great liturgical revival which we see in these days. What we may call the "archaisms" of the Missal are the expression of the faith of our fathers, which it is our duty to watch over and hand on to posterity.

In his book, *This Is the Mass*, Henri Daniel-Rops writes:

Therefore was it declared in the Catechism of the Council of Trent that no part of the Missal ought to be considered vain or superfluous: that not even the least of its phrases is to be thought wanting or insignificant. The shortest of its formularies, phrases which take no more than a few seconds to pronounce, form integral parts of a whole wherein are drawn together and set forth God's gift, Christ's sacrifice, and the grace which is dowered upon us. This whole conception has in view a sort of spiritual symphony in which all themes are taken as being expressed, developed, and unified under the guidance of one purpose. [5]

The beauty, the worth, the perfection of the Roman liturgy of the Mass, so universally acknowledged and admired, was described by Fr. Faber as "the most beautiful thing this side of heaven." He continues:

It came forth out of the grand mind of the Church, and lifted us out of earth and out of self, and wrapped us round in a cloud of mystical sweetness and the sublimities of a more than angelic liturgy, and purified us almost without ourselves, and charmed us with celestial charming, so that our very senses seem to find vision, hearing, fragrance, taste and touch beyond what earth can give.[6]

NOTES

1. Introduction to the Cabrol edition of *The Roman Missal.*

2. Cited in Ottaviani *et al, The Ottaviani Intervention: Short Critical Study of the New Order of the Mass (1969),* Fr. Anthony Cekada. trans. (Rockford. Illinois: TAN, 1992), p. 57. n. l.

3. Cited in T. Klauser, *A Shorter History of the Western Liturgy* (Oxford. 1952), p. 18.

4. From the Common of the Dedication of a Church, *The Roman Missal.*

5. H. Daniel Rops. *This Is the Mass* (New York: Hawthorn Books. 1958). p. 34.

6. Cited in N. Gihr, *The Holy Sacrifice of the Mass* (St. Louis: B. Herder. 1908). p. 337.

Address on the Occasion of the Tenth Anniversary of *Ecclesia Dei*

Joseph Cardinal Ratzinger
Rome, October 24, 1998

Ten years after the publication of the Motu proprio *"Ecclesia Dei,"* what sort of balance-sheet can one draw-up? I think this is above all an occasion to show our gratitude and to give thanks. The divers communities that were born thanks to this pontifical text have given the Church a great number of priestly and religious vocations who, zealously, joyfully, and deeply united with the Pope, have given their service to the Gospel in our present era of history. Through them, many of the faithful have been confirmed in the joy of being able to live the liturgy, and confirmed in their love for the Church, or perhaps they have rediscovered both. In many dioceses—and their number is not so small!—they serve the Church in collaboration with the Bishops and in fraternal union with those faithful who do feel at home with the renewed form of the new liturgy. All this cannot but move us to gratitude today!

However, it would not be realistic if we were to pass-over in silence those things which are less good. In many places difficulties persist, and these continue because some bishops, priests, and faithful consider this attachment to the old liturgy as an element of division which only disturbs the ecclesial community and which gives rise to suspicions regarding an acceptance of the Council made "with reservations," and more generally concerning obedience towards the legitimate pastors of the Church.

We ought now to ask the following question: how can these difficulties be overcome? How can one build the necessary trust so that these groups and communities who love the ancient liturgy can be smoothly integrated into the life of the Church?

But there is another question underlying the first: what is the deeper reason for this distrust or even for this rejection of a continuation of the ancient liturgical forms?

It is without doubt possible that, within this area, there exist reasons which go further back than any theology and which have their origin in the character of individuals or in the conflict between different personalities, or indeed a number of other circumstances which are wholly extrinsic. But it is certain that there are also other deeper reasons which explain these problems. The two reasons which are most often heard, are: lack of obedience to the Council which wanted the liturgical books reformed, and the break in unity which must necessarily follow if different liturgical forms are left in use. It is relatively simple to refute these two arguments on the theoretical level. The Council did not itself reform the liturgical books, but it ordered their revision, and to this end, it established certain fundamental rules. Before anything else, the Council gave a definition of what liturgy is, and this definition gives a valuable yardstick for every liturgical celebration. Were one to shun these essential rules and put to one side the *normae generales* which one finds in numbers 34-36 of the *Constitution De Sacra Liturgia* (SL), in that case one would indeed be guilty of disobedience to the Council! It is in the light of these criteria that liturgical celebrations must be evaluated, whether they be according to the old books or the new. It is good to recall here what Cardinal Newman observed, that the Church, throughout her history, has never abolished nor forbidden orthodox liturgical forms, which would be quite alien to the Spirit of the Church. An orthodox liturgy, that is to say, one which express the true faith, is never a compilation made according to the pragmatic criteria of different ceremonies, handled in a positivist and arbitrary way, one way today and another way tomorrow. The orthodox forms of a rite are living realities, born out of the dialogue of love between the Church and her Lord. They are expressions of the life of the Church, in which are distilled the faith, the prayer and the very life of whole generations, and which make incarnate in specific forms both the action of God and the response of man. Such rites can die, if those who have used them in a particular era should disappear, or if the life-situation of those same people should change. The authority of the Church has the power to define and limit the use of such rites in different historical situations, but she never just purely and simply forbids them! Thus, the Council ordered a reform of the liturgical books, but it did not prohibit the former books. The criterion which the Council established is both much larger and more demanding; it invites us all to self-criticism! But we will come back to this point.

We must now examine the other argument, which claims that the existence of the two rites can damage unity. Here a distinction must be made between the theological aspect and the practical aspect of the question. As regards what is theoretical and basic, it must be stated that several forms of the Latin rite have always existed, and were only slowly withdrawn, as a result of the coming together of the different parts of Europe. Before the Council there existed side by side with the Roman rite, the Ambrosian rite, the Mozarabic rite of Toledo, the rite of Braga, the Carthusian rite, the Carmelite rite, and best known of all, the Dominican rite, and perhaps still other rites of which I am not aware. No one was ever scandalized that the Dominicans, often present in our parishes, did not celebrate like diocesan priests but had their own rite. We did not have any doubt that their rite was as Catholic as the Roman rite, and we were proud of the richness inherent in these various traditions. Moreover, one must say this: that the freedom which the new order of Mass gives to creativity is often taken to excessive lengths. The difference between the liturgy according to the new books, how it is actually practiced and celebrated in different places, is often greater than the difference between an old Mass and a new Mass, when both these are celebrated according to the prescribed liturgical books.

An average Christian without specialist liturgical formation would find it difficult to distinguish between a Mass sung in Latin according to the old Missal and a sung Latin Mass according to the new Missal. However, the difference between a liturgy celebrated faithfully according to the Missal of Paul VI and the reality of a vernacular liturgy celebrated with all the freedom and creativity that are possible—that difference can be enormous!

With these considerations we have already crossed the threshold between theory and practice, a point at which things naturally get more complicated, because they concern relations between living people.

It seems to me that the dislikes we have mentioned are as great as they are because the two forms of celebration are seen as indicating two different spiritual attitudes, two different ways of perceiving the Church and the Christian life. The reasons for this are many. The first is this: one judges the two liturgical forms from their externals and thus one arrives at the following conclusion: there are two fundamentally different attitudes. The average Christian considers it essential for the renewed liturgy to be celebrated in the vernacular and facing the people; that there be a great deal of freedom for creativity; and that the laity exercise an active role therein. On the other hand, it is considered essential for a celebration according to the old rite to be in Latin, with the priest facing the altar, strictly and precisely according to the rubrics, and that the faithful follow the Mass in private prayer with no active role. From this viewpoint, a particular set of externals [*phénoménologie*] is seen as essential to this or that liturgy, rather than what the liturgy itself holds to be essential. We must hope for the day when the faithful will appreciate the liturgy on the basis of visible concrete forms, and become spiritually immersed in those forms; the faithful do not easily penetrate the depths of the liturgy.

The contradictions and oppositions which we have just enumerated originate neither from the spirit nor the letter of the conciliar texts. The actual Constitution on the Liturgy does not speak at all about celebration facing the altar or facing the people. On the subject of language, it says that Latin should be retained, while giving a greater place to the vernacular "above all in readings, instructions, and in a certain number of prayers and chants" (SL 36:2). As regards the participation of the laity, the Council first of all insists on a general point, that the liturgy is essentially the concern of the whole Body of Christ, Head and members, and for this reason it pertains to the whole Body of the Church "and that consequently it [the liturgy] is destined to be celebrated in community with the active participation of the faithful." And the text specifies "In liturgical celebrations each person, minister or lay faithful, when fulfilling his role, should carry out only and wholly that which pertains to him by virtue of the nature of the rite and the liturgical norms" (SL 28). "To promote active participation, acclamations by the people are favoured, responses, the chanting of the psalms, antiphons, canticles, also actions or gestures and bodily postures. One should also observe a period of sacred silence at an appropriate time." (SL 30).

These are the directives of the Council; they can provide everybody with material for reflection. Amongst a number of modern liturgists there is unfortunately a tendency to develop the ideas of the Council in one direction only. In acting thus, they end up reversing the intentions of the Council. The role of the priest is reduced, by some, to that of a mere functionary. The fact that the Body of Christ as a whole is the subject of the liturgy is often deformed to the point where the local community becomes the self-sufficient subject of the liturgy and itself distributes the liturgy's various roles. There also exists a dangerous tendency to minimalize the sacrificial character of the Mass, causing the mystery and the sacred to disappear, on the pretext, a pretext that claims to be absolute, that in this way they make things better understood. Finally, one observes the tendency to fragment the liturgy and to highlight in a unilateral way its communitarian character, giving the assembly itself the power to regulate the celebration.

Fortunately, however, there is also a certain disenchantment with an all too banal rationalism, and with the pragmatism of certain liturgists, whether they be theorists or practitioners, and one can note a return to mystery, to adoration and to the sacred, and to the cosmic and eschatological character of the liturgy, as evidenced in the 1996 "Oxford Declaration on the Liturgy." On the other hand, it must be admitted that the celebration of the old liturgy had strayed too far into a private individualism, and that communication between priest and people was insufficient. I have great respect for our forefathers who at Low Mass said the "Prayers during Mass" contained in their prayer books, but certainly one cannot consider that as the ideal of liturgical celebration! Perhaps these reductionist forms of celebration are the real reason that the disappearance of the old liturgical books was of no importance in many countries and caused no sorrow. One was never in contact with the liturgy itself. On the other hand, in those places where the Liturgical Movement had created a certain love for the liturgy, where the Movement had anticipated the essential ideas of the Council, such as, for example, the prayerful participation of all in the liturgical action, it was those places where there was all the more distress when confronted with a liturgical reform undertaken too hastily and often limited to externals. Where the Liturgical Movement had never existed, the reform initially raised no problems. The problems only appeared in a sporadic fashion, when unchecked creativity caused the sense of the sacred mystery to disappear.

This is why it is very important to observe the essential criteria of the Constitution on the Liturgy, which I quoted above, including when one celebrates according to the old Missal! The moment when this liturgy truly touches the faithful with its beauty and its richness, then it will be loved, then it will no longer be irreconcilably opposed to the new Liturgy, providing that these criteria are indeed applied as the Council wished.

Different spiritual and theological emphases will certainly continue to exist, but there will no longer be two contradictory ways of being a Christian; there will instead be that richness which pertains to the same single Catholic faith. When, some years ago, somebody proposed "a new liturgical movement" in order to avoid the two forms of the liturgy becoming too distanced from each other, and in order to bring about their close convergence, at that time some of the friends of the old liturgy expressed their fear that this would only be a stratagem or a ruse, intended to eliminate the old liturgy finally and completely.

Such anxieties and fears really must end! If the unity of faith and the oneness of the mystery appear clearly within the two forms of celebration, that can only be a reason for everybody to rejoice and to thank the good Lord. Inasmuch as we all believe, live and act with these intentions, we shall also be able to persuade the Bishops that the presence of the old liturgy does not disturb or break the unity of their diocese, but is rather a gift destined to build-up the Body of Christ, of which we are all the servants.

So, my dear friends, I would like to encourage you not to lose patience, to maintain your confidence, and to draw from the liturgy the strength needed to bear witness to the Lord in our own day.

"The Sanctuary"

Michael S. Rose
Ugly As Sin:
Why They Changed Our Churches
from Sacred Places to Meeting Spaces—
and How We Can Change Them Back Again
Sophia Institute Press, 2001

The sanctuary sets apart the holiest part of the church Just as all the sacraments are ordered toward the Holy Eucharist, the ark of salvation is ordered toward the sanctuary. Every aspect of the nave—pews, furnishings, architectural elements, and sacred art—ultimately leads to the sanctuary, the place in the church built especially for the altar of sacrifice. This is the Christian equivalent to the "Holy of Holies" of the tabernacle in the wilderness and in Solomon's Temple.[1] Although the sanctuary represents the apex of our pilgrim's journey and the summit of the Liturgy, the pilgrim merely approaches it. It isn't his dwelling place; it is God's.

In the Temple of Jerusalem, the sanctuary was also God's dwelling place, and only the ordained entered this most sacred of places: "While [Zechariah] was serving as priest before God when his division was on duty, according to the custom of the priesthood, it fell to him by lot to enter the temple of the Lord and burn incense. And the multitude of the people were praying outside at the hour of incense."[2] In like manner, the Christian sanctuary has always been the place for the clergy and those assisting the clergy at Mass, just as the nave is the place for the non-ordained faithful, whether praying the Rosary, adoring the Blessed Sacrament, or participating in the Liturgy of the Mass. In this way, our pilgrim is reminded that the Church is hierarchical, composed of different members—the head being Christ; with Pope, bishops, and priests each serving as alter Christus, "another Christ;" and with the religious and laity serving their own

---

[1] Cf. Heb. 9:3 ff. [50]

[2] Luke 1:8-9.

functions as part of the Church Militant.[3] That hierarchy is reflected in the Liturgy on earth as it is in Heaven. In an *ad limina* address in 1998, Pope John Paul II reminded a group of U.S. bishops that "the Liturgy, like the Church, is intended to be hierarchical and polyphonic, respecting the different roles assigned by Christ and allowing all the different voices to blend together into one great hymn of praise."[4] It only follows, then, that if the Church and the Liturgy are both hierarchical, the church building ought to reflect that hierarchy. This logic is reflected by the Church's stipulation that the "sanctuary should be marked off from the nave by a higher floor level and by a distinctive structure or decor."[5]

To put it simply and to reiterate the point: the sanctuary is meant to be a separate place in the church. It's the place where the priest offers the Holy Sacrifice of the Mass and where the Blessed Sacrament is reserved for adoration, an extension of the Holy Sacrifice.

The sanctuary is a raised area primarily for two reasons. The first is figurative: since the sanctuary represents Christ the head (and also the head of Christ), it's only natural that the head be higher than the body. Second, the sanctuary is elevated for a practical reason: so that the congregation can easily see the different parts of the Liturgy that take place in the sanctuary. If the nave is ordered toward the sanctuary, our pilgrim ought to be able to see it from the nave.

The sanctuary is also marked off from the nave by a "distinctive structure." In many churches, the sanctuary is not only differentiated from the nave, but it's also framed by the triumphal arch, the portion of the wall over the arch that separates nave from sanctuary. The name is taken from the grand arches built by emperors or governments typically to commemorate a military conquest. Two of the most well-known arches are the nineteenth-century *Arc de Triomphe* in Paris and the fourth-century Arch of Constantine in Rome. The first is a single grand arch, whereas the second is formed by a large central arch flanked by two smaller ones. Both forms have been adapted to churches. The triple-opening arch was applied to

---

[3] That is, the members of the Church on earth. The members in Heaven are known as the Church Triumphant and the members in Purgatory as the Church Suffering.

[4] *Ad limina* address to the Bishops of Washington, Oregon, and Alaska, October 9, 1998.

[5] General Instruction of the Roman Missal, no. 258.

those churches that have small side apses or chapels flanking the central apse of the sanctuary. The single-opening arch was used even since the first basilicas built in Rome. The oldest is probably the triumphal arch of Santa Maria Maggiore (435), which is decorated by mosaics that portray narrative scenes from the life of Christ.

Another common structure is the communion rail, or altar rail, usually a low balustrade made of carved wood, stone, wrought iron, stainless steel, or other precious materials. It not only serves to define the sanctuary; it is functional as well. Here our pilgrim, approaching the altar, kneels to receive the Holy Eucharist in adoration and humility.[6] At times outside of Mass, the pilgrim can give thanksgiving here, praying before the Blessed Sacrament in the tabernacle or exposed on the altar. At the rail, as in the pews, our pilgrim has the opportunity to assume the traditional Catholic posture of worship: kneeling.

From the sixteenth century to the late twentieth century, communion rails were almost universal in Catholic churches where the Roman rite is followed. Before the sixteenth century, in place of the communion rail, there was a low wall that functioned in much the same way as the balustrade and effectively separated the sanctuary from the nave without the two areas appearing or being disconnected. Even in fourth-century basilicas, these low walls, called *cancelli*, were extant. Since the faithful began to kneel at the rail for Communion, the altar rail has been understood as an extension of the altar, where the Holy Sacrifice of the Mass takes place, just as the reserved Blessed Sacrament is an extension of the Mass. For this reason, the design of the railing reflects the design and construction of the altar.

Finally, because the infinite act of the ultimate sacrifice is offered here, the sanctuary is differentiated by its decor. Sacred art and architectural elements, including the sanctuary's furnishings, express the majesty, grandeur, and sublimity of the Sacred Mystery enacted. St. Charles Borromeo, who called the sanctuary the "Chapel of the High Altar," recommended that the ceiling of the sanctuary be vaulted

---

[6] Although in some places the practice of kneeling at the altar rail to receive Communion has fallen by the wayside, it's still a normative method of reception. In *Eucharisticum Mysterium* (Instruction on the Worship of the Eucharistic Mystery, 1967) Pope Paul VI wrote, "When the faithful communicate kneeling, no other sign of reverence toward the Blessed Sacrament is required, since kneeling is itself a sign of adoration" (no. 34).

or at least be built of a rarer and richer form and material than that of the nave. The walls should he richly decorated with mosaics, paintings, frescoes, or stained glass. And all should "be proportioned to express harmonious unity."

The Reform of the Liturgy and the Position of the Celebrant at the Altar

Fr. Uwe Michael Lang
Turning Towards the Lord: Orientation in Liturgical Prayer
Ignatius Press, 2004

The reform of the Roman Rite of Mass that was carried out after the Second Vatican Council has significantly altered the shape of Catholic worship. One of the most evident changes was the construction of freestanding altars. The *versus populum* celebration was adopted throughout the Latin Church, and, with few exceptions, it has become the prevailing practice during Mass for the celebrant to stand behind the altar facing the congregation. This uniformity has led to the widespread misunderstanding that the priest's "turning his back on the people" is characteristic of the rite of Mass according to the Missal of Pope Saint Pius V whereas the priest's "turning towards the people" belongs to the *Novus Ordo* Mass of Pope Paul VI. It is also widely assumed by the general public that the celebration of Mass "facing the people" is required, indeed even imposed, by the liturgical reform that was inaugurated by Vatican II.

However, the relevant conciliar and post-conciliar documents present quite a different picture. The Council's Constitution on the Sacred Liturgy, *Sacrosanctum Concilium*, speaks neither of a celebration *versus populum* nor of the setting up of new altars. In view of this fact it is all the more astonishing how rapidly "*versus populum* altars" appeared in Catholic churches all over the world.[1] The instruction *Inter Oecumenici*, prepared by the *Consilium* for the carrying out of the Constitution on the Sacred Liturgy and issued on September 26, 1964, has a chapter on the designing of new churches and altars that includes the following paragraph:

> *Praestat ut altare maius exstruatur a pariete seiunctum, ut facile circumiri et in eo celebratio versus populum peragi possit.* [It is better for the main altar to be constructed away from the wall so that one can easily walk around the altar and celebrate facing the people.] [2]

It is said to be desirable to set up the main altar separate from the back wall, so that the priest can walk around it easily and a celebration facing the people is *possible*. Josef Andreas Jungmann asks us to consider this:

> It is only the possibility that is emphasized. And this [separation of the altar from the wall] is not even prescribed, but is only recommended, as one will see if one looks at the Latin text of the directive. . . . In the new instruction the general permission of such an altar layout is stressed only with regard to possible obstacles or local restrictions.[3]

In a letter addressed to the heads of bishops' conferences, dated January 25, 1966, Cardinal Giacomo Lercaro, the president of the *Consilium*, states that regarding the renewal of altars "prudence must be our guide," He goes on to explain:

> Above all because for a living and participated liturgy, it is not indispensable that the altar should be *versus populum*: in the Mass, the entire liturgy of the word is celebrated at the chair, ambo, or lectern, and, therefore, facing the assembly; as to the eucharistic liturgy, loudspeaker systems make participation feasible enough. Secondly, hard thought should be given to the artistic and architectural question, this element in many places being protected by rigorous civil laws.[4]

With reference to Cardinal Lercaro's exhortation to prudence, Jungmann warns us not to make the option granted by the instruction into "an absolute demand, and eventually a fashion, to which one succumbs without thinking."[5]

Inter Oecumenici permits the Mass facing the people, but it does not prescribe it. As Louis Bouyer emphasized in 1967, that document does not at all suggest that Mass facing the people is always the preferable form of Eucharistic celebration.[6]

Missal Rubrics

The rubrics of the renewed *Missale Romanum* of Pope Paul VI presuppose a common direction of priest and people for the core of the Eucharistic liturgy. This is indicated by the instruction that, at the *Orate, fratres*, the *Pax Domini*, the *Ecce*, *Agnus Dei*, and the *Ritus conclusionis*, the priest should turn towards the people.[7] This would seem to imply that beforehand priest and people were facing the same direction, that is, towards the altar. At the priest's communion the rubrics say *"ad altare versus,"*[8] which would be redundant if the celebrant stood behind the altar facing the people anyway. This reading is confirmed by the directives of the *General Instruction*, even if they are occasionally at variance with the *Ordo Missae*.[9] The third *Editio typica* of the renewed *Missale Romanum*, approved by Pope John Paul II on 10 April 2000 and published in spring 2002, retains these rubrics.[10]

This interpretation of the official documents has been endorsed by the Roman Congregation for Divine Worship. An editorial in its official publication, *Notitiae*, states that the arrangement of an altar that permits a celebration facing the people is not a question upon which the liturgy stands or falls (*"quaestio stantis vel cadentis liturgiae"*). Furthermore, the article suggests that, in this matter as in many others, Cardinal Lercaro's call for prudence was hardly heard in the post-conciliar euphoria. The editorial observes that changing the orientation of the altar and using the vernacular could become an easy substitute for entering into the theological and spiritual dimensions of the liturgy, for studying its history and for taking into account the pastoral consequences of the reform.[11]

The revised General Instruction of the Roman Missal, which was published for study purposes in the spring of 2000, has a paragraph bearing on the altar question:

> *Altare exstruatur a pariete seiunctum, ut facile circumiri et in eo celebratio versus populum peragi possit, quod expedit ubicumque possibile sit.* [Let the main altar be constructed separate from the wall so that one can easily walk around the altar and celebrate facing the people—which is desirable wherever possible.][12]

The subtle wording of this paragraph (*possit—possibile*) clearly indicates that the position of the celebrant priest facing the people is not made compulsory. The instruction merely allows for both forms of celebration. At any rate, the added phrase "which is desirable wherever (or whenever) possible (*quod expedit ubicumque possibile sit*)" refers to the provision for a freestanding altar and not to the desirability of celebration towards the people.[13]

Nonetheless various news reports about the revised *General Instruction* seemed to suggest that the position of the celebrant *versus orientem*—or *versus absidem*—was declared undesirable, if not prohibited.

This interpretation however has been rejected by the Congregation for Divine Worship in a response to a question submitted by Cardinal Christoph Schönborn, Archbishop of Vienna. The response is dated 25 September 2000 and signed by Cardinal Jorge Arturo Medina Estévez, then Prefect of the Congregation, and Archbishop Francesco Pio Tamburrino, its Secretary:

> In the first place, it is to be borne in mind that the word *expedit* does not constitute an obligation, but a suggestion that refers to the construction of the altar a *pariete seiunctum* (detached from the wall) and to the celebration *versus populum* (towards the people). The clause *ubi possibile sit* (where it is possible) refers to different elements, as, for example, the topography of the place, the availability of space, the artistic value of the existing altar, the sensibility of the people participating in the celebrations in a particular church, etc. It reaffirms that the position towards the assembly seems more convenient inasmuch as it makes communication easier (cf. the editorial in *Notitiae* 29 [1993] 245-49), without excluding, however, the other possibility.

> However, whatever may be the position of the celebrating priest, it is clear that the eucharistic sacrifice is offered to the one and triune God and that the principal, eternal, and high priest is Jesus Christ, who acts through the ministry of the priest who visibly presides as His instrument. The liturgical assembly participates in the celebration in virtue of the common priesthood of the faithful which requires the ministry of the ordained priest to be exercised in the eucharistic synaxis. The physical position, especially with respect to the communication among the various members of the assembly, must be distinguished from the interior spiritual orientation of all. It would be a grave error to imagine that the principal orientation of the sacrificial action is towards the community. If the priest celebrates versus populum, which is legitimate and often advisable, his spiritual attitude ought always to be *versus Deum per Iesum Christum* (towards God through Jesus Christ), as representative of the entire Church. The Church as well, which takes concrete form in the assembly which participates, is entirely turned *versus Deum* (towards God) as its first spiritual movement.[14]

Obviously, the relevant paragraph of the *General Instruction* must be read in light of this clarification.[15]

The Reform of the Liturgy and the Position of the Celebrant at the Altar

Early Critics of "facing the people"

Already in the sixties, theologians of international renown criticized the sweeping triumph of the celebration *versus populum*. In addition to Jungmann and Bouyer, Joseph Ratzinger, then professor of theology at Tübingen and *peritus* at the Council, delivered a lecture at the *Katholikentag* of 1966 in Bamberg that was received with much attention. His observations have lost nothing of their relevance:

> We can no longer deny that exaggerations and aberrations have crept in which are both annoying and unbecoming. Must every Mass, for instance, be celebrated facing the people? Is it so absolutely important to be able to look the priest in the face, or might it not be often very salutary to reflect that he also is a Christian and that he has every reason to turn to God with all his fellow-Christians of the congregation and to say together with them "Our Father"?[16]

The German liturgist Balthasar Fischer concedes that the turning of the celebrant towards the people for the entire celebration of the Mass was never officially introduced or prescribed by the new liturgical legislation. In post-conciliar documents it was merely declared possible. In view of this, however, the fact that the celebration *versus populum* has become the dominant practice of the Latin Church shows the astounding extent to which "the active role of the people in the celebration of the Eucharist" has been realized; for Fischer this is indeed the fundamental issue of the liturgical reform after Vatican II.[17]

"Face-to-face" or "Facing East"?

Two main arguments in favor of the celebrant's position facing the people during the Eucharist are usually presented. First, it is claimed that this was the practice of the early Church that should be the norm for our age. Second, it is maintained that the "active participation" of the faithful, a principle that was introduced by Pope Saint Pius X and is central to *Sacrosanctum Concilium*, demanded the celebration towards the people.[18]

The aim of this study will be to counter these arguments in a twofold way.

First, an examination of the historical evidence will show that the orientation of priest and people in the liturgy of the Eucharist is well-attested in the early Church and was, in fact, the general custom. It will be evident that the common direction of liturgical prayer has been a consistent tradition in both the East and the West.

Second, I should like to argue, relying on the thought of contemporary theologians, that the permanent face-to-face position of priest and people is not beneficial for a real participation of the faithful in the liturgy, as envisaged by Vatican II. Recent critical reflection on *participatio actuosa* has revealed the need for a theological reappraisal and deepening of this important principle.

Cardinal Ratzinger draws a useful distinction between participation in the Liturgy of the Word, which includes external actions, especially reading and singing, and participation in the Liturgy of the Eucharist, where external actions are quite secondary. He writes:

> *Doing* really must stop when we come to the heart of the matter: the *oratio*. It must be plainly evident that the *oratio* is the heart of the matter, but that it is important precisely because it provides a space for the *actio* of God. Anyone who grasps this will easily see that it is not now a matter of looking at or toward the priest, but of looking together toward the Lord and going out to meet Him.[19]

The statement of the Congregation for Divine Worship already quoted shows that speaking of "celebrating towards the people" indicates merely the position of the priest vis-à-vis the congregation at certain parts of the liturgy but does not refer to a theological concept.[20] The expression *versus (ad) populum* seems to have been used for the first time by the papal master of ceremonies, Johannes Burckard, in his *Ordo Missae* of 1502[21] and was taken up in the *Ritus servandus in celebratione Missae* of the *Missale Romanum* that Pope Saint Pius V issued in 1570. The *Ritus servandus* deals with the case where the altar is directed to the east and, at the same time, towards the people (*altare sit ad orientem, versus populum*). This is indeed the state of affairs in the major Roman basilicas with the entrance facing east and the apse facing west. Here *versus populum* is to be looked upon merely as an explanatory appositive, namely in view of the immediately following directive that in this case at the *Pax Domini* the celebrant does not need to turn around (*non vertit humeros ad altare*), since he already stands *ad populum* anyway.[22] It is in this topographical sense that the similar passages in Amalarius (ca. 830)[23] and Durandus (towards the end of the thirteenth century)[24] are also to be understood.

The Reform of the Liturgy and
the Position of the Celebrant at the Altar

When these texts use the phrase *versus populum*, they do not necessarily mean a visual connection between the people and the sacred action at the altar. It is by no means suggested here that nothing should limit, let alone block, the faithful's view of the ritual acts of the celebrant. Such an interpretation would have seemed alien to the understanding of the liturgy that was common from Christian antiquity until well into the Middle Ages and is still found in the Eastern Churches. Thus, it is hardly surprising to find that even with altars *versus populum* the sight was significantly restricted, for example, by curtains that were closed during certain parts of the liturgy or already by the architectural layout of the church.[25]

The guiding points of the Congregation for Divine Worship make clear that the expression *versus populum* does not convey the theological dimension of the Eucharistic liturgy. Each Eucharist is offered for the praise and glory of God's name, for the benefit of us and of the holy Church as a whole ("*ad laudem et gloriam nominis Dei, ad utilitatem quoque nostram, totiusque Ecclesiae suae sanctae*").

Theologically, the Mass as a whole, the Liturgy of the Word, and the Liturgy of the Eucharist, is directed at the same time towards God and towards the people. In the form of the celebration one must avoid a confusion of theology and topography, especially when the priest stands at the altar. The priest speaks to the people only during the dialogues at the altar. Everything else is prayer to the Father through Christ in the Holy Spirit. Evidently, it is most desirable that this theology should be expressed in the visible shape of the liturgy.[26]

Cardinal Ratzinger is equally emphatic that the celebration of the Eucharist, just as Christian prayer in general, has a trinitarian direction and discusses the question of how this can be communicated most fittingly in liturgical gesture. When we speak to someone, we obviously face that person. Accordingly, the whole liturgical assembly, priest and people, should face the same way, turning towards God to whom prayers and offerings are addressed in this common act of trinitarian worship. Ratzinger rightly protests against the mistaken idea that in this case the celebrating priest is facing "towards the altar," "towards the tabernacle," or even "towards the wall."[27] The catchphrase often heard nowadays that the priest is "turning his back on the people" is a classic example of confounding theology and topography, for the crucial point is that the Mass is a common act of worship where priest and people together, representing the pilgrim Church, reach out for the transcendent God.

Reinhard Meßner notes that what is at issue is not the *celebratio versus populum*, but the direction of liturgical prayer that has been known in the Christian tradition as "facing east."[28]

My claim is that the intrinsic sense of facing east in the Eucharist is the common direction of priest and people oriented towards the triune God. . . . [I]ts recovery is indispensable for the welfare of the Church today.

[**N.B.** Headings have been added in the text of the chapter.]

NOTES

1 J. A. Jungmann, 'Der neue Altar,' *Der Seelsorger* 37 (1967): 375.

2 Sacra Congregatio Rituum, *Instructio ad exsecutionem Constitutionis de sacra Liturgia recte ordinandam 'Inter Oecumenici,'* Acta Apostolicae Sedis 56 (1964): 898, no. 91. This translation is more literal than the one found in *Documents on the Liturgy*, 19631979: *Conciliar, Papal, and Curial Texts* (Collegeville, Minn.: Liturgical Press, 1982), 108, no. 383.

3 Translating Jungmann, 'Der neue Altar,' 375.

4 G. Lercaro, 'L'Heureux Développement,' *Notitiae* 2 (1966): 160; English translation: *Documents on the Liturgy*, 122, no. 428.

5 Translating Jungmann, 'Der neue Altar,' 380; see also C. Napier, "The Altar in the Contemporary Church," *Clergy Review* 57 (1972): 624. A. Lorenzer, *"Sacrosanctum Concilium:" Der Anfang der "Buchhalterei:" Betrachtungen aus psychoanalytisch-kulturkritischer Sicht,'* in *Gottesdienst-Kirche-Gesellschaft: Interdisziplinäre und ökumenische Standortbestimmungen nach 25 Jahren Liturgiereform*, ed. H. Becker, B. J. Hilberath, and U. Willers, *Pietas liturgica* 5 (St. Ottilien: EOS-Verlag, 1991), 158, argues that there is a significant difference between the conciliar documents and what came out of them. Whereas the texts carefully present a number of options, their implementation became an exercise in "total deforestation."

6 L. Bouyer, *Liturgy and Architecture* (Notre Dame, Ind.: University of Notre Dame Press, 1967), 1056.

7 *Missale Romanum ex decreto Sacrosancti Oecumenici Concilii Vaticani II instauratum auctoritate Pauli PP.VI promulgatum, editio*

typica (Vatican City: *Typis Polyglottis Vaticanis*, 1970), *Ordo Missae cum populo*, 391, no. 25 (*versus ad populum*), 473, no. 128 (*ad populum conversus*), 474, no. 133 (*ad populum versus*), and 475, no. 142 (*versus ad populum*).

8 Ibid., 474, no. 134.

9 Ibid., *Institutio Generalis*, nos. 107, 115, 116, 122, as well as 198 and 199 for concelebrated Masses. Cf. O. Nußbaum, "Die Zelebration *versus populum* und der Opfercharakter der Messe." *Zeitschrift für Katholische Theoligie* 93 (1971): 14950, who points out how little the liturgical reform wished to make *versus populum* celebration into the exclusive norm. This, he thinks, is clearly demonstrated by the fact that in the revision of the *Ritus servandus in celebratione Missae*, and subsequently also in the 1965 and 1967 versions of the *Ordo Missae*, the celebrant was still explicitly instructed to turn towards the people when addressing them directly, as for example in the liturgical greeting. The *Novus Ordo Missae* also keeps to this practice within the eucharistic liturgy. Nußbaum was certainly an advocate of *versus populum* celebration, and yet he concedes that, in the reform of the liturgy, this was not the preferred option let alone the only legitimate way of celebrating Mass.

10 *Missale Romanum ex decreto Sacrosancti Oecumenici Concilii Vaticani II instauratum auctoritate Pauli PP. VI promulgatum Ioannis Pauli PP. II cura recognitum, editio typica tertia* (Vatican City: *Typis Vaticanis*, 2002), *Ordo Missae*, 515, no. 28; 600, no. 127; 601, nos. 13233; 603, no. 141.

11 Congregatio de Cultu Divino, "*Editoriale: Pregare 'ad orientem versus*'," *Notitiae* 29 (1993): 247.

12 *Missale Romanum* (2002), *Institutio Generalis*, no. 299.

13 The text is carefully scrutinized by C.M. Cullen and J.W. Koterski, "The New IGMR and Mass *versus Populum*," *Homiletic and Pastoral Review*, June 2001, 5154.

14 Congregatio de Cultu Divino, 'Responsa ad quaestiones de nova *Institutione Generali Missalis Romani*,' *Communicationes* 32 (2000): 17172. Surprisingly, it has been published, not in *Notitiae*, but in *Communicationes*, the official publication of the Pontifical Council for the Interpretation of Legal Texts. The English translation is taken from *Adoremus Bulletin* Online Edition, vol. 6, no. 9 (December 2000

January 2001), (www.adoremus.org/12-0101cdw-adorient.html—acessed 5 January 2004).

15 Cf. The comments of J. Nebel, "Die *editio typica tertia des Missale Romanum*: *Eine Untersuchung über die Veränderungen*," *Ecclesia Orans* 19 (2002): 278, n. 72.

16 J. Ratzinger, "Catholicism after the Council," trans. P. Russell, *The Furrow* 18 (1967) 11-12.

17 B. Fischer, "Die Grundaussagen der Liturgie-Konstitution und ihre Rezeption in fünfundzwanzig Jahren," in Becker, Hilberath, and Willers, *Gottesdienst-Kirche-Gesellschaft*, 42223.

18 See, for instance, O. Nußbaum, *Der Standort des Liturgen am christlichen Altar vor dem Jahre 1000: Eine archäologische und liturgiegeschichtliche Untersuchung*, Theoph 18 (Bonn: Hanstein, 1965), 1:22, and B. Neunheuser, "*Eucharistiefeier am Altare versus populum: Geschichte und Problematik*," in *Florentissima proles Ecclesiae: Miscellanea hagiographica, historica et liturgica Reginaldo Grégoire O.S.B. XII lustra complenti oblata*, ed. D. Gobbi (Trento: Civis, 1996), 44243.

19 J. Ratzinger, *The Spirit of the Liturgy* (San Francisco: Ignatius Press, 2000), 174, cf. 17177. See also the critical remarks of M. Kunzler, '*La liturgia all'inizio del Terzo Millennio*,' in *Il Concilio Vaticano II: Recezione e attualità alla luce del Giubileo, ed. R. Fisichella* (Milan: San Paolo, 2000), 21724, and D. Torevell, *Losing the Sacred: Ritual, Modernity and Liturgical Reform* (Edinburgh: T and T Clark, 2000).

20 Congregatio de Cultu Divino, "*Editoriale*." 249.

21 Johannes Burckard, *Ordo Missae Ioannis Burckardi*, ed. J.W. Legg, Tracts on the Mass, HBS 27 (London: Harrison, 1904), 142; cf. Nußbaum, "*Die Zelebration versus populum*," 16061.

22 *Missale Romanum ex decreto Sacrosancti Concilii Tridentini restitutum Pii V Pont. Max. iussu editum, Ritus servandus in celebratione Missae*, V, 3. The 1570 *editio princeps* of this Missal is now accessible in a study edition: M. Sodi and A.M. Triacca, eds., *Missale Romanum: Editio Princeps* (1570), *Monumenta Liturgica Concilii Tridentini* 2 (Vatican City: *Libreria Editrice Vaticana*, 1998).

23 Amalarius uses the expressions *ad orientem* and *ad populum* for explaining that the celebrant stands in front of the altar facing east and turns around for the liturgical greeting: Liber *officialis* III, 9, ed. J.M. Hanssens, Studi e Testi, 139, 1:288–90. On Amalarius, see now W. Steck, *Der Liturgiker Amalarius: Eine quellenkritische Untersuchung zu Leben und Werk eines Theologen der Karolingerzeit*, MThS.H 35 (Munich: St. Ottilien: EOS-Verlag, 2000).

24 "*In ecclesiis vero ostia ab oriente habentibus, ut Rome, nulla est in salutatione necessaria conversio, quia sacerdos in illis celebrans semper ad populum stat converse*" *(Durandus, Rationale divinorum officiorum* V, II, 57: CChr. CM 140A, 424]).

25 Nußbaum, *Der Standort des Liturgen*, 1:418–19, and J. A. Jungmann, review of O. Nußbaum, *Der Standort des Liturgen am christlichen Altar vor dem Jahre 1000*, ZKTh 88 (1966): 447.

26 Congregatio de Cultu Divino, "Editoriale," 249.

27 J. Ratzinger, *The Feast of Faith: Approaches to a Theology of the Liturgy* (San Francisco: Ignatius Press, 1986), 139–43.

28 R. Meßner, "*Probleme des eucharistischen Hochgebets'*, in *Bewahren und Erneuern: Studien zur Meßliturgie: Festschrift für Hans Bernhard Meyer SJ zum 70. Geburtstag*, ed. R. Meßner, E. Nagel, and R. Pacik, IThS 42 (Innsbruck and Vienna: Tyrolia, 1995), 201, n. 99; likewise M. Wallraff, *Christus verus sol: Sonnenverehrung und Christentum in der Spätantike*, JAC.E 32 (Münster: Aschendorff, 2001), 72, n. 53.

Some Considerations on Holy Communion in the Hand

Fr. Paul McDonald
Christ to The World Magazine, 2007

Following your editor's request for information, here are some patristic and historical considerations on Communion on the hand, as well as an additional aspect.

Was it universal? The history of Communion in the hand is often presented in certain quarters as follows: From the Last Supper on, Holy Communion was, as the norm, continually given in the hand. So it was during the age of the martyrs. And it continued to be so during that golden age of the Fathers and of the liturgy after the peace of Constantine in 313 A.D. And it continued to be the common practice until at least the tenth century. Thus, for over half of the life of the Church it was the norm.

An argument for the above is held to be found in a text of St. Cyril of Jerusalem's fifth Mystagogic Catechesis (21f), which he preached to neophytes in 348 A.D., in which he counsels the faithful to "place your left hand as the throne of your right one, which is to receive the King [in Holy Communion]" (apud *L'Osservatore Romano*. English edition of June 14, 1973, p. 6). This Father of the Church further counsels great care for any Fragments which might remain on one's hands.

According to some critics' version of history, popular in certain quarters, Communion on the tongue became the universal norm in this way: During the Middle Ages certain distortions in the faith and/or in approaches to it gradually developed. These included an excessive fear of God and an over-concern about sin, judgment and punishment, as well as an over-emphasis on Christ's divinity—so emphasized as to down-play His sacred humanity or virtually deny it; also an over-emphasis on the priest's role in the sacred liturgy, and a loss of the sense of the community which the Church, in fact, is. In particular, because of excessive emphasis on adoring Christ in the Holy Eucharist and an over-strict approach to moral matters, Holy

Communion became more and more rare. It was considered enough to gaze upon the Sacred Host during the elevation. (In fact, in certain critics' minds the elevation, exposition and benediction of the Blessed Sacrament find their origins during the 'unfortunate' Middle Ages, a period whose liturgical practices we would do well—so they think—to rid ourselves of.) It was in this atmosphere and under these circumstances, they argue, that the practice of Communion in the hand began to be restricted. The practice of the priest placing the consecrated Bread directly into the mouth of the communicant thus developed and, they think, was unwisely imposed.

The conclusion is rather clear: We should get rid of this custom. We should forbid or at least discourage the Communion-on-the-tongue practice whereby the faithful are not allowed to "take and eat," and should return to the pristine usage of the Fathers and Apostles, namely, Communion in the hand.

It is a compelling story. It is too bad that it is not true.

The sacred Council of Trent declared that the custom whereby only the priest-celebrant gives Communion to himself (with his own hands), and the laity receive It from him, is an Apostolic tradition.

A more rigorous study of available evidence from Church history and from writings of the Fathers does not support the assertion that Communion in the hand was a universal practice which was gradually supplanted and eventually replaced by the practice of Communion on the tongue. Rather, facts seem to point to a different conclusion: Pope St. Leo the Great (440-461) is an early witness of the traditional practice. In his comments on the sixth chapter of St. John's Gospel he speaks of Communion in the mouth as the current usage: "One receives in the mouth what one believes by faith." The Pope does not speak as if he were introducing a novelty, but as if this were a well established thing.

A century and a half later Pope St. Gregory the Great (died in 604) is another witness. In his dialogues he relates how Pope St. Agapitus performed a miracle during Mass, after having placed the Body of the Lord into someone's mouth.

We are not claiming that under no circumstances whatever did the faithful receive by their own hands. But under what conditions did this happen? It does seem that from very early times on, it was usual for the priest to place the Sacred Host into the mouth of the communicant. However, during times of persecution, when priests were not readily available, and when the faithful took the Sacrament to their homes, they gave Communion to themselves by their own hand. Rather than be totally deprived of the Bread of Life, they could receive by their own hand. The same applied to monks who had gone out into the desert, where they would not have the services of a priest and would not want to give up the practice of daily holy Communion. St. Basil the Great (330-379) indicates that reception of Communion by one's own hand was permitted precisely because of persecution, or, as was the case with monks in the desert, when no deacon or priest was available to give It.

In his article on "Communion" in the *Dictionaire d'Archeologiae Chretienne*, Leclerq declares that the peace of Constantine in 313 A.D. served toward bringing the practice of Communion in the hand to an end. After persecution had ceased, evidently the practice of Communion in the hand persisted here and there. Church authority apparently judged that it invited abuse and deemed it contrary to the custom of the Apostles.

Thus, the Synod of Rouen, France, in about 878 directed: "Do not put the Eucharist in the hands of any layman or laywomen, but only in their mouths" ("*nulli autem laico aut feminae eucharistiam in manibus ponat, sed tantum in os eius*"). A non-ecumenical Council of Constantinople known as "*In Trullo*" in 692 A.D. prohibited the faithful from giving Communion to themselves (which is of course what happens when the Sacred Particle is placed in the hand of communicants), and decreed a censure against those who would do so in the presence of a bishop, priest, or deacon.

Promoters of Communion in the hand generally make little mention of the evidence we have brought forward, but do make constant use of the text attributed above to St. Cyril of Jerusalem, who lived in the fourth century at the time of St. Basil. But scholars dispute the authenticity of the St. Cyril text, according to Jungmann-Brunner, *op. cit.*, p. 191, n.25. It is not impossible that the text is really the work of the Patriarch John, who succeeded Cyril in Jerusalem. This John was of suspect orthodoxy, as we know from the correspondence of St. Epiphanius, St. Jerome, and St. Augustine.

But is it not a form of clericalism to allow the priest to touch the Sacred Host and to forbid the laity to do the same? But even priests were not allowed to touch the Blessed Sacrament except out of some need to do so. In fact, other than the celebrant of the Mass itself, no one else receiving Communion, not even a priest, could receive It in the hand. And so, in the traditional liturgical practice of the Roman Rite, if a priest were assisting at Mass (and not celebarating) and if he wished to receive Holy Communion, he did not do so by his own hand; he received on the tongue from another priest. The same would be true of a Bishop or even a Pope. When Pope St. Pius X was on his deathbed in August of 1914, and Holy Communion was brought to him as Viaticum, he did not and was not allowed to receive in the hand. He received on the tongue according to the law and practice of the Catholic Church.

This confirms a basic point: Out of reverence it seems better that there be no unnecessary touching of the Sacred Host. Obviously someone is needed to distribute the Bread of Life. But it is not needful to make each man, woman, and child into his own "eucharistic minister" and multiply the handling and fumbling and danger of dropping and loss of Fragments. Even those whose hands have been specially consecrated to touch the Most Holy Eucharist, namely the priests, should not do so needlessly.

As for the present situation, in those countries where the indult for Communion in the hand has been granted by the Holy See, an individual bishop may forbid the practice; but no Bishop has authority to forbid the traditional way of receiving Our Lord on the tongue.

But surely the Apostles received Communion in the hand at the Last Supper? It is usually presumed that this was so. Even if it were, though, we would point out that the Apostles were themselves priests, or even Bishops. But we must not forget a traditional custom of middle-eastern hospitality which was in practice in Jesus' time and which is still the case; that is, one feeds his guests with one's own hand, placing a symbolic morsel in the mouth of the guest. And we have this text of St. John's Gospel (13:26-30): "Jesus answered, 'It is he to whom I shall give this Morsel when I have dipped It.' So when He had dipped the Morsel, He gave It to Judas. . . . So, after receiving the Morsel, he [Judas] immediately went out . . . .'"

Did Our Lord place this wet Morsel into Judas' hand? That would be rather messy. Did He not perhaps extend to the one whom He addressed later in the garden as "friend" the gesture of hospitality spoken of above? And if so, why not with Holy Communion, "giving Himself by His own Hand"?

"Latin: Vehicle of Unity between Peoples and Cultures,"

Fr. Uwe Michael Lang
L'Osservatore Romano, 15 November 2007

The cultural and political unity of the Mediterranean world was a providential factor in the spread of the Christian faith. In particular, the diffusion of the Greek language in the urban centers of the Roman Empire facilitated the proclamation of the Gospel. The Greek spoken in East and West was not the classical idiom, but rather the simplified *koinè*, the common language of the various nations of the eastern part of the Mediterranean world: Greece, Asia Minor, Syria, and Egypt.

Koinè Greek was also the language of the urban proletariat of the West that had emigrated from the Eastern territories of the Empire. Rome had become a multi-ethnic and multi-cultural city. It also had a substantial Jewish population, which seems to have been mainly Greek-speaking. The language of the first Christian communities in Rome was Greek. This is shown by St. Paul's *Letter to the Romans* and by the first Christian literary works that originated in Rome, for instance, *First Letter of St. Clement*, *The Shepherd of Hermas,* and the writings of St. Justin Martyr.

In the first two centuries there were several popes with Greek names, and Christian tomb inscriptions were composed in Greek. During this period, Greek was also the common language of the Roman liturgy. The shift towards Latin did not begin in Rome, but in North Africa, where converts to Christianity were largely Latin-speaking natives rather than Greek-speaking immigrants. By the middle of the third century this transition had much advanced: members of the Roman clergy wrote to St. Cyprian of Carthage in Latin; Latin was also the language in which Novatian compose his *De trinitate* and other works, quoting from an existing Latin version of the Bible. No reference is made here to the so-called *Traditio Apostolica*, attributed to St. Hippolytus of Rome, because of uncertainties about its date, origin, and authorship.

It would seem that in the second half of the third century the stream of immigrants from the East to Rome diminished. This demographic change meant that the life of the Roman church began to be increasingly shaped by native Latin speakers. Nonetheless, Greek continued to be used in the Roman liturgy, at least to a certain extent, until the second half of the fourth century; this is implied by a Greek citation of the Eucharistic prayer in the Latin author Marius Victorinus, dating back to 360.

By that time, however, the transition to Latin was far on its way; this is evident from an otherwise unknown author writing between 374 and 382, who states that the Eucharistic prayer in Rome referred to Melchisedek as *summus sacerdos*—a title that is familiar to us from the later Canon of the Mass.

The most important source for the history of the early Latin liturgy is St. Ambrose of Milan. In his *De sacramentis*, a series of catecheses for the newly baptized held around 390, he quotes extensively from the Eucharistic prayer used at that time in Milan. The passages cited are earlier forms of the prayers *Quam oblationem, Qui pridie, Unde et memores, Supra quae*, and *Supplices te rogamus* of the Roman Canon. Elsewhere, in *De sacramentis*, Ambrose emphasizes his desire to follow the use of the Roman church in everything; for this reason, we can safely assume that this Eucharistic prayer was of Roman origin. There also is evidence in the sermons of St. Zeno, bishop of Verona from 362 to 372, which testifies to the geographical diffusion of this early form of the Roman Canon.

The wording of the prayers cited by Ambrose is not always identical with the Canon that was settled by St. Gregory the Great promulgated in the late sixth century and has come to us, with only a few minor changes, in the oldest extant liturgical books, especially the Old Gelasian Sacramentary, dating from the middle of the eighth century, but believed to reflect more ancient liturgical use. However, the differences between the two texts are far less remarkable than their similarities, given that the almost three hundred years lying between them were a period of intense liturgical development.

The shift from Greek to Latin in the Roman liturgy happened gradually and was completed in the pontificate of St. Damasus I (366-384). From then on the liturgy in Rome was celebrated in Latin, with the exception of a few reminders of the more ancient use, such as the *Kyrie eleison* in the *Ordo* and the readings in Greek in the Papal Mass. According to Optatus of Milevis, who wrote around 360, there were more than forty churches in Rome already before the Emperor Constantine's Edict of 313. If this information is correct, it would be reasonable to assume that there were Latin-speaking communities in the third century, if not before, celebrating the liturgy in Latin, notably the readings from Holy Scripture.

Psalms had been sung in Latin from early on, and the ancient version used in the liturgy had acquired such a sacrosanct status that St. Jerome only revised it with great caution. Later he translated the Psalter from Hebrew, as he said, not for liturgical use but to provide a text for scholarship and debate. Christine Mohrmann suggests that the baptismal liturgy was translated into Latin as early as the second century. There can be no certainty on these points, but it is clear that there was a period of transition, and that it was a long one.

Mohrmann introduces the useful distinction between, first, "purely prayer texts," where language is above all a means of expression, secondly, texts that are "destined to be read, the Epistle and Gospel," and, thirdly, "confessional texts," such as the Creed. In "prayers texts we are concerned with expressional form; in the others, primarily with forms of communication." Recent research on language and ritual, such as the work of Catherine Bell, confirm Mohrmann's insight that language has different functions in different parts of the liturgy, which go beyond mere communication or information. These theoretical reflections help us to understand the development of the early Roman liturgy: those parts where the element of communication was prevalent, such as the Scripture readings, were translated earlier, whereas the Eucharistic prayer continued to be recited in Greek for a much longer period.

The relatively new academic discipline of "sociolinguistics" alerts us to the fact that "the choice of one language over another is never a neutral or transparent one." (Maura K. Lafferty) Hence, it is important to see the transition from Greek to Latin in the Roman liturgy in its historical, social, and cultural contexts. Historians of antiquity have commented that the formation of liturgical Latin was part of a wide-ranging effort to Christianize Roman civilization.

In the second half of the fourth century, the leading bishops in Italy, above all Damasus in Rome and Ambrose in Milan, were striving to Christianize the dominant culture of their time. In the city of Rome, there was a strong pagan presence, and especially the aristocracy continued to adhere to old customs, even if they had become nominal Christians. Rome was no longer the center of political power, but its culture continued to have a hold on the thought-world of its elites.

The fourth century is now considered a period of literary rebirth, with a renewed interest in the "classics" of Roman poetry and prose. The emperors of the fourth century cultivated this *Latinitas*, and there was a revival of Latin even in the East. With characteristic tenacity, Rome maintained its ancient traditions.

In response, the popes of the late fourth century launched a conscious and comprehensive project to appropriate the symbols of Roman civilization for the Christian faith. Part of this attempt was the appropriation of public space through extensive building projects. After the emperors of the Constantinian dynasty had taken the lead with the monumental basilicas of the Lateran and St. Peter's, as well as the cemetery basilicas outside the city walls, the popes continued this building program that was to transform Rome into a city dominated by churches.

The most prestigious project was the construction of a new basilica dedicated to St. Paul on the Via Ostiensis, replacing the small Constantinian edifice with a new church that would match the size of St. Peter's. Another important aspect was the appropriation of public time with a cycle of Christian feasts throughout the year in place of pagan celebrations (see the Philocalian calendar of the year 354). The formation of liturgical Latin was part of this all-encompassing effort to evangelize late ancient Roman culture.

Christine Mohrmann sees here the fortuitous combination of a renewal of language, inspired by the newness of revelation, and of a stylistic traditionalism that was firmly imbedded in the Roman world. Liturgical Latin has Roman *gravitas* and avoids the exuberance of the Eastern Christian prayer style, which is found also in the Gallican tradition. This was not an adoption of "vernacular" language in the liturgy, since the Latin of the Roman Canon, of the collects and prefaces of the Mass was removed from the idiom of the ordinary people. It was a highly stylized language that would have been difficult to understand by the average Roman Christian of late antiquity, given especially that the rate of literacy was very low compared to our times. Moreover the development of the Christian *Latinitas* would have made the liturgy more accessible to the people of Milan or Rome, but not necessarily to those whose mother tongue was Gothic, Celtic, Iberian, or Punic.

It is possible to imagine a Western Church with local languages in its liturgy, as in the East, where, in addition to Greek, were also used Syrian, Coptic, Armenian, Georgian, and Ethiopian. However, the situation in the West was fundamentally different; the unifying force of the papacy was such that Latin became the only liturgical language. This was an important factor in furthering ecclesiastical, cultural, and political cohesion.

From the very beginning, liturgical Latin was a "sacred language" that was somewhat removed from the language of the people. However, the distance became greater with the development of national cultures and languages in Europe, not to mention mission territories. "The first real opposition to the Latin language," Christine Mohrmann wrote, "coincided with the end of medieval Latin as a 'living second language,' which was replaced by a truly 'dead' language, the Latin of the Humanists" ("The Ever-Recurring Problem of Language in the Church," in *Études sur le latin des chrétiens*, vol. IV, Rome, 1977).

The Second Vatican Council wanted to address this question by extending the use of the vernacular in the liturgy, above all in the readings (Constitution on the Sacred Liturgy *Sacrosanctum Concilium*, art. 36, n. 2). At the same time, it underlined that "the use of the Latin language . . . is to be preserved in the Latin rite" (*Sacrosanctum Concilium*, art. 36, n. 1; cf. also art. 54). The Council Fathers did not imagine that the sacred language of the Western Church would be completely replaced by the vernacular.

The linguistic fragmentation of Catholic worship in the post-conciliar period has been pushed so far that the majority of the faithful today can hardly pray the *Pater noster* together, as can be seen at international meetings in Rome or Lourdes. In an epoch marked by great mobility and globalization, a common liturgical language could serve as a vehicle of unity between peoples and cultures, apart from the fact that liturgical Latin is a unique spiritual treasure that has nourished the life of the Church for many centuries. Finally, it is necessary to preserve the sacred character of liturgical language in the vernacular translation, as the Holy See's instruction *Liturgiam authenticam* noted in 2001.

An extended version of this essay will be published under the title "Rhetoric of Salvation: The Origins of Latin as the Language of the Roman Liturgy" in the forthcoming volume *The Genius of the Roman Liturgy: Historical Diversity and Spiritual Reach: Proceedings of the 2006 Oxford CIEL Colloquium*, edited by U. M. Lang, Chicago: Hillenbrand Books.

Originally printed as "Latin: Vehicle of Unity between Peoples and Cultures," Fr. Uwe Michael Lang, *L'Osservatore Romano* (Italian edition), 15 November 2007. Reprinted courtesy of *L'Osservatore Romano*.

Letter to Bishops
Regarding the Apostolic Letter
"Summorum Pontificum"

Pope Benedict VI
July 7, 2007

My dear brother bishops,

With great trust and hope, I am consigning to you as pastors the text of a new apostolic letter "*motu proprio data*" on the use of the Roman liturgy prior to the reform of 1970. The document is the fruit of much reflection, numerous consultations, and prayer.

News reports and judgments made without sufficient information have created no little confusion. There have been very divergent reactions ranging from joyful acceptance to harsh opposition, about a plan whose contents were in reality unknown.

This document was most directly opposed on account of two fears, which I would like to address somewhat more closely in this letter.

In the first place, there is the fear that the document detracts from the authority of the Second Vatican Council, one of whose essential decisions—the liturgical reform—is being called into question.

This fear is unfounded. In this regard, it must first be said that the missal published by Paul VI and then republished in two subsequent editions by John Paul II obviously is and continues to be the normal form—the "forma ordinaria"—of the eucharistic liturgy. The last version of the "*Missale Romanum*" prior to the council, which was published with the authority of Pope John XXIII in 1962 and used during the council, will now be able to be used as a "*forma extraordinaria*" of the liturgical celebration. It is not appropriate to speak of these two versions of the Roman Missal as if they were "two rites." Rather, it is a matter of a twofold use of one and the same rite.

As for the use of the 1962 "*missale*" as a "*forma extraordinaria*" of the liturgy of the Mass, I would like to draw attention to the fact that this missal was never juridically abrogated and, consequently, in principle, was always permitted. At the time of the introduction of the new missal, it did not seem necessary to issue specific norms for the possible use of the earlier missal. Probably it was thought that it would be a matter of a few individual cases which would be resolved, case by case, on the local level. Afterward, however, it soon became apparent that a good number of people remained strongly attached to this usage of the Roman rite, which had been familiar to them from childhood. This was especially the case in countries where the liturgical movement had provided many people with a notable liturgical formation and a deep, personal familiarity with the earlier form of the liturgical celebration. We all know that, in the movement led by Archbishop Lefebvre, fidelity to the old missal became an external mark of identity; the reasons for the break, which arose over this, however, were at a deeper level. Many people who clearly accepted the binding character of the Second Vatican Council, and were faithful to the pope and the bishops, nonetheless also desired to recover the form of the sacred liturgy that was dear to them. This occurred above all because in many places celebrations were not faithful to the prescriptions of the new missal, but the latter actually was understood as authorizing or even requiring creativity, which frequently led to deformations of the liturgy which were hard to bear. I am speaking from experience, since I, too, lived through that period with all its hopes and its confusion. And I have seen how arbitrary deformations of the liturgy caused deep pain to individuals totally rooted in the faith of the church.

Pope John Paul II thus felt obliged to provide, in his "*motu proprio*" "Ecclesia Dei" (July 2, 1988), guidelines for the use of the 1962 missal; that document, however, did not contain detailed prescriptions but appealed in a general way to the generous response of bishops toward the "legitimate aspirations" of those members of the faithful who requested this usage of the Roman rite. At the time, the pope primarily wanted to assist the Society of St. Pius X to recover full unity with the successor of Peter and sought to heal a wound experienced ever more painfully. Unfortunately, this reconciliation has not yet come about. Nonetheless, a number of communities have gratefully made use of the possibilities provided by the "*motu proprio.*" On the other hand, difficulties remain concerning the use of the 1962 missal outside of these groups, because of the lack of precise juridical norms, particularly because bishops, in such cases, frequently feared that the authority of the council would be called into question. Immediately after the Second Vatican Council it was presumed that requests for the use of the 1962 missal would be limited to the older generation which had grown up with it, but in the meantime it has clearly been demonstrated that young persons, too, have discovered this liturgical form, felt its attraction and found in it a form of encounter with the mystery of the most holy Eucharist particularly suited to them. Thus, the need has arisen for a clearer juridical regulation which had not been foreseen at the time of the 1988 "*motu proprio.*" The present norms are also meant to free bishops from constantly having to evaluate anew how they are to respond to various situations.

In the second place, the fear was expressed in discussions about the awaited "*motu proprio,*" that the possibility of a wider use of the 1962 missal would lead to disarray or even divisions within parish communities. This fear also strikes me as quite unfounded. The use of the old missal presupposes a certain degree of liturgical formation and some knowledge of the Latin language; neither of these is found very often. Already from these concrete presuppositions, it is clearly seen that the new missal will certainly remain the ordinary form of the Roman rite, not only on account of the juridical norms, but also because of the actual situation of the communities of the faithful.

It is true that there have been exaggerations and at times social aspects unduly linked to the attitude of the faithful attached to the ancient Latin liturgical tradition. Your charity and pastoral prudence will be an incentive and guide for improving these. For that matter, the two forms of the usage of the Roman rite can be mutually enriching: new saints and some of the new prefaces can and should be inserted in the old missal. The "*Ecclesia Dei*" commission, in contact with various bodies devoted to the "*usus antiquior,*" will study the practical possibilities in this regard. The celebration of the Mass according to the missal of Paul VI will be able to demonstrate, more powerfully than has been the case hitherto, the sacrality which attracts many people to the former usage. The most sure guarantee that the missal of Paul VI can unite parish communities and be loved by them consists in its being celebrated with great reverence in harmony with the liturgical directives. This will bring out the spiritual richness and the theological depth of this missal.

I now come to the positive reason which motivated my decision to issue this "*motu proprio*" updating that of 1988. It is a matter of coming to an interior reconciliation in the heart of the church. Looking back over the past, to the divisions which in the course of the centuries have rent the body of Christ, one continually has the impression that, at critical moments when divisions were coming about, not enough was done by the church's leaders to maintain or regain reconciliation and unity. One has the impression that omissions on the part of the church have had their share of blame for the fact that these divisions were able to harden. This glance at the past imposes an obligation on us today: to make every effort to make it possible for all those who truly desire unity to remain in that unity or to attain it anew. I think of a sentence in the Second Letter to the Corinthians, where Paul writes: "Our mouth is open to you, Corinthians; our heart is wide. You are not restricted by us, but you are restricted in your own affections. In return . . . widen your hearts also!" (2 Cor 6:11-13). Paul was certainly speaking in another context, but his exhortation can and must touch us too, precisely on this subject. Let us generously open our hearts and make room for everything that the faith itself allows.

There is no contradiction between the two editions of the Roman Missal. In the history of the liturgy there is growth and progress, but no rupture. What earlier generations held as sacred remains sacred and great for us, too, and it cannot be all of a sudden entirely forbidden or even considered harmful. It behooves all of us to preserve the riches which have developed in the church's faith and prayer and to give them their proper place. Needless to say, in order to experience full communion, also the priests of the communities adhering to the former usage cannot, as a matter of principle, exclude celebrating according to the new books. The total exclusion of the new rite would not in fact be consistent with the recognition of its value and holiness.

In conclusion, dear brothers, I very much wish to stress that these new norms do not in any way lessen your own authority and responsibility, either for the liturgy or for the pastoral care of your faithful. Each bishop, in fact, is the moderator of the liturgy in his own diocese (cf. "*Sacrosanctum Concilium*," 22: "*Sacrae Liturgiae moderatio ab Ecclesiae auctoritate unice pendet quae quidem est apud Apostolicam Sedem et, ad normam iuris, apud Episcopum*").

Nothing is taken away, then, from the authority of the bishop, whose role remains that of being watchful that all is done in peace and serenity. Should some problem arise which the parish priest cannot resolve, the local ordinary will always be able to intervene, in full harmony, however, with all that has been laid down by the new norms of the "*motu proprio.*"

Furthermore, I invite you, dear brothers, to send to the Holy See an account of your experiences, three years after this "motu proprio" has taken effect. If truly serious difficulties come to light, ways to remedy them can be sought.

Dear brothers, with gratitude and trust, I entrust to your hearts as pastors these pages and the norms of the "*motu proprio.*" Let us always be mindful of the words of the apostle Paul addressed to the presbyters of Ephesus: "Take heed to yourselves and to all the flock, in which the Holy Spirit has made you overseers, to care for the church of God which he obtained with the blood of his own Son." (Acts 20:28).

I entrust these norms to the powerful intercession of Mary, mother of the church, and I cordially impart my apostolic blessing to you, dear brothers, to the parish priests of your dioceses, and to all the priests, your co-workers, as well as to all your faithful.

Given at St. Peter's, July 7, 2007.

Benedict XVI

Apostolic Letter
Summorum Pontificum
of the Supreme Pontiff

Pope Benedict XVI
Given Motu Proprio July 7, 2007

It has been the constant concern of the Supreme Pontiffs, and up to the present time, to ensure that the Church of Christ offers a worthy worship to the Divine Majesty, "to the praise and glory of His name," and "to the benefit of all His Holy Church."

Since time immemorial it has been necessary—as it is also for the future—to maintain the principle according to which "each particular Church must concur with the universal Church, not only as regards the doctrine of the faith and the sacramental signs, but also as regards the usages universally accepted by uninterrupted apostolic tradition, which must be observed not only to avoid errors but also to transmit the integrity of the faith, because the Church's law of prayer corresponds to her law of faith."[1]

Among the pontiffs who showed that requisite concern, particularly outstanding is the name of St. Gregory the Great, who made every effort to ensure that the new peoples of Europe received both the Catholic faith and the treasures of worship and culture that had been accumulated by the Romans in preceding centuries. He commanded that the form of the sacred liturgy as celebrated in Rome (concerning both the Sacrifice of Mass and the Divine Office) be conserved. He took great concern to ensure the dissemination of monks and nuns who, following the Rule of St. Benedict, together with the announcement of the Gospel illustrated with their lives the wise provision of their Rule that "nothing should be placed before the work of God." In this way the sacred liturgy, celebrated according to the Roman use, enriched not only the faith and piety but also the culture of many peoples. It is known, in fact, that the Latin liturgy of the Church in its various forms, in each century of the Christian era, has been a spur to the spiritual life of many saints, has reinforced many peoples in the virtue of religion and fecundated their piety.

Many other Roman pontiffs, in the course of the centuries, showed particular solicitude in ensuring that the sacred liturgy accomplished this task more effectively. Outstanding among them is St. Pius V who, sustained by great pastoral zeal and following the exhortations of the Council of Trent, renewed the entire liturgy of the Church, oversaw the publication of liturgical books amended and "renewed in accordance with the norms of the Fathers," and provided them for the use of the Latin Church.

One of the liturgical books of the Roman rite is the Roman Missal, which developed in the city of Rome and, with the passing of the centuries, little by little took forms very similar to that it has had in recent times.

"It was towards this same goal that succeeding Roman Pontiffs directed their energies during the subsequent centuries in order to ensure that the rites and liturgical books were brought up to date and when necessary clarified. From the beginning of this century they undertook a more general reform."[2] Thus, our predecessors Clement VIII, Urban VIII, St. Pius X,[3] Benedict XV, Pius XII, and Blessed John XXIII all played a part.

In more recent times, Vatican Council II expressed a desire that the respectful reverence due to divine worship should be renewed and adapted to the needs of our time. Moved by this desire our predecessor, the Supreme Pontiff Paul VI, approved, in 1970, reformed and partly renewed liturgical books for the Latin Church. These, translated into the various languages of the world, were willingly accepted by bishops, priests, and faithful. John Paul II amended the third typical edition of the Roman Missal. Thus, Roman pontiffs have operated to ensure that "this kind of liturgical edifice . . . should again appear resplendent for its dignity and harmony."[4]

But in some regions, no small numbers of faithful adhered and continue to adhere with great love and affection to the earlier liturgical forms. These had so deeply marked their culture and their spirit that in 1984 the Supreme Pontiff John Paul II, moved by a concern for the pastoral care of these faithful, with the special indult *"Quattuor abhinc anno,"* issued by the Congregation for Divine Worship, granted permission to use the Roman Missal published by Blessed John XXIII in the year 1962. Later, in the year 1988, John Paul II with the Apostolic Letter given as Motu Proprio, *"Ecclesia*

Dei," exhorted bishops to make generous use of this power in favor of all the faithful who so desired.

Our predecessor John Paul II having already considered the insistent petitions of these faithful, having listened to the views of the Cardinal Fathers of the Consistory of 22 March 2006, having reflected deeply upon all aspects of the question, invoked the Holy Spirit and trusting in the help of God, with these Apostolic Letters We establish the following:

Art. 1 The Roman Missal promulgated by Paul VI is the ordinary expression of the *Lex orandi* (Law of prayer) of the Catholic Church of the Latin rite. Nonetheless, the Roman Missal promulgated by St. Pius V and reissued by Bl. John XXIII is to be considered as an extraordinary expression of that same *Lex orandi*, and must be given due honour for its venerable and ancient usage. These two expressions of the Church's *Lex orandi* will in no any way lead to a division in the Church's *Lex credendi* (Law of belief). They are, in fact, two usages of the one Roman rite.

It is, therefore, permissible to celebrate the Sacrifice of the Mass following the typical edition of the Roman Missal promulgated by Bl. John XXIII in 1962 and never abrogated, as an extraordinary form of the Liturgy of the Church. The conditions for the use of this Missal as laid down by earlier documents *Quattuor abhinc annis* and *Ecclesia Dei*, are substituted as follows:

Art. 2 In Masses celebrated without the people, each Catholic priest of the Latin rite, whether secular or regular, may use the Roman Missal published by Bl. Pope John XXIII in 1962, or the Roman Missal promulgated by Pope Paul VI in 1970, and may do so on any day with the exception of the Easter Triduum. For such celebrations, with either one Missal or the other, the priest has no need for permission from the Apostolic See or from his Ordinary.

Art. 3 Communities of Institutes of consecrated life and of Societies of apostolic life, of either pontifical or diocesan right, wishing to celebrate Mass in accordance with the edition of the Roman Missal promulgated in 1962, for conventual or "community" celebration in their oratories, may do so. If an individual community or an entire Institute or Society wishes to undertake such celebrations often, habitually or permanently, the decision must be taken by the

Superiors Major, in accordance with the law and following their own specific decrees and statutes.

Art. 4 Celebrations of Mass as mentioned above in art. 2 may—observing all the norms of law—also be attended by faithful who, of their own free will, ask to be admitted.

Art. 5 § 1 In parishes, where there is a stable group of faithful who adhere to the earlier liturgical tradition, the pastor should willingly accept their requests to celebrate the Mass according to the rite of the Roman Missal published in 1962, and ensure that the welfare of these faithful harmonises with the ordinary pastoral care of the parish, under the guidance of the bishop in accordance with canon 392, avoiding discord and favouring the unity of the whole Church.

§ 2 Celebration in accordance with the Missal of Bl. John XXIII may take place on working days; while on Sundays and feast days one such celebration may also be held.

§ 3 For faithful and priests who request it, the pastor should also allow celebrations in this extraordinary form for special circumstances such as marriages, funerals, or occasional celebrations, e.g. pilgrimages.

§ 4 Priests who use the Missal of Bl. John XXIII must be qualified to do so [in good standing] and not juridically impeded.

§ 5 In churches that are not parish or conventual churches, it is the duty of the Rector of the church to grant the above permission.

Art. 6 In Masses celebrated in the presence of the people in accordance with the Missal of Bl. John XXIII, the readings may be given in the vernacular, using editions recognised by the Apostolic See.

Art. 7 If a group of lay faithful, as mentioned in art. 5 § 1, has not obtained satisfaction to their requests from the pastor, they should inform the diocesan bishop. The bishop is strongly requested to satisfy their wishes. If he cannot arrange for such celebration to take place, the matter should be referred to the Pontifical Commission "*Ecclesia Dei.*"

Art. 8 A bishop who, desirous of satisfying such requests, but who for various reasons is unable to do so, may refer the problem to the Commission "Ecclesia Dei" to obtain counsel and assistance.

Art. 9 § 1 The pastor, having attentively examined all aspects, may also grant permission to use the earlier ritual for the administration of the Sacraments of Baptism, Marriage, Penance, and the Anointing of the Sick, if the good of souls would seem to require it.

§ 2 Ordinaries are given the right to celebrate the Sacrament of Confirmation using the earlier Roman Pontifical, if the good of souls would seem to require it.

§ 2 Clerics ordained "*in sacris constitutis*" may use the Roman Breviary promulgated by Bl. John XXIII in 1962.

Art. 10 The ordinary of a particular place, if he feels it appropriate, may erect a personal parish in accordance with can. 518 for celebrations following the ancient form of the Roman rite, or appoint a chaplain, while observing all the norms of law.

Art. 11 The Pontifical Commission "Ecclesia Dei" (5), erected by John Paul II in 1988, continues to exercise its function. Said Commission will have the form, duties, and norms that the Roman Pontiff wishes to assign it.

Art. 12 This Commission, apart from the powers it enjoys, will exercise the authority of the Holy See, supervising the observance and application of these dispositions.

We order that everything We have established with these Apostolic Letters issued as Motu Proprio be considered as "established and decreed," and to be observed from 14 September of this year, Feast of the Exaltation of the Cross, whatever there may be to the contrary.

From Rome, at St. Peter's, 7 July 2007, third year of Our Pontificate.

---

1. General Instruction of the Roman Missal, 3rd ed., 2002, no. 397.
2. John Paul II, Apostolic Letter "*Vicesimus quintus annus*," 4 December 1988, 3: *Acta Apostolicae Sedis* 81 (1989), 899.

3. Ibid.

4. St. Pius X, Apostolic Letter Motu propio data, "*Abhinc duos annos*," 23 October 1913: *Acta Apostolicae Sedis* 5 (1913), 449-50; cf John Paul II, Apostolic Letter "*Vicesimus quintus annus*," no. 3: AAS 81 (1989), 899.

5. Cf. John Paul II, Apostolic Letter *Motu proprio data* "*Ecclesia Dei*," 2 July 1988, 6: *Acta Apostolicae Sedis* 80 (1988), 1498.

Cum Amore Ac Timore:
On Holy Communion on the Tongue

H. E. Athanasius Schneider
Auxiliary Bishop of Karaganda, Kazakhstan
L'Osservatore Romano, January 8, 2008

1. In his last encyclical, the great Pope John Paul II gave the Church a strong warning which sounds like a real testament: "We must carefully avoid underestimating any dimension or requirement of the Holy Eucharist. We thus show our awareness of the greatness of this gift . . . there is no risk of exaggerating in respect for this Mystery."

Awareness of the greatness of this mystery is shown in the way in which Christ's Body is given and received. Being aware of the importance of the moment of Holy Communion, the Church in her bimillenary tradition has tried to find a ritual expression to testify to her faith, love, and respect in the most perfect possible way. Thus, in the wake of an organic development, by at least as early as the 6th century, the Church began to give the Holy Eucharist directly into the mouth. This is testified in the biography of Pope Gregory the Great, who reigned from 590 to 604, and by an indication of the Pope himself.

The Synod of Cordova, which took place in 839, condemned the sect of the so-called Casians for their refusal to receive Holy Communion directly into the mouth. After this the Synod of Rouen of 878 confirmed the current practice of placing the Body of Christ on the tongue, threatening priests with suspension from their office should they give the Eucharist to lay people by placing it in their hands.

In the West the custom of kneeling and prostrating oneself before receiving the Eucharist was established in monasteries as early as the 6th century (e.g., in the monasteries of St. Colombanus). Later, in the 10th and 11th centuries, this custom became even more widespread.

Cum Amore Ac Timore: On Holy Communion on the Tongue

At the end of the patristic age, the practice of receiving Holy Communion directly into the mouth became so widespread as to be almost universal. This organic development can be traced back to the spirituality and Eucharistic devotion of the Fathers of the Church. As early as the first millennium, owing to the highly sacred nature of Eucharistic bread, the Western and Eastern Church in unison and almost instinctively realized the urgency of giving the Eucharist to lay people in their mouth.

The well-known liturgist J. A. Jungmann explained that, thanks to the distribution of Holy Communion directly into the mouth, several problems were sorted out: the necessity for those about to receive the Eucharist to clean their hands, the even more serious problems of preventing fragments of consecrated bread from being lost, and the necessity of purifying the patens of the hands after receiving the sacrament. The cloth and, later on, the paten were expressions of greater respect for the Eucharist.

2. As John Paul II pointed out in the encyclical *Ecclesia de Eucharistia:* "In the wake of this great sense of mystery it becomes clear how the Church's faith in the Eucharistic mystery has found expression, through the centuries, not only in the exhortation to an attitude of inner devotion, but also in a series of outer gestures."

The most adequate attitude towards this gift is receptivity, the centurion's humility, the attitude of someone ready to receive food, i.e., a child's attitude. The word of Christ, which invites us to receive the Kingdom of Heaven like children, can find its most suggestive expression in our gesture of receiving the Eucharistic bread kneeling and directly into the mouth.

John Paul II highlighted the necessity of outer expressions of respect for the Eucharist: "Although the banquet connotes the idea of familiarity, the Church has never given in to the temptation of banalizing this 'familiarity' with her Bridegroom, forgetting that He is also her Lord . . . The Eucharistic banquet is a real sacred banquet where underlying the simplicity of signs is God's unfathomable holiness. The bread broken on our altars is the angels' bread, which we can only approach with the centurion's humility."

The child's attitude is the Christian's deepest and most authentic attitude towards his Savior, who nourishes him with His Body and Blood. As Clement of Alexandria points out in a moving passage:

"The Word is everything to the child: father, mother, pedagogue, nourisher: 'Eat My Flesh and Blood, says Jesus!' . . . What an amazing mystery!"

Another biblical reflection is found in the story of the Prophet Ezekiel's calling. Ezekiel received God's word in his mouth symbolically: "Let your stomach make a meal of it and let your inside be full of this roll which I am giving to you. I looked, and lo, a hand outstretched towards me was holding a roll. Then I took it, and it was sweet as honey in my mouth" (Ezekiel 2, 8-9; 3, 2-3).

In Holy Communion we receive the Word-made-Flesh, food for us little children. When we receive the Eucharist, therefore, we can remember the gesture of the Prophet Ezekiel.

Christ's giving us real nourishment with His Body and Blood in Holy Communion was compared to breastfeeding in the patristic age, as shown by St. John Chrysostom's impressive words: "Through the Eucharistic mystery, Christ unites with each believer; he Himself nourishes those he gave life to, without entrusting them to anybody else. Do you not see how newborn children rush to their mother's breast? We must approach this sacred banquet and take this spiritual drink with the same fervor; rather, with an even more burning desire than a baby."

3. The most typical manifestation of worship is the biblical gesture of kneeling down, as understood and practiced by the early Christians.

According to Tertullian, who lived between the 2nd and 3rd century A.D., the highest form of prayer is the worship of God, which is also to be manifested in the act of kneeling: "The angels pray, all creatures pray, cattle and wild beasts pray and bend their knees."

St. Augustine warned believers that they sinned unless they adored Christ's body when receiving it in the Eucharist.

As established in an ancient *Ordo communionis* of the liturgy of the Coptic Church: "Let all, young and old alike, prostrate themselves and in this way begin the distribution of the Eucharist."

According to the *Mystagogic Catecheses* ascribed to St. Cyril of Jerusalem, the believer was to receive Holy Communion with a gesture of worship and veneration: "Do not hold out your hands, but with a gesture of worship and veneration come close to the cup which contains Christ's blood."

St. John Chrysostom invited those on the point of receiving Christ's Body in the Eucharist to imitate the Magi of the East in their spirit and gesture of worship: "Let us therefore come close to Him with fervor and burning love. The Magi themselves worshipped Him even though they found Him in a manger. Those men worshipped the Lord with awe and respect, though being Gentiles and barbarians. So we, who belong to the Kingdom of Heaven, must at least try to imitate those barbarians! Unlike the Magi, you do not only see this body, but have also experienced its strength and power of salvation. Let us therefore spur ourselves to show greater awe, reverence and devotion than the Magi."

Benedict XVI speaks about the same close link between worship and Holy Communion in his recent post-synodal exhortation *Sacramentum caritatis:* "Receiving the Eucharist involves an attitude of worship towards the One we receive." (n. 66)

Even as a cardinal, Joseph Ratzinger stressed this point: "Receiving the Eucharist is a spiritual event affecting the whole of human reality . . . Holy Communion affects us completely only when supported and understood by worship."

In the *Apocalypse*, the book of the heavenly liturgy, the 24 elders prostrating themselves before the Lamb of God provide a model of how the Church is to treat the Lamb when believers come into contact with Him in the Eucharist.

4. The Fathers of the Church showed the greatest concern to prevent even the smallest piece of Eucharistic bread from being lost, as St. Cyril of Jerusalem exhorted with highly suggestive words: "Be careful not to lose any part of the Lord's body. Should you drop anything, it would be as though you had severed a limb from your own body. Pray, tell me, if anyone were to give you gold beads, would you not keep them with the greatest care so as not to lose any of them? Should you not be more careful and vigilant to prevent even the smallest crumb of the Lord's body from falling to the floor, this being far more precious than gems and gold?"

As early as the 2nd and 3rd centuries, Tertullian voiced the great anguish and concern of the Church to prevent any fragment of bread from being lost: "We are exceedingly worried to avoid dropping the smallest crumb of bread or spilling the smallest drop of wine."

This is what Saint Ephrem, who lived in 4th century, taught: "Jesus filled the bread with Himself and the Spirit and called this bread His living Body. What I have given to you, Jesus said, you must not regard as bread or tread on any fragment of it. The smallest fragment can sanctify millions of men and is enough to give life to all those who eat it."

A warning in the liturgical tradition of the Coptic Church reads as follows: "There is no difference between larger and smaller pieces of the Eucharist; even fragments so small as to be invisible are worthy of the same veneration and have the same dignity as the unbroken bread."

In some Eastern liturgies the consecrated bread was referred to as *pearl (margarita)*. The *Collectiones Canonum Copticae* read as follows: "God forbid it! No pearl of consecrated bread must fall on the floor or stick to the fingers!"

The great care of the early Church in preventing fragments of Eucharistic bread from being lost was all over the Christian world: Rome (see Hippolytus, *Traditio apostolica,* 32), North Africa (see Tertullian, *De corona* 3, 4), Gaul (see Caesarius Arelatensis, *sermo* 78, 2), Egypt (see Origenes, *In Exodum hom.* 13, 3), Antioch and Constantinople (see John Chrysostom, *Ecloga quod non indige accedendum sit ad divina mysteria),* Palestine (see Hieronymus, *In Ps* 147, 14), Syria (see Ephraem *In hebd. Sanctam, s.* 4, 4).

5. In the early Church, men had to wash the palms of their hands before receiving the Eucharist. Also, believers had to take a deep bow and receive Christ's Body directly in the palm of their right, but not their left, hand. The palm of the right hand was used, so to speak, as a paten or as a corporal (especially for women).

A sermon by St. Caesarius of Arles reads as follows: "All men who desire to receive Holy Communion are to wash their hands. All women are to bring a linen cloth upon which Christ's Body is to be placed."

The palm of the hand was usually washed after reception of the Eucharist, as is still the case in the Communion of the clergy in the Byzantine liturgy.

The ancient canons of the Chaldean Church prohibited even the priest from bringing the Eucharist to his mouth with his fingers. He was to take the Lord's Body from the palm of his hand; the reason for this was that it was not ordinary, but heavenly food: "The priest is commanded to take the piece of bread directly from the palm of his hand; he is to take it directly with his mouth, as it is heavenly food."

6. In the ancient Syriac Church, the distribution of the Eucharist was a rite compared to the scene of Isaiah's purification at the hands of a seraph. In one of his sermons, St. Ephrem puts the following sentences into Jesus' mouth: "The coal sanctified Isaiah's lips. Now, I, who have come to you in the appearances of bread, have sanctified you all. The fire tongs whereby the coal was taken from the altar and which the Prophet Isaiah saw were an image of Me in the great sacrament. Isaiah saw Me, in the same way as you see Me when you hold out your right hand and bring the living Bread to your mouth. The tongs are My right hand. I am in the seraph's place. The burning coal is My Body. All of you are Isaiah."

In the Liturgy of St. James, before distributing Holy Communion to the congregation, the priest said this prayer: "May the Lord bless us all and make us worthy to receive the burning coal with immaculate hands and bring it to our mouth."

7. If every liturgical celebration is a sacred act *par excellence* (see *Sacrosanctum Concilium,* n. 7), this applies most of all to the rite of Holy Communion. The great Pope John Paul II stressed the need for the Church to take into particular consideration the sacred nature of the Eucharist, given the tendency of contemporary culture to ignore the sacred: "We must always remember, perhaps most of all in times like these when we perceive a tendency to obliterate the distinction between *sacrum* and *profanum,* given the widespread inclination (in certain areas at least) to desecrate all things."

In this context, the Church is called on to secure and strengthen the sense of the sacredness of the Eucharist. In our pluralistic, and in certain respects deliberately secularized society, the living faith of the Christian community secures the right of citizenship for this sense of sacredness. As a result of the experience of the early Church, of the increase in the overall theological understanding of the Eucharistic mystery and the ensuing changes in the liturgy, the distribution of Holy Communion was limited, at the end of the patristic age, as is still the case in the Eastern liturgy. For the laity, the distribution of Eucharistic bread directly into the mouth began to come into use. In the East only non-consecrated bread, called *antidoron,* was laid on the palm of the hand. The difference between Eucharistic bread and simply blessed bread was thus clearly shown. The most frequent warning of the Fathers of the Church about the attitude towards Holy Communion was expressed thus: *"Cum amore et timore!"* ("With love and awe!"). At the end of ancient times, the organic development of Eucharistic devotion by the Fathers of the Church, in the West and East alike, resulted in the distribution of the Eucharist into the mouth and the gestures of prostrating oneself (in the East) and kneeling (in the West).

Would it not be consistent with the innermost nature of consecrated bread if, even today, believers prostrated themselves and opened their mouth before receiving Christ's Body and let themselves be nourished like children, Holy Communion being food for the spirit? Such a gesture would also be an impressive manifestation of faith in God's Real Presence amongst the congregation. Should any non-believer find himself there and see such an act of worship, perhaps he too "would prostrate himself and worship God, proclaiming that the Lord is really amongst you." (1 Cor 14:24-25)

Papal Press Conference

Pope Benedict XVI
En Route to France, September 12, 2008

Q. What do you say to those in France who are worried that the motu proprio "Summorum Pontificum" is a step backward with regards to the great institutions of the Second Vatican Council?

Benedict XVI: It is baseless fear; because this "motu proprio" is simply an act of tolerance, with a pastoral objective, for people who have been formed in this liturgy, who love it, who know it, who want to live with this liturgy. It is a small group, because it supposes an education in Latin, a formation in a certain type of culture. But it seems to me a normal requirement of faith and pastoral practice for a bishop of our Church to have love and forbearance for these people and allow them to live with this liturgy.

There is no opposition between the liturgy renewed by Vatican II and this liturgy. Every day, the council fathers celebrated the Mass following the old rite and at the same time they conceived a natural development for the liturgy throughout this century, since the liturgy is a living reality, which develops and keeps its identity within its development.

So there is certainly a difference of emphasis, but a single fundamental identity that excludes any contradiction or antagonism between a renewed liturgy and the preceding liturgy. I believe there is a possibility for both types to be enriched. On the one hand, the friends of the old liturgy can and should know the new saints, the new prefaces of the liturgy, etc. But on the other hand, the new liturgy emphasizes the common participation, but it is not just the assembly of a particular community, but rather it is always an act of the universal Church, in communion with all the believers of all time, an act of adoration. In this sense, it seems to me that there is a mutual enrichment, and it is clear that the renewed liturgy is the ordinary liturgy of our time.

To the Bishops of France

Pope Benedict XVI
Lourdes, September 14, 2008

Liturgical worship is the supreme expression of priestly and episcopal life, just as it is of catechetical teaching. Your duty to sanctify the faithful people, dear Brothers, is indispensable for the growth of the Church. In the *Motu Proprio "Summorum Pontificum,"* I was led to set out the conditions in which this duty is to be exercised, with regard to the possibility of using the missal of Blessed John XXIII (1962) in addition to that of Pope Paul VI (1970). Some fruits of these new arrangements have already been seen, and I hope that, thanks be to God, the necessary pacification of spirits is already taking place. I am aware of your difficulties, but I do not doubt that, within a reasonable time, you can find solutions satisfactory for all, lest the seamless tunic of Christ be further torn. Everyone has a place in the Church. Every person, without exception, should be able to feel at home, and never rejected. God, who loves all men and women and wishes none to be lost, entrusts us with this mission by appointing us shepherds of his sheep. We can only thank him for the honour and the trust that he has placed in us. Let us therefore strive always to be servants of unity!

Appendix:
The Canon of the Mass

TE ígitur, clementíssime Pater, per Jesum Christum Fílium tuum Dóminum nostrum súpplices rogámus ac pétimus (*osculatur altare*) uti accépta hábeas, et benedícas (*jungit manus, deinde signat ter super oblata*), hæc ✠ dona, hæc ✠ múnera, hæc ✠ sancta sacrifícia illibáta (*extensis manibus prosequitur*): in primis quæ tibi offérimus pro Ecclésia tua sancta cathólica: quam pacificáre, custodíre, adunáre, et régere dignéris toto orbe terrárum, una cum famulo tuo Papa nostro *N.* et Antístite nostro *N.* et ómnibus orthodóxis, atque cathólicæ et apostólicæ fídei cultóribus.

WHEREFORE, O most merciful Father, we humbly pray and beseech Thee, through Jesus Christ Thy Son, our Lord (*he kisses the altar*), that Thou wouldst vouchsafe to receive and bless (*he joins his hands together, and then makes the sign of the Cross thrice over the offerings*) these ✠ gifts, these ✠ offerings, this ✠ holy and unblemished sacrifice (he extends his hands and continues), which in the first place we offer Thee for Thy holy Catholic Church, that it may please Thee to grant her peace: as also to protect, unite, and govern her throughout the world, together with Thy servant *N.*, our Pope *N.*, our bishop, as also all orthodox believers who keep the catholic and apostolic faith.

The Commemoration for the living.

MEMÉNTO, Dómine, famulórum famularúmque tuárum *N.* et *N.*

BE mindful, O Lord, of Thy servants and handmaids, *N.* and *N.*

He joins his hands, prays a little while for those he wishes to pray for, then with his hands stretched out he continues:

ET ómnium circumstántium, quorum tibi fides cógnita est, et nota devótio: pro quibus tibi offérimus, vel qui tibi ófferunt hoc sacrifícium laudis, pro se,

AND of all here present, whose faith and devotion are known unto Thee; for whom we offer, or who offer up to Thee, this sacrifice of praise for themselves

suísque ómnibus, pro redemptióne animárum suárum, pro spe salútis et incolumitátis suæ; tibíque reddunt vota sua ætérno Deo, vivo et vero.

and theirs, for the redeeming of their souls, for the hope of their safety and salvation, and who pay their vows to Thee, the eternal, living, and true God.

Infra actionem.

Within the action.

COMMUNICÁNTES, et memóriam venerántes, in primis gloriósæ semper Vírginis Maríæ, genitrícis Dei et Dómini nostri Jesu Christi: sed et beatórum Apostolórum ac Mártyrum tuórum, Petri et Pauli, Andréæ, Jacóbi, Joánnis, Thomæ, Jacóbi, Philíppi, Bartholomæi, Matthæi, Simónis et Thaddæi, Cleti, Cleméntis, Xysti, Cornélii, Cypriáni, Lauréntii, Chrysógoni, Joánnis et Pauli, Cosmæ et Damiáni et ómnium sanctórum tuórum: quorum méritis precibúsque concédas, ut in ómnibus protectiónis tuæ muniámur auxílio. (*Jungit manus.*) Per eúmdem Christum Dóminum nostrum. Amen.

COMMUNICATING, and reverencing the memory first of the glorious Mary, ever a virgin, Mother of our God and Lord Jesus Christ; likewise of Thy blessed apostles and martyrs, Peter and Paul, Andrew, James, John, Thomas, James, Philip, Bartholomew, Matthew, Simon, and Thaddeus; of Linus, Cletus, Clement, Xystus, Cornelius, Cyprian, Lawrence, Chrysogonus, John, and Paul, Cosmas and Damian, and of all Thy saints; by whose merits and prayers grant that in all things we may be guarded by Thy protecting help. (*He joins his hands together.*) Through the same Christ our Lord. Amen.

With his hands spread over the offerings, he says:

HANC ígitur oblatiónem servitútis nostræ, sed et cunctæ famíliæ tuæ, quæsumus Dómine, ut placátus accípias, diésque nostros in tua pace dispónas, atque ab ætérna damnatióne nos éripi, et in electórum tuórum júbeas grege numerári. (*Jungit manus.*) Per Christum Dóminum nostrum. Amen.

WE therefore beseech Thee, O Lord, to be appeased, and to receive this offering of our bounden duty, as also of Thy whole household; order our days in Thy peace; grant that we be rescued from eternal damnation and counted within the fold of Thine elect. (*He joins his hands together.*) Through Christ our Lord. Amen.

QUAM oblatiónem tu, Deus, in ómnibus, quæsumus,

WHICH offering do Thou, O God, vouchsafe in all things.

He makes the sign of the Cross three times over the offerings.

bene ✠ díctam, adscrí ✠ ptam, ra ✠ tam, rationábilem, acceptabilémque fácere dignéris:

to bless ✠, consecrate ✠, approve ✠, make reasonable and acceptable:

He makes the sign of the Cross once over the host and once over the chalice.

ut nobis Cor ✠ pus et San ✠ guis fiat dilectíssimi Fílii tui Dómini nostri Jesu Christi.

that it may become for us the Body ✠ and ✠ Blood of Thy most beloved Son our Lord Jesus Christ.

QUI prídie quam paterétur (*accipit hostiam*), accépit panem in sanctas ac venerábiles manus suas (*elevat oculos ad cœlum*), et elevátis óculis in cœlum, ad te Deum Patrem suum omnipoténtem, tibi grátias agens,

WHO the day before He suffered took bread (*he takes the host*) into His holy and venerable hands (*he raises his eyes to heaven*), and with His eyes lifted up to heaven, unto Thee, God, His almighty Father, giving thanks to thee,

He makes the sign of the Cross over the host.

bene ✠ díxit, fregit, dedítque discípulis suis, dicens: Accípite, et manducáte ex hoc omnes.

He blessed ✠, brake, and gave to His disciples, saying: Take and eat ye all of this,

Holding the host between the first fingers and thumbs of both hands, he says the words of consecration, silently with clearness and attention, over the host, and at the same time over all the other hosts, if several are to be consecrated.

Hoc est enim Corpus meum.

For this is My Body.

As soon as the words of consecration have been said, he kneels and adores the consecrated host. He rises, shows it to the people,

puts it on the corporal, and again adores.
Then, uncovering the chalice, he says:

Símili modo postquam cœnátum est,	In like manner, after He had supped,

He takes the chalice with both hands.

accípiens et hunc præclárum Cálicem in sanctas ac venerábiles manus suas, item tibi grátias agens,	taking also this excellent chalice into His holy and adorable hands; also giving thanks to Thee,

Holding the chalice with his left hand, he makes the sign of the Cross over it with his right.

bene ✠ díxit, dedítque discípulis suis, dicens: Accípite, et bíbite ex eo omnes:	He blessed ✠, and gave It to His disciples, saying: Take, and drink ye all of this;

He utters the words of consecration over the chalice silently, attentively, carefully, and without pausing, holding it slightly raised.

Hic est enim Calix Sánguinis mei, novi et ætérni testaménti; mystérium fidei: qui pro vobis et pro multis effundétur in remissiónem peccatórum.	For this is the Chalice of My Blood, of the new and eternal testament; the mystery of faith: which shall be shed for you and for many unto the remission of sins.

As soon as the words of consecration have been said, he puts the chalice on the corporal, and says silently:

Hæc quotiescúmque fecéritis, in mei memóriam faciétis.	As often as ye shall do these things, ye shall do them in memory of Me.

He kneels and adores; then rises, shows it to the people, puts it down, covers it, and again adores. Then holding his hands apart, he says:

Unde et mémores, Dómine, nos servi tui, sed et plebs tua sancta,	Wherefore, O Lord, we Thy servants, as also Thy holy people,

ejúsdem Christi Fílii tui Dómini nostri, tam beatæ passiónis, necnon et ab ínferis resurrectiónis, sed et in cœlos gloriósæ ascensiónis: offérimus præcláræ majestáti tuæ de tuis donis ac datis,

calling to mind the blessed passion of the same Christ Thy Son our Lord, and also his rising up from hell, and his glorious ascension into heaven, do offer unto Thy most excellent majesty, of Thine own gifts bestowed upon us,

He joins his hands and makes the sign of the Cross three times over the host and chalice together.

hóstiam ✠ puram, hóstiam ✠ sanctam, hóstiam ✠ immaculátam,

a pure ✠ victim, a holy ✠ victim, a spotless ✠ victim,

He makes the sign of the Cross once over the host and once over the chalice.

Panem ✠ sanctum vitæ ætérnæ, et Cálicem ✠ salútis perpétuæ.

the holy ✠ Bread of eternal life, and the Chalice ✠ of everlasting salvation.

He continues with his hands stretched out:

SUPRA quæ propítio ac seréno vultu respícere dignéris: et accépta habére, sícuti accépta habére dignátus es múnera púeri tui justi Abel, et sacrifícium patriárchæ nostri Ábrahæ, et quod tibi óbtulit summus sacérdos tuus Melchísedech sanctum sacrifícium, immaculátam hóstiam.

Upon which do Thou vouchsafe to look with a propitious and serene countenance, and to accept them, as Thou wert graciously pleased to accept the gifts of Thy just servant Abel, and the sacrifice of our patriarch Abraham, and that which Thy high priest Melchisedech offered to thee, a holy sacrifice, a spotless victim.

Bowing low with his hands joined together and then laid on the altar, he says:

SÚPPLICES te rogámus,

We most humbly beseech thee,

omnípotens Deus: jube hæc perférri per manus sancti Ángeli tui in sublíme altáre tuum, in conspéctu divínæ majestátis tuæ: ut quotquot (*osculatur altare*), ex hac altáris participatióne, sacrosánctum Fílii tui,

almighty God, to command that these things be borne by the hands of Thy holy angel to Thine altar On high, in the sight of Thy divine majesty, that as many of us (*he kisses the altar*) as, at this altar, shall partake of and receive the

He joins his hands together and makes the sign of the Cross over the host and once over the chalice.

Cor ✠ pus et Sán ✠ guinem sumpsérimus (*seipsum signat*), omni benedictióne cœlésti, et grátia repleámur (*jungit manus*). Per eúndem Christum Dóminum nostrum. Amen.

most holy Body ✠ and ✠ Blood of Thy Son (h*e makes the sign of the Cross on himself*), may be filled with every heavenly blessing and grace (*he joins his hands together*). Through the same Christ our Lord. Amen.

The Commemoration for the dead.

MEMÉNTO étiam, Dómine, famulórum famularúmque tuárum *N.* et *N.* qui nos præcessérunt cum signo fídei, et dórmiunt in somno pacis.

Be mindful, O Lord, of Thy servants and handmaids *N.* and *N.*, who are gone before us, with the sign of faith, and sleep in the sleep of peace.

He joins his hands, prays a little while for those dead whom he means to pray for, then with his hands stretched out, continues:

Ipsis, Dómine, et ómnibus in Christo quiescéntibus, locum refrigérii, lucis et pacis, ut indúlgeas, deprecámur.

To these, O Lord, and to all that rest in Christ, we beseech thee, grant a place of refreshment, light, and peace.

He joins his hands together, and bows his head.

Per eúmdem Christum Dóminum nostrum. Amen.

Through the same Christ our Lord. Amen.

He strikes his breast with his right hand,
and slightly raising his voice, says:

NOBIS quoque peccatóribus, fámulis tuis, de multitúdine miseratiónum tuárum sperántibus, partem áliquam et societátem donáre dignéris, cum tuis sanctis Apóstolis et Martyribus: cum Joánne, Stéphano, Mathía, Bárnaba, Ignátio, Alexándro, Marcellíno, Petro, Felicitáte, Perpétua, Ágatha, Lúcia, Agnéte, Cæcília, Anastásia, et ómnibus sanctis tuis; intra quorum nos consórtium, non æstimátor mériti, sed véniæ, quæsumus, largítor admítte. Per Christum Dóminum nostrum. Per quem hæc ómnia, Dómine, semper bona creas, sanctíficas, vivíficas, benedícis, et præstas nobis.

TO us sinners, also, Thy servants, hoping in the multitude of Thy mercies, vouchsafe to grant some part and fellowship with Thy holy apostles and martyrs: with John, Stephen, Matthias, Barnabas, Ignatius, Alexander, Marcellinus, Peter, Felicity, Perpetua, Agatha, Lucy, Agnes, Cecily, Anastasia, and with all Thy saints, into whose company we pray thee admit us, not considering our merit, but of Thine own free pardon. Through Christ our Lord; through whom, O Lord, Thou dost create, hallow, quicken, and bless these Thine ever-bountiful gifts and give them, to us.

He uncovers the chalice, kneels, takes the Blessed Sacrament
in his right hand, and holding the chalice in his left, makes
the sign of the Cross three times over it from lip to lip, saying:

Per ip ✠ sum, et cum ip ✠ so, et in ip ✠ so,

By ✠ Him, and with ✠ Him, and in ✠ Him,

He makes the sign of the Cross twice between the chalice and his
breast.

est tibi Deo Patri ✠ omnipoténti, in unitáte Spíritus ✠ sancti,

is to Thee, God the Father ✠ almighty, in the unity of the Holy ✠ Ghost,

Lifting up the chalice a little with the host, he says:

omnis honor et glória.

all honour and glory.

*He puts back the host, covers the chalice,
kneels, rises, and sings or reads:*

Per ómnia sǽcula sæculórum. R.
Amen.

Orémus. Præcéptis salutáribus et
divína institutióne formáti,
audémus dícere:

For ever and ever. R. Amen.

Let us pray. Taught by the
precepts of salvation, and
following the divine commandment,
we make bold to say:

He stretches out his hands.

Pater noster, qui es in cœlis,
sanctificétur nomen tuum:
advéniat regnum tuum: fiat
volúntas tua, sicut in cœlo et in
terra panem nostrum quotidiánum
da nobis hódie; et dímitte nobis
débita nostra, sicut et nos
dimíttimus debitóribus nostris: et
ne nos indúcas in tentatiónem.

Our Father, who art in heaven,
hallowed be Thy name: Thy
kingdom come; Thy will be done
on earth as it is in heaven. Give
us this day our daily bread: and
forgive us our trespasses, as we
forgive them that trespass against
us. And lead us not into
temptation.

R. Sed líbera nos a malo.

R. But deliver us from evil.

The priest says, Amen.
He takes the paten between his first and middle finger, and says:

Líbera nos, quæsumus Dómine,
ab ómnibus malis prætéritis,
præséntibus, et futúris, et
intercedénte beáta et gloriósa
semper Vírgine Dei genitríce
María, cum beátis Apóstolis tuis
Petro et Paulo, atque Andréa, et
ómnibus sanctis,

Deliver us, we beseech Thee, O
Lord, from all evils, past, present,
and to come; and by the
intercession of the blessed and
glorious, Mary ever virgin,
Mother of God, together with
Thy blessed apostles Peter and
Paul, and Andrew, and all the
saints,

*He makes the sign of the Cross with the paten
from his forehead to his breast and kisses it.*

da propítius pacem in diébus
nostris: ut ope misericórdiæ tuæ

mercifully grant peace in our
days: that through the help of

adjúti, et a peccáto simus semper líberi, et ab omni perturbatióne secúri.

Thy mercy we may always be free from sin, and safe from all trouble.

He puts the paten under the host, uncovers the chalice, kneels, rises, takes the host and breaks it in half over the chalice, saying:

Per eúmdem Dóminum nostrum Jesum Christum Fílium tuum,

Through the same Jesus Christ Thy Son our Lord,

He puts the portion that is in his right hand on to the paten; he then breaks off a small piece from the portion which is in his left hand, saying:

qui tecum vivit et regnat in unitáte Spíritus sancti Deus.

who liveth and reigneth with thee in the unity of the Holy Ghost, one God.

He puts the other half with his left hand on to the paten, and holding the particle over the chalice in his right hand, and the chalice with his left, he says:

Per ómnia sæcula sæculórum. R. Amen.

For ever and ever. R. Amen.

He makes the sign of the Cross three times over the chalice with the particle of the host, saying:

Pax ✠ Dómini sit ✠ semper vobís ✠ cum.

The peace of the Lord be ✠ always with ✠ you.

R. Et cum spíritu tuo.

R. And with Thy spirit.

He puts the particle into the chalice, saying silently:

Hæc commíxtio et consecrátio Córporis et Sánguinis Dómini nostri Jesu Christi, fiat accipiéntibus nobis in vitam ætérnam. Amen.

May this mingling and hallowing of the Body and Blood of our Lord Jesus Christ avail us that receive it unto life everlasting. Amen.

He covers the chalice, kneels, rises, and bowing before
the Blessed Sacrament, with his hands joined together
and striking his breast three times, says:

AGNUS Dei, qui tollis peccáta mundi, miserére nobis.

LAMB of God, who takest away the sins of the world, have mercy on us.

Agnus Dei, qui tollis peccáta mundi, miserére nobis.

Lamb of God, who takest away the sins of the world, have mercy on us.

Agnus Dei, qui tollis peccáta mundi, dona nobis pacem.

Lamb of God, who takest away the sins of the world, grant us peace.

At mass for the dead, instead of saying: miserére nobis, *he says:* dona eis réquiem, rest. *And the third time he adds*, sempitérnam, everlasting.

Then with his hands joined together above the altar
he bows down and says the following prayers:

Dómine Jesu Christe, qui dixísti Apóstolis tuis: Pacem relínquo vobis, pacem meam do vobis: ne respícias peccáta mea, sed fidem Eccelésiæ tuæ: eámque secúndum voluntátem tuam pacificáre et coaduráre dignéris. Qui vivis et regnas Deus, per ómnia sæcula sæculórum. Amen.

O Lord Jesus Christ, who didst say to Thy apostles, Peace I leave with you, My peace I give unto you; look not upon my sins, but upon the faith of Thy Church; and vouchsafe to her that peace and unity which is agreeable to Thy will; who livest and reignest God for ever and ever. Amen.

If the kiss of peace is to be given,
the priest kisses the altar, and giving the kiss of peace, says:

Pax tecum.

Peace be with you.

R. Et cum spíritu tuo.

R. And with Thy spirit.

At masses for the dead the kiss of peace is not given,
neither is the above prayer said.

DÓMINE Jesu Christe, Fili Dei vivi, qui ex voluntáte Patris, cooperánte Spíritu sancto, per mortem tuam mundum vivificásti: líbera me per hoc sacrosánctum Corpus et Sánguinem tuum, ab ómnibus iniquitátibus meis, et univérsis malis, et fac me tuis semper inhærére mandátis, et a te numquam separári permíttas. Qui cum eódem Deo Patre et Spíritu sancto vivis et regnas Deus in sæcula sæculórum. Amen.

PERCÉPTIO Córporis tui, Dómine Jesu Christe, quod ego indígnus súmere præsúmo, non mihi provéniat in judícium et condemnatiónem: sed pro tua pietáte prosit mihi ad tutaméntum mentis et córporis, et ad medélam percipiéndam. Qui vivis et regnas cum Deo Patre in unitáte Spíritus sancti Deus, per ómnia sæcula sæculórum. Amen.

O LORD Jesus Christ, Son of the living God, who, according to the will of Thy Father, through the co-operation of the Holy Ghost, hast by Thy death given life to the world, deliver me by this, Thy most holy Body and Blood, from all my iniquities and from every evil; and make me always cleave to Thy commandments, and never suffer me to be separated from thee; who with the same God the Father and Holy Ghost livest and reignest God for ever and ever. Amen.

LET not the receiving of Thy Body, O Lord Jesus Christ, which I, all unworthy presume to take, turn to my judgement and damnation: but through Thy loving-kindness may it avail me for a safeguard and remedy, both of soul and body. Who with God the Father, in the unity of the Holy Ghost, livest and reignest God for ever and ever. Amen.

The priest kneels down, rises, and says:

PANEM cœléstem accípiam, et nomen Dómini invocábo.

I WILL take the Bread of heaven, and call upon the name of the Lord.

Then, bowing a little, he takes both parts of the host with the thumb and first finger of his left hand, and the paten between his first and middle finger. He strikes his breast with his right hand, and, slightly raising his voice, says three times reverently and humbly:

DÓMINE, non sum dignus, ut intres sub tectum meum: sed tantum dic verbo, et sanábitur

LORD, I am not worthy that Thou shouldst enter under my roof; say but the word, and my soul shall

ánima mea.

be healed.

He makes the sign of the Cross with the host in his right hand over the paten, and says:

CORPUS Dómini nostri Jesu Christi custódiat ánimam meam in vitam ætérnam. Amen.

MAY the Body of our Lord Jesus Christ preserve my soul unto life everlasting. Amen.

He receives both portions of the host reverently, joins his hands together, and remains for a little while quietly meditating on the most holy Sacrament. Then he uncovers the chalice, kneels, gathers up the crumbs, if there are any, and wipes the paten above the chalice, whilst he says:

QUID retríbuam Dómino pro ómnibus, quæ retríbuit mihi? Cálicem salutáris accípiam, et nomen Dómini invocábo. Laudans invocábo Dóminum, et ab inimícis meis salvus ero.

WHAT return shall I make to the Lord for all He hath given unto me? I will take the Chalice of salvation, and call upon the name of the Lord. Praising I will call upon the Lord, and I shall be saved from my enemies.

He takes the chalice into his right hand, and making the sign of the Cross on himself with it, he says:

SANGUIS Dómini nostri Jesu Christi custódiat ánimam meam in vitam ætérnam. Amen.

MAY the Blood of our Lord Jesus Christ keep my soul unto life everlasting, Amen.

He receives the precious blood with the particle. Then, if there are any communicants, he should give them communion before purifying. Afterwards he says:

QUOD ore súmpsimus, Dómine, pura mente capiámus; et de múnere temporáli fiat nobis remédium sempitérnum.

GRANT, Lord, that what we have taken with our mouth we may receive with a pure mind; and that from a temporal gift it may become for us an eternal remedy.

Meanwhile, he passes the chalice to the server, who pours into a little wine, with which he cleanses his fingers; then he continues:

CORPUS tuum, Dómine, quod sumpsi, et Sanguis quem potávi, adhæreat viscéribus meis: et præsta; ut in me non remáneat scélerum mácula, quem pura et sancta refecérunt sacraménta. Qui vivis et regnas in sæcula sæculórum. Amen.

MAY Thy Body, O Lord, which I have received, and Thy Blood which I have drunk, cleave to my bowels; and grant that no stain of sin may remain in me, whom Thy pure and holy sacraments have refreshed; who livest and reignest world without end. Amen.

He washes his fingers, wipes them, and takes the ablution; he wipes his mouth and the chalice, which he covers, and after folding up the corporal, arranges it on the altar as before. Then he continues mass. After the last Postcommunion the priest says:

Dóminus vobíscum.

The Lord be with you.

R. Et cum spíritu tuo.

R. And with Thy spirit.

Then either:

Ite, missa est.

Go, you are dismissed.

or, according to what mass is being said:

Benedicámus Dómino.

Let us bless the Lord.

R. Deo grátias.

R. Thanks be to God.

At mass for the dead, he says:

Requiéscant in pace.

May they rest in peace.

R. Amen.

R. Amen.

After saying, Ite missa est *or* Benedicámus Dómino, *the priest bows down at the middle of the altar, and with his hands joined above it, says:*

Pláceat tibi, sancta Trínitas, obséquium servitútis meæ: et præsta; ut sacrifícium quod óculis

May the homage of my service be pleasing to thee, O holy Trinity; and grant that the

tuæ majestátis indígnus óbtuli, tibi sit acceptábile, mihíque, et ómnibus pro quibus illud óbtuli, sit, te miseránte, propitiábile. Per Christum Dóminum nostrum. Amen.

sacrifice which I, though unworthy, have offered in the sight of Thy majesty, may be acceptable to thee: and through Thy mercy win forgiveness for me and for all those for whom I have offered it. Through Christ our Lord. Amen.

Then he kisses the altar, and raising his eyes upward, stretching out, lifting up, and joining his hands, bowing his head before the cross, he says:

Benedícat vos omnípotens Deus,

May God almighty bless you,

and turning towards the people, he blesses them once only, even at high mass, and continues:

Pater, et Fílius ✠ et Spíritus sanctus. R. Amen.

Father, and Son and Holy ✠ Ghost. R. Amen.

At a bishop's mass a triple blessing is given. At mass for the dead no blessing is given. Then at the Gospel corner, after saying Dóminus vobíscum, *and* Inítium *or* Sequéntia sancti Evangélii, *and making the sign of the Cross on the altar, or on the book and on himself as at the Gospel in the mass, he reads the Gospel of St. John, as below, or another Gospel as appointed.*

✠ Inítium sancti Evangélii secúndum Joánnem.
R. Glória tibi, Dómine.

✠ The beginning of the holy Gospel according to St. John.
R. Glory be to thee, O Lord.

In princípio erat Verbum, et Verbum erat apud Deum, et Deus erat Verbum. Hoc erat in princípio apud Deum. Ómnia per ipsum facta sunt, et sine ipso factum est nihil quod factum est. In ipso vita erat, et vita erat lux hóminum, et lux in ténebris lucet, et ténebræ eam non comprehendérunt. Fuit homo

In the beginning was the Word, and the Word was with God, and the Word was God: the same was in the beginning with God. All things were made by Him, and without Him was made nothing that was made: in Him was life, and the life was the light of men; and the light shineth in darkness, and the darkness did not

missus a Deo, cui nomen erat Joánnes. Hic venit in testimónium, ut testimónium perhibéret de lúmine, ut omnes créderent per illum. Non erat ille lux, sed ut testimónium perhibéret de lúmine. Erat lux vera quæ illúminat omnem hóminem veniéntem in hunc mundum. In mundo erat, et mundus per ipsum factus est, et mundus eum non cognóvit. In própria venit, et sui eum non recepérunt; quotquot autem recepérunt eum, dedit eis potestátem fílios Dei fíeri; his qui credunt in nómine ejus, qui non ex sanguínibus, neque ex voluntáte carnis, neque ex voluntáte viri, sed ex Deo nati sunt. (*Hic genuflectitur.*) ET VERBUM CARO FACTUM EST, et habitávit in nobis: et vídimus glóriam ejus, glóriam quasi Unigéniti a Patre, plenum grátiæ et veritátis.

R. Deo grátias.

comprehend it. There was a man sent from God, whose name was John. This man came for a witness to give testimony of the light, that all men might believe through him. He was not the light, but was to give testimony of the light, that was the true light which enlighteneth every man that cometh into this world. He was in the world, and the world was made by Him, and the world knew Him not. He came unto His own, and his own received Him not. But as many as received Him, He gave them power to become the sons of God: to them that believe in His name, who are born not of blood, nor of the will of the flesh, nor of the will of man, but of God. AND THE WORD WAS MADE FLESH (*here the people kneel down*), and dwelt among us; and we saw His glory, the glory as it were of the only-begotten of the Father, full of grace and truth.

R. Thanks be to God.

Acknowledgements

Thanks are extended to His Excellency Auxiliary Bishop Athanasius Schneider, Fr. John T. Zuhlsdorf, Fr. Uwe Michael Lang, Fr. Paul McDonald, and Michael S. Rose for permission to reprint their work.

Thanks are also extended to Jeffrey Tucker, editor of the quarterly *Sacred Music*, for assistance in reprinting Fr. Zuhlsdorf's 1993 commentary and to Mary Frances Lester of TAN Books and Publishers for permission to reprint from Michael Davies' *A Short History of the Roman Mass*.

Thanks also go to Sr. Mary Elizabeth Lariviere of *L'Osservatore Romano* for permission to reprint Father Lang's article "Latin: Vehicle of Unity between Peoples and Cultures" and to Fr. Joseph Fessio and Laura Dittus of Ignatius Press for permission to reprint the first chapter of Fr. Lang's *Turning Towards the Lord: Orientation in Liturgical Prayer.*

Made in the USA
San Bernardino, CA
28 June 2014